Exchange Rate Policies in Developing and Post-Socialist Countries

THE INTERNATIONAL CENTER FOR ECONOMIC GROWTH is a nonprofit research institute founded in 1985 to stimulate international discussions on economic policy, economic growth, and human development. The Center sponsors research, publications, and conferences in cooperation with an international network of correspondent institutes, which distribute publications of both the Center and other network members to policy audiences around the world. The Center's research and publications program is organized around five series: Sector Studies; Country Studies; Studies in Human Development and Social Welfare; Occasional Papers; and Reprints.

The Center is affiliated with the Institute for Contemporary Studies and is headquartered in Panama; the administrative office is in San Francisco, California.

For further information, please contact the International Center for Economic Growth, 243 Kearny Street, San Francisco, California, 94108, USA. Telephone (415) 981-5353; Fax (415) 986-4878.

ICEG Board of Overseers

Exchange Rate Policies in Developing and Post-Socialist Countries

Edited by
Emil-Maria Claassen

An International Center for
Economic Growth Publication
ICS Press
San Francisco, California

Inquiries, book orders, and catalog requests should be addressed to ICS Press, 243 Kearny Street, San Francisco, California, 94108. Telephone: (415) 981-5353; fax: (415) 986-4878. For book orders and catalog requests, call toll free in the contiguous United States: **(800) 326-0263.**

Cover design by M.R.P. Design.

Index by Shirley Kessel.

Distributed to the trade by National Book Network, Lanham, Maryland.

Library of Congress Cataloging-in-Publication Data
Exchange rate policies in developing and post-socialist countries /
    edited by Emil-Maria Claassen.
        p.   cm.
    Proceedings of the Second Monetary Conference of the Freie
Universität Berlin and the Landeszentralbank Berlin, held
05/10–12/90, at the Berliner Bank, and sponsored by the
International Center for Economic Growth.
    "An International Center for Economic Growth publication."
    Includes bibliographical references and index.
    ISBN 1-55815-146-X (pbk.)
    1. Foreign exchange—Congresses.   2. Monetary policy—Developing
countries—Congresses.   I. Claassen, Emil-Maria, 1934–   .
II. International Center for Economic Growth.   III. Monetary
Conference of the Freie Universität Berlin and the Landeszentralbank
Berlin (2nd : 1990 : Berliner Bank)
HG3877.E93   1991
332.4'56—dc20
                                                            91-5029
                                                            CIP

CONTENTS

LIST OF TABLES

LIST OF FIGURES

PREFACE

Exchange Rate Policies in Developing and Post-Socialist Countries looks at one of the most important questions that all countries—both developing ᴧnd developed—must answer: What is the optimal exchange rate regime?

Answering this question appropriately and following through with policy are now vital for economic progress in the developing and former socialist countries. Developing countries are coping with a history of import substitution, overvalued currencies, and hyperinflation. Meanwhile, the countries of Eastern Europe face a legacy of price controls, repressed inflation, and currencies that cannot be converted into goods. Both groups of countries are dealing with the effects of capital-intensive forms of production and rudimentary financial systems.

All of these problems are related to exchange rate policies. But reforming such policies is a large and difficult job. In what order should reforms be instituted? Should the exchange rate be fixed or managed? How can currency reform be made credible? And, for Germany, how can the monetary systems of two countries best be unified? Emil-Maria Claassen and the contributors to this volume—several of whom are helping the countries of Eastern Europe restructure their economies— bring their expertise and experience to bear on these hard questions.

This book presents the discussions that took place at a conference held May 10–12, 1990, in Berlin. The ideas presented in *Exchange Rate Policies in Developing and Post-Socialist Countries* will surely be useful for policy makers and economists playing a role in the changes still to come. We are pleased to have cosponsored the conference and to publish this important book.

Nicolás Ardito-Barletta
General Director
International Center for Economic Growth

November 1991
Panama City, Panama

Acknowledgments

This volume is the outcome of the Second Monetary Conference of the Freie Universität Berlin and the Landeszentralbank Berlin, which took place May 10–12, 1990, at the Berliner Bank. The conference was made possible by the financial support of the following institutions (in alphabetical order):

Banca d'Italia (Rome)
Berliner Bank (Berlin)
Commerzbank (Berlin)
Deutsche Bank (Berlin)
Deutsche Stiftung für Internationale Entwicklung (Berlin)
Dresdner Bank (Berlin)
Flick Stiftung (Düsseldorf)
Freie Universität Berlin
International Center for Economic Growth
  (Panama City and San Francisco)
Landeszentralbank Berlin
Repap Enterprises Inc. (Montreal)
Senat der Stadt Berlin
Sparkasse der Stadt Berlin

My special thanks are addressed to these donors and to all the institutions of Berlin.

Emil-Maria Claassen

PART ONE

INTRODUCTION

EMIL-MARIA CLAASSEN

Exchange Rate Policies in Developing and Post-Socialist Countries: An Overview

The year 1989 was probably as decisive for world history as the year 1789 was two hundred years earlier. The political democratization and the economic liberalization of Eastern Europe constitute a challenge to any third-way solution between capitalism and socialism. It took seventy years after the rise of Marxism-Leninism in the Soviet Union for the world to recognize that democracy and the market economy are among the least of evils for the political and economic organization of society.

The countries of the third world passed through a shorter period of painful experience. Many of them, having become independent during the 1950s (except mainly those in Latin America), went through the experimental phase of the economic third-way solution that was widely preached in that decade by the universities of Oxford, Cambridge, and Paris. Beginning in the 1980s, under the pressure of twenty or thirty years of mismanagement, they began to turn to a more liberalized economy. The recent experience of liberalization by the South (developing countries) can serve as a lesson for the transition of the East (socialist countries).

For both the South and the East, microeconomic or structural reforms (in terms of the legal and fiscal framework, of privatization, of commercial banking and financial markets, and of the proper relative price structure among tradables, between tradables and nontradables, and among factors of production) seem to be more urgent than macroeconomic policies. They are even prerequisites for the success of stabilization policies. If stabilization policies are broadly defined as monetary, fiscal, and exchange rate policies, this volume on exchange rate policies must view them necessarily in the larger context of macroeconomic policies.

In the first section of this chapter, I begin by describing the similarities and differences between the developing countries and the socialist (or former socialist) countries in Central and Eastern Europe. One of the main differences between these two groups of countries is their organizing principle. One relies (or relied) on a centrally planned economy and the other on a market economy with a huge public sector and many disruptive state interventions. The organizing principle of socialist economies leads to the lack of internal and external convertibility common to all Central and Eastern European currencies, as seen in the second section.

An implication of the shortage of goods in a planned economy, which is the main cause of inconvertibility, is the existence of a monetary overhang, which gives rise to repressed inflation or to open inflation during the transition period. Both inflationary situations could be corrected by a properly administered currency reform. In the third section, it is seen that past experiences in industrialized countries, as well as in developing countries, should provide some policy guidelines.

For any economic policy and, in particular, for any fundamental liberalization reform, the question of credibility is a decisive criterion for success in both developing countries and socialist countries. The choice of an exchange rate regime rests upon the decision as to whether the exchange rate or the quantity of money (that is, the internal conduct of monetary policy) has been selected as the nominal anchor of the monetary system. Currency reforms are probably only credible when they are accompanied by a fixed (equilibrium) exchange rate. The recent tendency within the third world toward more flexible exchange rate arrangements is welcomed when it leads to the external adjustment needed to absorb external shocks, but it could also be the result of internal mismanagement. In the latter case, more flexible exchange rates could mean the loss of a credible nominal anchor as a yardstick for monetary discipline, as discussed in the fourth section.

An important issue for the South, as well as for the East, is the sequencing of economic reforms. We have already mentioned the sequencing of microeconomic (structural) and macroeconomic (stabilization) policies. Whether liberalization reforms should be gradual or radical is another basic question for both types of economies. This choice is decisive for the length of the transition period. More fundamentally, gradualism may lack credibility and lead to a complete failure of reforms. If we look at specific sequencing issues, such as those of trade account and capital account liberalization, there are consistent arguments, given in the fifth section, that trade liberalization should come before financial convertibility.

The phenomenon of overvaluation has plagued many countries of the third world. Recognition of an overvalued currency presumes knowledge of the fundamental real equilibrium exchange rate, which is important to know for all types of economies. The extent of disequilibrium has to be judged according to the proper mix of stabilization policies, since the current account not only depends on the relative price of tradable to nontradable goods but also on the level of domestic expenditures and therefore on the fiscal stance. Overvaluation can be seen as the source of the growth collapse of several countries during the 1980s. A deliberate overvaluation policy can sometimes be of fiscal origin. In the sixth section, it is seen that a dual exchange rate regime, with an official overvalued exchange rate and a black-market rate, can provide considerable tax revenues derived from export revenues being sold at the official rate.

The exchange rate policy of the newly industrialized countries of East Asia is a special case among developing countries. The seventh section discusses whether these countries should peg to the U.S. dollar or freely float, or whether they should follow a common policy of a managed float or even form a currency area.

The chapter concludes with a discussion of the central theme of this volume: the optimal exchange rate regime. In restrospect, the choice between fixed and flexible exchange rates has been changed to one between fixed and managed floating exchange rates. Candidates for a pegged exchange rate are small open economies, such as those of Eastern Europe. A managed floating exchange rate can be combined with the formation of a currency area. The worst of all exchange rate regimes is a fixed and overvalued exchange rate, as has been observed in many developing countries in the past.

Differences and Similarities between Developing and Socialist Economies

According to the World Bank's classification of developing countries, the socialist countries are generally upper middle-income economies having a per capita gross national product (GNP) below US$6,000 (while low-income economies are below US$400 and middle-income economies are below US$2,000). Thus Czechoslovakia, Hungary, and Yugoslavia are approaching the level of Portugal, whereas the former German Democratic Republic is above it.

The main difference beween the third world and the second world probably lies in the importance of the public sector and therefore in the organizing principle of the overall economy. The dream for the classical Soviet-type model was to run the whole economy like one huge factory. Even though many developing countries have in common an important public sector, with all accompanying distortions, the differences in their nature rest upon the organizing principle of their economy. For developing countries, important sectors are more likely run as in a market economy. Consequently, structural adjustment measures in the South, though extremely painful, are still milder than those involved in the transition of the Eastern economies toward a rudimentary market economy.

The second difference, a corollary of the first, is the degree of openness of the economy: the socialist economies are closed, while the developing economies are relatively open. It is also necessary to distinguish large and small economies, since both India and the Soviet Union are rather closed. However, even the small Central European countries are highly closed economies, because of the bilateral trade (or barter) relationships among them and because of the external inconvertibility of their currencies not only with respect to the industrialized countries but also among themselves. Exchange controls can also exist in the South, but there international trade is predominantly multilateral. The closed nature of the socialist economies is the result of their refusal to participate in any international division of labor, implying an adherence to the principle of autarky. The most striking example is Albania.

On the other hand, many similarities exist between the South and the East. Unbalanced growth is one example. Both the South and the East gave priority to industrialization, which was pursued in many cases at the expense of agriculture. The East stressed heavy industry (investment goods), while the South favored light industry (consumption goods) through a policy of import substitution. In addition, the socialist countries discouraged production of nontradable goods (such as housing, transport, and handicrafts).

Another similarity between the two types of countries involves the allocation of resources. Disguised unemployment is one common feature. Capital-intensive production, resulting from the artificially low price of capital, is another. Two particular characteristics of the East are related to the quality of their production factors (labor and capital). On the one hand, workers are highly qualified, at least in Central Europe, because of the education system inherited from the precommunist past. On the other hand, the investment ratio is high (mostly above 20 percent), owing to the necessity for inventory stocks in a monetary system of limited domestic convertibility. Since money cannot buy goods, firms are forced to stock all kinds of primary and intermediate goods in order to maintain production.

A final common element between the East and the South is the rudimentary structure of the financial system. Both types of economies generally possess financial assets consisting only of currency, bank deposits, and treasury bonds, largely because of financial repression. In the East, repressed inflation, the subsequent limited internal convertibility of the domestic currency, and the nonexistence of property rights are the culprits. In the South, credit controls, credit selection, interest ceilings, and the predominance of the rural sector over the urban sector are the main reasons for financial underdevelopment.

Internal and External Convertibility

With price controls still in effect, the domestic currency in any former socialist economy is prevented from functioning as a means of payment and a store of value. Consequently, goods take on the functions of money. On the one hand, a large share of domestic transactions takes the form of barter. On the other hand, goods are hoarded by households and firms as a store of value. Thus, a paradoxical situation arises: goods are in abundance as far as hoardings are concerned, and they are simultaneously in shortage because they are purchasable in a limited amount of (soft) goods against the domestic currency. Ronald McKinnon has estimated the inventories of firms for the Soviet Union for 1985. They amounted to 82 percent of national income, while U.S. firms accumulated inventories equal to 31 percent for the same year.

The share of Eastern Europe and the Soviet Union in total world trade was under 8 percent in the late 1980s. Roughly half of it was traded among the members of the Council for Mutual Economic Assistance (CMEA). Despite the formal existence of a common socialist currency, called the transfer ruble, trade among CMEA members was basically bilateral (which is merely barter), while multilateral trade accounted only for 1 percent of total CMEA trade. The basic idea of the transfer ruble was that a country could be a net exporter to one country and use its transfer ruble surpluses as a net importer from another CMEA country. However, that type of multilateral trade arrangement was never achieved (except for the 1 percent mentioned), simply because a country with balances in transfer rubles could not use them for buying goods in another member country that was not disposing of any available goods. In reality, the transfer ruble was not convertible in goods and thus was not transferable. Similarly, the domestic currencies on the internal market were not convertible into domestic goods, as a result of the shortage of goods.

Bilateral trade negotiations consisted mainly of five-year trade agreements, which were detailed in yearly trade protocols. Each country tried to obtain *hard* goods (goods in short supply within the CMEA region, such as raw materials and food products) by selling *soft* goods (mostly machinery, which could not be sold easily to the West). As Marie Lavigne notes in Chapter 7, the specific trade pattern was revealed to have some subsidizing elements by the Soviet Union in favor of its trading partners, at least until 1986–1988. On the one hand, the terms of trade were favorable. The Soviet Union sold oil at low prices, compared with prices of acquired Eastern European machinery. However, this trend was revised in the late 1980s because of the worldwide decline in oil prices. On the other hand, having experienced a long-time trade surplus (with a corresponding accumulation of transfer rubles), the Soviet Union moved toward a deficit position with the granting of foreign trade rights to a growing number of Soviet enterprises, which could earn foreign currencies in order to import on their own account.

In early 1990, the CMEA members agreed (or expressed the hope) to shift toward foreign trade based on world prices and settled in convertible currencies from 1991 on. The dominant view in the West is that Eastern Europe should be increasingly integrated into the world economy, while the Soviet Union may be disjoined from Eastern Europe because of the uncertainty about its future economic reform. Consequently, a revival of the CMEA as a regional union would not be desirable. External currency convertibility would be an important part of the transition process toward a market economy and toward integration into the Western world economy, so that any further efforts for intraregional convertibility within Eastern Europe would be redundant.

However, this view is not shared by Marie Lavigne. She is concerned about the time frame of the transition, which she believes should be a gradual process, in particular as regards intraregional trade relationships. Reducing trade within the CMEA from the present 50 percent average of total trade to, for instance, 20 percent of total trade would be devastating, since foreign trade could not be diverted to the West because of the lack of competitiveness. One possible scheme for providing additional multilateral trade would be monetary arrangements involving settlement in domestic currencies, provided that they become progressively convertible within each economy, within the CMEA area, and outside the area.

Repressed versus Open Inflation and Currency Reforms

Repressed inflation refers to a situation in which the price level is fixed (by price controls), and there is a simultaneous excess supply of money (the monetary overhang) and a corresponding excess demand for goods. This phenomenon expresses the shortage of goods within the economy or the imperfect convertibility of the domestic currency into domestic goods (that is, lack of internal convertibility).

If one opts to avoid open inflation, it is necessary to eliminate the monetary overhang. There are many technical ways to do so, as emphasized by Robert Mundell in Chapter 2. The simplest, but probably also the least popular, way would be to confiscate a part of the outstanding volume of bank deposits. A less harmful method would be to freeze bank deposits and to wait to determine what to do with the frozen deposits in the future. They could be converted later into property titles of physical assets during the privatization process of state-owned enterprises and land. They could also be converted into new government bonds, implying a fiscal deterioration as to future debt service. Until 1990, no Eastern country, except East Germany, had chosen to confiscate or freeze deposits. The conversion rate of East German mark prices and wages into West German mark prices and wages was 1:1, while the conversion rate of East German mark currency into West German mark currency was 1.6:1, according to my calculation.

Two important observations must be made with respect to a price-level peg. On the one hand, after the elimination of the monetary overhang, prices can and should be decontrolled in order to introduce the necessary change in relative prices. At that stage, the price-level peg can be replaced by an exchange rate peg, so that the domestic relative prices of tradable goods would reflect those of the international economy. On the other hand, as Robert Mundell emphasizes, a monetary overhang cannot be eliminated by canceling one or two zeros of the outstanding quantity of money (examples are the New French franc or the new pesos) and by also reducing prices by the same proportion, since the excess supply of money would be maintained, but expressed by another numeraire.

An open inflation is the alternative to equilibrating the money market through decontrol of prices. The money supply is not reduced, but the money demand is increased as a result of rising prices. The subsequent (short-lived) hyperinflation (as in Poland or Yugoslavia) could also be regarded as a silent confiscation of the monetary overhang, since its real value is reduced to zero through the price-level increase. Robert Mundell points out that inflation is usually preferred to direct confiscation, since it operates by deceit on an unsuspecting public. However, as Reuven Brenner remarks in Chapter 6, confiscation through open inflation is not all that dramatic, since people were already used to high prices in black markets. The official price level was largely understated, and real wages were overstated. The high prices in black markets actually were nominal bribes to avoid the long queues or years of waiting.

If the country opted for open inflation, a currency reform that would promote the credibility of future monetary policy could be adopted. Since open inflation restores internal convertibility, a monetary anchor in the form of a fixed exchange rate could guarantee some kind of external convertibility and, therefore, confidence in future price-level stability.

This type of currency reform occurred in Poland and Yugoslavia. As Roman Frydman, Stanislaw Wellisz, and Grzegorz Kolodko describe the Polish situation in Chapter 4, the exchange rate was set on January 1, 1990, above the free market rate at 9,500 zlotys to the U.S. dollar. Zlotys were freely convertible into dollars. In the first months of 1990, there was a considerable shift from dollars into zlotys, since the latter were made attractive by high interest rates on zloty deposits. Poland's open inflation took place mainly from August 1989 to February 1990, with a retail price index of 1,640 (December 1988 = 100), while afterward monthly inflation rates were less than double digit. Yugoslavia's open inflation represented several thousand percentage points in 1989 and early 1990. Yugoslavia then introduced a new convertible dinar for 10,000 old dinars and pegged the new dinar to the deutsche mark at 7:1. As in the case of Poland, there was a considerable shift from deutsche mark holdings into holdings of the new dinar, since the latter shared equally high returns on deposits. The Yugoslavian currency reform resembles Germany's currency reform of November 1923 (see Chapter 5), when one trillion paper marks were exchanged for one gold mark (or Rentenmark) and where the exchange rate of the gold mark to the U.S. dollar was set at 4.2:1.

As all contributors on the inflation issue emphasize, a currency reform is only fully successful with a proper mix of monetary, fiscal, and exchange rate stabilization. Since, in many cases, monetary financing of the budget deficit is the main cause of hyperinflation, fiscal austerity is a precondition for success. For Eastern countries, however, the fiscal picture looks far more varied. There are two monetary sources for open inflation: (1) the monetary overhang built up during the period of repressed inflation and (2) the additional money creation during the transition phase.

This latter aspect is demonstrated in this book by Ronald McKinnon for the Soviet Union, but it is equally applicable to other Eastern socialist countries. In the absence of an elaborate fiscal system, the main government revenue of socialist countries was derived in former times from the surpluses of enterprises. The central planning authorities fixed prices according to cost (labor, intermediaries, etc.), plus transfer of the so-called surplus to the government. When the first price deregulations went into effect and certain enterprises were allowed to set prices freely, the surpluses disappeared. The Soviet budget deficit rose progressively from 1.8 percent of GNP in 1985 to 10 percent in 1989 (to 14 percent according to Reuven Brenner in this book). According to Roman Frydman, Stanislaw Wellisz, and Grzegorz Kolodko, the Polish budget deficit was 7 percent of GNP in 1989 and was estimated to be reduced to 1.5 percent in 1990 owing to various fiscal reforms and to the cut in subsidies.

There is a third inflationary source in many Eastern countries (provided that the banking system has not been reformed), as both Ronald McKinnon and Reuven Brenner show. In the planned economies, firms had full access to bank credits at zero or low interest rates in order to finance the purchase of inputs they needed to fulfill the plans. In the terminology of the Hungarian economist Kornai (1986), enterprises had *soft* budget constraints. To the extent that bank reforms are slowed down, this specific lack of financial constraint constitutes another source of inflation.

Open inflation can lead to hyperinflation, as in Yugoslavia and to a lesser extent in Poland. Among developing countries, Latin America is the most frequent candidate for hyperinflation, and Argentina is the most obvious example of the failure of various anti-inflation plans. The traditional approach to stabilization in Argentina was the announcement of fiscal discipline plus price controls, and the traditional result was increasing inflation after a short period of stabilization. The Austral Plan of June 1985 confirmed this tradition. The lack of fiscal discipline, together with unsound monetary management, accelerated inflation in 1986–1987. The consequences of the Austral Plan lasted for several years, with the result that credibility in the government's announcements vanished completely.

The Primavera Plan, which was introduced some months before spring 1988, had some positive aspects for the liberalization of foreign exchange controls and of commercial policy. When the authorities abandoned the idea of heterodox policies (in terms of the income-policy approach) and moved gradually to more orthodox measures, such as the reduction of the budget deficit and sound monetary management, it was too late. The strong credibility available at the beginning of the Austral Plan was gone. The lack of credibility and the fear of repudiation of the government debt increased interest rates to over 30 percent for operations in U.S. dollars—that is, four times the LIBOR (London interbank offered rate).

Roque Fernández makes an interesting point in Chapter 11 on the choice between using debt financing or money creation to finance a budget deficit. Under normal circumstances, it is believed that more debt finance and less money creation reduces the inflation rate. However, to the extent that an increased stock of public debt involves higher real interest rates, as was the case for Argentina, the budget deficit deteriorates, implying higher monetary finance and a higher inflation rate. The impact of greater borrowing on the stock of public debt and on the real interest rate requires more inflation to pay for it than the alternative of not borrowing (depending on which side of the Laffer curve the economy is located). Consequently, the decisive anti-inflationary measure is again reducing the budget deficit.

Choice of the Nominal Anchor

Among the lessons to be drawn from open macroeconomics over the past three decades is the recognition that policy makers can fix only one nominal variable, while the others become endogenous (provided that markets clear). According to Robert Mundell, among the nominal variables available as the single exogenous one (that is, the nominal anchor of the system) are the quantity of money, the nominal exchange rate, the price level, and the nominal wage rate. The Western industrialized countries normally choose between the first two variables (that is, either the outstanding quantity of money or the exchange rate). The first monetary system consists of a fixed quantity of money and a flexible exchange rate. The second system is just the contrary: a fixed exchange rate and a flexible quantity of money.

The idea of targeting the money supply can be ascribed to the monetarist school. When the rate of growth of the money supply is fixed, all other nominal variables adjust as endogenous magnitudes: the price level, the nominal exchange rate, and the nominal wage rate. Furthermore, these three endogenous nominal variables have to move in such a way that the resulting real exchange rate and real wage rate ensure an equilibrium in the real sector of the economy (goods market and labor market, respectively). The money supply target can be motivated by the ultimate goal of price-level stability or a low inflation rate. The three present monetary areas in the world economy (the dollar, deutsche mark, and yen areas) could be interpreted so that the center countries in each area fix the growth rate of the money supply according to the desired price-level evolution, while all other nominal variables float correspondingly.

The second monetary system consists of a fixed nominal exchange rate that is attained by letting all other nominal variables float. Its ultimate goal could also be price-level stability or a low inflation rate. Since a country can fix only one exchange rate $(n-1)$ among the various exchange rates (n representing the number of currencies in the world), it would choose the exchange rate of the country with which it has important trade relationships and which succeeds relatively well in pursuing price-level stability. The evolution of the European Monetary System (EMS) toward a German monetary area is a striking example.

The choice between a fixed and a floating exchange rate is not a matter of indifference if the monetary authorities of the country have a lack of credibility as a consequence of their past inflation-prone behavior. Pegging to the deutsche mark involves following the monetary policy of the Deutsche Bundesbank, which has gained a high level of credibility with respect to the maintenance of price-level stability over the past four decades.

Pegging the price level is probably the most inconvenient method, since it would not only imply price control of thousands, if not millions, of goods, but it would result primarily in the distortion of relative prices. The control of a single price would be the other extreme, consisting of pegging the exchange rate as the simplest device if the specific currency is convertible on the domestic and international level. The choice of nominal wages is the ultimate ratio in the Keynesian case of wage rigidities.

Since the late 1970s, developing countries as a whole have moved toward more flexible exchange rate arrangements. These arrangements could be managed floating or be independently floating. In most cases, however, these terms do not accurately describe the underlying exchange rate policy, since the exchange rate is ultimately set by the authorities, even though it is frequently adjusted. Until the mid-1970s, the overwhelming part of the third world pegged to a single currency. As Bijan Aghevli and Peter Montiel show in Chapter 8, during 1976–1989, the proportion of countries pegging to a single currency fell from 63 percent to 38 percent, while the proportion of countries relying on flexible arrangements more than doubled (to exactly one-third).

Three main factors contributed to the more flexible arrangements of exchange rates. With the wide fluctuations in the exchange rates of the industrialized countries, a number of countries opted to peg to a basket of currencies and made frequent adjustments of the exchange rate vis-à-vis the intervention currency (mostly the single currency to which they had previously pegged). A second factor, particularly for countries in Latin America, was the sharp acceleration of domestic inflation during the 1980s. Rapid depreciation of their currencies was inevitable in order to avoid a deterioration in their external competitiveness. Finally, during the same period, the emergence of external shocks (slowdown in the growth of industrialized countries, increase in the international interest rate, the debt crisis, and adverse terms-of-trade effects) forced many developing countries into depreciation as one element of a generalized stabilization program.

An interesting question, also raised by Bijan Aghevli and Peter Montiel, concerns the use of the exchange rate as the nominal anchor, a practice that had been abandoned by countries that shifted toward increased flexibility of nominal exchange rates. Since nominal devaluations may undermine financial discipline, the result can be a strong domestic inflationary pressure, giving rise to a real appreciation and thus to a loss in international competitiveness.

The generalized movement toward more flexible exchange rate arrangements could imply higher inflationary tendencies as a consequence of the abandonment of the exchange rate as the nominal anchor. If nothing can anchor the domestic price level, attempts to achieve a real depreciation through nominal devaluations may simply end in accelerated domestic inflation. This lesson should also be taught to Eastern European countries in their attempt to establish external competitiveness and to maintain price stability, at least for the small open economies of Central Europe in contrast to the large and relatively closed economy of the Soviet Union. For the developing countries as a whole, Aghevli and Montiel show that the real exchange rate appreciated during 1978–1982, stabilized up to 1985, and depreciated only in the second half of the 1980s, despite a considerable acceleration of inflation during the last period.

If the nominal exchange rate is used as the nominal anchor to avoid inflationary pressure, any necessary adjustment in terms of a depreciating real exchange rate must stem from domestic financial policies to decelerate the domestic price level. However, the need to reverse the general tendency of more flexibility and replace it with more rigid nominal exchange rates in developing countries raises the question of credibility. Once countries are accustomed to altering the nominal exchange rate, the decision to peg it persistently may not be perceived by the public as a credible policy action. The time dimension of the inflationary past may constitute the main element for monetary confidence in the future. Once the authorities have proceeded to a nominal devaluation without changing the real exchange rate, the confidence in stable future monetary policy may be broken. Ideally, it could be argued, nominal devaluation should have been used in the past only for mitigating external shocks while excluding any ratification of domestic inflationary pressure.

Sequencing of Reforms and Convertibility

The sequencing of macroeconomic and microeconomic reforms is rather simultaneous in the case of Germany. It is precisely for that reason that the deutsche mark was introduced, in order to make possible all other economic reforms. The labor market played a predominant role in the monetary and economic unification of East and West Germany. Because there was perfect labor mobility from East Germany to West Germany, after the removal of the wall between them on November 9, 1989, gradual adjustment measures would not have stopped the labor migration. Even under the adopted shock therapy (monetary union, implementation of the Western legal, fiscal, and social system, and progressive privatization of combinates that were not doomed to bankruptcy), a unified labor market with low wage differences is still an enormous danger for increasing unemployment in both East and West Germany. I conclude that both East and West Germany did not have any other viable and credible alternative than the German monetary union.

Reuven Brenner, as he states in Chapter 6, thinks that macroeconomic policies (such as monetary, fiscal, and exchange rate stabilization) should come after implementation of basic legal and economic reforms (such as the introduction of property rights, bankruptcy laws, and a simple tax system). Thus, the policy of decontrolling prices would be meaningless if no legal decentralized framework exists for determining prices by privatized enterprises. If the bureaucracy is not abolished, the well-established tradition of corruption (similar in many developing countries) will continue the misallocation of resources.

An important issue in the appropriate sequencing of liberalization policies is liberalization of trade and capital flows. Conventional wisdom suggests that trade account reforms should be implemented first and that the liberalization of the capital account should be realized afterward. The reason for this is that the abolishment of capital controls (and a well-functioning domestic capital market) may lead to net capital inflows and, therefore, to a real appreciation that would not favor the tradable goods sector and the current account. On the other hand, the liberalization of foreign trade through the suppression of trade impediments and tariffs would necessitate a compensating devaluation. As a consequence, trade liberalization should come first in order to consolidate the industrial or tradable goods sector. Simultaneous capital liberalization would endanger only the structural reform of the trade account. Furthermore, the capital inflows would be unsustainable in the future, provided that the tradable goods sector has not been sufficiently restructured, as is needed for future debt service.

In Chapter 9 Sebastian Edwards confirms the above sequencing of liberalization measures on the basis of an intertemporal framework. By reviewing empirical studies on Argentina, Chile, Colombia, and Uruguay, he comes to the following results. On the one hand, for these four countries, trade liberalization required a depreciation of the equilibrium real exchange rate (the real exchange rate being defined as the relative price of tradables to nontradables). On the other hand, development of a liberalized, nonrepressed domestic capital market produced an appreciation of the equilibrium real exchange rate. These results are not only of extreme importance for the stabilization and structural adjustment policies in the South, but they should also constitute a guideline for the sequencing of liberalization reforms in the East. Capital liberalization tends to frustrate the depreciation that is necessary to sustain trade reform. The capital account should be opened up after the current account is fully liberalized.

The Phenomenon of Overvaluation

Until the early 1970s, the world economy experienced a "golden age" of growth. Then, various real shocks emerged: the oil price rise of 1973, the boom and fall in commodity prices (terms-of-trade effects), increasing unemployment in the industrial world, the second oil-price shock, large fluctuations in capital flows, the debt problem, and high real interest rates. Many of them were common to a great number of developing countries, but economic performance and, in particular, growth performance diverged sharply. Out of a sample of twenty-one developing countries chosen for a World Bank study entitled "The Political Economy of Poverty, Equity, and Growth," Deepak Lal observes in Chapter 10 a growth collapse in eleven of them (Brazil, Costa Rica, Ghana, Indonesia, Jamaica, Madagascar, Mexico, Nigeria, Peru, Turkey, and Uruguay).

One of the common causes for the growth collapse was an overvalued real exchange rate, indicating a fall in competitiveness. There were several reasons for this misalignment. Many countries were confronted by accelerating inflation, resulting from huge budget deficits with an increasing ratio of public debt to gross domestic product (GDP). In general, the nominal exchange rate adjustment and the inflation path led to an overvaluation of the real exchange rate.

Another reason for growth collapses in countries with only moderate inflation (for example, Nigeria and Jamaica) is related to the real exchange rate effect of the "Dutch disease" phenomenon. In general, an external shock arising from a favorable terms-of-trade evolution for specific export commodities or arising from heavy capital inflows led to a real appreciation of the exchange rate. The causal link was generally fiscal expansion through the windfall profits of the primary export sector or through easier borrowing abroad. In many cases, since the additional public expenditures were partly for nontradable goods, the domestic prices of nontradable goods rose, leading to a real appreciation. When there was a reversal of the terms of trade or a cessation of foreign borrowing, public expenditures had to be reduced (that is, there was a fall in absorption) and the real exchange rate had to return to its original level. If there were nominal wage rigidities or sluggishness in price movements of nontradable goods, the last resort would be a nominal devaluation. Maintenance of an overvalued real exchange rate, as observed, must be explained either by an insufficient reduction in government expenditures or by an insufficient adjustment of the price of nontradable goods and of the nominal exchange rate.

Price controls arrived at by setting official prices below equilibrium prices imply rationing (for instance, through queueing up) and the formation of black markets. Exchange controls that set the official exchange rate below the equilibrium one (overvaluation) also imply rationing and the emergence of black foreign-exchange markets. In the past, many socialist and developing countries have lived with this everyday phenomenon.

This type of a dual regime of official and black market exchange rates misallocates resources through tax-subsidy effects. Provided that all commercial foreign exchange transactions take place at the official exchange rate, exporters are taxed and importers are subsidized. One part of the export revenues comes from smuggling, while the other part of export revenues is sold at the official exchange rate. The tax rate on these official export revenues is equal to the black market premium on foreign exchange. It is an implicit tax from which importers and the government profit. According to Brian Pinto in Chapter 12, importers are rationed through import licenses sold by the government at the official exchange rate. Domestic prices of tradables reflect those of the black foreign-exchange market. Consequently, importers receive a rent linked to the difference between the black market and the official rate. Taxation of exports at the premium rate creates disincentives to produce exports and lowers the ability to import (in particular, to import intermediate goods), which leads to the phenomenon of import compression. On the other hand, to the extent that the government is a net buyer of foreign exchange for its proper purchases of imported goods and for the service on its foreign debt, the other part of the implicit tax on export producers is used by the government. This phenomenon has been studied by Brian Pinto for various anglophone African countries.

Exchange rate unification (that is, the increase of the official rate to approximate the black market rate) raises a policy dilemma. On the one hand, unification leads to benefits for resource allocation by increasing exports and eliminating import compression. On the other hand, for an unchanged volume of public expenditures, the government needs more tax revenues. If more ordinary taxes cannot be raised, the alternative is to increase the inflation tax (provided that the money-demand elasticity with respect to the inflation rate is still less than unity). Consequently, a trade-off occurs between the benefits for resource allocation and the inflation costs of unification. This trade-off can be avoided only when the new exchange rate policy is combined with fiscal reforms to reduce the budget deficit, as Brian Pinto demonstrates for Ghana and Sierra Leone. Gradual exchange rate unification would be ineffective without matching fiscal reform.

Exchange Rate Policy of Newly Industrialized Countries

What is the appropriate exchange rate policy for developing countries that are close competitors, whose development strategy is based on manufactured, export-led growth, whose prices are stable, and whose growth performance has been around 10 percent a year over the past two decades? These countries are the East Asian newly industrialized countries (NICs): Hong Kong, South Korea, Singapore, and Taiwan. All four countries have been running a persistent trade deficit with Japan and a surplus with the United States. For the 1980s, a synchronized movement of their real effective exchange rates is evident. Until 1985, they remained rather stable. When the U.S. dollar began to depreciate against the yen and the deutsche mark, the currencies of the NICs appreciated significantly less with respect to the dollar than did the yen, leading to a depreciation of their currencies in real effective terms. From that moment onward, the NICs (in particular, Korea and Taiwan) were increasingly criticized for exercising trade protection through currency depreciation.

In Chapter 13, Yung Chul Park and Won-Am Park discuss two exchange rate proposals. The first consists of the establishment of an Asian Monetary System, with Japan as the center, along the pattern of the European Monetary System (EMS). One of the main arguments against such an Asian monetary integration is the relatively small size of intra-regional trade among Asian economies in comparison to the trade dominance of the NICs with the United States and Europe for exports and with Japan for imports. Having a peg to the yen, the NICs are forced to revalue their currencies with respect to nonyen currencies whenever the yen appreciates.

The second proposal is a managed joint float of the currencies of the NICs (and probably of some other East Asian currencies) with respect to a trade-weighted basket of key currencies. A joint float with respect to a common basket would eliminate the problem of competitive depreciation among NICs. According to Park and Park, the joint float could repesent a first step toward the establishment of a currency area in the Asian Pacific region. However, no political leadership now exists that is strong enough to bring about such a scheme among the East Asian NICs.

Concluding Remarks on the Optimal Exchange Rate Regime

John Williamson's advice in the concluding chapter on the choice of an adequate exchange rate regime is a rate between a fixed or managed floating exchange rate. He discourages floating rates, pointing out the huge misalignments of exchange rates and the existence of speculative bubbles that he says characterized the 1970s and, in particular, the 1980s.

He recommends a fixed rate for a country that satisfies three conditions: (1) it should have a small open economy, (2) the currency to which it pegs should play the role of a stable anchor, (3) the central bank should be replaced by a currency board, or alternatively, an independent central bank committed to the fixed rate should be established. He answers the question of whether a country should choose a single-currency peg or a multicurrency peg in a pragmatic way. If 50 percent or more of a country's trade is with one single country, it should peg to the currency of that country (provided that the latter is also a stable anchor in terms of monetary stability). Otherwise, it should opt for a currency basket of the currencies of its most important trading partners.

In all other cases, the priority should be given to a managed exchange rate, either with close bands (as in the EMS) or with wide bands (as envisaged by John Williamson's target zone proposal). Monetary policy or nonsterilized interventions in the foreign exchange market should be the instruments of exchange rate management. Also here, the question is whether the management of the exchange rate should have as a peg a single currency or a basket of currencies. A single-currency peg stabilizes the bilateral rate, while considerable changes can occur in the effective exchange rate. A multi-currency peg stabilizes the effective exchange rate (macroeconomic stability), while considerable fluctuations can occur in the bilateral rates (microeconomic instability).

The real difficulty of a managed exchange rate regime is to know precisely the fundamental equilibrium exchange rate that should indicate the target level of the managed exchange rate. John Williamson's answer has been known for a decade. It is the rate that reconciles internal equilibrium (highest level of domestic activity with continued control of inflation) and external equilibrium in the medium term (sustainable current account imbalances). Sebastian Edwards is more explicit about the current account criterion, since it is derived from a maximization of intertemporal welfare within an intertemporal current account constraint.

With respect to developing countries, John Williamson's yardstick of an overvalued currency depends on an examination of the evolution of nontraditional exports. If they are nonexistent, stagnant, or declining, this is prima facie evidence of overvaluation and of medium-term balance-of-payments problems. As far as socialist countries are concerned, he believes that a convertible currency is the most promising way of reforming the price structure of tradable goods. However, the commitment to a fixed nominal exchange rate for an indefinite future implies the danger of a future overvaluation, and thus of a future loss of credibility, if the underlying macroeconomic conditions cannot be fulfilled. As John Williamson remarks in the concluding chapter, "credibility is too precious to be squandered."

Stabilization Policies in Developing and Socialist Countries

The topic of stabilization policies is a subject of both theoretical and practical interest. Like all topics with strong policy implications, it raises considerable controversy. Theoretical controversy centers on the appropriate model to be used for analysis. Policy controversy centers on the various objectives of stabilization policies, distributional implications of alternative policies, and differing views of the way the economy works. Stabilization policies in this chapter refer to macroeconomic policies designed to eliminate excess liquidity and to reduce or eliminate open or repressed inflation.

This topic concerns both socialist and developing economies. There are important similarities. No stabilization policy can be successful unless the overhang of liquidity that arises from price, wage, or exchange controls is eliminated; nor can equilibrium with comparatively stable prices be brought about without anchoring the rate of growth of the quantity of money at low inflation rates. The latter requires balanced budgets in countries where there is no market, at home or abroad, for government debt. These features—low and stable money growth and balanced budgets—are common denominators of stabilization policies in both socialist and developing countries.

There are also significant differences between the two groups of countries in levels of technological development, labor-force skills, and incentive systems. If the developing countries lack the technological development and skilled labor force of some of the socialist countries, they have, on the other hand, more open production systems in the private sector. It is doubtful whether the socialist (or former socialist) countries can achieve the microeconomic supply-side response that can be stimulated in the wake of successful macroeconomic stabilization policies unless drastic changes are made in regulations inhibiting the expansion of firms in the private sector. Much adaptation needs to be made in deregulation and privatization before stabilization policies that work in the developing countries will work in the socialist countries. Although the emphasis in this chapter is on macroeconomic stabilization policies, I do note those microeconomic supply-side policies that should accompany the macroeconomic policies as rapidly as possible.

One basic difference between the economies of socialist countries and all other economies is their vast government control or ownership. In the course of decontrolling the economy, it is expected that real estate will be privatized and that many state enterprises will be allowed to fail or to be sold to the private sector. These vast resources under the control of the governments of the socialist economies present a unique opportunity for making a link between the goals of privatization and the achievement of asset convertibility for the domestic currency.

The theme of stabilization policies is a little different from the focus of this book, which is exchange rate policies, but the difference is more superficial than fundamental. Any given exchange rate is the most likely pivot around which all other policies of the government of an open economy revolve. In any general equilibrium system, only one degree of freedom exists. If that single freedom is used to fix the exchange rate, other macroeconomic instruments must become variables. In general, only one level of prices, wages, and monetary aggregates can be associated with full employment and balance of payments equilibrium in an economy where the exchange rate is fixed.

The first part of the chapter discusses the architecture of macroeconomic stabilization policies. The second part discusses the microeconomic and institutional changes that should accompany stabilization policies.

Architecture of Stabilization Policies

This part develops a grammar for macroeconomic stabilization policies in developing and socialist economies, both of which lack a developed capital market. The basic approach is the general equilibrium method, with explicit attention focused on monetary, exchange rate, and price and wage variables.

General equilibrium and the four numeraires

In any economy, critical monetary or price vectors are relevant to stabilization policies. These include money prices (p), money wage rates (w), money supplies (m), and exchange rates (e). For purposes of static analysis, the stock of capital and land (K) and full employment output (Y) are assumed constant.

The vectors p, w, m, and e contain the number of elements needed for the discussion of stabilization policies. Prices (p) can be disaggregated into broad categories of import prices, export prices, domestic (nontraded) goods prices, wholesale prices, consumer goods prices, or gross domestic product (GDP)–deflator prices. Wage rates (w) can be disaggregated into the various categories of labor. The components of the money supply (m) can range from currency and bank reserves to demand, time, and savings deposits and various categories of other liquid financial instruments. The vector of exchange rates (e) includes the price of each foreign currency in the world market.

Corresponding to these four vectors are four classes of markets. The excess demands for goods, labor, money, and foreign exchange are denoted respectively by X, N, L, and F. The excess demands are functions of the four variables, and in equilibrium each is equal to zero:

$$
\begin{array}{llll}
\text{(goods)} & X &= X\,(p,\, w,\, m,\, e;\, K,\, Y) &= 0 \\
\text{(labor)} & N &= N\,(p,\, w,\, m,\, e;\, K,\, Y) &= 0 \\
\text{(money)} & L &= L\,(p,\, w,\, m,\, e;\, K,\, Y) &= 0 \qquad (1) \\
\text{(foreign exchange)} & F &= F\,(p,\, w,\, m,\, e;\, K,\, Y) &= 0.
\end{array}
$$

The four markets are connected by Walras's Law:

$$
pX + wN + L + eF \equiv 0.
$$

According to this law, the sum of the values of all excess demands is zero. Walras's Law would imply that the system is underdetermined (only three independent equations in four variables). However, the homogeneity postulate ensures that there are only three independent variables. If, for example, prices, wages, money, and the exchange rate are all increased in the same proportion, excess demands would remain unchanged. It is possible, therefore, to reduce the number of equations to three because of Walras's Law and also to reduce the number of variables to three because of the homogeneity postulate. The choice of the variables and equations (if any) to eliminate is less a matter of logic than a matter of convenience.

For purposes of clarification of stabilization theory, it is desirable to keep under observation each of the four markets. This leaves four interdependent equations. The choice of variable to use as numeraire is, again, a matter of convenience. Under a regime of fixed exchange rates, it would be convenient to use foreign exchange as the numeraire. Under a system where money wage rates are predetermined, it would be convenient to use wage rates as the numeraire (as in Keynesian analysis). Under a monetarist regime of fixed money supplies and flexible exchange rates, the money supply can be used as the numeraire. Under a regime where the target of stabilization policy is the domestic price level, that could be selected as numeraire. It is convenient to use the variable that is rigid or targeted as the numeraire.

In the case where the price level is a target of policy, all the variables can be deflated by the price level:

$$
\begin{aligned}
X &= X\,(1,\, w/p,\, m/p,\, e/p) &= 0 \\
N &= N\,(1,\, w/p,\, m/p,\, e/p) &= 0 \\
L &= L\,(1,\, w/p,\, m/p,\, e/p) &= 0 \\
F &= F\,(1,\, w/p,\, m/p,\, e/p) &= 0,
\end{aligned}
\tag{2}
$$

where the variables are real wage rates, real money balances, and real exchange rates.

In the case where the wage rate is fixed, the variables can be deflated by the wage rate (as in Keynes's general theory):

$$
\begin{aligned}
X &= X\,(p/w,\, 1,\, m/w,\, e/w) &= 0 \\
N &= N\,(p/w,\, 1,\, m/w,\, e/w) &= 0 \\
L &= L\,(p/w,\, 1,\, m/w,\, e/w) &= 0 \\
F &= F\,(p/w,\, 1,\, m/w,\, e/w) &= 0.
\end{aligned}
\tag{3}
$$

An alternative is to use the money supply as the numeraire. This approach may be helpful under monetarist policies of fixing the monetary target. The system then becomes:

$$
\begin{aligned}
X &= X\,(p/m,\, w/m,\, 1,\, e/m) &= 0 \\
N &= N\,(p/m,\, w/m,\, 1,\, e/m) &= 0 \\
L &= L\,(p/m,\, w/m,\, 1,\, e/m) &= 0 \\
F &= F\,(p/m,\, w/m,\, 1,\, e/m) &= 0.
\end{aligned}
\tag{4}
$$

Foreign currency is a convenient numeraire under a system of fixed exchange rates. In this case, the system becomes:

$$
\begin{aligned}
X &= X\,(p/e,\, w/e,\, m/e,\, 1) &= 0 \\
N &= N\,(p/e,\, w/e,\, m/e,\, 1) &= 0
\end{aligned}
$$

$$L = L \ (p/e, \ w/e, \ m/e, \ 1) \ = 0 \qquad (5)$$
$$F = F \ (p/e, \ w/e, \ m/e, \ 1) \ = 0.$$

The choice among these four constructions depends on the problems of the economy under analysis. In many large democratic and unionized countries, it is impossible or not expedient to alter money wages. This means that the other variables—the price level, the money supply, and the exchange rate—must perform as required by the level of wage rates. In small open economies, on the other hand, the domestic price level is likely to be dominated by the exchange rate. Fixing the exchange rate or its rate of change[1] is therefore a good mechanism for stabilizing the rate of growth of the domestic price level, making the last system a convenient one for analysis.

The anatomy of disequilibrium

From a position of equilibrium, changes in prices create a disequilibrium. The first step in devising policies to restore equilibrium is to identify the pattern of disequilibrium. Therefore, the four equations of the non-normalized system (1) are differentiated to arrive at:

$$dX = X_p dp + X_w dw + X_m dm + X_e de$$
$$dN = N_p dp + N_w dw + N_m dm + N_e de$$
$$dL = L_p dp + L_w dw + L_m dm + L_e de \qquad (6)$$
$$dF = F_p dp + F_w dw + F_m dm + F_e de.$$

The pattern of signs of the matrix formed by the coefficients on the right-hand side of (6) reflect the assumption of gross substitutes: the diagonal terms X_p, N_w, L_m, and F_e are negative, while all the off-diagonal terms are positive. Thus, an increase in the money-price level (other things constant) shifts excess demand away from commodities to labor services, money balances, and foreign exchange. An increase in the wage rate shifts excess demand away from labor to goods, money, and foreign exchange; an increase in the money supply creates an excess supply of money and an excess demand for goods, labor, and foreign exchange; and an increase in the price of foreign exchange (depreciation) creates an excess supply of foreign exchange and an excess demand for goods, labor, and domestic money. From Euler's Theorem, the row coefficients sum to zero; and, from Walras's Law, the column coefficients (when weighted by prices) sum to zero.

For purposes of exposition, it is convenient to study two markets at a time, combining the two remaining markets by assuming that the relative price of the other things is fixed. For example, fixed exchange rates can be assumed and then domestic and foreign money as a composite good can be combined along lines of the Hicks-Leontief theorem that commodities whose prices move together can be analyzed as if they are a single commodity. This procedure permits analysis of the commodity and labor markets and the formation of prices and wages, a problem analyzed in the subsection "The real wage under fixed exchange rates."

Let us assume first that prices and wages move proportionately together, so that real wages are constant. This assumption amalgamates the commodity and labor markets and collapses the wage and price variables into a single price variable p–w. If it is also assumed, provisionally, that the money stock is constant, the system can be depicted in the price-wage and exchange rate variables. In Figure 2.1, the exchange rate or the price of foreign exchange, e, is placed on the ordinate and the price-wage level, p–w, is placed on the abscissa.

The equilibrium lines for what are now three markets—goods and labor, foreign exchange, and domestic money—have the slopes depicted, on the assumption that foreign money, domestic money, and goods and labor are gross substitutes for one another. The XN schedule has a positive slope, because an increase in the price-wage level reduces the excess demand for goods and labor and an increase in the price of foreign exchange increases it. Similarly, an increase in the wage-price

FIGURE 2.1   The Anatomy of Disequilibrium

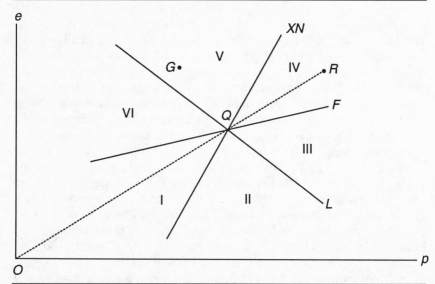

level increases the excess demand for foreign exchange, while a rise in the exchange rate decreases it. The liquidity equilibrium line, on the other hand, has a negative slope because an increase in the price-wage level increases the demand for money, while a decrease in the exchange rate decreases it.

The three lines have a common intersection at point Q, where there is equilibrium in the money, foreign exchange, and the combined goods and labor markets. It must be noted, however, that the position at Q is not inconsistent with an excess supply of goods and an equal value of the excess demand for labor. There will be full equilibrium in all markets only if the real wage rate is at the equilibrium level.

Figure 2.1 can then be used to exhibit some of the problems that stabilization policies are designed to correct. Each point has associated with it a specific disequilibrium configuration. Point Q, for example, is the point at which the excess demands have a common value, equal to zero. Point G, on the other hand, represents a point of disequilibrium where there is an excess demand for goods and labor, an excess supply of foreign exchange (balance of payments surplus), and an excess demand for money. The other points can be distinguished according to whether they lie on or off one of the lines. Any point of the F line implies an excess supply of (demand for) money exactly equal to the excess demand for (supply of) goods and labor. Similarly, a point on the XN schedule implies an excess demand for (supply of) foreign exchange exactly balanced by an excess supply of (demand for) domestic money.

It is also important to know the relative values of the XN and F slopes. This can be inferred by combining the information implicit in Walras's Law and the homogeneity postulate (under the assumption of gross substitutes). Consider the ray OQ extended to a typical point in Zone IV, such as point R. At this point, the prices of foreign exchange, wage rates, and commodity prices have increased in proportion, reducing real money balances and thus creating an excess demand for money. The increase in the prices of labor, commodities, and foreign exchange, in fact, can be regarded as equivalent, in the general equilibrium system described above, to a fall in the value of money that, under the gross substitutes assumption, must increase the demand for money. Therefore, an excess demand for money exists at point R, implying that the XN curve is steeper than the F curve.[2]

At points in the zones not on any of the lines, all three markets exhibit disequilibrium. The six zones correspond to the following situations of excess demand:

Zone I. $XN > 0; F > 0; L < 0$
Zone II. $XN < 0; F > 0; L < 0$

Zone III. $XN < 0; F > 0; L > 0$
Zone IV. $XN < 0; F < 0; L > 0$
Zone V. $XN > 0; F < 0; L > 0$
Zone VI. $XN > 0; F < 0; L < 0.$

How should a disequilibrium be interpreted and inferred from available economic data? Consider again the situation at G, where there is an excess demand for goods and labor, an excess supply of foreign exchange, and an excess demand for money. If prices and exchange rates are flexible, prices should rise and exchange rates should fall (appreciation) until equilibrium at Q is restored. On the other hand, if prices are rigid, inventories would fall to satisfy the excess demand, firms would experience excess profits and an accumulation of money that if hoarded, would shift the equilibrium configuration at Q down and to the left. If, instead, the exchange rate was fixed, the central bank would accumulate foreign exchange and, assuming no sterilization, would increase the supply of money, shifting the equilibrium configuration at Q upward and to the right. Whichever process is at work, the zones of disequilibrium are unambiguously identifiable.

The anatomy of disequilibrium provides the raw material for determining the appropriate stabilization policy. Because each country has a different type of disequilibrium, optimum stabilization policies differ. The specific stabilization policy suitable for each country can be determined by the characteristics of the disequilibrium.

The case of repressed inflation

One important case of disequilibrium—typical in many of the planned economies—is that of repressed inflation. There is an excess supply (an overhang) of money, coupled with shortages of goods and foreign exchange. The exchange rate is fixed, but foreign exchange is rationed. Commodity prices and wages are fixed, but the shortages result in long waiting lines and inadequate production.

Figure 2.2 reproduces the structure of Figure 2.1. The equilibrium is at Q, but price-wage controls restrict the price-wage level to OH. The overvalued exchange rate is OG, so that the intersection at R determines the actual position in e–p space. At R there is an excess demand for goods, labor, and foreign exchange and an excess supply of money.

There are two basic approaches for restoring equilibrium. One approach is open inflation, leading to a movement of the price-wage and exchange rate levels to the equilibrium level indicated by Q. The other approach is deflation of excess demand for goods and foreign exchange, involving a movement of the equilibrium configuration corresponding

FIGURE 2.2   Repressed Inflation

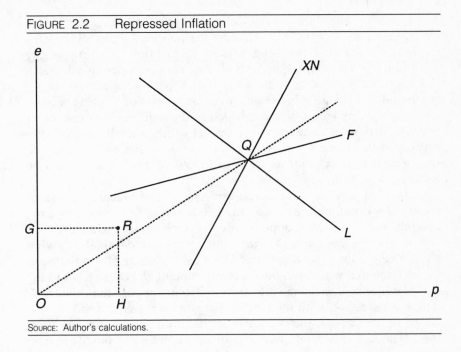

SOURCE: Author's calculations.

to the existing price-wage levels and the exchange rate. Between these two are hybrids representing various combinations of the two basic approaches.

In early 1990, both the Soviet Union and Poland faced situations like that depicted. Consider first the open inflation approach. There are three ways of getting to equilibrium Q: (1) the free market, (2) the planning mechanism, and (3) a hybrid approach that combines that two methods. By the free-market method, prices and exchange rates are decontrolled, and market forces bring about equilibrium at Q. Through the planning method, the state controls on the price-wage levels and the exchange rate are adjusted to the new equilibrium levels.

The free-market method has an advantage over the planning method in that it works best where the actual equilibrium position is not known. If the actual equilibrium levels of prices and exchange rates are not known, the free market will find them. A possible defect of the free-market method is that it can result in inefficient overshooting and temporary false pricing. In countries where the inhabitants are unfamiliar with the price mechanism, there will be many false steps in the process of interpreting the information inherent in free-market prices. In the early stages of stabilization, it would be especially difficult to prevent an undervaluation of the exchange rate in a free market.[3]

Because of the different nature of the commodity and foreign exchange markets, it is better to consider the policies appropriate to each market in isolation. The exchange rate is a single price,[4] affecting directly the whole class of internationally traded goods and indirectly all goods. The commodity market, on the other hand, represents millions of diverse units that make it impossible to adjust prices to changing scarcity relationships, making rational calculation difficult. For this and other reasons, it is safer to adopt a free-market solution for the commodity market while setting the exchange rate, perhaps after an initial period of fluctuation, at a point as close to the equilibrium level as can be estimated.

What is the adjustment mechanism under fixed exchange rates? To answer this question, consider Figure 2.3, which again reproduces some essentials of Figure 2.1. Suppose now that the plan for the stabilization policy involves decontrol of prices, but a one-time devaluation. What should be the new exchange rate? Obviously, the rate OW is the equilibrium rate that would put the economy at point Q, but mistakes in the choice of the new exchange rate are inevitable. Suppose that the devaluation is excessive, with the new exchange rate at ON, instead of OW. Given flexible prices, the new quasi-equilibrium will be at point M on the XN line. At this point, there is equilibrium in the commodity market

FIGURE 2.3   Open Inflation

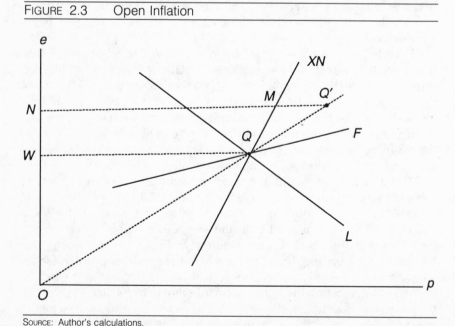

SOURCE: Author's calculations.

but an excess demand for money combined with an excess supply of foreign exchange. The central bank could let the exchange rate appreciate to correct the mistake. A government's prestige, however, is often committed to a given exchange rate parity and further adjustment in it might lead to dangerous outward speculation.

An alternative plan is to let the automatic adjustment mechanism work itself out. The new exchange rate (ON) will lead to a new equilibrium at point Q', if the automatic adjustment mechanism is allowed to take its course. To prevent appreciation, the central bank buys foreign exchange, creating an equivalent amount of domestic currency. The three schedules, drawn up on the assumption of a constant stock of money, now shift. The increasing money supply shifts all three schedules so that their intersection point remains on OQ extended, a ray from the origin through Q. The equilibrium at the new exchange rate (ON) will be at Q', where NQ' intersects OQ'. At this position, the balance of payments and all other markets will be in equilibrium at the fixed exchange rate.

The adjustment process under fixed exchange rates

Whether exchange rates should be flexible, but with a fixed stock of money or whether the money supply should be flexible, but with a fixed exchange rate, has been the subject of an enduring controversy between advocates of flexible and fixed exchange rates. In this section the adjustment process under fixed exchange rates is described in more detail.

In Figure 2.4, the money supply is on the ordinate and the price-wage level is on the abscissa. The three schedules (XN, L, and F) now have slopes different from that in the first three figures because of the change of variable on the ordinate. The XN line has a positive slope because an increase in the money supply increases the excess demand for domestic goods, whereas an increase in the price level reduces it. The L line has a positive slope because an increase in the money supply reduces the excess demand for money, while an increase in the price level increases it. The F schedule has a negative slope because an increase in the money supply creates an excess demand for foreign exchange, while a reduction in the domestic price level reduces it. Moreover, it can be shown that the XN schedule is steeper than the L schedule. This is because, at a point like Q', on the ray OQ extended, there is, because of the homogeneity postulate, an excess demand for foreign exchange. An increase in m and p has all the characteristics of a rise in the exchange rate that must create an excess supply of money and commodities. The three lines demarcate six zones of disequilibrium,

FIGURE 2.4   Equilibrium under Fixed Exchange Rates

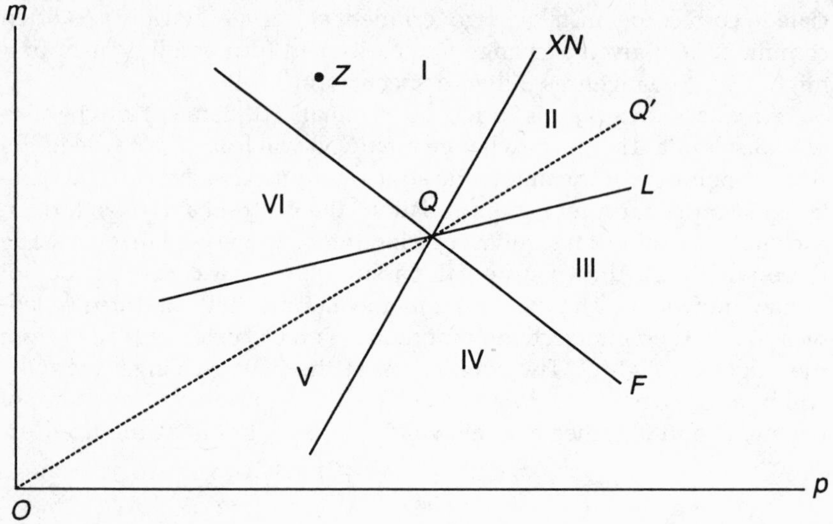

SOURCE: Author's calculations.

labeled according to the excess demands indicated in the discussion of Figure 2.1.

Consider now a typical disequilibrium point, such as Z. At this point, there is an excess demand for goods that will tend to increase the price level. There is also a balance of payments deficit (an excess demand for foreign exchange) that will reduce the money supply. Associated with these forces is an excess supply of money that will be expended partly on commodities and partly on foreign exchange. These pressures will move the m–p configuration closer to equilibrium, either directly or after moving into another zone of disequilibrium. The system is necessarily stable, moving ever closer to equilibrium.

Consider now in Figure 2.4 the position of equilibrium at Q. From this point, devaluation will shift each of the curves to a new intersection point. It is easy to see from the homogeneity postulate that the new equilibrium will be a point such as Q' on the ray OQ extended. Devaluation creates an excess demand for goods and labor, an excess demand for money, and an excess supply of foreign exchange. The central bank's purchases of foreign exchange that are made necessary by the new parity increase the money supply and the price level until the new equilibrium is reached. Exchange rate changes can thus be the cause, as well as the result, of inflation.

FIGURE 2.5   Real Wage Adjustment

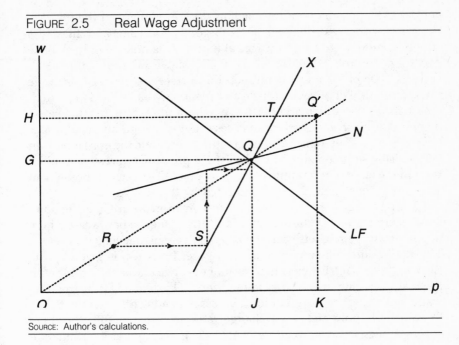

SOURCE: Author's calculations.

The real wage under fixed exchange rates

The stabilization policy adopted in Poland in early 1990 involved decontrol of prices, unification of the exchange rate, and devaluation, not unlike the example given above. However, a special feature of the Polish stabilization was a wage freeze that brought about scarcities and strikes. To analyze that special feature, it is necessary to relax the assumption that wages and prices move together and to reopen the distinction between the commodity and labor markets that was sidestepped for analysis of the real wage situations discussed earlier.

To analyze the real wage problem, consider Figure 2.5, which plots the level of money wages on the ordinate and the price level on the abscissa. The exchange rate is assumed to be fixed, so that there is no other degree of freedom in the system. Given the exchange rate, there are unique levels of the money supply, money-wage rates, and prices at which all markets will clear. Because the exchange rate is fixed, foreign exchange and domestic money are combined in a composite commodity, delineating a composite schedule LF.[5] In Figure 2.5, the X, N and LF schedules are drawn on the assumption of the fixed exchange rate and the equilibrium money supply.

Consider now a situation where, from a position of excess liquidity, the exchange rate has been set at the specific level that corresponds to the equilibrium appropriate to the existing stock of money. At the position R, there is an excess demand for both goods and labor and an excess supply of money. Prices and wages at R can be maintained only by price and wage controls. Now, as in the Polish stabilization policy in 1990, suppose that prices are decontrolled but a freeze is imposed on wage rates. Decontrol of prices results in an inflationary movement to point S, where the commodity markets are in equilibrium. At S there is an excess demand for labor, matched by an excess supply of liquidity. Real wages have fallen, and there is an even greater excess demand for labor than before. This situation should lead to wage pressures to restore equilibrium in the labor market, until eventually point Q is reached, possibly in sequential steps along the path indicated by the arrows.

The real wage is given by the slope of a ray from the origin to the point in w–p space; thus at Q, the real wage is OG/OJ. Consider now a case where the money wage rate has been put at a relatively high level, such as OH. The equilibrium full-employment real wage, however, is given by the slope of the ray OQ. It is clear that the money-wage rate is compatible with the real wage rate only at the point Q' on OQ extended. If the money-wage rate cannot be lowered, it is necessary to adjust the parameters— the money supply and the exchange rate—in order to shift the three curves in such a way as to intersect at Q'. This act requires a devaluation (an increase in the price of foreign exchange) in the proportion Q'Q/OQ = JK/OJ. In the absence of devaluation, there would be a temporary equilibrium at point T, where there would exist an excess supply of labor and an excess demand for money. The excess demand for money would induce a reduction of expenditure below income, a balance of payments surplus, and an increase in the money supply through the automatic mechanism of reequilibration of the balance of payments.

Draining the overhang

Up to now the alternatives associated with accommodating the overhang of money and unleashing price inflation to reduce its real value to the equilibrium level have been explored. This section considers the alternative approaches that involve lowering the stock of money to the point where the actual controlled level of prices will be the equilibrium level.

It must first be emphasized again that equilibrium cannot be achieved by deflationary policies if relative prices are not at their equilibrium values. If prices and wages are controlled, full equilibrium by deflation can only be achieved if real wages are at the equilibrium level. Otherwise, there would be an excess demand for (or supply of) labor, depending on whether real wages were below or above the equilibrium level.

FIGURE 2.6   Draining the Overhang

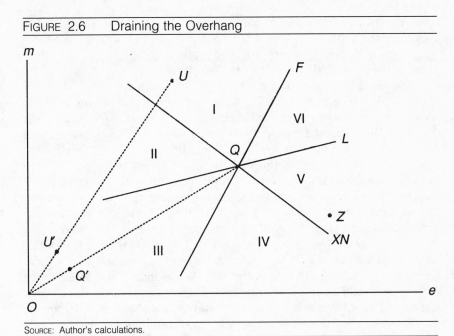

SOURCE: Author's calculations.

In Figure 2.6, $e–m$ space is plotted, with money wages and prices assumed to be constant. The F, L, and XN lines have the usual meaning, and the six zones of disequilibrium are designated again by the numerical code discussed in connection with Figure 2.1. For example, point Z in Zone V would indicate an excess demand for money, an excess demand for goods and labor, and an excess supply of foreign exchange. Since it would alleviate pressures in all markets, the correct therapy is an appreciation of the exchange rate, combined with a small increase in the money supply.

In countries with histories of excess liquidity and price-wage controls, a more usual initial position requiring stabilization policy is that of excess demand for goods and services, excess demand for foreign exchange, and excess supply of money. The point U in Zone I represents a more typical point of disequilibrium. The predominant problem is the "overhang" of money represented by the vertical distance between U and Q. The combination of money supply reduction and a slight change in the exchange rate would suffice to achieve equilibrium.

How should the money supply be reduced? The surgical method is a currency reform.[6] The current money is demonetized. Old currency is exchanged for new. In the age of hard money, the sequence of devaluation and debasement largely involved the substitution by the government of inferior money for good money in the process of debasement. In the modern age of soft paper or bank money, the substitution of good money to replace bad money is accomplished when confidence in the old money has broken down.

The most famous example is the substitution in Germany of 1 rentenmark for 1 trillion reichmarks. Recent examples include the postwar exchanges of 10 reichmarks for 1 deutsche mark in Germany and 10 yen for 1 yen in Japan. Currency conversions have also taken place more recently, but with mixed success, in Argentina, Brazil, and Israel.

It is necessary to distinguish between different types of currency conversions. Nominal conversions do not fit into stabilization policies because they leave liquidity the same before and after the conversion. An exchange of ten units of old currency for one unit of new currency does not alone reduce liquidity, if all prices and debts are scaled down in proportion. In the case of pure accounting conversions, the public does not experience any psychological loss of wealth and the reform amounts to nothing more than moving the decimal place on currency bills, prices, and financial instruments. Such measures may have transactional convenience and psychological impact, but they do not alter the fundamentals of the disequilibrium. If, for example, there was an overhang of liquidity of the old currency at the time of the conversion, there would be an equivalent overhang of real liquidity after the conversion. In Figure 2.6, a nominal currency reform of one unit for ten units would shift the equilibrium point from Q to a point Q', one-tenth of the way from O to Q; it would also, however, shift the disequilibrium point U to one-tenth the distance on the ray OU—that is, to the point U'. This amounts to nothing more than a relabeling of the axes. The case of the conversion of the franc in 1959 illustrates the point where a simple change in the name of the currency was involved.[7]

Real conversions involve a reduction in liquidity. There are different ways of effecting them. One way is to confiscate the portion of the money supply that constitutes the overhang. Another way, relevant in a command economy, is to conduct the nominal conversion as above, but to leave prices denominated in the new currency the same as those that were expressed in the old currency. For example, if the overhang amounts to five times the money supply, a conversion of five old units for one new unit, combined with no change in nominal wages and prices, would eliminate the excess liquidity. Alternatively, a ten-for-one currency exchange could be accompanied by a halving of prices expressed in the new units to achieve the same result as in the preceding case.

Asset conversions constitute a third (and very important) category of conversions. Instead of confiscating part of the real liquidity held by the public—whether directly or by inflation—the authorities can sell

FIGURE 2.7   Undervalued Labor

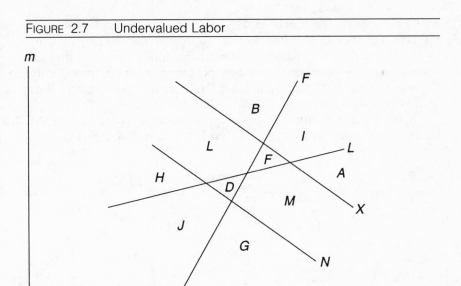

SOURCE: Author's calculations.

government assets in order to retire the excess liquidity. By this solution, the national assets are not changed, but they are redistributed from the government to the private sector. In the case of the former communist countries, the government owns most of the land and the process of privatizing the land could be partly used to retire the excess liquidity. The government could, indeed, make the currency convertible into hectares of land. An alternative possibility is to sell other government-owned assets, such as gold, silver, platinum, foreign exchange, or equities in government enterprises. A more familiar case of asset conversions is the sale of government bonds, a vehicle not likely to have much success in countries where inflation has destroyed confidence in financial assets.

Employment equilibrium

In the preceding analysis, the labor and goods markets were amalgamated, and it was merely noted that equilibrium in each market individually would hold only if real wages were set at the full employment level of marginal productivity. This section considers the situation where the real wage rate is out of equilibrium. Figure 2.7 illustrates the problems resulting from a single relative price, in this case, the real wage rate, fixed below its equilibrium level. Four schedules correspond to the four markets, but they do not intersect at a common equilibrium point. Indeed, there are no less than five intersections and ten zones of disequilibrium. The five intersections indicate loci of m and e at which two of the markets are in equilibrium. The letters indicate the zones in which no market is in equilibrium.

In all, there are fourteen zones of disequilibrium. These can be identified by the sign of the excess demand in the following tabulation:

	X	N	L	F
A	+	+	+	−
B	+	+	−	+
C	+	−	+	+
D	−	+	+	+
E	+	−	−	−
F	−	+	−	−
G	−	−	+	−
H	−	−	−	+
I	+	+	−	−
J	−	−	+	+
K	+	−	+	−
L	−	+	−	+
M	−	+	+	−
N	+	−	−	+

Not all of these zones are illustrated in Figure 2.7, because some are not consistent with the possibility that real wages are below the equilibrium level. An excess supply of labor and an excess demand for every other thing (as in Zone C) are inconsistent with the basic model. Similarly, excess demand for goods and an excess supply of every other thing (as in Zone E) are inconsistent when the real wage is below equilibrium. These zones are excluded from Figure 2.7.[8]

How would the figure be changed if the real wage rate was too high? In this case, the relative positions of the X and N curves would be reversed. It would then be found that Zones C and E, which were ruled out when real wages were too low, are now possible, but Zones D and F are ruled out.[9] These positions are indicated in Figure 2.8, which is drawn on the assumption that the real wage is too high. Zones D and F are sign opposites and are compatible with undervalued, but not overvalued, labor.

The Stabilization-Privatization Link

General equilibrium theory provides the possibility set of alternative stabilization policies, but it cannot replace the work of the political econ-

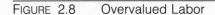

FIGURE 2.8   Overvalued Labor

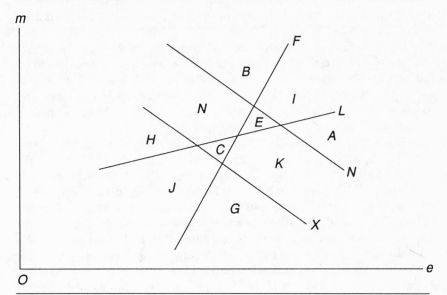

SOURCE: Author's calculations.

omist in adapting it to take into account the historical, social, political, and psychological characteristics of the country under consideration. Political economy replaces economics in deciding between actual stabilization policies.

If a stabilization policy starts out with a round of inflation, the expectation is created that a future stabilization policy, if one should prove necessary, will follow the same procedure and thus invite counterproductive speculation that will prejudice the success of the next plan. For example, the abortive Austral Plan in Argentina and the Cruzado Plan in Brazil made it more difficult to establish credibility for the next attempt at stabilization. The history of a nation's money forms part of its mental landscape. Because stabilization affects future expectations, every plan must take historical experience into account.

Both good and bad experiences affect policies in the present and future. Repeated historical experiences of monetary instability make it difficult to create new sets of expectations. Many countries in South America have histories of inflation extending over a century. It would be foolish to attempt to apply even a good plan for stabilization without a serious attempt to convince the public that the current stabilization plan is going to be the last. The situation is different in countries that have suffered monetary cataclysms following long periods of monetary stability. The distasteful memory of the German hyperinflation in the 1920s benefits attitudes toward monetary policy in Germany today and gives the Deutsche Bundesbank greater freedom to carry out anti-inflationary policies.[10]

In countries with controls and an overhang of liquidity, it is first necessary to decide whether price levels and exchange rates should be adjusted to the existing stock of money or whether the stock of money should be adjusted to the existing level of prices and exchange rates. The decision is partly political, because it affects the distribution of income and wealth.

The inflation-devaluation method, tried in Poland in early 1990 under the supervision of the International Monetary Fund, has the disadvantage that it destroys individual savings held in financial assets.[11] Coupled with this approach is the defect of freezing money-wages and undervaluing labor, resulting in labor unrest and low productivity. Like all inflation, the Polish solution was a capital levy, not very different in its final effects from an overt confiscation of capital. There is also the moral hazard, referred to above, of creating an unfavorable precedent for future stabilization plans.[12] The inflation method, rather than the confiscation method is usually adopted because it operates by deception on an unsuspecting public, and thus arouses less overt dissent.

No stabilization plan should be implemented without defining carefully and establishing firmly the characteristics of the monetary regime after stabilization. In order to generate confidence in money, it is necessary to establish an anchor for monetary policy. The money supply will not suffice as an anchor, and a system of flexible exchanges will not be successful. Flexible exchange rates have not been successful in developing countries and are not likely to be successful in former socialist countries. In order to restore confidence in the currency after stabilization, it is necessary to give it a credible and prestigious anchor. The only plausible anchor is a major foreign currency or a monetary commodity, such as gold or some other precious metal. In most countries, however, with only minute gold stocks and no gold production, gold is not an option.[13]

The choice between the alternatives of confiscation or inflation depends partly on the economic system. The solutions open to the market-oriented developing economies are different from those open to the former socialist countries. In the developing countries, the government has no direct control over the factors of production. The unhappy choice between outright confiscation of the overhang and its real reduction by inflation has to be based on the political possibilities of the two alternatives. The confiscation approach has the possible merit of achieving equilibrium at existing prices.[14]

In the former socialist countries, the government still has substantial control over the factors of production, although most of them have indicated the intention of privatizing government assets, including real estate, factories, and farms. This presents an opportunity to link privatization with stabilization. Government assets can be sold, and the financial proceeds can be retired, destroying liquidity without reducing private wealth. Since the value of privatizable assets greatly exceeds the excess stock of liquidity, only a part of the sales proceeds needs be allocated to the stabilization problem. Privatization of government assets, combined with destruction of the excess liquidity, has the advantage of preserving the value of public savings and at the same time permitting the restoration of convertibility of the currency. It represents no cost to governments that have already made plans for privatization. There is no reason why the privatization and stabilization operations cannot be linked.

The concern here has been mainly with achieving stabilization. It is necessary, however, to maintain stability after equilibrium has been established. Again, it is necessary to have a budget that is balanced (except for foreign loans) in order to gain control over the money supply. If there is no prospect of a balanced budget, there can be no successful stabilization policy.

As already noted, there must be an anchor for the money supply. The best means of establishing this anchor is to make the currency convertible. Two main types of convertibility are currency convertibility and asset convertibility. With respect to currency convertibility, there are two major currency groups—the U.S. dollar area and the European currency unit–deutsche mark (ecu-DM) area—and a third emerging bloc around the yen. The choice among currency areas depends on financial, commercial, social, and political ties. The countries of Central Europe naturally gravitate to the ecu-DM bloc. The countries of Eastern Europe will choose between the ecu-DM and the U.S. dollar. The countries in Asia will choose between the dollar and the yen. The countries of Africa will choose between the dollar and the ecu-DM. The currency area will determine the rate of inflation of the country choosing it.

Asset convertibility involves conversion of the currency on demand into a hard asset. One possibility would be to take a model from the French revolution and make currency convertibility into land (and/or factories) at fixed prices, taking care not to commit the mistakes made by the revolutionary government.[15] Provided that the requirements of a balanced budget rule out the future excess issues of money, this plan would have considerable credibility. However, it would be an administrative nightmare. The difficulty of establishing fixed prices for millions of diverse assets outside the framework of the free market would render that solution unfeasible. Asset convertibility is, in fact, only feasible if the asset chosen is homogeneous and stable relative to all other commodities.

Gold is attractive for convertibility because it has maintained its purchasing power over the long term better than any currency. Nevertheless, gold is not a possibility for most of the developing or socialist countries because, with the exception of the Soviet Union, they lack sufficient stocks of gold or the foreign exchange with which to buy it. Another objection is that gold is not monetized in any of the major countries of the world (although it is conceivable that the vast stocks of gold held by central banks might, in the future, be utilized for global social purposes). For this reason, convertibility into gold should follow, rather than precede, convertibility into currencies, and it should take place only as part of an international monetary agreement to utilize gold in a reform of the international monetary system.

Microeconomic and Institutional Preconditions

The axioms implicit in the theory of general equilibrium are based on responses of individual agents to economic incentives. These incentives, however, may not be operative in certain economies. A typical case is where private enterprise is prohibited, as in some former socialist economies and in some that have not yet made (or are not intending to make) the transition to free-enterprise capitalism. Even if prohibitions on private enterprise are lacking, regulations and taxes can discourage it. In some of the least developed countries and in former socialist economies, entrepreneurship itself may still be lacking. It is necessary, therefore, for stabilization policies to take into consideration the social, institutional, technological, and psychological factors that govern economic incentives and yield the required increase in production.

Although an important feature of every stabilization policy must be the demand-side elimination or absorption of excess liquidity, its long-term success depends on an adequate supply-side response. The basic pay-off from monetary stabilization policy is the supply response attracted by a stable monetary unit and the increased allocative efficiency of economic activity organized around the market principle. The success of the macroeconomic stabilization is therefore predicated on the creation of conditions under which the microeconomic preconditions are established. The following points suggest factors that need to be considered as preconditions for achieving the wider long-term goals of stabilization policy.

Budgetary policy

Stabilization policies that are restricted to elimination of excess liquidity often fail because they do not provide a mechanism for cutting off the source of future monetary disturbances. The main source of failure to control the money supply is the inability to balance the budget. If the budget cannot be balanced by taxation or foreign borrowing and if there is no domestic capital market, recourse will be made to inflationary finance from the central bank. Because, in nearly every country, the central bank is subservient to the Ministry of Finance, it is necessary to discipline the government by creating an institutional block—preferably a very visible one—that prohibits or severely restricts central bank finance of government spending. A possible device is a constitutional amendment that denies (or at least limits) holdings of government securities. The assets of the central bank would be restricted to gold, special drawing rights (SDRs), foreign exchange, and assets of the private sector (loans).[16] No stabilization policy will be successful if the central bank is required to finance budget deficits.

There is much scope, particularly in communist countries, for reducing the size of government by privatizing government industry. Obviously, such a policy has deep political implications. The industries to privatize should first be the least efficient, proceeding from there to industries where government management has performed better.

Government sector and privatization

The scale of government activity is limited by the resources of the economy. In many countries, national resources that form the base of the tax system are too small to support the size of government that is consistent with the consumption expectation of the population. Bloated and unproductive government regulatory agencies doubly inhibit economic efficiency by creating bureaucratic barriers to economic freedom and place an undue tax burden on the private sector.[17] Successful stabilization policy requires a freeze or limitation on the growth of government spending and, in many cases, an outright reduction.

Tax revenue policy

After government spending has been pared to the optimum, the tax system must provide sufficient revenue to balance the budget.[18] In socialist countries, where the government has been the landlord, government revenue was maintained as much from revenues from state enterprises as from taxation. After privatization, it will be necessary to recover part of the income by means of taxes on expenditure or income. Tax reform is inevitable in achieving a balanced budget—a requirement for the success of stabilization policies.

Supply-side tax principles

It would be desirable for both socialist and developing economies to profit from the mistakes made in other countries. The tax systems in North America and Europe are a good example. Before the 1980s, marginal income tax rates in the United States and Europe were as high as 80–90 percent. As a result of the supply-side revolution (beginning in Canada, the United States, and England,[19] but extending to most of the industrial countries), marginal income tax rates have been drastically cut, with beneficial effects for growth and efficiency. Both the developing and socialist countries would benefit by creating national tax systems that will maintain incentives for production and efficiency, subject to the need for sufficient revenue to balance the budget. No single formula can apply to every country, but a good rule is to keep maximum marginal tax rates below a maximum of 40 percent and at no more than 30 percent for the middle-income groups. Above that level, inefficiency, tax avoidance, and evasion, and erosion of the tax base sets in. The point of maximum revenue, where increases in tax rates leave revenue unaltered, is already beyond the optimum level.[20] Incentives must be taken into account in constructing appropriate tax policies. It would be a mistake to imitate the bad practices of taxation in the Western countries.[21]

Another aspect of taxation relates to the foreign sector. Stabilization policies should be combined with trade liberalization. The private sector should be encouraged, by low tariff policies, to develop industries in line with the country's future comparative advantages, making the best use of national resources. Only by export orientation of production and import orientation of consumption can a country that is newly entering the world economy expect to earn most-favored-nation (MFN) status and preferential trading agreements with other countries.

Private commercial banking

The banking system is a data system. Bankers have access to private information about clients. Private enterprise and free competition require access to credit under circumstances that preserve important elements of corporate privacy. The strategies relating to corporate products, investment, sales, personnel, and taxes require confidentiality between banker and client, and this is not possible with state-controlled banking. In the absence of a private domestic banking system, many corporations in the private sector would have to forgo the convenience of ready credit from a government-monopoly bank. The allocation of rationed credit by civil servants would undermine the free competitive structure of a dynamic private sector.[22] Public banks can coexist with private banks, but the option of private banking must be permitted.

Foreign banks

Foreign banks provide contacts and credit links to the rest of the world that would otherwise be unavailable. By the nature of the industry, banking experiences economies of scale that favor concentration of large banks or banking groups. Foreign banks create competition and incentives for modernization and innovation in domestic banks.

Capital markets

The banking system provides access to short-term credit, but it is also necessary to develop efficient markets for long-term capital. A capital market in both equities and bonds is a great benefit if countries are sufficiently large to support such institutions. In smaller countries, where there are insufficient economies of scale to make a daily stock exchange viable, less frequent periodic markets can be set up.

Venture capital and merchant banking

It is a great benefit to establish institutions for the formation of risk capital. Particularly in the early stages of the transformation from a socialist to a market economy, there is a need for providing venture capital to promising entrepreneurs. Apart from capital imports, this venture capital must come from within the economy. In the transition period, it will be probably be necessary for the state, which was the sole capitalist, to establish one or more institutions for venture capital to provide to willing and able entrepreneurs the medium-term credits necessary to launch risky enterprises.

Property and leasing rights

Property rights should be clarified, and markets should be opened for the free exchange of property and titles to it. In the absence of private property, the incentive for economic success is unnecessarily limited. Financial reward is a basic motivation for entrepreneurial activity.

Free enterprise

Entrepreneurs must be enabled to create firms and to go into bankruptcy with a minimum of bureaucracy. They must be allowed to increase the size of their firms by hiring whatever labor and other resources are needed for the economies of scale that are necessary to achieve efficient and profitable operations. Firms must be allowed to price their products without restriction in the open market (subject only to control of monopolies and cartels that artificially restrict supply and restrain trade). An efficient private sector is impossible in countries that continue to prohibit or limit the number of employees in a firm or the land and capital resources of a firm. Once the government phases out some of its state monopolies, it must allow private sector alternatives to develop.

Increasing and decreasing the number of employees

While some socialist countries are guilty of the sin of prohibiting increases in employment in private enterprises, some market economies have been guilty of the opposite sin of forbidding individual firms from firing labor. Efficiency requires that enterprises be permitted to add or release labor as conditions require, subject to the usual clauses protecting workers against unfair treatment. An employment policy of some countries is to prohibit all firing, a practice that has the defects of preventing changes in the skill mix of a labor force and inhibiting the attainment of new optimum factors as market conditions change. Because it imposes an implicit fixed cost of hiring labor, it has the opposite effect from the one intended because it encourages the substitution of capital for labor and reduces equilibrium employment.[23]

Wage and salary ceilings

Wage and salary ceilings for entrepreneurs, as well as workers, only result in under-the-table payments, if evaded, or in the export of the undervalued personnel, if enforced. In the 1970s, Portugal lost thousands in its entrepreneurial force, partly because of low ceilings on entrepreneurial salaries.

Supply of entrepreneurship and management

Without adequate entrepreneurship and management expertise in the private sector, there would be no alternative to retention by the government of a considerable part of the processes of production. Although entrepreneurial talent is both born and made, its spirit has withered in the communist countries, and it will take some time before it is recreated. To accelerate the process, it will be necessary to create managerial and entrepreneurial schools on a suitably modified model of the schools in Western countries.

Future monetary and exchange rate policies

Confidence in current monetary policy is essential to the success of any stabilization policy. It is also necessary, however, to create a monetary system to generate confidence that the future monetary policy can be trusted. There must be a mechanism to create confidence that the reform will last. Once confidence begins to break down, all the problems associated with uncertainty will come again to the forefront, including hoarding, shortages, and reduced production.[24] It is not sufficient to establish the equilibrium quantity of money and then leave the rate of credit creation up to the discretion of either the head of the central bank or the minister of finance. The simplest requirement would be that the central bank follow a monetary policy designed to maintain equilibrium in the balance of payments at a fixed exchange rate.

Without confidence in the future exchange rate, there will be a flight from domestic money to foreign exchange and real assets, leading to a breakdown of the stabilization program. The successful stability of the gold standard over long periods was due to confidence in the mechanism for eliminating disequilibrium quickly when it arose. A similar feature is required for a country expecting long-term success for its stabilization policies. For most countries, the best anchor would be the U.S. dollar or the ecu-DM.[25] Gold would also be a suitable anchor, but no country now could be advised to proceed alone with gold convertibility.

National indebtedness

Most of the socialist and developing countries have borrowed to the limit, up to or beyond their capacity to repay. Most face serious difficulties in servicing their foreign debts. The dilemma for these countries is that, the more successfully the economy performs after its stabilization policy, the more it will be obliged to keep its debt service current. This places a heavy "tax" on the proceeds of success at the time when the population has made the greatest sacrifices for that success.

The moral hazard is that countries may prefer to remain insolvent rather than maintain current debt payments. This is not a new problem. In the 1920s, Germany let its economy slip into hyperinflation rather than arrange for the financing of its bill for punitive reparations.

Germany finally stabilized only after negotiation of a drastically reduced debt-service payment. Again, in the late 1940s and 1950s, Marshall Plan aid was distributed by the Organization for European Economic Cooperation (OEEC), partly according to need, as indicated by a country's balance of payments difficulties—thus creating a subsidy for incompetent financial management. It is still true that a country's claim on foreign aid or support from the World Bank or the International Monetary Fund is partly contingent on a country's having balance of payments difficulties.[26]

To avoid these disincentives, some countries have chosen to put an upper limit on the proportion of national income or exports that they will allocate to service the debt. Debts have already been scaled down, and it is now only a question of what proportion of debts will be repaid in the long term. It might be desirable for countries to try to negotiate a substantial scaling down of their external debts to levels that correspond to the country's capacity to pay comfortably, providing some form of collateral for the remainder of the debt.

Notes

1. Many small countries attempted to fix the rate of change in the exchange rate, publishing the schedule for future spot exchange rates. The *tablita*, as the schedule was called in Latin America, was used in attempts to adjust smoothly for domestic inflation rates greater than those abroad. They were never, in practice, used in the opposite way—that is, to make the domestic price level rise at a slower rate than the price level in the intervention currency area.

2. Under the dynamic postulates that exchange rates move in proportion to excess demands for foreign exchange and that prices and wages move in proportion to excess demands for goods and labor, it is a necessary condition for a stability that XN be steeper than F. More simply, an excess demand for money at point R requires an excess supply of either goods or foreign exchange that is ruled out if the slopes are reversed.

3. The social costs of undervaluation of the exchange rate involve underpricing of land and capital assets and their expatriation, sacrificing part of a country's wealth.

4. As noted earlier, this is not strictly true in the post–Bretton Woods era of multiple currency areas. Even so, most countries can peg to the dominant currency of a large currency area or to a basket of currencies.

5. While a position on line LF implies equilibrium in the combined money and foreign exchange markets, it does not ipso facto imply equilibrium in both markets. There would be equilibrium in each market taken singly only if the money supply was set at the level appropriate to the given exchange rate.

6. A dictator could simply confiscate the redundant currency.

7. The exchange of 100 French francs for 1 new franc differs from the German and Japanese conversions in that it was an accounting measure adopted for purposes of prestige rather than an economic change that altered liquidity. This is not to deny the importance of psychological reasons and transaction convenience for nominal conversion. The extreme case of the trillion to one conversion in 1923 illustrates its importance for both motives. More important, however, is the announcement effect of a profound change in policy. The Reichbank stopped financing government deficits and thus wrested control of monetary policy from the fiscal authorities. By the same token, the currency conversions in Latin America have not been successful because there was no change in the system of using the central banks to finance budget deficits. The failure of one reform creates the expectation that the next attempt will also fail.

8. Zones K and N, which are not indicated on Figure 2.7, cannot be ruled out because of the possibility that schedules N and X intersect, yielding one or the other of those zones of disequilibrium.

9. Again, we should note that in the case of overvalued labor, Zones L and M cannot be ruled out a priori because of the possibility that N and X will intersect.

10. The history of England affords good examples of how monetary experiences have salutary effects on future policy. After 1066, William the Conqueror used the inflation tax to finance his revenues by devaluing the coinage every year, until his new subjects voted taxes on themselves to replace the revenues from devaluation. This concern for stable money was reinforced by centuries of comparatively stable monetary conditions. In 1558, Elizabeth (the Virgin Queen) conducted a recoinage without inflation, a method that kept the pound stable until nearly the end of her reign. Almost a century and a half later, during the great recoinage controversy of the 1690s, Elizabeth's decision was held up as an example that won the day (over Newton's objections) in financing the recoinage out of taxation rather than by devaluation. Britain's restoration of the pound after the Napoleonic Wars at the same parity was influential in preserving confidence in the pound throughout the nineteenth century and even during World War I, when the public was encouraged to believe that the pound would be restored after the war at the old parity. A century of confidence in the pound stood England in good stead in World War I, enabling the country to float sterling loans at comparatively low rates of interest, despite the lapse of convertibility, so strong was the belief that the traditional parity would be restored after the war. For a discussion of other episodes, see Mundell (1990).

11. It could be argued that there was no real counterpart to these savings because money was overvalued at the regulated price level. However, these savings may have a real counterpart in the increase in capital stock financed by the implicit tax on cash balances.

12. The answer frequently given is that the current plan will be successful and that there will be no need for future stabilization plans. History, however, does not bear this out.

13. Only in the Soviet Union would gold be an option—in fact, an option proposed by Wayne Angell, governor of the U.S. Federal Reserve System, and

Jude Wanniski, president of Polyconomics (see Wanniski 1989). The merits of this alternative are discussed later in this chapter.

14. It is a merit from the standpoint of discouraging future inflationary expectations.

15. Between 1789 and 1795, the French Republic issued *assignats*, so-named because they were secured by confiscated crown, noble, and church property. The first issue had been 400 million francs, followed by a second issue of 800 million francs, followed rapidly by several more until, by December 1795, the total accumulated issue reached the vast sum of 37 billion francs. Under the stabilization plan, the *assignats* were converted into *mandats* (warrants) at one-thirtieth of their face value. These, in turn, were converted in 1796 at one-seventieth part of the value of coin, implying a total depreciation of 2,100. Because of the high inflation associated with the *assignats*, the experiment of backing money by land has generally been judged a failure. However, the inflationary finance may have accomplished its purpose when no politically feasible alternatives existed. The basic idea of backing currency by assets was sound, but it was misconceived in its execution. The *assignat* scheme collapsed for three reasons: (1) as no prices of the land securing the *assignats* were set, with inflation the worth of *assignats* fell, (2) it was believed that someday the priests and aristocrats would return to claim land thus acquired, and (3) the overissues of *assignats* to finance the budget were so great that they lost all credibility. If the government had actually sold property to the public at fixed prices, inflation could have been avoided in the early periods, provided that government spending did not exceed the amount the public would be willing to invest in confiscated property.

16. An alternative would be to create a monetary branch of the government to provide new checks and balances along with the executive, judiciary, and legislative branches. An alternative in countries with two heads of state (president and chairman, king and prime minister, president and premier) would be to place the central bank under the authority of the branch in charge of the budget (for example, congressional or parliamentary). Still another alternative in countries where constitutions can be altered too easily or overturned by a military coup is to abolish the central bank and use a major foreign currency for domestic reserve money.

17. Many socialist countries have lower taxes than many market economies because the government receives implicit rent as ubiquitous landlord, reflected in the "profits" of state enterprises. McKinnon makes this point in Chapter 3.

18. Balanced "budget" means that government spending is equal to the sum of taxes and direct foreign loans to the government. Thus, it allows for an excess of expenditure over taxes, if the excess can be financed by loans from abroad.

19. Canada was one of the first countries to implement supply-side tax principles when, in 1973, tax brackets were indexed for inflation. I had made that same recommendation in a paper presented to the Ottawa Economics Club in September 1972. Nevertheless, the Canadian government failed to lower high marginal tax rates until 1989; federal rates in Canada are as low as in the United

States, but provincial rates make the combined income tax rates higher in Canada than in the United States. The Reagan government lowered the maximum marginal tax rate from 70 percent to 50 percent in 1981, and from 50 percent to 28 percent (with a segment rising to 33 percent) in 1986. To these rates, state and local income taxes must be added. The Thatcher government was slow in implementing supply-side economics, but now maximum income tax rates have been reduced to 40 percent. Most countries in the Organization for Economic Cooperation and Development (OECD) have now lowered maximum income tax rates.

20. The proof of this theorem follows, mutatis mutandis, from the famous argument in international trade theory that the tariff that maximizes government revenue is higher than the tariff that maximizes economic welfare.

21. A characteristic example is double taxation in the United States, where corporate income is taxed at both the corporate and personal level. Corporate profits are taxed at 34 percent at the corporation level and up to 33 percent at the federal personal level and then at levels hovering around 10 percent at the state and local levels, amounting to a combined marginal income tax rate of 77 percent, a flagrant violation of supply-side tax principles.

22. The alternative of semipublic banks on the Italian model, however, is a second-best alternative, providing that competition is sufficient. Even the Italian public banks compete with one another, as well as with domestic and foreign private commercial banks.

23. A less restrictive, more benign form of these laws would permit employers to hire and fire while maintaining the firm's level of employment.

24. Under conditions of inflation, the liquidity spectrum from money through financial assets to goods, property, and land shifts to make physical assets and land more liquid than money.

25. Many countries choose to stabilize their currency to a basket that usually involves a combination of the U.S. dollar, ecu-DM, and the yen, or the SDR, which is an "alloy" of the currencies of the Group of Five industrial countries. There are great disadvantages to fixing to a basket rather than to a usable currency from the standpoint of capital market transactions, but this may have small weight in countries with undeveloped capital markets.

26. The Articles of Agreement of the International Monetary Fund provide for a country's drawing of foreign currencies "needed" for its balance of payments.

Comments

JUERGEN B. DONGES

Robert Mundell has given an analytical overview of the basic issues of stabilization programs. Since I agree completely with his analysis, I can only make some general remarks that may help to focus the discussion.

First, I would like to stress that developing countries typically have open inflation, whereas most former socialist countries have repressed inflation and a monetary overhang. Open inflation is often considered to be more favorable for policy action, but the evidence shows that this is not always the case. The reason is that, in spite of the well-known economic costs and social hardships of high rates of inflation, the government can derive some advantage. It can, and does, use inflation both as a tax and to reduce the real burden of its outstanding debt. Repressed inflation, by contrast, is worse for the government, because it does not provide revenues and the monetary overhang can become politically dangerous (as it is normally accompanied by goods rationing and empty shelves), especially in an environment of political transformation from authoritarian regimes to pluralist democracies. This situation may encourage reforms.

Second, persistent and high rates of inflation are rooted in both groups of countries in the monetization of fiscal deficits. Hence, the key to a successful stabilization policy is to reduce the budget deficit to sustainable levels and to switch to noninflationary sources of financing of what is considered an unavoidable deficit. The problem that a stabilization-minded government will face is fiscal rigidity. In developing countries, this rigidity is created mainly by powerful interest groups that effectively oppose cuts in public spending, especially wages and subsidies. In socialist countries, fiscal rigidity often originates more in the lack of a tax system through which sufficient revenues can be raised. Therefore, the temptation toward continued monetization of the budget deficit is great. Financial discipline could be imposed by adopting a fixed exchange rate (after a one-time devaluation to realign relative prices, as part of the stabilization program). However, for that to occur, the fixing of the exchange rate would have to be irrevocable, which, in practice, is not easy to achieve. Hence, overall inflationary expectations are not reversed, but reinforced. This is particularly the case when the government pursues an exchange rate policy of managed crawling peg rates, but is not able to avoid a real appreciation of the currency thereby implying that it is unable to consolidate the budget. Stabilization attempts, despite initial successes, will then end in failure. Evidence can be taken from recent experience in Argentina (Austral Plan) and Brazil (Cruzado Plan) as well as in East Germany (before the monetary union with West Germany) and the Soviet Union. An encouraging counter-example is Bolivia, where the government ended an extreme fiscal crisis and hyperinflation within two months in 1985. Whether the resolute stabilization program adopted in early 1990 in Poland will become another success story remains to be seen.

Third, it has long been known that stabilization policies in inflation-ridden countries must be combined with economic reforms that aim at a more efficient allocation of resources. Moreover, such reform packages can generate credibility for the new anti-inflationary course. The removal of the many microeconomic domestic distortions and the opening of the economy to foreign trade and international capital movements are difficult tasks. Reform is dramatic in the socialist countries because these countries are, for systemic reasons, much further from allocative efficiency than any middle-income developing country. The main complications stem from the privatization of economic activities that is the core of any market-oriented reform. Little is known about how to address and handle crucial issues such as market structure (to value assets), property rights (that are diffused), principal-agent relations (for the sake of efficient control over firm management), and the creation of capital markets (to channel savings and attract private capital from abroad).

Fourth, the implementation of economic reforms poses complicated policy choices to the government with regard to speed and sequencing. To do the reforms at one stroke is good for credibility, but such action may create high costs of adjustment that are politically intolerable. The shock approach could even prove politically explosive in the socialist countries because an abrupt freeing of prices probably triggers a too-painful inflationary push and because sharp competition in markets presumably leads to dramatic unemployment. A gradual approach makes adjustment easier, but it provides domestic interest groups with the opportunity to oppose and the government with the opportunity to fall back. Evidence on this abounds in Latin America, as well as in Eastern Europe. In socialist countries, the risk that economic reforms, when implemented gradually, may be diluted (if not forestalled) is especially great because many citizens, being unfamiliar with the functioning of a market system, will balk at the price rises and layoffs that inevitably accompany the transition period. With regard to sequencing, there is broad agreement among economists that domestic markets should be deregulated first and that the liberalization of external relations should follow in a second step, with the liberalization of the current account preceding that of the capital account. Frequently, however, governments tend to reverse the order, to delay the domestic reforms too much, or to put off unpopular measures, so that doubts arise abroad about the irreversibility of the reform process—thus, in turn, reducing capital inflows. The Eastern European countries, including the Soviet Union, are experiencing this now.

What lesson can be drawn from past experience for the future? Mundell has presented a comprehensive catalogue of domestic economic policies that must be adopted if stabilization of the price level and structural adjustment with growth are to be achieved. I basically agree. Probably not everything has to be done immediately, but it is crucial for the success of both sets of policies—stabilization and economic reform—that a feasible path for the implementation of the various measures be preannounced. The whole policy package must be widely perceived as consistent and sustainable. It is obvious that the shaping and implementation of such programs requires not only a high degree of technical expertise but also, and above all, political determination. This determination is nowhere in ample supply. It should, therefore, not come as a surprise if macroeconomic and microeconomic policies are also inappropriately mixed in the future, so that new waves of inflation (including galloping inflation and near-hyperinflation) arise. The tendency toward stability is not firmly embedded everywhere in society and cannot be imposed by fiat or by constitutional rules.

Similar concerns hold for the prospect of true economic reforms. Economic theory does not provide unambiguous guidelines about how to make the transition from severely distorted markets toward undistorted, well-functioning markets. There is a great diversity of conceptual frameworks and policy prescriptions. The objectives and full implications of the reforms are not easily understood. It is by no means certain that the people really want a comprehensive economic reform or, in case they do, that they will agree on the details and the path or policy implementation. Consequently, governments may not act in an enlightened way but may base their reform decisions only on political convictions. Therefore, the needed process of liberalization and deregulation of the economy in question may slow down or be realized only partially or discontinued, so that the crisis is prolonged, if not accentuated.

My final remark concerns the external environment. The main responsibility for ridding an economy of inflation and distortions rests with the government of the country. The efficacy of well-designed and executed domestic stabilization and reform policies also crucially depends on favorable external conditions. Apart from the availability of external financing (and the ability to cope with the external debt problem), a proper functioning of the world trading system is of great importance. An efficiency-increasing reallocation of resources must accompany an expansion and diversification of exports of developing and socialist countries. The governments of the industrial countries can provide support by offering full access to their markets. Will they do so? Again, I am skeptical. There is no evidence to indicate a removal of the many selective nontariff trade barriers that often discriminate against exports from developing and socialist countries. The recent trade agreements that the European Community has concluded with Eastern European countries all keep the well-known elements of selective protectionism.

Part Two

Socialist Countries

Stabilizing the Ruble:
The Problem of Internal
Currency Convertibility

The political economy of the Soviet Union is in crisis. The old authoritarian model of allocating economic resources based on central planning has been discredited, but, despite the enormous political shift in favor of restructuring (that is, perestroika), the financial conditions necessary for a workable market economy are still elusive. Instead, as fiscal deficits and the domestic money stock spiral out of control (Table 3.1), a potentially explosive internal inflation is forcing Soviet authorities to reimpose controls on prices and output. The success of perestroika depends on monetary and fiscal discipline, and that, in turn, requires a radically new tax and banking system for the Soviet Union. Before charting a course for stabilizing the ruble in order to attain economic liberalization, let us trace the origins of the present impasse back to the nature of money and taxation under central planning.

Implicit Taxation in the Planned Economy

In the traditional Soviet economy, which was the prototype for other communist countries in Eastern Europe and Asia, what is the nature of the fiscal process? How is revenue raised to support the ordinary functions of government—the military, judiciary, education, the civil service, old-age pensions, and so on? Although turnover taxes are

Table 3.1   Financial Statistics for the Soviet Economy, 1979–1989

Year	Government budget deficit[a]		Government debt[b]		Household savings deposits		Enterprise deposits[c]
	Billions of rubles	% of GNP	Billions of rubles	% of GNP	Billions of rubles	Ratio to retail sales	Billions of rubles
1979	n.a.	n.a.	64	n.a.	146.2	0.576	n.a.
1980	12	1.9	76	12.2	156.5	0.579	n.a.
1981	9	1.4	85	13.1	165.7	0.579	n.a.
1982	15	2.2	100	14.4	174.3	0.589	n.a.
1983	10	1.4	110	15.1	186.9	0.611	n.a.
1984	9	1.2	119	15.7	202.1	0.639	n.a.
1985	14	1.8	133	17.1	220.8	0.680	n.a.
1986	46	5.8	179	22.4	242.8	0.731	n.a.
1987	52	6.3	231	28.0	266.9	0.782	n.a.
1988	81	9.3	312	35.7	296.7	0.810	100.0
1989	92	9.9	404	43.4	337.7	0.837	100.0 +

n.a. = not available.
a. Soviet officials claimed that they were implementing emergency measures to bring the deficit down to 6.1% of GNP in 1990.
b. Government debt includes private savings deposits, other government indebtedness to the State Bank, and very small amounts of government bonds in the hands of the nonbank public.
c. Balances of state-production enterprises in the State Bank. For 1988, 100 billion rubles are a minimal estimate, in the sense that the deposits of cooperatives and a wide variety of state agencies are excluded. This "missing" money could amount to another 250 billion rubles.
Source: Jan Vanous, ed., *PlanEcon Report* (Washington, D.C.: PlanEcon Inc., February 21, 1990); Gregory Grossman, "Problems of Monetary Reform," Hoover-Rand Symposium, March 29–30, 1990.

sometimes levied explicitly on goods passing from the wholesale to the retail level, the traditional tax-collecting mechanism is largely *implicit*.

Under old-style central planning, the capital stock of virtually all significant economic enterprises is owned and controlled by the central government. Thus, economic surpluses of enterprises are effectively "revenue" in the fiscal sense. Depending on its revenue needs, the government simply sets average prices for goods and services at a considerable markup over money wages, although these profit margins may vary widely from one firm to the other. This average markup determines the collective economic surplus, which is automatically deposited with the State Bank and becomes revenue to be used for general government support or to be reinvested in designated industries.

Thus, under central planning, *the Soviet government never had to formalize the nature of the tax system on which it was implicitly relying*. Discussion about principles of taxation, which is commonplace among Western economists, was largely unnecessary. There was no need for a general corporate profits or value-added tax when the legal tax liabilities of enterprises were well defined. Allowances for corporate depreciation and deductibility of interest payments from taxable enterprise profits were not critical issues. Nor was any formalized personal income tax necessary, because almost all workers were employed directly by state-owned enterprises; by keeping wages low, the government acted as if it withheld personal income tax at the source.

True, turnover taxes were collected from enterprises on many consumer goods before they passed on to the retail stage. Because of long-standing price controls, however, turnover taxes tended to reduce surpluses at the margin, making such levies part of the process of surplus extraction. As long as the economy remained centrally planned, this automatic sequestering of surpluses neatly avoided the resource costs and political pain of levying explicit taxes.

With the advent of perestroika, however, this implicit tax-collecting mechanism tended to break down. First, as the effective ownership and control of industrial property passes from the central government to private farmers, independent industrial cooperatives, or local governments, the implicit tax base of the central government (the surpluses of the enterprises it owns) naturally erodes. No formal tax-collecting mechanism (other than the heterogeneous and inconsistent levies on various activities at different rates that now characterize Soviet tax policy) exists, therefore, for recapturing the loss in revenue.

Second, insofar as the remaining state-owned enterprises become more independent and profit-oriented in making decisions outside of the apparatus of central planning, the old government policy of simply appropriating surpluses of enterprises becomes incompatible with microeconomic incentives for these enterprises to operate efficiently. Why should managers strive to economize on resource use if 100 percent of "profits" are to be expropriated? Realizing this truth, the Soviet government has allowed state-owned enterprises to begin accumulating innumerable "special funds" in the form of credit money with the State Bank (Table 3.1); these funds may be spent for investment within the enterprise, for employee social purposes, or (with more strict limits) for a wages fund that is convertible into cash in order to pay workers. But the spending of each enterprise is officially monitored and often restricted, so that *the convertibility of its credit money into domestic goods and services (and also into foreign exchange) is partially blocked.* Nevertheless, these funds are no longer part of "pure" tax revenue in the old sense—in other words, a clear diversion of economic spending power from enterprises to the government.

Table 3.2 shows clearly that, from 1985 to 1989, the rapidly increasing Soviet fiscal deficit was mainly due to an increasingly serious shortfall in revenue, which fell from 48.0 percent of gross national product (GNP) in 1985 (when Gorbachev assumed power) to 41.7 percent in 1989—a fall of more than 6 percentage points. This shortfall in revenue

TABLE 3.2   Soviet Government Expenditure and Revenue,
1980–1989 (percentage of GNP)

Year	Expenditure	Revenue	Deficit
1980			1.9
1981			1.4
1982			2.2
1983			1.4
1984			1.2
1985	49.8	48.0	1.8
1986	52.2	46.5	5.7
1987	52.3	45.9	6.4
1988	52.5	43.3	9.2
1989	51.6	41.7	9.9

NOTE: Expenditure and revenue figures are not available separately before 1985.
SOURCE: Derived from Jan Vanous, ed., *PlanEcon Report* (Washington, D.C.: PlanEcon Inc., February 21, 1990).

is consistent with the basic hypothesis that perestroika itself tends to undermine the central government's traditional "implicit" tax-collecting mechanism based on appropriating the surpluses of enterprises.

This Soviet fiscal decline may not be at an end. The People's Republic of China liberalized its economy over a much longer period, beginning in 1978, although liberalization might have ended in 1989. Table 3.3, taken from an important International Monetary Fund study of the Chinese economy (Blejer and Szapary 1989), shows that the revenues of the central government fell from 34.4 percent of GNP in 1978 to just 20.4 percent in 1988. Even more remarkable, Table 3.3 shows that the revenue of the Chinese central government from enterprises fell from 20.6 percent of GNP in 1978 to just 7 percent in 1988. Also, since 1985, the country's loss of monetary control, with consequent inflationary pressure, has been similar to that experienced in the Soviet Union.

In summary, as in the other liberalizing socialist economies of Eastern Europe and Asia, the ability of the Soviet government to collect tax revenue has greatly diminished as a result of the liberalization itself (that is, the growth of economic activity outside the government sector and the attempt to give state-owned enterprises better incentives for making their own investment and production decisions). Although the numbers are necessarily rather uncertain, Table 3.1 shows the rapid buildup of the fiscal deficit, from 1.8 percent of GNP in 1985 (when Gorbachev assumed power) to an estimated 9.9 percent of GNP in 1989. Correspondingly, the debt-to-GNP ratio increased extraordinarily, from 17.1 percent in 1985 to 43.4 percent in 1989.

Because a market in government bonds hardly exists, this outstanding debt was largely financed by borrowing against household savings

TABLE 3.3   Government Revenue in the People's Republic of China, 1978–1988 (percentage of GNP)

Type of revenue	1978	1979–1981	1982–1984	1985–1987	1988
Total revenue[a]	34.4	30.0	27.0	24.8	20.4
Revenue from enterprises	20.6	17.1	12.5	8.3	7.0
Profit remittances	19.1	16.1	11.4	0.4	0.3
Profit tax	1.5	1.0	1.1	7.9	6.7
Taxes on					
Income and profits[b]	21.5	17.8	13.3	7.9	5.5
Goods and services[c]	11.3	10.6	10.1	10.6	9.1
International trade	0.8	0.9	1.1	1.8	1.1
Other taxes	—	—	1.5	3.2	3.0
Nontax revenue[d]	0.8	0.8	1.0	1.3	1.7

Dash indicates negligible percentage.
a. Total revenue includes nontax revenue.
b. Includes profit remittances.
c. Includes product, value-added, and business taxes.
d. Excluding profit remittances.
SOURCE: Data from the People's Republic of China, Ministry of Finance, as compiled in Mario I. Blejer and Gyorgy Szapary, "The Evolving Role of Fiscal Policy in Centrally Planned Economies under Reform: The Case of China," IMF Working Paper 0407 (Washington, D.C.: International Monetary Fund, 1989).

deposits (Table 3.1) and by issuing coin and currency to households (the exact outstanding amount of which is unknown). Thus, the fiscal deficit of the government is responsible for the major and rapidly growing amount of money and near-money owned by households. To understand the overall magnitude of the monetary overhang in Table 3.1, the huge stocks of partially blocked credit money of enterprises (about which information is scarce) should be added, but on a basis of less than one for one, to the more liquid cash and savings deposits of households. As estimated by Gregory Grossman (1990), these balances of operating enterprises were in excess of 100 billion rubles in 1989 (Table 3.1). This is an extremely conservative estimate, as it excludes another 250 billion rubles held on deposit by various government entities.

Money and Credit in the Planned Economy

Other than fiscal decline, in the traditional system of money and credit what might lead to a further loss of financial control with the advent of economic liberalization?

Under central planning, the monetary system facing enterprises is necessarily *passive*. The flow of funds, which is duly recorded as debits or credits with the state bank, fulfills an important auditing function to ensure that the purchases and sales of goods by each enterprise conform with the plan. However, neither the outstanding deposit money of enterprises nor their outstanding indebtedness to the state bank inhibit bidding for real resources.

For example, if any enterprise has a shortage of credit money for buying the inputs it needs as approved by the planners, this shortfall is no constraint. The state bank automatically advances the credit, at a zero or very low rate of interest, so that the enterprise may buy the inputs it needs to fulfill the approved plan.

Similarly, reflecting this passivity, the optimal stock of deposit money for enterprises to keep inflation under control is indeterminate in a centrally planned economy. Unlike households, enterprises cannot freely spend the deposit balances they nominally own. As long as the traditional planning apparatus for controlling resource flows among enterprises remains in place, however, the supply and demand for producer goods is more or less balanced.

The problem arises when the monetary system serving enterprises remains passive after liberalization begins (after the apparatus of central planning is weakened). Once decision making is shifted to the enterprises themselves, they begin to bid for scarce resources as if they have no effective budget constraint. Indeed, the faster their deposits with the state bank can be drawn down, the less likely it is that these surpluses will be subject to an arbitrary tax. Similarly, old and established credit lines—particularly for loss-making state-owned enterprises—are likely to remain open at very low rates of interest. The upshot is that, once a few producer goods are freed of centralized controls and can be bid for openly, their market prices might rise far beyond a level that reflects their relative economic scarcity.

Consider a rather dramatic recent example of overbidding for foreign exchange by well-established Soviet enterprises with soft budget constraints. It is common knowledge that the official commercial rate of exchange over the past twenty years (0.64 rubles for one U.S. dollar) greatly overvalues the ruble. Indeed, in late October 1989, the Soviet government introduced a new exchange rate for tourists that values the dollar at 6.26 rubles—a tenfold devaluation. Then, on November 3, 1989, in a first-ever official auction (albeit quite small) for foreign currency, enterprises bid 13–15 rubles per dollar, or twenty-two times the official rate. Does this market test imply that an appropriate official exchange rate should similarly be twenty-two times the old rate, in order to value the ruble at just 6.7 U.S. cents?

Not at all. The dollar's ruble value was bid up sharply because, in part, enterprises faced weak domestic financial constraints. Market processes cannot work properly when budget constraints remain soft because of too much domestic money. If price controls are removed and open bidding for key producer or consumer goods becomes more frequent, the traditionally passive Soviet monetary system is likely to accommodate explosive, confusing, and demoralizing increases in prices, without any well-defined upper limit.[1]

Deadlock in Decontrolling Prices

How then have the Soviet authorities reacted to this "excessive" monetary demand for domestic goods and services by households and enterprises without imposing financial constraints?

Reform of the traditional system of price controls—where relative prices have been wildly irrational, as, for example, the grotesque underpricing of energy resources to enterprises and the underpricing of some basic foodstuffs to consumers—has been continually delayed and is now deferred until after 1991.[2] In late April 1990, after intense internal discussions, the Soviet government officially announced that plans for further liberalization of the price mechanism were abandoned because of fear of an inflationary explosion. Even those economists who are most committed to reform are hesitant to promote decontrol of prices until the necessary fiscal and financial constraints are in place.

> . . . Stanislav S. Shatalin, an economist in Mr. Gorbachev's cabinet and an ardent proponent of change, [told] the daily *Izvestia* that the country must first take time to create a banking system, [new] fiscal and monetary policies and other measures.
> "Without all this, to introduce a market today would only be suicide," he said (*New York Times*, April 25, 1990).

Indeed, price controls are being extended to cover previously independent cooperatives. Because of the monetary overhang, many of these cooperatives are unseemingly profitable because they charge prices many times those charged for similar goods and services (of limited availability) sold through traditional government stores. In addition to greater production efficiency, however, these profits may well reflect the ability of cooperatives to evade the price controls that are still largely enforced on state-owned enterprises. Therefore, much "rent seeking," corruption, and wastage of resources goes into this evasion process, as entrepreneurs try to engage in arbitrage between the parallel controlled and liberalized sectors of the economy.

Suppose, however, that this excess macroeconomic demand is absent. In this case, the introduction of cooperatives, private farms, or other enterprises that are free to set their own prices would generate less disparity in relation to controlled prices in the state-owned enterprises. Not only would the current strong populist reaction against further privatization in the Soviet economy be muted, but the private or cooperative sectors would give a much better idea of what equilibrium relative prices should be. In addition, such a balanced market could better separate the liberalized enterprises that were truly more efficient in an economic or productive sense from those that were simply living off the income associated with a distorted price system. Surely, a large number of legally established cooperatives, as well as much of the burgeoning activity in the black market economy, would disappear as soon as macroeconomic equilibrium is established.

From the welfare theory of the second-best solution, therefore, populist resentment toward current Soviet efforts to liberalize the economy is not entirely misplaced. In the face of a monetary overhang, economic efficiency might worsen as liberalization proceeds. The monetary imbalance makes the transition to a more market-oriented economy too difficult to achieve and makes the transitional welfare costs too heavy. Thus, the Soviet government and the governments of the republics are forced to continue existing price controls as a second-best method of pinning down the nominal price level, even though *relative* prices are badly misaligned and greatly distort the economy (Shmelev and Popov 1989). A fully liberalized economy, in which enterprises with hard budget constraints are free to determine their own prices, would naturally be the first-best solution.

State Orders and Wholesale Trade

With the price system paralyzed and price reform indefinitely deferred, how are production and allocation decisions being made? The centerpiece of perestroika (the 1987 Soviet Law on State Enterprises and related legislation) was to make enterprises increasingly independent of the planning process (Aslund 1989:123). Detailed planning controls over thousands of commodities (traditionally exercised by Gosplan) were to be drastically truncated.

> According to Academician Nikolai Federenko in 1984, Gosplan elaborated about 4,000 material balances, Gossnab[3] 18,000, and the ministries 40–50,000. The number of balances increases lower down the hierarchy as they are disaggregated. Deputy Chairman of Gosplan, Leonard Vid, alleged that the number of material balances elaborated by Gosplan had been reduced to 2,117 in 1987 and that there would only be 415 in 1988. Vadim Kirichenko, who appears to be

one of the last competent Soviet economists to believe in central
planning, favoured a limited number of central balances—250–300
at the central level that would imply 3,000–5,000 material balances at
the ministerial level (Aslund 1989:122).

The development of what reformists like to call wholesale trade was
to be the counterpart of this stage-by-stage reduction in the centralized
allocation of resources. Enterprises were to negotiate directly with each
other on the terms and delivery dates for supplies, without using Gossnab as intermediary. Goods could be legally bought and sold among
state enterprises and private firms (mainly collectives of various forms)
at negotiated prices that could differ somewhat from the official ones. If
new firms or cooperatives were to succeed in manufacturing, they had
to be able to bid for industrial inputs or raw materials from the existing
state enterprises. Of course, entrants into personal service activities,
such as barbers, would not suffer greatly from being excluded from
wholesale trade.

The 1987 Soviet Law on State Enterprises intended that only a portion of each firm's output would be subject to state orders, that is,
traditional delivery quotas mandated by Gosplan. The remainder could
then flow into a freer market at the wholesale level.

Unfortunately, the 1987 Law on State Enterprises has not yet succeeded in developing wholesale trade and freer markets for industrial
goods as was promised. In 1987, Soviet economists projected that state
orders would initially account for some 20–40 percent of the activity of
traditional enterprises. Instead, throughout 1988, state orders absorbed
closer to 85 percent or 90 percent. In 1989, the situation was no better
with regard to producer goods; and on November 20, 1989, Leonid
Abalkin, Gorbachev's principal economic adviser, announced emergency measures to reimpose rigidly comprehensive state orders on a
wide variety of consumer goods, including foodstuffs and basic household necessities, that were especially affordable items for children and
pensioners. Moreover, it appears that most deposit money of enterprises remains effectively blocked, except when used for officially designated purposes. Thus, most managers of traditional enterprises have
not perceived any real change from full-scale central planning. Apart
from illicit trade, a substantially free wholesale market—absolutely crucial in the transition from a planned to a market economy—does not yet
exist.

Why did the 1987 Law on State Enterprises not work as intended?
Soft budget constraints on enterprises, government fiscal deficits, and
the monetary overhang in households made its failure inevitable.

In the face of general excess demand, the ministries that retained the responsibility for achieving a coordinated allocation of the resources under their jurisdiction were probably "forced" to use their remaining discretionary control over resource use in order to prevent economic chaos.[4] In the face of irrational prices and soft budget constraints on enterprises, the predominance of state orders was necessary to prevent the mismatch of production decisions, including a further excessive buildup of inventories.

Excess Inventories and Productivity of Capital

In the Soviet economy, to what extent are the low productivity of capital, in general, and inventory accumulation at the enterprise level, in particular, financial problems?

Certainly, disappointing growth in real output antedates by more than two decades the accelerated loss of monetary control caused by perestroika. Indeed, beginning in 1985, perestroika itself was largely a response to the Brezhnev years of stagnation under the classical Stalinist planned economy. And as glasnost allows increasingly open scrutiny of Soviet statistics, realistic assessments of how low Soviet output is, and has been, are getting progressively more pessimistic:

> The actual condition of the Soviet economy is worse than that indicated by data either from the Kremlin or the (American) Central Intelligence Agency . . . said several senior Soviet economists today.
> The Agency said that the Soviet Gross National Product was about half that of the United States. . . .
> Viktor Belkin, a prominent economist from the Soviet Academy of Sciences, said that Soviet output was no more than 28 percent of American GNP and might be substantially less (*New York Times*, April 23, 1990).

And since 1985, Soviet real economic growth seems to have slowed down even more, with overall GNP growing by less than 1.5 percent a year and actually falling by 1 percent or so in 1989, according to Central Intelligence Agency (CIA) estimates. GNP per capita seems to have been slowly falling in the 1980s, on the order of 1–2 percent a year, with the recent decline being a bit sharper (Vanous 1990).

Nevertheless, the problem is *not* the conventional one of mobilizing financial intermediaries to increase aggregate saving. All observers agree that the Soviet saving-investment effort as a share of national income has been truly enormous for many decades. For the first half of the 1980s, Shmelev and Popov (1989:149) estimate that net Soviet investment (saving) has been over 20 percent of net national income, whereas the comparable figure for net national investment in the United States is less than 6 percent. Nor is there any reason to believe that this discrepancy was any less in the late 1980s. Indeed, the Soviet saving-investment effort in the postwar period probably exceeded that of Japan. Why then did the pay-off from this enormous capital investment turn out to be so abysmal?

The sheer impossibility of efficiently allocating hundreds of thousands of industrial goods and raw materials by central planning is now evident. Without a market mechanism for evaluating equilibrium prices for inputs and outputs, planners must specify some form of targets of gross output for each enterprise and then allocate inputs from other enterprises according to crudely specified norms of what usage should be. Enterprises thus have no incentive to economize on inputs in meeting their targets of gross output, and these targets are not subject to effective quality control through market discipline. In their insightful book *The Turning Point: Revitalizing the Soviet Economy*, Shmelev and Popov (1989) have a long chapter entitled "Black Holes That Swallow Resources." They provide incredible detail on specific irrationalities and waste arising from perverse managerial responses to ministerial or Gosplan directives.

This massive social waste of resources in enterprises is an outcome not only of quantitative central planning per se, but it is also affected by the system of money and credit. Because not all the details of resource use can be planned from the center, managers have considerable discretionary latitude in their use of supplies, especially since perestroika began. If the enterprises have no liquid domestic monetary asset bearing an attractive real rate of return, however, their managers will opt to hold excess inventories of all kinds: raw materials, semifinished goods, their own outputs, and then fixed assets, such as excess capacity in plant and equipment, and semifinished structures. With hidden price inflation now on the order of 5–10 percent a year, and without an offsetting rate of interest being paid on deposits with the state bank (deposits that are semiconvertible and subject to being frozen or otherwise restricted), enterprises will naturally opt to build up excess inventories as a substitute monetary store of value. These excess commodity stocks and the spare production capacity serve as a hedge against threatened shortages of inputs of key materials, if official allocations prove inadequate or late. If some unanticipated shortage arises, excess stocks of other commodities can be informally bartered in the extensive "gray" market among enterprises for parts the firm really needs, or even for consumer goods to distribute directly to its employees.

If the firm has access to further credit from the state bank at a very low rate of interest, this tendency to hold excess inventories is exacerbated. Similarly, if the credit is designated for fixed capital investments, construction projects will be delayed because of the low opportunity cost of not bringing them to completion.[5] Unfinished structures are in themselves an inflation hedge, although much less liquid than commodity inventories. Partly because excess stocks continue to proliferate, the incremental Soviet net output-capital ratio seems to be approaching zero.

Shmelev and Popov (1989) calculate that Soviet industrial inventories relative to national income rose from 50 percent in 1960 to 82 percent in 1985, compared with just 31 percent in the United States in 1985 (Figure 3.1). In addition, farm inventories are also relatively high and are still rising in the Soviet Union. Because Soviet inventories are increasing faster at the margin, Shmelev and Popov (1989:135) further estimate that

FIGURE 3.1   Soviet and U.S. Inventories as a Percentage of National Income, 1960–1985

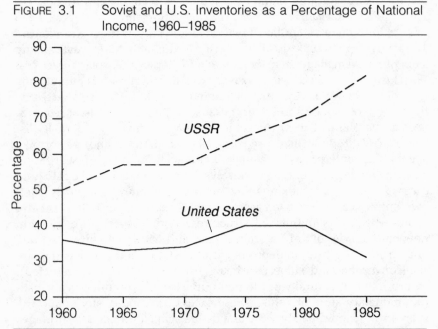

NOTE: USSR—Year-end inventories, excluding collective farm inventories (almost 9 percent of national income in 1988), as a percentage of utilized national income.
United States—Year-end inventories as a percentage of national income in the business sector; national income of business sector calculated on the assumption that its share in the total national income is the same as in the gross national product.
SOURCE: Nikolai Shmelev and Vladimir Popov, *The Turning Point: Revitalizing the Soviet Economy* (New York: Doubleday, 1989), 305.

"almost 6 percent of created national income goes toward increasing inventories in our country in the 1980s, while in the United States this figure is less than 1 percent."

Because wholesale markets are not open at equilibrium prices, the liquidity of enterprise deposits is reduced. In the long run, the syndrome of excess accumulation of inventory and fixed capital is thereby worsened. In the presence of a monetary overhang, however, any attempt to open wholesale trade could greatly exacerbate this syndrome of excess holding of stocks in the short run:

> Yet it will be difficult for us to move away from the direct, central allocation of capital goods to a system of wholesale buying and selling for the simple—ostensibly contradictory—reason that enterprises currently have too much money at their disposal. As soon as they would be allowed to buy what they please, the acquisitive instinct they have developed over the years would come into play, and they would increase stocks out of all proportion.
>
> Such apprehensions are not simply speculation. A large scale experiment conducted in 1984–1986 has shown that as soon as enterprises were given the go-ahead to make special purchases, they bought equipment and material for the "rainy days" ahead. The value of the stock (inventories) in all our enterprises exceeds 460 billion rubles—almost as much as the State's entire annual budget! Moreover, the stocks are growing twice as fast as production. Because enterprises acquired material resources largely by credit, there were years when enterprise production increased by 3 to 4 percent and debt by 10 to 15 percent. As a result, there is an enormous amount of spare money not geared to the real requirements of production. For this reason alone, the introduction of wholesale trade is necessary, and must go hand-in-hand with the reform of finance and credit discussed at the 27th CPSU Congress (Abel Aganbegyan 1988:36).

Before the Soviet government proceeds much further with perestroika, therefore, the domestic Soviet monetary and fiscal systems need to serve as active constraints on the ability of enterprises, households, and governments to bid for scarce resources. Going one step further, any new system of money and credit should prompt massive dishoarding by enterprises of excess commodity stocks in open wholesale trade at equilibrium prices, while encouraging more efficient use of existing fixed capital and curtailing cheap credit for new projects. Indeed, the general dishoarding of excess inventories and their replacement by new domestically convertible enterprise money could be important elements in a macroeconomic process of disinflation that would simultaneously increase the productivity of capital.

The attainment of sufficient financial control to promote disinflation of this kind requires: (1) the imposition of fiscal and monetary constraints on the cash flows of both enterprises and households, and (2) monetary measures to deal with excessive existing stocks of various monies or near-monies.

Taxing Value Added Rather Than Profits

On the tax side, resolving the problem of cash flow is conceptually straightforward, although politically difficult. To help limit the excess issue of new money, major reforms in enterprise and personal income taxation are needed to eliminate the fiscal deficit of the Soviet government. The rapid fiscal decline can be turned around only by a massive effort to: (1) cut government expenditures, particuarly the massive resources devoted to defense[6] and food subsidies, and (2) to replace the old implicit revenue system and the more recent ad hoc levies with a comprehensive and uniform system of explicit business and personal income taxes, according to well-established canons of taxation.

Clearly, a liberalizing socialist economy should restructure tax arrangements for enterprises so that: (1) revenue does not fall simply because ownership and management of industrial enterprises move away from the direct control of the central government, and (2) the new tax system is fully consistent with hardening the budget constraints of enterprises by avoiding the arbitrary expropriation of their surpluses.

To satisfy these principles, I have suggested elsewhere that the value-added tax (VAT) is best suited to be the main pillar of a reformed system of taxation (McKinnon 1989). Even without detailed institutional information on the Soviet system of production and distribution, a VAT permits the central government to tax all forms of income uniformly. Profits, interest, rents, wages, and salaries can all be taxed at flat rate (say, 20 percent), without having to make distinctions among them at a time when accounting conventions have yet to be established in socialist enterprises.[7]

The VAT is particularly advantageous for a socialist economy in transition. First, it avoids the conceptual and accounting difficulties associated with defining "profit" that plague business income taxes, and it therefore has the great advantage of being neutral with respect to any corporate form that might develop in the liberalized enterprises. By levying the VAT on all enterprises—whether they are state-owned agencies, cooperatives, joint-stock companies, or sole proprietorships—the

Soviet government could collect revenue without committing itself to any legal ground rules defining ownership and control (rules that seem to be in a state of flux). The creation of thousands of new small firms or cooperatives, some of which compete with the large state-owned enterprises, would not undermine the revenue position of the Soviet government.

Second, the VAT is neutral between domestic and foreign trade. If the VAT is to be applied on the "destination" principle, imports would be taxed at the same uniform rate as domestically produced goods. Government revenue would rise automatically, as foreign trade is liberalized and imports increase. Provided that the exchange rate is "right" (a big issue to be discussed later), enterprises having access to foreign inputs, including joint ventures with foreign firms, would not have a great advantage over those without such access.

In contrast, the proliferation of new enterprises in China, many of which operate in free-trade zones or have come under the control of the state and local government, has undermined the ability of the central government to collect tax revenue and has weakened its control over the flow of credit in the Chinese economy. Indeed, one of the main arguments against uncontrolled free-trade zones is that the central government finds it more difficult to collect taxes. For example, customs officials normally collect the VAT levy on imported goods as they cross the border, but in a pure free-trade zone, goods come through the initial port of entry without being checked by the customs. By the late 1980s, the resulting inflationary pressure forced the Chinese to begin retrenching on liberalization and to take control of enterprises that had been given their independence.

Third, with an easily understood, uniform VAT in place in the Soviet Union, each potential new firm would know its tax liabilities before deciding whether to go into business. Thus, ex post changes in the tax rules to recapture surpluses of the most profitable enterprises could be minimized or even avoided altogether. For fully liberalized enterprises that are financially independent (to be discussed more fully in the section "Hardening the System of Money and Credit"), taxes on enterprise profits could be officially abandoned. Because of the unfortunate history of arbitrary seizure of profits by the Soviet and other communist governments, eliminating taxes on profits altogether would be a highly visible—not to say draconian—step for the Soviet government toward committing itself to a more stable future tax regime for enterprises.

If a firm's output prices are tightly controlled, however, the VAT may not be collectible because it could not be shifted forward and incorporated in the price paid by the final user. In fact, the incidence of the tax could be shifted backward and might reduce the firm's profit on a one-for-one basis. After paying their VAT in the absence of price controls, many potentially profitable enterprises might find themselves with a negative cash flow if the VAT is levied with price controls in place. The authorities would find that they had not escaped from the syndrome of arbitrary taxation of profits or the seizure of surpluses. Indeed, with an arbitrary disequilibrium pattern of price controls in place, the *only* feasible method of taxing enterprises may well be the seizure of surpluses or profits in the Stalinist mode.

Hence, the introduction of a broad and uniform VAT cannot be effected without simultaneously decontrolling prices. Successful monetary and price reforms thus facilitate the collection of taxes on enterprises, and vice versa.

Tax Position of Households

Although a carefully designed VAT levied on enterprises would be a major resource for fiscal revenue, a broad-based personal income tax could also bring in badly needed revenue. After standard deductions to keep the poorest people off the tax rolls, a uniform basic rate on the order of 25–35 percent could be levied on the consolidated personal income, including wages and interest or profits actually paid out to each household.

In the present state of the Soviet economy, however, much household income is imputed rather than in the form of cash. In housing, for example, many people pay low rents for ample housing services. Similarly, the social funds in enterprises often provide substantial returns, through canteens and other amenities, to employees at their place of work. Because of the monetary overhang, resulting in long queues at retail shops, Soviet enterprises often distribute a wide variety of consumer goods directly to their employees. Until all these noncash sources of household income are properly calculated, their value should be imputed for inclusion in the base of the personal income tax. Realized capital gains accruing to households should also be included in the base of the personal income tax, provided that the marginal tax rate remains moderate. However, neither unrealized capital gains of households nor capital gains by enterprises should be in the personal income tax net.

Specific commodity taxes on consumer luxuries (such as alcohol, gasoline, and jewelry) at the retail level are also necessary for revenue purposes. Insofar as the base for the personal income tax remains weak at the beginning of perestroika, a wide range of specific consumer levies could generate additional revenue. Like the personal income tax itself, these specific commodity taxes should apply to informal distribution channels (factory sites, for example), as well as to formal retail outlets.

Finally, negative commodity taxes, such as the vast array of subsidies on consumer and producer goods, should be discontinued or phased out, both to help balance the government budget and to further reduce the discretionary power of the Soviet government to intervene ex post facto after markets have been ostensibly liberalized. The mechanisms of monetary reform are discussed later in this chapter.

In summary, the issues involved in tax reform are conceptually straightforward in a technical economic sense. The key idea is to identify a tax base for enterprises and households that is as broad as possible (covering all forms of income) and then to tax it moderately. Unfortunately, successful implementation would require major new administrative bureaucracies for collecting both the VAT and the personal income tax. Also, achieving the necessary political consensus would undoubtedly be difficult. Nevertheless, the reformers have no choice. A comprehensive new tax system is simply a necessary condition for the success of perestroika.

How do the above suggestions for tax reform in evolving socialist economies differ from what might be advocated for an advanced industrial economy where market processes, including borrowing and lending in the capital market, are better established? The only substantial difference lies in the treatment of profits accumulated within enterprises. I suggested that the liberalizing socialist economy should avoid levying a separate profits or capital gains tax on domestic enterprises that were otherwise properly registered for paying their VAT. For many years, the Soviet system ran better without the equivalent of a corporate profits tax as is typical in mature capitalist economies. In the absence of any separate profits tax on retained earnings, self-financed capital accumulation *within* enterprises that were liberalized could then be better promoted as the centerpiece of a general monetary program for hardening the system of money and credit for the economy in transition—the all-important conundrum, to which we now turn.

Hardening the System of Money and Credit

The amount that liberalized enterprises—those that are free to make their own decisions regarding output, employment, input, prices, and wages—can borrow in either domestic or foreign financial markets must be strictly limited during the transition to a full-fledged market economy. Because Soviet bankers have little experience evaluating domestic credit risks and foreign bankers have little knowledge of the Soviet economy (and also because examples of bank lending to loss-making enterprises have been horrendous), a strong case can be made for considering new enterprises (whether state-owned, cooperative, or private) *ineligible* for bank credit. For investment finance, both rural and urban enterprises would be constrained to rely mainly on retained earnings that could possibly be supplemented by nonmonetary sources of capital, such as loans from private credit cooperatives or the sale of commercial bills.

Liberalized enterprises could participate in the monetary system as depositors but *not* as borrowers—at least not for several years, until inflation is under control and the banking system is operating profitably in a commercial environment. In addition to nontaxation of retained earnings, self-financed capital accumulation would be greatly facilitated if enterprises could hold *liquid* ruble deposits bearing an attractive real rate of interest. Indeed, the key to reducing excess inventories of Soviet enterprises and the general excessive hoarding of physical capital would be to allow liberalized enterprises to hold bank deposits at an attractive real rate of interest (McKinnon 1973). Such deposits should be freely convertible into domestic goods and services or into the coin and currency that households own. Once enterprises are given attractive financial assets in which to invest and free wholesale trade in producer goods is opened up, voluntary dishoarding of excess inventories would quickly develop.

Similarly, credit subsidies to nonliberalized enterprises remaining under state ownership and control would be phased out as soon as possible. As long as traditional enterprises operated with negative cash flows covered by borrowing from the state bank and other enterprises, they would remain under central ministerial supervision and could not freely spend any bank deposits they might accumulate. In the transition period, the domain of liberalized enterprises, with hard budget constraints on the use of domestically convertible rubles, would expand relative to traditional enterprises with soft budget constraints under centralized control. For some years to come, the lending resources of the deposit banks would be fully utilized for financing the current government deficits (until they are phased out) and for capital expenditures in rebuilding the depleted infrastructure in transportation, the environment, etc.

Liberalized Enterprises and State Ownership

In the optimum order of economic liberalization, privately owned enterprises (that is, those in which the residual profits accrue to private owners), would be in the liberalized sector. Otherwise, if price controls and quantitative restrictions on outputs and inputs remain, privatization is counterproductive and rather pointless. (Some Soviet leaders, such as Boris Yeltsin of the Russian republic, advocate rapid privatization while, perversely, keeping price controls in place.) Small-scale private capitalism (small shopkeepers, farmers, artisans, etc.) could quickly flourish in decontrolled markets when macroeconomic equilibrium is established, as the experience of China from 1979 to 1984 suggests. Some years later, larger-scale private industrial activity would naturally develop, as the most successful "home-grown" entrepreneurs succeed in accumulating sufficiently large amounts of capital to permit a substantial expansion in their operations. As Kornai (1990) emphasizes, capitalism cannot spring in full scale from some "big bang" type of liberalization; it must arise from small beginnings, in which a sorting process eventually separates good entrepreneurs from their less-successful counterparts.

In an optimally organized transition, therefore, some liberalized enterprises may well remain government-owned. For example, the government need not immediately break up large-scale manufacturing activities that are successful and could possibly remain viable in a competitive environment. If the private capitalist sector is still a small-scale one, with no concentration of wealth among individuals with proven entrepreneurial skills, no efficient means for the privatization of large manufacturing complexes would yet exist, although that situation would not preclude the future sale of some state-owned enterprises at fair market prices. In the meantime, any state-owned enterprise that is free to determine its own prices for output and can bargain freely over prices of inputs, including wages, could be treated like a private firm. Such liberalized, but state-owned, enterprises would be cut off from government subsidies, special tax treatment, credit from the monetary system, etc., in order to ensure a hard budget constraint similar to that imposed on private firms.

The important caveat is that *the state must assert its role as owner*: to be the recipient of any residual profits and to demand a fair claim on the firm's capital—perhaps after a once-and-for-all recapitalization of the kind to be discussed in the section "A One-Time Adjustment in Nonmonetary Stocks." Like a private owner protecting his capital, the government would have to oversee wage bargaining within the state-owned firm in order to minimize wage claims to the market level necessary for securing needed labor inputs. Indeed, given the precarious fiscal position of most socialist governments, the net profits of state-owned enterprises are best returned to the government, which would have the incidental advantage of gradually reducing the size of the state-owned sector relative to the private one.

Why should not state-owned firms be self-managing, or simply be turned over to worker cooperatives in the Yugoslavian mode, where any residual surplus accrues to those who currently work for the firm? In his important paper, "Issues in the Introduction of Market Forces in Eastern European Socialist Economies," Manuel Hinds (1990) demonstrates that neither the capital market nor the labor markets will operate efficiently if firms are self-managing but the ownership of capital is ambiguous. Let us consider a typical socialist enterprise with a large capital stock that had previously been financed by government loans or grants. In a liberalized system, the enterprise is freed of government controls, so that it is self-managed. Hinds demonstrates that internal pressure to pay excessive wages (in cash or in kind) to managers or workers would tend to decapitalize the firm, unless the government reasserts its ownership interest. Workers (or managers) would act as if they had a claim on the assets of the self-managed enterprise, but the firm's employees could only exercise this otherwise illiquid claim if: (1) above-market wages and salaries are paid out to existing employees, who in turn must remain with the firm if they are to collect, and (2) new entrants—employees who would potentially share in this economic surplus—are excluded.

Thus, self-managed or worker-managed enterprises are induced to deplete the capital stock through excessive wage payments. As Kornai (1990) observed in Hungary, this situation has been a well-known feature of Yugoslavian labor-managed firms for many years. True, existing workers could be given equity claims on the capital stock of the enterprise rather than higher wages. That might solve the problem of wasting capital or interfering with labor mobility, but direct diversion of the capital to the existing labor force would be manifestly unfair, as some workers in highly capitalized or natural-resource-based enterprises would be unduly enriched. More important, the precarious fiscal position of the government would be further impaired if it failed to earn revenue from its accumulated capital stock.

Thus, in the proper order of liberalization, the government must claim the residual profits of state-owned firms (even those in the liberalized sector); this is the hypothesis maintained in the following summary of alternative financial arrangements for traditional and liberalized enterprises in the transition period.

Alternative Financial Constraints

Before the transition to a full-fledged market economy is effected, both traditional and liberalized enterprises would coexist under somewhat different monetary and tax regimes. Table 3.4 presents a summary of financial arrangements consistent with the degree of liberalization (that

TABLE 3.4   Alternative Domestic Financial Arrangements for Enterprises in Transition

Financial arrangement	Traditional enterprises[a]	Liberalized enterprises	
		State-owned	Private
Taxation	Expropriation of surpluses	Uniform value-added tax	Uniform value-added tax
Deposit money	Restricted convertibility[b]	Domestically convertible[b] and interest-bearing	Domestically convertible[b] and interest-bearing
Credit eligibility	State bank	Nonbank capital market	Nonbank capital market
Wages	Government-determined	Government-determined	Market-determined
Residual profits	Accrue to government	Dividends to government; retained earnings for reinvestment	Dividends to owners; retained earnings for reinvestment or lending to other private enterprises[c]

a. Traditional enterprises are those whose output and pricing decisions are still determined by a central-government authority or planning bureau with centrally allocated inputs and credits from the state bank to cover any negative cash flows.
b. Convertibility here means the freedom to spend for domestic goods and services only (not necessarily convertibility into foreign exchange).
c. Dividends would be subject to the personal income tax when paid out to private owners, but retained earnings would not be taxed.
SOURCE: Author.

is, mode of operation) of each class of enterprise. It distinguishes three relatively large classes.

First are traditional enterprises that are state-owned, subject to direct price controls on their outputs and perhaps to direct allocations of materials for some inputs, including credits from the state banking system. They could include both natural public enterprises, such as utilities, energy-producing resource-intensive industries, and firms engaging in infrastructure activities, such as roads or irrigation facilities. In addition, traditional enterprises include industrial "basket cases"—those having negative cash flows in a domestically liberalized environment, but not shut down by the government immediately for social reasons.

The distinction between liberalized enterprises with hard budget constraints and traditional enterprises need not preclude substantial rationalization of relative prices in the latter. For example, in the energy sector, which would be expected to remain under state ownership and control, much like a public utility, a sharp increase in the economy-wide price of energy to approximate world levels should be charged to the liberalized enterprises at the outset of the transition period. Otherwise, they will continue to use energy wastefully. Higher energy prices would allow the government to better collect the economic rents (tax the surplus) associated with the exploitation of this valuable natural resource.

Second are state-owned liberalized enterprises, where output and input decisions on prices and quantities are freely determined by management in pursuit of higher profits, after payment of the value-added tax. The government would exert its ownership claim over the return to capital (residual profits), as described above.

Third are private liberalized enterprises, where there are no government restraints on enterprise behavior in making output, price, and wage decisions in the pursuit of higher profits, except for the obligation to pay the value-added tax at the enterprise level and to cooperate with the government authorities in the collection of the personal income tax through tax withholding on any wages, interest, dividend, or capital-gains payouts to individuals.

For each of these three enterprise classifications, the columns in Table 3.4 list mutually consistent tax, monetary, credit, wage, and profit arrangements. Each set of financial arrangements is more or less self-explanatory in the preceding analysis. For example, it may well not be feasible to collect a broad-based value-added tax from traditional enterprises, although that would be the prime mode for taxation of enterprises in the liberalized sector.

It should be noted, however, that the differential treatment of money and credit in traditional enterprises has implications for macroeconomic control in the system as a whole. Traditional enterprises could borrow from the state bank at a positive real rate of interest, although they would be strictly rationed under central government supervision. Their deposits would remain blocked, being only partially convertible for domestic purposes, as part of the centralized financial control by the government. In effect, the bank accounts of traditional enterprises would simply be part of the government treasury accounts that are naturally subject to centralized official supervision. In Western economies, such accounts are typically *not* counted as part of the general money supply of the nonbank public—that is, these blocked balances would be excluded from any general monetary measure, such as M1, M2, M3, etc., that is normally considered to influence the spending behavior of the nonbank sector.

The domestically convertible deposits of the liberalized enterprises, as well as coin, currency, and savings deposits held by households, would be part of these generalized monetary measures. Indeed, as the monetary circuits of liberalized enterprises and households would be fully integrated, there would be no official restrictions on transactions between them. Either could hold coin and currency and the same classes of deposits.

Transactions between traditional and liberalized enterprises would certainly occur, but they would be subject to the official payments and convertibility restrictions on the former. Indeed, insofar as the traditional enterprises ran payments deficits in relation to the liberalized enterprises and household sectors (probably covered by loans from the state bank), the general supply of fully convertible money, as measured by M1, M2, or M3, would increase. Inflationary pressure would be correspondingly greater, much in the same way that a government deficit financed by bank borrowing would expand the supply of domestically convertible money in the system.

In summary, the key to controlling the supply of effective domestic "money" in a partially liberalized economy is, first, to measure the consolidated net deficits of both the general government and the traditional enterprises and, next, to take fiscal and other restrictive measures to keep that net deficit as small as possible. It is assumed here that a generalized domestic market in government bonds does not exist, so that the consolidated fiscal deficit cannot be offset by selling government bonds directly to the nonbank public. Moreover, neither liberalized enterprises nor households can borrow from the banks, so that the government need not worry about additional money creation from borrowing. Therefore, this consolidated public sector deficit should remain the main focus of attention for balancing monetary flow, if price inflation is to be eliminated and macroeconomic equilibrium is to be established.

A One-Time Adjustment in Monetary Stocks

Resolving the stock problem—the excess monetary overhang—is conceptually much more complex. Nothing much can be done before the necessary fiscal and credit-market reforms for correcting the flow imbalances of the economy are implemented. Once the yield on deposit money available to both enterprises and households has been made much more attractive, a determination must be made as to how great the monetary overhang actually is, presuming that the current price level is, on average, to be maintained when price controls are removed.

If a once-and-for-all stock adjustment seems necessary, a natural place to start would be with the quasi-convertible deposit money of state-owned enterprises that opted, or were forced, to become "liberalized." In the process of their recapitalization, both their debts *and* deposits with the state bank in all the many categories of wages funds, working capital funds, social funds, etc., could be written off. Each newly liberalized enterprise could then be given a small starting fund of "new" rubles that are fully convertible and unrestricted for making domestic payments in any category and are fully convertible into coin and currency.

After this recapitalization, however, the newly liberalized enterprises could not borrow from the state bank or from other state enterprises. To build up their liquidity for making investments over the longer term, liberalized enterprises would be forced to raise their profitability (raising output prices, cutting down on labor, reducing their use of raw materials, etc.), so that untaxed retained earnings would increase in the steady state. To ease their initial liquidity squeeze in the short run, however, many would strive to auction off their excess inventories in the burgeoning wholesale markets for all manner of industrial goods. Most important, because such liberalized enterprises—whether agricultural or industrial—would be forced to build up their cash-balance positions for some years, they would help to finance the remaining deficit sectors of the economy in a noninflationary manner.

The above measures focusing on the cash position of enterprises may or may not be sufficient to deal with the inflationary overhang for the economy as a whole, as empirical data on the stock of currency held by households is not currently available. If these measures are not sufficient, the liquidity of households could be reduced by substituting for part of their outstanding ruble balances less liquid government bonds, at an attractive rate of interest in real terms. Because of the acute political and administrative difficulties involved, however, it would be desirable to avoid tampering with the cash position of households. Indeed, the mere raising of interest rates on saving and time deposits available to households and to liberalized enterprises (in the hypothetical new monetary regime) well above any expected inflation may be sufficient to prevent net cash dishoarding after price controls are removed.

Basically, however, the various forms of domestic money should be unified and have stable domestic purchasing power. As budget constraints of enterprises are hardened in the liberalized sector, convertibility restrictions should all be eliminated among different categories of deposits and between money of enterprises and household cash balances. Only after this monetary consolidation can perestroika succeed in creating open markets, where state-owned or more liberalized enterprises, including small private firms, can compete freely for goods and services within the Soviet economy at market-determined prices.

Flows of Foreign Capital and Foreign Trade

Free convertibility of rubles into foreign exchange would come later, possibly much later. Deflecting attention from the current *domestic* fiscal and monetary disarray and leaping to a convertible "gold" ruble, as suggested by Wanniski (1989) and Angell (1989), can do more harm than good. Unrestricted convertibility into gold or foreign exchange is not sustainable in the face of internal fiscal and financial hemorrhages.

To keep domestic financial constraints binding while liberalization proceeds, the absorption of large amounts of foreign capital is also best avoided, even as the economy moves toward freer foreign trade in goods and services. Apart from the problem of servicing foreign debt in the future, the absorption of large net capital inflows from abroad at the beginning of a liberalization program will cause the economy to be flooded with foreign goods. Overall, the relative prices of internationally tradable goods, in general, and of potentially new manufactured exports, in particular, would be artificially depressed in the fledgling market economy. New entrepreneurs in the Soviet traded-goods sectors would have even greater difficulty in coping with this subsidized international competition. Also, the apparently low cost of capital to those individuals or firms with favored access to foreign sources of finance could induce them to overborrow.[8]

Nevertheless, the rationalization of foreign trade on current account could still proceed with deliberate speed through the establishment of an appropriate unified exchange rate for importing and exporting and a well-defined commercial policy. What sort of tariff regime is appropriate in a liberalizing socialist economy is heavily dependent on what the preexisting system of implicit protection actually was. This important question is taken up in some detail in McKinnon (1991:ch. 12).

Next, some limited forms of convertibility could be developed, where, say, authorized importers could bid for foreign exchange certificates with which to buy foreign goods, but capital flight or overborrowing abroad would be inhibited (McKinnon 1989). Indeed, liberalized enterprises with hard budget constraints could be allowed to bid freely for foreign exchange certificates in order to import, whereas state-owned enterprises and other government agencies in the traditional sector would be more strictly rationed as to the certificates they purchase. Rather than being held abroad, foreign exchange proceeds from exports by either group should be fully repatriated into rubles in the same centralized market for exchange certificates. Thus, both groups would always use the same unified exchange rate.

In 1989 and 1990 Soviet foreign exchange policy was the worst of both worlds. On the one hand, contracting for imports has been decentralized to enterprises and other government agencies with soft budget constraints. On the other hand, multiple and arbitrarily administered exchange rates proliferated and differed greatly from one transaction to the next. Not only were the social gains from trade greatly eroded, but in 1990 and 1991, many Soviet enterprises cannot make the foreign exchange payments for which they are liable. The foreign exchange bank is refusing to honor many of these independently negotiated contracts, probably for good reasons. Clearly, the whole foreign payments regime must again be centralized, but at a uniform exchange rate.

Only after the domestic capital market is fully liberalized, with well-defined financial and fiscal constraints on firms and individuals in place, so that unrestricted borrowing and lending at equilibrium domestic interest rates becomes feasible, could the ruble be safely made fully convertible into foreign exchange on capital account. Many years hence, individuals and enterprises, including joint ventures with foreign firms, could possibly be allowed to choose freely between domestic and foreign sources of finance. This is the last, rather than the first, step in the overall process of liberalization.[9]

The Wrong Kind of Monetary Reform: An Addendum

In early 1991, after this manuscript was virtually completed, the Soviet government tried a quick fix on the economy's monetary overhang. The authorities had become increasingly desperate about empty shelves and severe shortages of consumer necessities in the official price-controlled outlets, high inflation in the legal cooperative market outlets where prices are only "monitored," and very high inflation in rapidly proliferating black-market activities. Thus on January 23, 1991, the government announced that:

1. Ruble bank notes in large denominations of 50 and 100 rubles were no longer legal tender—perhaps one-quarter to one-third of the outstanding supply of currency was thereby canceled.

2. People were given just three working days to turn in large ruble notes (presumably for smaller denominations or for credit to their savings accounts) up to a maximum governed by a worker's monthly salary (which averaged about 250 rubles per month in 1990) or 1,000 rubles—whichever was less. Pensioners were restricted to converting a maximum of 200 rubles.

3. Personal savings accounts (which in practice are very large relative to the coin and currency held by households—Table 3.1) were frozen. Individuals could withdraw no more than 500 rubles per month from these accounts.

Insofar as they can demonstrate that their large notes were acquired by bringing hard currency into the country, foreigners are exempted from these restrictions on money changing; and individuals who were about to make a documented large-scale purchase from an official outlet could still transfer the money. The authorities claimed that they were mainly out to confiscate the cash hoards of black-market traders and profiteers who deal in large denomination notes.

However, many of the Soviet republics, including the huge Russian republic, immediately moved to undermine or soften the decree. Within each republic's jurisdiction, banks were variously required to extend the number of days for transferring money and to increase the amounts that could be transferred in different categories. Indeed, because they didn't trust savings accounts, pensioners turned out to be major holders of large denomination bank notes, and their great economic distress was the most obvious.

The full empirical consequences of this dramatic monetary action cannot be assessed before this chapter goes to press. The reform could even be reversed. Nevertheless, in light of the analytical framework provided above, whether or not the reform is conceptually well founded ex ante can still be assessed.

Over the years, the Soviet government has continually intervened to freeze or confiscate the cash positions of state enterprises. Even cooperatives, which were supposedly made independent by the 1987 Law on Cooperatives, were subject to intervention in their cash positions. What then was novel about the decree of January 23, 1991? The unusual element was the direct confiscation and reduction in the internal convertibility of household and small enterprise money that had heretofore been on a separate, unrestricted monetary circuit. (True, goods might not be available in government shops, but there had been no restraint on spending household money per se.)

In effect, this most recent decree cuts in the *opposite* direction to our optimum program for stabilizing the Soviet price level while simultaneously increasing the productivity of capital in the Soviet economy. The optimum program, as sketched above, focused on raising the stock demand for money and on curtailing the flow imbalances that created excess supplies of money. The goal is to extend the domain of internally convertible rubles to encompass liberalized enterprises—in other words, to unify the monetary circuits of households and firms. Then, by increasing interest paid on deposits, reducing expected inflation, and eliminating the threat of arbitrary confiscation of the monetary holdings of households and liberalized enterprises, the increased demand for money would itself tend to reduce inflationary pressure. Households and enterprises would sell off their excess inventories of physical goods in order to build up their real cash balances.

Although it aims to reduce the monetary overhang from the supply side (by canceling outstanding money), the decree of January 23, 1991, could well reduce the future stock demand for money even more. Households and enterprises will be even more loathe to hold rubles because of their heightened fear of expropriation and instead will strive harder to hold their wealth in the form of "excess" inventories of physical goods and foreign exchange. Thus, if the demand for rubles falls by more than the outstanding stock is reduced, net inflationary pressure from the monetary reform could actually increase. Either way, however, the economy will become more demonetized and the productivity of physcial capital could well fall further.

In addition, the Soviet government did not supplement the one-time adjustment in the stock of rubles with any signfiicant action to stem the economy's more fundamental flow imbalances: the fiscal deficit and the overextension of bank credit. These will inevitably lead to more inflationary pressure in the future. Because people know that the one-time stock adjustment of January 23 will not correct the ongoing inflation in the longer run, their current demand for rubles is further undermined.

Notes

Acknowledgment is due to Gregory Grossman, Ed Hewett, Janos Kornai, Lawrence Lau, John Litwack, and Judy Shelton for their great help, although they need not necessarily agree with all the arguments advanced. This chapter is a much extended and revised version of my "Stabilizing the Ruble," which appeared in *Communist Economies*, June 1990. Further elaborations on this same theme are contained in my book *The Order of Economic Liberalization: Financial Control in the Transition to a Market Economy*, Johns Hopkins University Press, 1991.

1. Janos Kornai has made us familiar with the concept of the "soft" budget constraint on socialist enterprises. He emphasized how soft budget constraints make resource use by state-owned enterprises immune to changes in relative prices. If a controlled price change (say, an increase in the price of an important input) creates a potentially negative cash flow, the socialist firm will simply borrow more from the state bank, seek remission of taxes, or seek permission to raise the price of its own output—all without much changing the use of the now more expensive input (Kornai 1986a and 1986b).

The dual meaning of Kornai's important insight, emphasized here, is that in a world of enterprises with soft budget constraints, but one where the government stops setting prices from the center, any open bargaining process would leave both relative and absolute prices indeterminate.

2. Indeed, many authors, such as Ed Hewett (1988:356) in *Reforming the Soviet Economy*, have previously noted the peculiarity of delaying price reform to 1990–1991 or beyond.

3. State Committee for Material and Technical Supplies, the trading agency directly responsible for distributing (and rationing) industrial inputs to producers—both in taking deliveries and making allocations, according to Gosplan.

4. John Litwack (1991) suggested this particular, and fairly benign, interpretation of bureaucratic behavior.

5. John Litwack (1991) has suggested that the apparent proliferation of unfinished construction projects in the formal accounts may be somewhat exaggerated, because the soft credits have actually been diverted to other uses.

6. For the 1980s, Rowen and Wolf (1990) estimate that Soviet military expenditures, narrowly defined, were about 15–17 percent of Soviet GNP, while military expenditures, broadly defined, could have been as high as 22–28 percent. If one recalls that U.S. defense expenditures were only 6–7 percent of GNP at the height of President Reagan's buildup, these estimates of the Soviet defense burden are staggering. Analysis of defense and other potential areas for the Soviet government to reduce expenditures, while critical for the success of the fiscal reforms, exceeds the scope of this chapter.

7. The tax collector need not actually calculate wages, profits, interest, etc., as separate categories. Instead, in order to determine gross tax liability, he need only verify that the firm is correctly stating its gross sales and apply the uniform rate of (tentatively) 20 percent. Then, to get tax credit on intermediate goods—raw materials and capital goods—purchased from other enterprises, the taxpaying enterprise must itself provide proof that the 20 percent VAT had been paid on these supplies. If such documentation is complete, the net tax liability of the enterprise can be correspondingly reduced.

8. The distortions arising from trying to absorb large amounts of foreign capital into an imperfectly open economy—i.e., where free arbitrage in all goods and factor markets has not yet become well established—was one of the main themes of my book *Money and Capital in Economic Development* (Washington, D.C.: Brookings Institution, 1973). See especially Chapters 11 and 12.

9. The fact that the international convertibility of the ruble on capital account comes last rather than first in the optimal order of economic liberalization is well recognized by Abel Aganbegyan (1988).

Roman Frydman, Stanislaw Wellisz,
and Grzegorz W. Kolodko   Chapter Four

Stabilization Policies
in Poland:
A Progress Report

The Solidarity-led government that assumed office in Poland on September 12, 1989, inherited a system molded by forty-five years of Communist rule. It also faced a massive government deficit and rapidly accelerating inflation. It soon became clear that radical reform of the system was fraught with technical and political difficulties. However, there was great pressure, both from the public and from international organizations, including the International Monetary Fund (IMF) and the World Bank, for immediate control of the hyperinflation that was beginning to disorganize the economy. Moreover, it appeared that hyperinflation could quickly be controlled by standard, purely technical, measures, allowing the new government to achieve its first economic success before it tackled the more difficult issues of structural adjustment. What was difficult to predict, however, was how the inherited structure of the economy would affect macroeconomic adjustment. This chapter gives a progress report based on preliminary data for the first four months of Poland's stabilization program, which began January 1, 1990.

Poland's economy is highly distorted and rigid. Therefore, measures to curb inflation had to be undertaken simultaneously with upward price adjustments. To balance the budget, it was necessary to cut subsidies on basic products and to raise their prices. Still other prices had to be increased to eliminate shortages and relative price distortions.

The economy is dominated by enterprises in the public sector that account for all the country's finance and for almost all manufacturing, transport, and wholesale and retail trade. The enterprises are autonomous and represent a high degree of monopoly. The profit motive operates very weakly. Since managers of enterprises are in close alliance with labor, it was difficult to predict their response to demand management measures. The private sector consists mainly of small units and, despite recent vigorous growth, plays a marginal role. Last but not least, the financial market is nonexistent, and the labor market is rudimentary.

The current stabilization program is, of necessity, a step without precedent. Poland is the first country to apply orthodox fiscal and monetary remedies to an economy in an early stage of transition from "real socialism" to a market system.

Background

It is useful to sketch briefly the origins of the crisis that gripped the Polish economy at the time of the transition from Communist to Solidarity rule.[1] Following the seizure of power at the close of World War II, the Polish United Workers party (PZPR) nationalized industry and commerce and pressured farmers to join collectives.[2] The plan replaced the market. Industrialization became a major goal, and priority was given to the producer goods sector.

Under Soviet-type fixed-price planning, the growth of aggregate wages tended to outpace the production of consumer goods, especially food. The government's periodic attempts to restore equilibrium by raising food prices were seen by the workers as an attack on their standard of living. Food riots that also had a strong political element erupted in 1970 and again in 1976. On both occasions, the government rescinded the price increases. In place of them, it resorted to farm subsidies, which rose from about 10 percent of national income in 1970 to about 17 percent in 1975 and 20 percent in 1977. Increasing reliance was also placed on imports of agricultural products and, in particular, high-protein fodder.

In the 1970s, the government borrowed heavily abroad to achieve a simultaneous rise in investment and consumption. A temporary period of prosperity was bought at the cost of foreign indebtedness that rose from negligible levels in 1970 to US$12 billion in 1976, when investments and nonfood imports were curbed in order to correct the external imbalance. Economic growth stopped and then declined. Net national income fell by 2.3 percent in 1979 and by a further 4 percent in 1980. Meanwhile, Poland's external debt continued to mount, rising from

US$12 billion at the end of 1976 to US$24 billion at the end of 1979. In 1980 debt-service payments required 96 percent of Poland's exports in convertible currency (World Bank 1987:5). The situation was obviously not sustainable. The Polish United Workers party tried to institute austerity measures, but an announcement of meat price increases in July 1980 led to riots that contributed to the success of Solidarity.

During an eighteen-month period of struggle, the Solidarity government sought to loosen the control of the Communist party, which sought to retain its power. The two sides reached a number of compromises, one of which was to have a long-lasting effect. In September 1981, the Polish parliament adopted a measure giving wide powers to Workers' Councils, among them the power to hire and dismiss managers, although the power to fix the salaries of the managers was retained by the government. The resulting blurring of the line between the management of capital resources and the defense of workers' interests became an impediment to the rationalization undertaken by the Solidarity government.

While the government temporized on political issues, it readily acceded to workers' demands for higher wages, and it extended to enterprises the credits required to meet the growing wage bills. The fiscal balance, slightly positive throughout the 1970s, turned negative in 1980 and in 1981. Prices rose by 9.6 percent in 1980 and by 21.2 percent in 1981. Goods were more and more scarce, indicating an increase in the "inflationary overhang."

Under the shield of martial law, declared in November 1981, the regime attempted to find a cure for the country's economic ills. In 1981, prices were raised drastically (the consumer price index rising by 101 percent), while restaints were imposed on wages, resulting in a 25 percent decrease in real wages. The current account budget turned positive. Production and exports rose sharply, and a trade surplus was achieved.[3]

At the same time, the government embarked on a long-term program to decentralize the economy and to reestablish market mechanisms. The classic Soviet-type model was abandoned. (Strumilin, a leading Soviet economist of the Stalinist period, expected that the whole economy would be run "like one big factory.") Direct allocation of raw materials was curtailed, and overall production planning was deemphasized. Enterprises were to have a large degree of autonomy. Within limits, they could negotiate wages, set prices, and make assortment decisions. They could decide how to reinvest retained profits. They also received the right to conclude their own export arrangements and to retain part of the export proceeds.[4] The percentages that could be retained differed across economic sectors, as did the amount of centrally allocated foreign exchange.[5] This, in effect, meant that exchange rates had a wide range.

The reforms were tempered by the Communist party's determination to retain its power, and they met with indifference or hostility on the part of the politically alienated public. The restructuring remained incomplete. The planning system was dismantled, but it was not replaced by a functioning market mechanism. Public sector enterprises were left in limbo, with ownership legally undefined. Though the National Bank of Poland was broken up into a central unit (that continued under its old name) and a number of commercial banks, each of the latter retained monopoly rights within its region or special area of activity. Thus, every enterprise continued to have just one source of credit, and credit continued to be rationed. There was no financial market.

Despite the gradual wage liberalization, prices remained below market-clearing levels. Although enterprises became self-sustaining, in principle, those unable to meet their financial targets could easily obtain subsidies. There was little incentive to eliminate shortages, because profit played a minor role in the determination of a manager's pay. Indeed, high profits were regarded by administrators as a sign of exploitation and managers could be ordered to reduce prices. On the other hand, less-than-equilibrium pricing had its advantages. The product could readily be sold, regardless of quality, and managers could grant (and obtain) favors by giving priority to preferred customers.

With shortages persisting throughout the economy, workers found jobs without difficulty. There was, therefore, no unemployment. Labor discipline was lax, especially since the managers appointed by the workers' council had little incentive to punish shirkers or to dismiss supernumerary workers.

After the repeal of martial law, the government lost its will or its ability to enforce fiscal discipline. It tried to stem the inflationary spiral by imposing a steeply progressive tax on wage increases that exceeded a certain threshold or that were not matched by improved productivity, but, in practice, exemptions were so easy to obtain that this policy was virtually ineffectual. To mitigate the cost impact, the government raised subsidies (mainly for coal mining and the food sector), thus causing the budget to remain in deficit throughout the 1980s, while money creation steadily outpaced the growth of output.

In 1988 the credit centrally allocated to enterprises proved insufficient, because it was based on anticipated price increases that were much smaller than actual price increases. Thus, the enterprises had to extend credit to each other. To avoid backruptcies, the authorities decided in the second half of the year to grant additional credit to enterprises—in effect, monetizing the private debt. Fuel was added to the inflationary process in November when the newly installed Rakowski government raised agricultural procurement prices, making the increases retroactive to July.

In 1989 a series of measures further unbalanced the budget. The replacement (as of January 1) of the profit tax by a "dividend," calculated as a percentage of enterprise capital, initially reduced budgetary revenues.[6] On January 31, the average remuneration of civil servants was raised from 74.4 percent to 97 percent of the average remuneration in the "productive" sector, increasing the size of budgetary expenditure by 11.8 percent in the first half of the year (Gomulka 1990). To stem the rise of energy prices, coal subsidies were also sharply increased.

As it grew weaker, the government was less and less able to resist workers' demands. Even before the start of the round table talks in February 1989 enterprise managers found it politic to raise wages and to delay, if need be, the settlement of other bills and the payment of taxes. Wages rose, while the government raised procurement prices in response to farmers' demands for parity. The round table agreements, concluded in April 1989, institutionalized the price-wage spiral. Wages were thereafter indexed on a quarterly basis to the extent of 80 percent of the cost of living increase, the adjustment being multiplied by any wage concessions won by the workers from the employers.

The result was a budgetary deficit that, during the first six months of the year, averaged 29 percent of the budgetary expenditure (Table 4.1).[7]

The deficit was financed through money creation. During the first six months of the year, the nominal money stock (as measured by M2) increased by 44 percent, while the real value of the money stock declined by 10 percent.[8]

In August 1989, the government lifted price controls on food. Because of the inefficiency of the distribution network, dominated by monopolistic "cooperatives," there was almost no increase in the quantity of food supplied to urban areas. Retail food prices rose by 80 percent and, since food accounts for about 50 percent of household expenditure, the cost of living index rose by 40 percent (Figures 4.1, 4.2, and 4.3). Nominal wages (including bonuses) climbed in August by 100 percent (Figure 4.3), and real wages rose by 40 percent (Figure 4.4). An accommodating money policy turned inflation into hyperinflation (Table 4.2).

With the accelerating inflation, the flight from money speeded up. Between the end of the first quarter and the end of the fourth quarter of the year, the real value of the money stock declined by 50 percent. Demand and time deposits of households fell, in real terms, from 3,412 billion zlotys to 1,150 billion zlotys (at December 1988 prices), while deposits of enterprises declined from 2,815 billion zlotys to 1,050 billion

Table 4.1   Fiscal Budget Balance in Poland, January 1989–March
             1990 (percentage of government expenditure)

Month	Consolidated budget surplus (+) or deficit (−)	Central budget surplus (+) or deficit (−)
1989		
January	−41.9	n.a.
February	−35.5	−45.9
March	−30.3	−37.8
April	−51.5	−58.2
May	−25.0	−49.5
June	−2.6	+16.3
July	+45.4	+80.0
August	+5.8	+23.0
September	−26.0	−20.3
October	−5.0	−22.1
November	−5.7	−27.9
December	+2.5	+10.5
1990		
January	−9.9	−15.8
February	+6.4	+35.6
March	+15.8	+3.5

n.a. = not available.
Source: Poland, Central Statistical Office.

zlotys (at December 1988 prices).[9] Consumers accelerated their buying
and hoarded goods, as well as dollars. The free-market price of dollars
rose astronomically. Enterprises, prevented by shortages and import
regulations from purchasing machinery, invested in inventories and
construction. Despite the depressed economy, aggregate investment actually rose. With rising inflation, enterprises also delayed tax payments,
further eroding the fiscal balance.

Implementation of the Stabilization Program: Phase I

The Solidarity-led government decided on a two-stage strategy (Poland,
Council of Ministers 1989). During Phase I, the preparatory stage (fall of
1989), the government sought to regain a degree of control over the
budget in order to correct some price distortions. It also made institutional changes, such as the creation of an unemployment compensation
system and bankruptcy procedures.

   A comprehensive stabilization and liberalization program, backed
by the IMF, was to be launched on January 1, 1990. The major purpose

Monthly Price Indexes of Foodstuffs in Poland, January 1989–April 1990

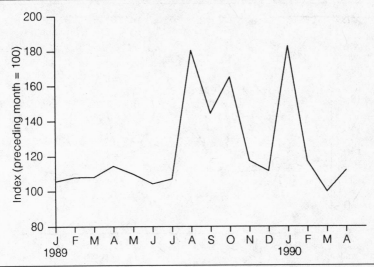

SOURCE: Poland, Central Statistical Office.

FIGURE 4.2   Monthly Expenditure for Foodstuffs by Households in Poland, January 1989–April 1990

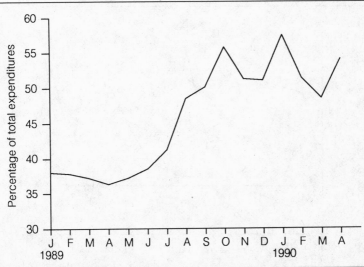

SOURCE: Poland, Central Statistical Office.

FIGURE 4.3 Monthly Retail Prices and Wage Indexes in Poland, January 1989–April 1990

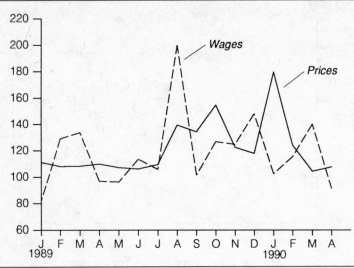

SOURCE: Poland, Central Statistical Office.

FIGURE 4.4 Index of Real Wages in Poland's Socialized Sector January 1989–April 1990

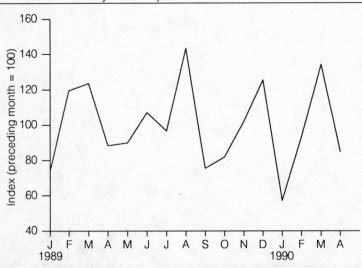

SOURCE: Poland, Central Statistical Office.

TABLE 4.2   Retail Prices in Poland, January 1989–April 1990

Month	Price index 1 (December 1988 = 100)	Price index 2 (Preceding month = 100)
1989		
January	111.0	111.0
February	119.8	107.9
March	129.5	108.1
April	142.2	109.8
May	152.4	107.2
June	161.7	106.1
July	177.1	109.5
August	247.0	139.5
September	331.8	134.4
October	513.5	154.8
November	628.3	122.4
December	739.6	117.7
1990		
January	1,320.9	178.6
February	1,636.7	123.9
March	1,710.7	104.7
April	1,850.4	108.1

SOURCE: Poland, Central Statistical Office.

of this Phase II was to put a stop to inflation. Although the imposition of a standard stabilization package, involving fiscal and monetary restraints and the use of "anchors" (a fixed exchange rate and a wage freeze), carried the risk of aggravating existing distortions (Blejer and Cheasty 1988), it was hoped that such measures would also foster the restructuring of the economy. The expectation was that the transition from a shortage-driven, soft-budget economy to a system constrained on the demand side, as well as on the finance side, would drive the inefficient units to bankruptcy and would spur the surviving ones to greater efficiency. Unemployment was expected to rise, but this fact seemed favorable, as unemployment was expected to improve labor discipline.

The new government, enjoying the confidence of the workers, was able to win important concessions. In October 1989, indexation was moved to a monthly basis, but the automatic raises applied up to a maximum of 80 percent of the cost of living increase and could no longer be compounded with wage concessions won by the workers. The workers acquiesced to a forthcoming drastic reduction of indexation in Phase II. In December 1989, backward indexation was abandoned in order to avoid the danger of real wage overshooting when inflation would be subsiding. Instead, forward indexation (linking wage increases to the next month's expected price rise) was adopted. The

FIGURE 4.5   Real Free-Market and Official Rates of Exchange in
              Poland, January 1989–April 1990 (December 1988 = 100)

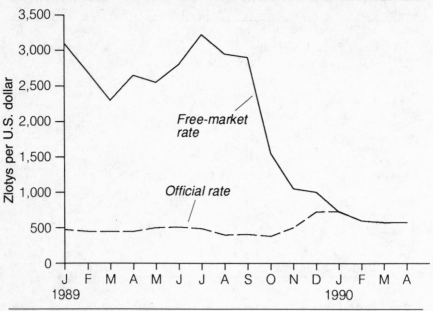

SOURCE: Poland, Central Statistical Office.

December wages were, in effect, indexed twice: once to the preceding month's price rise and once to the next month's. Since wages in Poland are paid monthly toward the end of each month, the resulting 25 percent surge in real wages (Figure 4.4) fed the price increase that occurred in the first month of Phase II of the program (January 1990).

To rationalize the price structure and to reduce the fiscal deficit, the government in October 1989 increased the administered prices of coal, metals, and transportation. Throughout Phase I, adjustments also took place in the value of foreign exchange. The policy of the Rakowski government (from which the Solidarity-led government took over) was to maintain the real exchange rate at an approximately constant level (Figure 4.5) and to approach equilibrium by gradually increasing the sphere of free-market transactions. The new government sought, instead, to reduce the official rate to the market-clearing level and to liberalize trade. In preparation for this move, the nominal exchange rate was devalued between September and December 1989 by 390 percent.[10] Apparently, it was expected that, after liberalization, the dollar exchange rate would be fixed below the September 1989 free-market rate. The free-market rate declined in October and November 1989, but the

FIGURE 4.6   Nominal Free-Market and Official Rates of Exchange in Poland, January 1989–April 1990

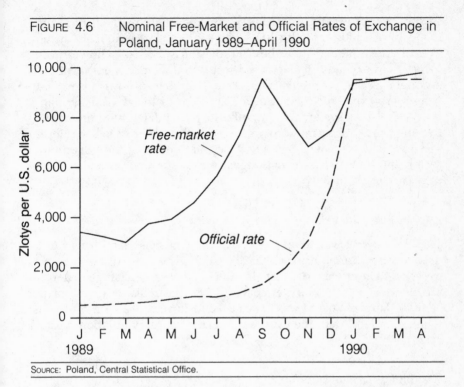

SOURCE: Poland, Central Statistical Office.

market undershot; the rate eventually fixed was approximately at the September free-market level (Figure 4.6).

The cuts in subsidies and other drastic economy measures permitted the government to reduce the budgetary deficit. Inflation appeared to be cooling off. In December 1989, prices rose by 17.7 percent relative to November—the lowest rate of increase since August.

Implementation of the Stabilization Program: Phase II

On January 1, 1990, a comprehensive stabilization program with IMF backing came into effect. The package contained the standard measures: budgetary deficit reduction, devaluation and foreign exchange unification, monetary and credit restraint, and the use of exchange rate and wage restraint "anchors."

Reduction of the fiscal deficit

The program called for a fiscal deficit reduction from 7 percent of gross national product (GNP) in 1989 to 1 percent of GNP in 1990. Substantial savings were to result from the elimination of virtually all remaining food and agricultural production subsidies, as well as from the reduction in coal and transport subsidies.[11] Provision was made, however, for increases in expenditures on social security, unemployment insurance, and debt-service payments. On balance, reductions in fiscal expenditures were expected to amount to 3 percent of the GNP. Although a reform of the tax system was put off until a later date, the elimination of the numerous tax exemptions was expected to give rise to a significant increase in government revenue. The total deficit of the government sector (the budget plus extrabudgetary expenditures) was also drastically curtailed.

Interest rate policy

The interest rate was to be positive in the real sense, and it was to be used as an instrument for credit allocation. The positive real rate was expected to induce a switch from individual foreign exchange to deposit accounts in zlotys. As of January 1, 1990, the rediscount rate of the National Bank of Poland was to be raised to 36 percent a month—that is, to a higher level than the expected January–February inflation rate.

The foreign exchange anchor

On December 22, 1989, the official exchange rate stood at 5,560 zlotys per U.S. dollar, the auction rate averaged 6,000 zlotys per U.S. dollar, and the free-market rate ranged from 8,000 zlotys to 9,000 zlotys per U.S. dollar. As of January 1, 1990, the exchange rate for all commercial transactions was set at 9,500 zlotys per U.S. dollar, and foreign exchange accounts of enterprises were eliminated.[12] Enterprises were permitted to retain their accounts denominated in foreign currency, but they could not make any additional deposits. Proceeds from export sales were to be immediately converted into zlotys. On the other hand, importers could henceforth freely buy foreign exchange from the National Bank of Poland at the official selling rate. The unification of the exchange rate was accompanied by the elimination of export subsidies. Individuals and households were permitted to retain their accounts in foreign currency and to buy and sell currency on the parallel market.

The government intended to maintain a fixed exchange rate for a three-month period that would be followed, if necessary, by realignment. Stability of the exchange rate was to be assured through the use of interest rates, and a US$1 billion stabilization fund was to provide additional exchange support. A deviation of more than 10 percent between the parallel market and the official rate that lasted more than three weeks was to be a signal for an increase in interest rates and other measures to defend the exchange rate or for devaluation. Given the probable price trend, an accumulation of reserves was forecast for the initial period of one or two months, followed by a drawing down of reserves. An excessive reduction of reserves would be another signal of the need for possible further devaluation.

The wage anchor

The government did not want to freeze wages administratively because a wage freeze would be reminiscent of policies of previous governments. Nonetheless, they had to restrain wages for both external and internal reasons. Externally, the IMF insisted on such restraint as part of the standard anti-inflationary procedure. Internally, it was probable that, in the absence of a government ruling, managers of enterprises in the socialized sector would not resist workers' wage demands. A responsive credit policy would spell the end of the anti-inflationary program, while a highly restrictive policy was likely to generate massive unemployment. Furthermore, since the pay of government employees was directly linked to wages in the socialized ("productive") sector, a policy of wage restraint helped to balance the budget.

The solution that was adopted called for a reduction of the degree of indexation to 30 percent in January and to 20 percent in February, March, and April. A tax of 200 percent was imposed on increases in wage funds not exceeding the wage guidelines by more than 3 percent, and a tax of 500 percent was also imposed on increases in excess of 3 percent.[13] An enterprise could raise wages by reducing its labor force, although the practical importance of such an "escape route" may be doubted. Workers' councils have a strong say in management, and they are unlikely to agree to dismissals for the sake of wage increases.[14] The taxes apply to private firms, as well as to socialized firms, crippling the formation of an effective labor market.

Early Effects of Phase II Stabilization Measures

During the first four months of 1990, the fiscal budget was balanced. The "anchors" held firm. The dollar rate of the free market deviated by only a few percentage points from the official rate held at 9,500 zlotys per U.S. dollar. Reserves accumulated, obviating the need for a devaluation at the end of the three-month period. Money wages rose less than was permitted under the indexation rule, but inflation was not completely

TABLE 4.3   Monthly Interest Rates in Poland, January–April 1990
(percentages)

	January	February	March	April
Discount rate of National Bank	36	20.0	10.0	8.0
Six-month time deposits	17	13.0	6.5	5.0
One-year credit				
Minimum rate	36	20.0	9.0	7.5
Maximum rate	62	23.0	12.0	9.5
Monthly retail price index	106	5.3	6.1	6.3

NOTE: Monthly retail price index is estimated by Dariusz Jaszczynski.
SOURCE: Poland, Central Statistical Office.

extinguished, with retail prices continuing to rise at some 5 percent a month. Data pertaining to "real" aspects of the economy also revealed a disturbing picture. Production in the socialized sector declined by close to 30 percent. Employment in the socialized sector also declined, though at a much slower pace, suggesting that enterprises retained too many workers. Somewhat unexpectedly, for the first four months, there was only one bankruptcy; the desired "purge" had not yet taken place.

Our purpose here is not to assess the program's success. Instead, we shall attempt to show that the idiosyncracies of the system's reactions to the stabilization measures stem from the peculiarities of the structure of the Polish economy. Clearly, however, it is much too early to reach definite conclusions. In the next few months, there may be drastic turns of events that would require a thorough revision of our judgment. Thus, our remarks are in the form of suppositions.

Interest rates and credit

Interest rate policy is one of the keystones of Phase II of the stabilization program. High positive interest rates were aimed at restricting borrowing and serving as an allocative device that would help to eliminate the economically weak units. Positive real rates were also expected to encourage monetary savings, thus slowing down the velocity of circulation.

The discount rate of the National Bank of Poland for January 1990 was set at 36 percent a month, with the intention of achieving a positive real rate (Table 4.3). The actual price rise was much faster than was forecasted, and the ex post real rate was negative. Nevertheless, since the new rate applied to old debt, as well as to new debt,[15] the large increase in the nominal rate had a strongly contractionary effect. Both the socialized sector and the private sector significantly reduced their indebtedness in January. The discount rate was progressively lowered during the next four months (the new rates applying to both old and new credit) but, with lower inflation, the ex post real rate turned strongly positive. Nevertheless, net debt repayment stopped in February, and net indebtedness of enterprises increased in March.[16]

The monetary and credit targets agreed upon with the IMF were also predicated on a smaller January price rise than actually occurred. Consequently, the January credit squeeze was particularly severe. Between the end of December 1989 and the end of January 1990, M1 at constant December 1989 prices declined 18 percent. A similar drop occurred in M2, while M3 (M2 plus foreign currency deposits) fell by 43 percent. No further contraction of M2 took place in February, and an increase of 13 percent was registered in March.

Setting of the January discount rate at 36 percent created an enormous interest rate differential between the zloty and the dollar deposits, which were only paying about 0.75 percent a month. Enterprises liquidated US$900 million in dollar deposits, thus strengthening the domestic currency. (It should be recalled that the entire stabilization fund amounted to US$1 billion.) They used an estimated 87 percent of the zlotys obtained from the liquidation to rebuild their demand deposits, which increased by 10 percent in real terms, and they used the balance to reduce their indebtedness. Since enterprises are not allowed to exchange zlotys into dollars, except for import purposes, the move to zlotys was clearly not speculative, and could not, therefore, contribute to the collapse of the currency (as happened in Argentina).

Remarkably, although households were allowed to exchange zlotys into dollars, the interest rate differential did not cause a massive switch to zloty deposits. The reduction of their foreign currency holdings by US$300 million was apparently mainly for consumption purposes. During the month of January, demand and time deposit of households in zlotys fell by 29 percent in real terms.

Wages

Many observers thought that, during the first months of 1990, the restrictive monetary policy was the cause of the wage restraint exercised by enterprises in the socialized sector. It appeared that the demand management policies were beginning to affect the enterprises, so that they were unable to pay the maximum wages permitted under the indexation rule. This evidence also suggested that, as hoped, demand management was putting pressure on enterprises to restructure. A closer examination of the data casts serious doubts on this interpretation.[17]

Under the existing arrangements, enterprises must pay a penalty tax if wage increases exceed the limit determined on the basis of the *actual*

TABLE 4.4   Indexation and Nominal Wage Increases in Poland, January–April 1990

	January	February	March	April
Cost of living increase				
Forecast	45.0	23.0	6.0	6.0
Actual	78.6	23.9	4.7	8.1
Indexation coefficient	0.3	0.2	0.2	0.2
Permissible wage increase				
Based on forecast	13.5	4.6	1.2	1.2
Based on actual consumer price index	23.6	4.8	0.9	1.6
Actual wage increase[a]	11.1	5.4	10.5	4.8

a. Net of bonus, relative to the indexation base for December 1989.
Source: Calculations by Dariusz Jaszczynski on the basis of data from the Central Statistical Office of Poland.

cost of living increase. However, since wages are set a month in advance, they are based on a forecast. The January forecast of price inflation issued by Poland's Ministry of Finance was 45 percent. The indexation rule would have permitted enterprises to raise wages by 13.5 percent relative to the indexation base for December 1989. The actual increase was 11.1 percent over the base—an increase that is remarkably close to the forecasted maximum.[18] In fact, January prices rose much faster than forecasted, leaving a wide margin of wages that could subsequently be paid out without penalty. In February the forecast indicated that enterprises could raise wages by 4.6 percent; they actually raised wages by 5.4 percent, beginning a process of recovering from the January shortfall. In March the forecast permitted an increase of 1.2 percent, while enterprises granted an increase of 10.5 percent. The recovery continued in April (Table 4.4).

Thus, during the first four months of 1990, wages were restricted by the indexation. The monetary policy does not seem to have affected wage behavior. It also failed to have a significant effect on employment in the socialized sector.

Prices

Price increases during the first four months of 1990 exceeded the targets. The January price increase is the easiest to explain, since the forecast for that month neglected to take into account several factors that contributed to the cost push. Although the retail price index for December 1989 rose by only 17 percent relative to the preceding month, price increases for producer goods were much higher. For instance, the prices in the metal-working industries rose 61 percent, those in the machine tool

FIGURE 4.7   Weekly Rate of Inflation of Consumer Goods and
Services in Poland, January–April 1990

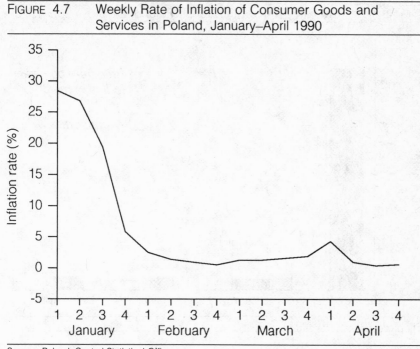

Source: Poland, Central Statistical Office.

industry rose 56 percent, and those in the chemical industry rose 60 percent, while prices of construction materials rose 52 percent. The December increases undoubtedly affected the January production costs. Interest rate increases also added to costs. To be sure, in January 1990 money wages were restrained by punitive taxes, but the raises granted in late December 1989 amounted to 48 percent in nominal terms and to 25 percent in real terms. The cost effect of such raises was strongly felt in January.

Much as expected, the price jump was the steepest at the very beginning of the program. During the first week, prices rose by 28 percent, and they continued to increase very rapidly during the second and third week (Figure 4.7).

It was expected that, after the initial jump in prices caused by the cost push, prices would quickly stabilize and remain stable for several months. Such, indeed, was the typical course of other stabilizations, including some that ultimately proved unsuccessful.[19] In Poland, the rate of inflation declined at the end of January, but prices continued to rise during the subsequent months. The estimated increase measured from the end of January to the end of February amounted to only 4

FIGURE 4.8   Monthly Rate of Inflation in Poland, January–April 1990

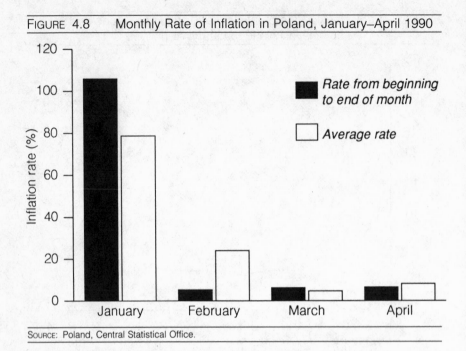

SOURCE: Poland, Central Statistical Office.

percent. The lowest point was reached by the fourth week in February. The estimated monthly inflation rate rose to 6.1 percent in March and to 6.3 percent in April (Figures 4.7 and 4.8). To be sure, food prices usually rise during the Easter holiday season, and this time the demand for food was boosted by the unusually high March wage payments, but prices did not fall after the holidays were over. Therefore, we suspect that the explanation comes, in part, from the behavior of enterprises.

Production

Throughout 1989, production of the socialized sector was declining and, with the exception of December, output sold was lower than in the corresponding month of the preceding year.

At the beginning of Phase II of the program, output sold by the socialized sector fell precipitously (Figure 4.9). A decline was expected at the beginning of the year because, in anticipation of price rises, enterprises and households made purchases in December ahead of their needs, pushing sales to an exceptionally high level (Table 4.5). The January sales stood at 68.4 percent of those in December and at 69.3 percent of the sales in January 1989. What is more significant, February sales were only 69 percent of those in the corresponding month of 1989. March figures showed a slight increase over February but a further (very

FIGURE 4.9   Index of Output Sold in Poland's Socialized Sector,
January 1989–April 1990 (constant 1984 prices)

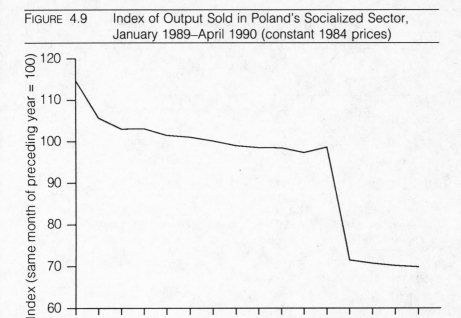

SOURCE: Poland, Central Statistical Office.

slight) decline relative to the results of a year earlier. Although it is too early to predict with any degree of certainty, the slide appears to be slowing down (Table 4.5).

Employment

In 1989 employment in the socialized sector declined in step with declining output (Table 4.6). Workers released found jobs in the expanding private sector. There was no recorded unemployment.

During the first three months of 1990, in the face of a drastic drop in output sold, there was only a very slight acceleration of the decline (Figures 4.9 and 4.10). The number of workers employed in the socialized sector fell by 209,000. In contrast to the past, however, not all the workers found other jobs. Unemployment at the end of April stood at 351,000, and it seemed to be rising at about 100,000 per month.

According to Table 4.7, of the 351,000 unemployed as of the end of April, only 27,000 were workers who had been laid off,[20] while 170,000 quit work or were dismissed for cause. Almost as many (154,000) seem never to have held a job. Some of them may be new entrants into the

TABLE 4.5   Sales and Net Profits of Poland's Socialized Sector, January 1989–March 1990

Month	Sales (billions of 1988 zlotys)	Net profits (billions of 1988 zlotys)	Net profit/ sales ratio (percentage)
1989			
January	4,498	504	11.2
February	4,108	551	13.4
March	5,379	550	10.2
April	3,764	430	11.4
May	4,328	632	14.6
June	6,000	896	14.9
July	2,841	320	11.3
August	4,028	439	10.9
September	5,493	746	13.6
October	3,517	711	20.2
November	4,221	794	18.8
December	5,013	1,904	38.0
1990			
January	3,315	425	12.8
February	3,050	467	15.3
March	3,414	535	15.7

Source: Poland, Central Statistical Office.

TABLE 4.6   Employment in Poland's Socialized Sector, January 1989–March 1990

Month	Employment (thousands of workers)	Change from preceding month	
		Thousands of workers	Percentage
1989			
January	7,180.0		
February	7,176.3	−3.7	−0.05
March	7,100.4	−75.9	−1.07
April	7,069.8	−30.6	−0.43
May	6,995.9	−73.9	−1.06
June	6,933.6	−62.3	−0.90
July	6,925.8	−7.8	−0.11
August	6,853.4	−72.4	−1.06
September	6,814.1	−39.3	−0.58
October	6,809.1	−5.0	−0.07
November	6,790.2	−18.9	−0.28
December	6,706.9	−83.3	−1.24
1990			
January	6,636.2	−70.7	−1.07
February	6,564.6	−71.6	−1.09
March	6,496.0	−68.6	−1.06

Source: Poland, Central Statistical Office.

labor force; others are either outside the labor force or have casual jobs, but they register in order to collect unemployment compensation.

During the first three months of 1990, output sold per employed worker was 26 percent lower than during the corresponding period in the preceding year. There are several reasons for the retention of excess labor. Under existing rules, group reductions require sixty to ninety days' notice. Workers' councils, as well as unions, exercise pressure on

FIGURE 4.10   Index of Employment in Poland's Socialized Sector, January 1989–April 1990

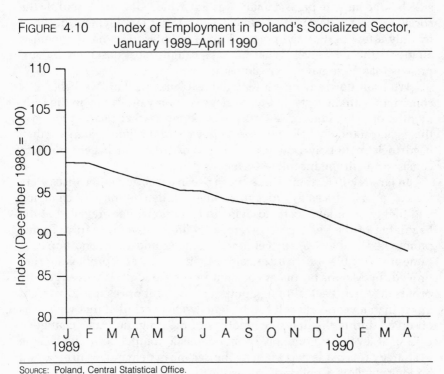

SOURCE: Poland, Central Statistical Office.

TABLE 4.7   Unemployment in Poland, January–April 1990

	January 31	February 28	March 31	April 30
Number laid off	n.a.	n.a.	15,110	27,371
Other separations	n.a.	n.a.	171,462	169,922
Unemployed for more than 3 months before registration	n.a.	n.a.	80,000	153,845
Total unemployed	55,774	152,191	266,572	351,138

n.a. = not available.
SOURCE: Poland, Ministry of Labor.

management not to discharge workers. The expectation that the anti-inflationary squeeze will rapidly lead to rationalization of labor use has been proved untrue.

Behavior of enterprises

During the first four months of the stabilizaton program, inflation subsided, but complete price stability was not achieved. Output sold by the socialized sector declined by almost a third, but employment declined by only a few percentage points. Profits of enterprises have remained almost at the 1989 level. What perhaps caught most observers by surprise is that there have been almost no bankruptcies.

We shall now advance a tentative explanation that, we believe, is consistent with the facts. In the shortage economy prevailing in the early months of 1989, enterprises set prices below market-clearing levels— that is, substantially below the price they could profitably charge if they used their monopoly power. As observed earlier, such behavior was consistent with the incentive system at that time.

In January 1990, there was a sharp rise in costs, and enterprises were forced to raise prices in order to survive. Under the rapidly changing and highly uncertain cost and demand conditions that prevailed at the beginning of the year, prices were set more or less arbitrarily. Profits plummeted (Table 4.6). In February, demand and cost conditions became more stable. Enterprises raised their prices, and profitability improved. By March, profits at constant prices stood at 97 percent of the profits in March 1989, although output at constant prices was 27 percent lower than a year earlier. It can be tentatively concluded that what was observed during the first three months of the program was a change to pricing at levels of monopoly or monopolistic competition. The change in strategy was made necessary by the decline in demand, as firms could no longer follow a policy of underpricing and still survive.

There seem to be three other explanations of the price and output behavior of enterprises during the first few months of the stabilization program. The possibility that the achievement of constant profits with declining sales reflects improvements in productivity can be rejected, since output per worker actually declined. The facts are also at variance with the assertion that enterprises in the socialized sector engage in simple-minded cost-plus pricing, because, if true, aggregate profits would be proportional to sales (but they are not). It also is not sufficient to observe that monopolies dominate the socialized sector. If the firms were pricing all the time at a profit-maximizing level, their profits would have declined with output. The actual behavior, as explained above, is consistent with the hypothesis that the stabilization measures induced the monopolies dominating the socialized sector to *change* their pricing behavior.

The nature of the enterprises in the public sector also explains why hoarding of labor occurs. In the shortage economy, managers sought out workers, who were in short supply. In a demand-constrained situation, workers pressured managers to avoid layoffs. Interestingly, although output per worker declined since the end of 1989, labor discipline has improved. Workers now fear to be dismissed for cause, and both absenteeism and sick leaves have declined.

It was widely expected that the credit squeeze would either force firms to produce more efficiently or would drive them into bankruptcy. The idea that a tight money policy will force firms to rationalize or will drive them to bankruptcy assumes the presence of competition. In the Polish context, internal competition outside of agriculture is extremely weak. The opening of the economy to trade does not suffice. A country can be economically open *and* highly inefficient. Moreover, the policy instruments that were expected to induce bankruptcies turned out to be weak. An enterprise goes bankrupt if it is incapable of paying its "dividend," after having met its nondeferrable obligations. (Let us recall that the dividend is a 32 percent tax on the founding capital of the firm, adjusted for inflation.) As it turns out, the founding capital represents a small proportion of capital for most firms, and thus this obligation is relatively low.[21] Moreover, few enterprises are critically affected by the rise in interest rates on old debt, another element of the restrictive monetary policy. The reason is that debt of enterprises was virtually wiped out by the 1989 inflation.[22] In 1989, wage payments in industry represented only 17 percent of total costs.[23] Since the recent decline in real wages lowered labor costs still further, overmanning is relatively inexpensive. It is possible that, as in the past, some firms are not paying their suppliers and that arrears are again mounting.[24] If a credit crunch should occur, it is not probable that it would eliminate the inefficient firms. More probably, it would lead to mass bankruptcies or to the abandonment of the restrictive monetary policy. Another serious danger is that, since other payments (and, in particular, equipment maintenance) can be put off, instead of going bankrupt or improving their productivity, inefficient enterprises will become progressively decapitalized.

Foreign trade and the balance of payments

The pessimistic appraisal of the socialized sector's response to the stabilization policies should be modified by taking into account their foreign trade behavior. The January 1990 devaluation of the zloty, and the decrease in domestic demand increased the profitability of exports. The response of industry was quite dramatic. In January exports to both the ruble area and the convertible currency area actually declined. In the next three months, ruble exports recovered, while exports to the convertible currency area expanded rapidly, with all the major sectors of the economy sharing in the growth.[25] In April they surpassed the level of April 1989 by more than 30 percent.

At the same time, despite the abolition of quantitative import restrictions, imports declined. The deepest cuts occurred in imports of producer goods from the convertible currency area—strongly suggesting that there was substitution with domestic or ruble area goods that became relatively cheaper.

In the January–April 1990 period, the current account balance with both the convertible currency and the ruble areas was positive. This strengthened the Polish currency. Despite the continuing internal inflation, reserves accumulated, and recourse to the currency stabilization fund was unnecessary. Ironically, since Poland is seeking substantial debt relief, the surplus is something of an embarrassment. Consequently, import tariffs are being reduced, and there is even some speculation about revaluation of the zloty.

Concluding Remarks

The devaluation of the Polish currency and fiscal restrictions induced enterprises to seek foreign markets and to curtail imports from abroad. However, in many important respects the behavior of socialized enterprises appeared to be pathological. There were sharp cuts in output, but there was also hoarding of labor. In the face of a decrease in demand, prices seemed to rise. Aggregate profits remained on a satisfactory level, and the expected wave of bankruptcies did not materialize. This behavior is consistent with the incentives that guide managerial decisions. The pathology lies in the nature of the enterprises inherited from the Communist regime.

The Polish experience shows how difficult it is to stabilize a highly distorted economy. The socialized sector does not have a strong incentive to become more efficient. Managers, controlled by labor councils, find it difficult to shed unnecessary labor—the only way to increase efficiency in a situation where new investments are prohibitively expensive. Wage restraints leave no room for incentive wages. The tight credit impedes the growth of enterprises in the private sector.

We believe that measures to revive demand are very likely to fail. If wages are permitted to rise, enterprises will again attempt to increase prices. A relaxation in monetary policy would validate those price increases; it is possible that this, in fact, happened in April.[26] On the other hand, failure to validate the price increases would ultimately lead to the reduction of profitability of firms and to a high level of unemployment. High interest rates are also likely to impede the development of the private sector. There are indications that this has already happened.[27] Therefore, it seems that structural reform and strong supply-side policies are the only way to escape from this morass. The monopolies must be dismantled, and enterprises in the public sector must be remolded into genuine firms guided by the profit motive. However, structural transformation, as is known from world experience, is a difficult task that includes overcoming social and political obstacles much greater than those that stand in the way of macroeconomic stabilization.

Notes

We would like to thank Dariusz Jaszczynski for his extensive help and the C. V. Starr Center for Applied Economics for its partial support of this project.

1. For a more comprehensive treatment, see the following: World Bank (1987, 1989), Nuti (1990), and Lipton and Sachs (1990).

2. The collectivization drive was abandoned in 1956, although indirect pressure continued to be used to induce farmers to join cooperatives and to sell land to state farming enterprises.

3. The recovery rapidly lost momentum; the level of production achieved in the late 1970s was not to be reached for the balance of the 1980s.

4. Enterprises were permitted to open foreign currency accounts. The retained foreign currency earnings could be used for imports, and they could also be sold at auction and purchased by other enterprises.

5. Throughout the Communist rule, the official rate of the zloty in terms of dollars exceeded the black market rate by a wide margin; at times the two rates differed by a factor of five to six. The authorities generally had a tolerant attitude toward the black market. They ran "dollar" stores and made it possible for Polish citizens to maintain dollar accounts in the Polish bank. Until the 1980s, however, all commercial transactions had to be carried out at the official rate, and foreign currency allocations were guided by the plan.

6. The "dividend" is paid on the capital provided by the founding authority; the capital created through reinvestments of enterprise profits is not subject to the tax. As a consequence, the dividend has a differential effect that depends on an enterprise's past investment history.

7. Because of a strong seasonality of expenditures and tax collections, the monthly figures in Table 4.1 should be interpreted with caution.

8. Computed by deflating M1 by the retail price index.

9. Enterprises reduced their time deposits from 912 billion zlotys to 44 billion zlotys at December 1988 prices, while households reduced their time deposits from 3,090 billion zlotys to 962 billion zlotys at December 1988 prices.

Demand deposits of enterprises and households were reduced, respectively, from 1,903 billion and 322 billion zlotys to 1,006 billion and 188 billion zlotys at December 1988 prices. Thus, there was a substantial shortening of the maturity of deposits.

10. At constant December 1988 prices, this devaluation amounted to 75 percent.

11. The reduction in coal subsidies was accompanied by a 400 percent increase in industrial coal prices and in a 200 percent increase in tariffs on electricity. The price of domestic coal was raised 600 percent and the freight charges were raised 200 percent.

12. The zloty was also devalued relative to the ruble, but by a smaller margin.

13. A tax was also imposed on increases in bonus payments in excess of the index limit.

14. Initially, the limit on the wage bill was interpreted to mean that an enterprise would have to pay the penalty tax if it increased its wage bill by hiring more workers; it was later clarified, however, that this was not the intent of the law.

15. Debtors were permitted to capitalize 60 percent of the interest payments on old debt, reckoned at the new rate. In the case of debt in agriculture, half of the remaining 40 percent was to be paid as interest by the debtor and half was given as subsidy, whereas, in the case of building credit, the subsidy was to amount to 32 percent and the debtor was to be responsible for 8 percent.

16. The tight credit policy appears, however, to have had an adverse effect on private enterprise. The evidence is purely anecdotal, since the official statistics virtually ignore the private sector.

17. We are indebted to Dariusz Jaszczynski for this point.

18. Wages are indexed on the basis of September 1989. According to the rules prevailing in the fall of 1989, the indexation base for December 1989 was 556,400 zlotys. The actual wage, reflecting backward and forward indexation in December was 606,600 zlotys. However, 556,400 zlotys formed the indexation base for January 1990. This explains why the January wage of 618,300 zlotys was 11.1 percent higher relative to the December base and only 1.9 percent higher than the actual December wage. This discrepancy contributed to the impression that the January wage increases were much lower than permitted.

19. This was the case of the 1924 German stabilization, the 1923 Austrian stabilization, and the Polish stabilizations of the 1920s, as well as of the 1947 Italian stabilization. See Dornbusch and Fischer (1986).

20. Approximately three times as many were, however, on forced paid or unpaid holidays.

21. It is currently estimated that 155 of the 7,000 national enterprises and 370 of the (mainly small) provincial and local enterprises will not be able to pay the dividend payments due in the first half of 1990.

22. Total enterprise indebtedness toward banks is estimated at 7 percent of GNP.

23. Inclusive of coal mining, the figure is 20 percent.

24. Exact information on this important issue is not available.

25. For the first four months of 1990, ruble exports were 4 percent higher than in the corresponding four months of 1989, and dollar exports were 11.3 percent higher.

26. It might be recalled that real wages increased in March by 28 percent. In April nominal interest rates on new debt, as well as on old debt, were substantially reduced. As a result, M2 in real terms rose by close to 14 percent.

27. It should be recalled that in 1989 reductions in employment in the socialized sector were matched by employment increases in the private sector. In the first three months of 1990, the rate of labor absorption by the private sector appears to have declined.

Comments

EDMUND S. PHELPS

According to news reports, a pithy slogan is being used by the government in Moscow these days: "The market, yes. Unemployment, no." The slogan implicitly assumes that, without the proper safeguards, market capitalism yields a much higher equilibrium unemployment rate than does socialism (even decentralized socialism—the sort of quasi-market socialism—found in some Eastern European countries in the past decade). In fact, as observers have noted, following the introduction of a number of reforms, the unemployment rate in Poland that was at first negligible has begun to rise steeply, although it is not known yet whether all or most of this rise is purely transitional. The widespread worry on this score had led me to wonder whether there are good theoretical reasons for believing that the unemployment rate that is "natural" to market socialism is markedly lower than the natural rate under market socialism of a nonwelfare state.

It is with this question in mind that I comment on the chapter on stabilization in Poland by Frydman, Wellisz, and Kolodko. As this chapter follows soon after the publication of a wide-ranging paper on Poland by Lipton and Sachs (1990), it would be somewhat confining to comment on one without the other. I will discuss both of them.

Comparison with Lipton and Sachs

The chapter by Frydman, Wellisz, and Kolodko posits that, in the reform socialism of the 1980s, Poland's managers of enterprises have shown an aversion to high profits, preferring to set prices below profit-maximizing levels and, further, that they generally find advantages in setting their prices below market-clearing levels as well. The Brookings paper by Lipton and Sachs also depicts, in much the same spirit, a kind of upward price inflexibility—a refreshing change from the downward price and wage inflexibility that was for many years the vogue in American macroeconomic discussions.

I have to quarrel a little, however, with the nature of the model used by Lipton and Sachs to analyze the consequences of nonmarket-clearing in the product market. Their paper builds a general equilibrium model of the level of excess demand, or shortage, in the product market and the level of queuing, or rent seeking, in the labor market. The model is built, however, on the unexpected device of a supposed rigidity of the *nominal* price level. This modeling feature was evidently intentional. The authors speak of "repressed inflation" as a "fundamental factor" in "chronic shortages," and they say: "A strong dose of macroeconomic austerity (tight money and fiscal policies) can substantially alleviate many problems that are misinterpreted as structural rather than monetary." The original draft of the chapter by Frydman, Wellisz, and Kolodko seemed to endorse the view that at least a large part of the "excess demand" has been monetary, although monetary factors have been put firmly in the background in the final version.

It is clear to me that it is a theoretical error to view excess demand in such monetary terms—but the error may not be serious for the authors' purposes. In the formulation by Lipton and Sachs, it is implied that firms are devoted to a particular nominal price that may cause the real volume of cash balances to be large enough to create excess demand for output. It would seem to me more reasonable to suppose that the managers want a lower markup over costs rather than the fetish of a particular nominal price level. If, when prices are imagined initially to be marked down, nominal wages rise because (as the authors argue) the ensuing shortages harm workers more than the lower prices help them, the price level will then be adjusted upward to adhere to the desired markup. On the other hand, if nominal wages fall because the lower prices help workers more than the shortages harm them, the price level will be adjusted downward. In the former case, there would be indefinite deflation unless the unemployment rate is allowed to decline, and in the latter case, there would be inflation unless the unemployment rate is allowed to increase. In this way the managers' behavior is modeled as free of money illusion—a desirable move in the context of a sort of repetitive game.

A nonmonetary model?

I would go further by advocating that, as a first approximation, money be omitted altogether from the model. If a nonmonetary model is built of Poland in the 1980s, would that model be incapable of generating excess demand? Could the government in one stroke abolish the curse of shortage simply by the device of banishing "outside money," leaving the economy to function as a pure credit economy? Of course not! To ask the question is to see how false such a notion is. There is no lack for goods and things that can serve as the numeraire in terms of which prices—or the vector of prices—can be expressed. The managers can be modeled as setting such "real prices."

Such a nonmonetary model might considerably downgrade the importance attached to fiscal austerity as a weapon to lessen shortages. Fiscal policy would be seen as altering wealth and various after-tax prices, and thus altering the mix of output among the various kinds of goods, but not necessarily having much effect, if any, on average excess demand. Some fiscal measures conventionally seen as "tight" would have an effect and some would not, or would have a perverse effect.

Model of natural unemployment rate

Let me propose two simple models of the natural unemployment rate under the real-life market socialism discussed in these two recent reports on Poland. In the paper by Lipton and Sachs, discussed here first, the managers do not exactly have an aversion to profit, but they prefer to maximize some linear combination of profit and output.

In such a model, the firm chooses its own output (y) so as to maximize the sum of the two terms shown in the equation below: (1) profit—real revenue less cost, both measured in units of labor, with the wage rate as the numeraire—and (2) output weighted by a positive constant (Y) that represents the manager's valuation of the worth of additional output in terms of profit.

$$\text{Max}_{y} \quad [h(y,\hat{y}) - l(y)]\,\hat{y} + Yy, \quad Y > 0.$$

Here the firm chooses its own output (y) with the knowledge (or correct expectation) of the average output of the other firms, denoted by $\hat{y}$. The function h gives the demand price faced by the firm as a function of y and $\hat{y}$, and the function l gives the labor per unit of output that the firm will require as an increasing function of the tightness of the labor market that is, in turn, increasing in $\hat{y}$.

Now find the first-order condition for the maximizing y. In the symmetrical case that I will focus on and that I believe entails no serious loss of generality, economywide equilibrium requires that $\hat{y}$ be such as to make the maximizing y equal to $\hat{y}$. To find that equilibrium, the first-order condition may be used to calculate how y changes with a small change of $\hat{y}$, as represented by the derivative dy/dy, and it is required for existence and uniqueness that this derivative be less than unity at the fixed point where $\hat{y}$ and y equal the equilibrium level, say y^*. It is then simple to show that, using the last-mentioned condition, an increase of Y implies an increase of equilibrium output y^*.

I interpret this result as follows. There is, unseen in the background, a labor market described by efficiency-wage considerations or (to use the term I prefer) incentive-wage considerations. Corresponding to any given unemployment rate, with the regrettable temptations for workers to shirk, quit, drink, etc., is a level of the real wage that vice-presidents over personnel calculate will instill the incentives necessary to minimize overall unit cost. This required wage rate—the wage needed to "support" an economic equilibrium at a specified unemployment rate—becomes higher as the given unemployment rate becomes lower. There is, in addition, another relationship between wages and employment—that is, unemployment—that comes from the demand side. The actual equilibrium is the intersection of these two relationships.

The hypothetical decision of socialist-minded managers to abandon as their sole objective the maximization of profit, in favor of giving some weight to output as well, serves to shift outward the demand relationship between wages and employment. Managers drive down the real price of output (in units of labor), thus effectively raising the real wage they are willing to pay to workers at any given level of employment. The result is an increase of the equilibrium real wage and a decrease of the unemployment rate.

However, the above model of the reduced natural rate of unemployment depending on a preference of managers for output or sales, as well as profit, is not at all the sort of model apparently imagined in the two reports on Poland that are being discussed here. In the above model, the product market continues to clear, following the attack of socialist conscience, but at a reduced markup—further down the real demand curves. The two reports see a world of shortage and rationing.

The chapter by Frydman, Wellisz, and Kolodko is particularly interesting in its all-too-brief remarks on the theory of socialist shortage. The authors point out that a manager, by the stratagem of pricing the product under the demand price to create an excess demand, can then proceed to allocate the goods to some or all customers as desired and thus earn favors in return from the recipients. Since the profit is not the manager's to dispose of, the consequent decline of profit costs the manager nothing. If the profit would have been a stigma, this decline is the relief of a burden, while the favors are a clear benefit. The practice of pricing below market-clearing prices could equally well be described as a form of extortion, where, like blackmail, the extorter is paid for not doing what he threatens to do if not paid.

Model of general equilibrium shortage

I will try to model general equilibrium shortage in a nonmonetary economy, in order to see what it suggests about the effects of such rationing on the equilibrium rate of unemployment. Now it is necessary to distinguish between the real demand price, $h(y,\hat{y})$, again in units of labor, and the real price asked by the manager, to be denoted by p. Here each firm's manager is supposed to maximize a linear combination of the profit earned by the firm, again measured in units of labor, and the favors "produced" by the device of rationing the output. The latter should be understood to be expressed likewise in units of labor because the favors are personal services performed by worker-consumers in return for their (equal) allotted shares of the firm's output. The manager solves the two-variable problem:

$$\underset{p,y}{\text{Max}}\ \Theta\ \{\ [p - \mathbf{1}(\hat{y})]\ y\} + F\{\ [h(y, \hat{y})-p]y\ \},\quad F'(.) > 0,\ \Theta > 0.$$

The first-order conditions with regard to p and y, respectively, are:

$$0 = [\Theta - F'(.)]y$$

$$0 = \Theta\{\ [1/\Theta]F'[.][h(y,\hat{y}) - p] + p - 1 + yh_1[y, \hat{y}\ ]\ \}$$

Assuming that that there is a maximum at some $y > 0$, the two conditions imply:

$$0 = [\ h(y, \hat{y}) - 1 + yh_1(y, \hat{y}\ )\ ].$$

This last condition is none other than the condition for a profit maximum in the classic problem where F gets zero weight (rather than $1/\theta$ weight) relative to profit. It says that output is to be pushed to that level at which the excess of the demand price over marginal cost just counterbalances the loss of profit resulting from the price concession that must be made to sell additional output. Therefore, if $\hat{y}$ does not change when the managers hypothetically discover the opportunity to sell for favors, the newly recalculated y will not change, and none of the managers will be induced to depart from the initial output level, despite the increased gain (to them) from adopting the new shortage policy. Hence, both the labor required to produce and the unemployment rate do not change either.

On the surface, it seems that, as workers now have higher wages in real terms, they would be less willing then before, given the same unemployment rate, to take the risk of prolonged unemployment by quitting their jobs or "shirking." In that case, the firms will find that their cost function has improved, and both employment and output will be increased somewhat. But the correct view, I believe, is that the workers will see that they can work shorter hours for the same real take-home pay, but they must then work performing favors in return for their allotments of the products they are permitted to buy at prices below market-clearing prices. The result is that, as they are no better or worse off than before, the cost function is not affected, and the analysis stands.

A frequently heard point in the present context is that costs are affected, and adversely, by the shortages, because the workers now must take time away from their desks and machines in order to acquire the rationed goods being allotted by the various firms. However, this queuing model is rather different from the favors model. If your name is in the manager's book, you don't have to queue.

That fact suggests to me that it is important to give emphasis also to the other idea expressed in the chapter by Frydman, Wellisz, and Kolodko on the matter of shortage. The authors say that a firm, by charging less than the market-clearing price, can get away with offering low quality. I think they mean that reliability, or "quality control," becomes less important for the firm if the firm creates an excess demand for its product. For example, no one will bring back a vacuum cleaner, even though it does not work well, because the purchaser is fortunate that it works at all. But exactly what benefit does the manager get from such a policy?

Until there is a microeconomic queuing model of shortage, it will be difficult to be persuaded about what the effects on unemployment are in that model.

To summarize, the first model predicts a lower unemployment rate under market socialism and the second model predicts no effect at all. No model based on queuing is yet available.

The typical socialist worker

Although some progress has been made, there is another point of considerable importance that may be the main answer to my question of why the natural rate of unemployment is lower under market socialism. Workers under capitalism dare to quit and dare to shirk because they have positive quantities of wealth that serve as a cushion to fall back on.

If I am rich, I can take the risk of being unemployed for a few weeks or months. (Only after several months would the risks of alcoholism and, later, suicide become considerations.) However, under the socialism of Poland and similar countries, even under the reform socialism of the past decade, the workers do not have the liquidity for tiding themselves over if unemployed.

To be more precise, the socialist worker suffers from a low ratio of wealth to wages. There have been restrictions on the kinds of wealth that the worker might invest in, so that the rates of return on the remaining available stores of wealth are extraordinarily low. Workers could always hold cash at a zero or somewhat negative return, but there are risks of losing it or having it stolen. They could hold bank accounts, but they might not like the authorities to know about this for fear of a capital tax. Also, the population has been so poor in recent years that much of the wealth is in the form of assets that could not be sold for tiding over except at great inconvenience. Selling the winter coat or the refrigerator or the motorbike for food and children's clothes may not seem to be a real palliative.

If this suggestion is on the mark, then the equilibrium, or natural, rate of unemployment in Poland should rise during the move to market capitalism. This would take place partly because the workers will become capitalists and will thus be better able to afford to take the risks of spells of unemployment.

Gradual or Radical Transformation? The Case of the German Monetary Union

The political and economic division of Germany was the result not of World War II but of the Cold War. After World War II the four Allies did not pursue the goal of a divided Germany. Rather, the division of Germany emerged as a consequence of the rivalry between East and West. Over the years, the so-called German question, which is that of German unity, became subordinated to the question of worldwide peace. Those who spoke for German unity risked the breakdown of peace. The eventual détente between East and West signified a renunciation of the goal of German reunification, and the price of peace was paid by those who remained under the socialist dictatorship. Certain intellectuals in the West predicted that a "third way" or "socialism with a human face," combining the advantages of both economic systems, would arise.

The silent revolution in the streets of Leipzig was not dominated by the German question. In the beginning of the revolutionary movement, at least, the coexistence of the two German states was not challenged, and the identity of the German Democratic Republic (GDR) could still be sustained by the illusion of the third way. The elections of March 18, 1990, however, made it evident that those "virtues" long ago stigmatized by Bertolt Brecht—the greatest of German socialist writers—were still influential: people prefer a better standard of living; morality is a luxury good if one has too little to eat; and another "system experiment" for the next generation is not sustainable. At the same time, the Federal Republic of Germany had to digest the daily inflow of two thousand settlers. Under these circumstances, the idea of the peaceful coexistence of the two German states was no longer feasible and it became evident that rapid economic integration was a necessity for both East and West Germany.

Monetary unification is one way to foster the rapid transformation of the East German socialist economy into a market economy and to accelerate the economic integration of East and West Germany. This chapter will highlight four issues. The first section reviews and compares past and present German currency reforms. The second section emphasizes West Germany's rising unemployment rate as that country's main economic motivation for radical rather than gradual economic measures. Next, the chapter discusses the pros and cons of monetary union compared with alternative monetary arrangements for East Germany. The final section deals with the implications of German monetary union for the probable future evolution of European monetary union. I have chosen these four issues rather arbitrarily, based on my interests. Property rights, fiscal reform, and other issues may be of equal importance. But at the time of this writing, in early 1990, we must begin to apply our knowledge of economic theory to the problem of transforming socialist economies, and one part of that is currency reform.

Three Currency Reforms in Four Generations

November 1923, June 1948, and July 1990 are the decisive dates of the various German currency reforms.

The rentenmark

On November 23, 1923, bank notes of paper marks amounted to 224 quintillion marks (224×10^{18}). One week earlier a parallel currency, the rentenmark, had been introduced, which was backed by mortgage bonds denominated in gold marks and yielding an interest rate of 5 percent. The exchange rate between the two currencies was fixed at 1 trillion paper marks for 1 gold mark, with 4.2 gold marks equal to 1 dollar, implying 4.2 trillion paper marks = 4.2 rentenmarks = 1 dollar. The value of the outstanding amount of paper mark notes was only equal to 224 million gold marks as the result of hyperinflation and the extremely high velocity of paper marks. The total stock of gold held by the Reichsbank corresponded to 467 million gold marks (Pfleiderer 1976: 192–93).

The rentenmark was not issued by the Reichsbank but by a new semipublic institution, the Rentenbank. The total amount of the new currency issue was limited to 2.4 billion gold marks—an amount ten times higher than the real value of the outstanding volume of paper marks, but a considerable increase in the demand for gold marks in the following months was expected, which was indeed the case. The price level became stabilized, as expressed in either paper marks or gold marks. Half of the Rentenbank note issue was granted as a loan to the government, of which 300 million served to retire short-term debt held by the Reichsbank. Government long-term debt had already been confiscated by the former inflation process. The end of hyperinflation (the so-called Tanzi effect), together with the implementation of a new tax system, resulted in a government budget surplus in 1924 (Dornbusch 1987). Gradually all paper marks were converted into gold marks and finally the rentenmark was renamed the reichsmark. The currency reform was fully successful because of the proper mix of monetary, fiscal, and exchange rate stabilization.

The deutsche mark

Twenty-five years later, in June 1948, the second currency reform took place; this replaced reichsmarks (RM) with deutsche marks (DM) at an initial conversion rate of 10:1. The main difference of 1948 compared with 1923 was repressed inflation due to a wage and price freeze and rationing of goods and foreign exchange. By the end of June, DM 4.4 billion were circulating in the economy—twice the amount of rentenmarks issued during the initial phase of the first currency reform (Mayer and Thumann 1990). Also in June 1948, half of outstanding demand deposits were frozen. During the following months the general price level rose by approximately 15 percent, implying that the former monetary overhang had not been cancelled completely. Consequently, in September 1948, 70 percent of the frozen deposits were annulled. The conversion rate of RM into DM was finally 10:0.65—the stock of money had been cut by 93.5 percent instead of the planned 90 percent.

The currency reform was implemented on June 20, 1948, in the three occupational zones of Western Germany. Three days later, Soviet Marshal Sokolovsky announced a currency reform for the Soviet occupational zone and Greater Berlin. The *coupon mark*—the reichsmark with a special coupon attached—was introduced, which, some weeks later, was replaced by the "deutsche mark." Consequently, in June 1948, the uniform currency area of the reichsmark had been split into two separate currency areas, those of the deutsche mark (West) and the deutsche mark (East).

One could advance the hypothesis that the monetary partition of 1948 was a decisive element in the process of the political division of Germany in the same way that the monetary union of 1990 constitutes an important step toward political unification. In 1948, however, the banking system had been split since May 1945, when the interbank payments system between the Soviet occupational zone and the three Western zones had been interrupted. Furthermore, all existing banks in the Soviet zone had been abolished and consequently all existing deposits—sight, time, and saving—canceled. The official argument for the dismantling of the banking system was that financial bank claims had no value because of destruction in the war and that bank liabilities no longer had any intrinsic value (Stucken 1964:187). In 1945, the remaining quantity of money in the Soviet zone consisted of only coins and Reichsbank notes. Consequently, in 1945, an important part of the monetary overhang was reduced in the Soviet zone, although the overhang continued to exist in the Western zones. In the following years, the newly installed centralized banking structure (the state bank with its branches in the form of saving banks and cooperative banks) produced a volume of deposits, which in June 1948 was nearly equal to the amount of currency in circulation. The currency reform in the East was handled with a conversion rate of 5:1 for deposits under 1,000 marks and 10:1 for deposits above 1,000 marks.

In the initial stages of the West German currency reform, the Western Allies did not include West Berlin in the DM area. Wishing to maintain the unified city government, a uniform currency for greater Berlin constituted an important condition for avoiding a political division. The Soviet army considered greater Berlin an economic component of the Soviet zone and the ostmark (OM) was intended to be legal tender in West Berlin. The Western Allies would have agreed with such an approach provided that the OM was put under quadripartite control. That proposal seemed unacceptable to the Soviets, since it implied that the Western Allies also controlled the OM in the entire Soviet zone. On June 25, 1948, the Western occupational authorities integrated West Berlin in the currency area of West Germany, but admitted the OM as a restricted parallel legal currency in West Berlin. The blockade of West Berlin was the immediate reaction of the Soviets.

The legal tender aspect of the OM was limited to two types of transactions: the purchase of basic goods in West Berlin and the wage bill of East Berlin workers commuting to West Berlin. Both currencies were declared of equal value. Basic goods and services were bread, potatoes, flour, meat, lard, sugar, malt-coffee, salt, public transportation, postal services, electricity, gas, taxes, and municipal fees (Collier and Papell 1988:532). The convertibility of the OM for this category of goods was conceived mainly for workers living in West Berlin and commuting to East Berlin or the Soviet zone. As far as the commuters from East to West were concerned, one quarter of their wages were paid in DM and the rest in OM.

On July 27, 1948, the establishment of exchange bureaus (Wechselstuben) was permitted. One week later the first office opened with a free-market exchange rate of OM 2.2 per DM while official parity remained at 1:1. In November 1948, hope of maintaining a unified municipal administration collapsed. Gresham's law did the rest (many West Berliners paid for basic goods with OM), and on March 20, 1949, the OM was suspended as parallel legal tender, and the DM was declared the sole currency of West Berlin.

Since the Soviet zone and the later GDR were not considered a foreign country under West German law, exchanges of DM and OM were not regarded as foreign exchanges. Foreign exchange controls that continued to exist in West Germany after the currency reform were not applicable, and consequently a free-market rate could be established. It was one of the first examples of floating exchange rates in the postwar world economy (as was the Canadian dollar in the 1950s). Figure 5.1 illustrates the yearly average exchange rate of the OM with respect to 1 DM for the years 1948–1990; the average monthly rate is represented for September 1989 to June 1990.

German monetary union

There are certain similarities between the degree of monetary value of the RM in early 1948 and the OM in early 1990. Both lacked the quality of internal and external convertibility. In both economies the combination of rationing and a price freeze gave rise to a monetary overhang, with the consequent repressed inflation. Many goods served as a means of payment and store of value in place of money. Consequently, as is also true in many socialist countries, there was the paradoxical situation that goods existed in "abundance," but were in shortage since they were hoarded as "near money" by households and firms. In the case of East Germany since at least the mid-1970s, the DM circulated as a parallel currency in addition to goods.

Both currencies, RM and OM, completely lacked any characteristics of external convertibility. The foreign-trade monopoly of the East German government excluded any exchange of OM into foreign currencies. In a similar way, the military powers in West Germany managed all foreign-trade transactions. The external convertibility of the DM (as of many other European currencies) was reestablished gradually and fully realized only in 1958 (Moeller 1976). In this context it is interesting to

FIGURE 5.1 Exchange Rates of East and West Germany, 1948–1990

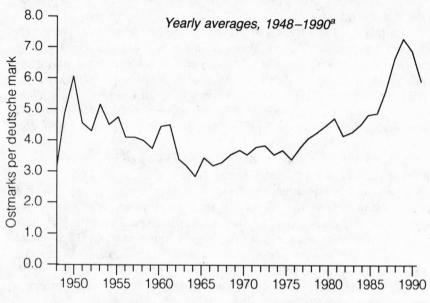

Yearly averages, 1948–1990[a]

Ostmarks per deutsche mark

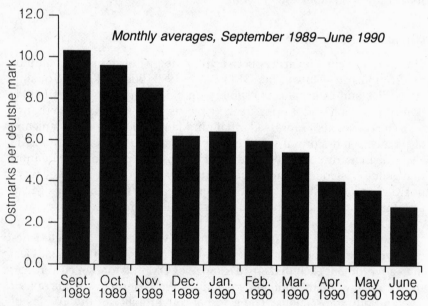

Monthly averages, September 1989–June 1990

Ostmarks per deutshe mark

a. Data for 1990 are for the first quarter only.
SOURCE: Berliner Bank.

TABLE 5.1   Quantity of Money of the Federal Republic of Germany (FRG) and Estimated Demand for Money by the German Democratic Republic (GDR), Mid-1990

Monetary aggregates	Quantity of money of the FRG		Demand for the money by the GDR (billions of DM)
	Billions of DM	Percentage of GDP	
Monetary base			
Currency	150	6.2	19
Bank reserves	70	2.9	9
Total	220	9.1	28
M1			
Currency	150	6.2	19
Sight deposits	280	11.7	35
Total	430	18.0	54
M3			
M1	430	18.0	54
Time deposits	920	38.3	115
Total	1,350	56.2	169
	FRG		GDR
Estimated nominal GDP (billions of DM)	2,400		300

SOURCES: Deutsches Institut für Wirtschaftsforschung, *Wochenbericht*, April 12, 1990; International Monetary Fund, *International Financial Statistics*, 1990.

note that Lloyd Metzler (1979) calculated in 1946 for the Colm-Dodge-Goldsmith Committee (whose plan was the basis of the 1948 currency reform) the adequate exchange rate of the deutsche mark to be in the range of DM 2.8 to 4.2 per dollar. In June 1948, it was fixed at DM 3.3 and one year later, after the devaluation of the pound sterling, at DM 4.2, a rate identical to that of the rentenmark in 1923.

There is no doubt that the monetary overhang of the GDR is far lower than that of West Germany in early 1948. In Table 5.1 we have estimated the demand for money in the GDR on the basis of two restrictive assumptions. We assume that the various money-to-income ratios are the same as those of the Federal Republic. The other assumption involves the uncertainty of nominal gross domestic product (GDP), which is unknown for the past, much less the present. The Deutsches Institut für Wirtschaftsforschung (1990) estimated it to be 300 billion shortly after the currency reform and other reforms.

Toward the end of April 1990, the West German government proposed a 1:1 conversion rate for up to OM 4,000 per person (but only 2,000 marks for children under fifteen years and 6,000 marks for people age sixty and over), and a 2:1 rate for remaining ostmarks. The total M3 money supply at the end of 1989 amounted to OM 252.6 billion (see the appendix to this chapter). With a population of 16.1 million, the maximum amount of Eastern M3 to be converted at a 1:1 rate is equal to DM 64.4 billion. The remaining OM 188.2 billion, when converted at 2:1, make a total M3 of DM 158.5 billion and a global conversion rate of 1.6:1 (compensation of households with savings deposits being converted at 2:1 is envisaged; in the later phase of privatization, they will be given priority access to property titles). In Table 5.1, the GDR's demand for M3 is estimated to be 169 billion DM. The total hypothetical increase of M3 in the GDR (158.5 billion) related to M3 in the Federal Republic amounts to 11.7 percent.

It should be noted that the inflationary danger of the monetary union for the Federal Republic is rather limited. Assume that the Bundesbank overestimates the demand for money in the GDR and creates an excess liquidity of 10 percent of East Germany's GDP. Since the GDP of the GDR is estimated to be roughly one-tenth of that of the Federal Republic, the inflationary impact for the whole monetary area of Germany would be approximately 1 percent. This conclusion results from our knowledge about the determination of the inflation rate in open economies that are linked by fixed exchange rates. It follows from the law of one price per tradable good, that the inflation rate will tend to be equalized, at least for tradable goods. Furthermore, for the size of the common inflation rate, the country of origin of the inflationary pressure is completely irrelevant.

The argument of the Bundesbank for the conversion rate of 2:1 was conducted in terms of the asset side rather than the liability side of the consolidated balance sheet of the East German banking sector (see the appendix). At the end of 1989, East German enterprises (mainly the state-owned combinates, which conduct various activities for producing inputs) were indebted to the Staatsbank (the head of the centralized banking system) by a net amount of OM 200 billion, while the net volume of deposits by households amounted to OM 150 billion. According to the Bundesbank, a conversion rate of 1:1 for the liabilities of enterprises would give rise to an unsustainable burden of debt service, such that many of them would face bankruptcy after the currency reform. Consequently, the Bundesbank proposed a conversion rate of 2:1 for all financial assets and liabilities. If the conversion rate of 1:1 had been maintained for claims and liabilities of the banking system, one part of the deposits should have been frozen and eventually nullified at the moment the danger of bankruptcy became real, or else some additional assets would have to be transferred to the banking system.

The currency reform of 1948 involved a conversion rate for prices of goods, wages, and pensions of 1:1, as does the currency reform of the GDR. In principle, one could argue that the precise conversion rate for prices and incomes may be considered as rather irrelevant to the extent that the emerging market economy will determine them. To the extent that the GDR's economy opens and has to adopt the relative prices of tradables in the Western countries, the GDR's relative price structure of tradable goods has to be altered overnight. This is in contrast to West Germany in 1948, which, like many other European economies, was still a closed economy as a consequence of the worldwide postwar disintegration of foreign trade. The main characteristics of the GDR, as well as all other socialist countries, concern the present relative price structure—basic consumption goods are highly subsidized and industrial goods extremely overpriced. The high price level of industrialized goods is not only an outcome of high production costs (or low productivity), but in particular is the consequence of the fiscal system. Since most government revenues are provided by the "surpluses" of enterprises, a monetary union and the subsequent reversal of the total relative price structure implies a simultaneous fiscal reform to replace the transfer of surpluses with ordinary taxes.

The issue of the conversion rate for wages has been intensively debated in East and West Germany. Monthly gross wages for industrial workers in 1988 were OM 1,290 in the GDR—over one-third of West German wages (DM 3,660) at a conversion rate of 1:1. To the extent that the consumer price index may increase by 50 percent after the price reform of tradable goods (the prices of nontradable goods such as housing and transport will probably be maintained for a certain time, as they were in the 1948 currency reform), real wages will fall correspondingly— except for a one-time compensation payment to cancel the fall in real wages. Nevertheless, the decisive element for wage setting in the GDR will be determined by the labor market and the producitivity differential between the GDR and the Federal Republic. A discussion of the appropriate conversion rate for wages becomes relevant only at the moment nominal wage rigidities are assumed.

On the Two Labor Markets

Figure 5.2 indicates migration flows in Germany before and after the fall of the Berlin wall. The highest outflow took place in the weeks immediately after the removal of the Berlin wall on November 9, 1989. It is interesting to note that two subsequent events slowed the migration flow: the announcement of the monetary union on February 6, 1990, and the victory of the Christian Democrats in the parliamentary elections of the GDR on March 18, 1990.

In Figure 5.3 we illustrate the unified labor market with three possible

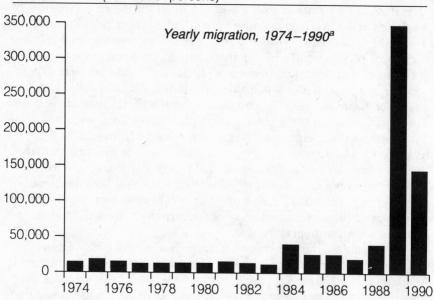

Yearly migration, 1974–1990[a]

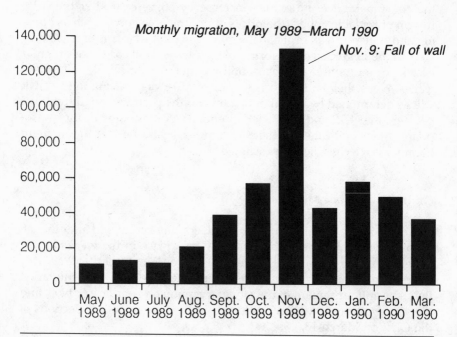

Monthly migration, May 1989–March 1990

Nov. 9: Fall of wall

(continued)

FIGURE 5.2 (*continued*)

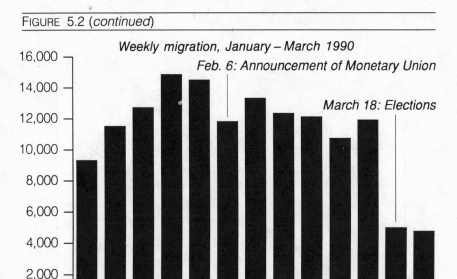

Weekly migration, January – March 1990

Feb. 6: Announcement of Monetary Union

March 18: Elections

SOURCE: Statistisches Bunderamt, Wiesbaden.

outcomes for labor migration from East to West. Before migration starts, we assume that there is no unemployment in either country. The active population in the West (P_w) is measured from left to right and the active population in the East (P_e) from right to left. The marginal productivity of labor of each region is represented by the downward sloping schedules, MPL_w and MPL_e. Before the fall of the wall, the distribution of the active population was at P, where labor productivity in East Germany (point B) is estimated to be one-third of West Germany's labor productivity (point A).

By opening the West German labor market to East German labor, the optimal migration level would be determined by the intersection of both marginal labor productivities, point C. At this point, wage levels in East and West are equal. An amount of East German labor equal to PP_o would migrate to West Germany, and the whole area would have a net benefit of an increase in GDP equal to the area of triangle ABC. At the same time, a considerable number of East German firms would close, decreasing Eastern GDP, by BPP_oC, to $CP_oO'D$.

This optimal solution is unlikely to happen. What is optimal for both regions as a whole is not optimal from the point of view of West German

FIGURE 5.3   Model for Migration from East to West Germany

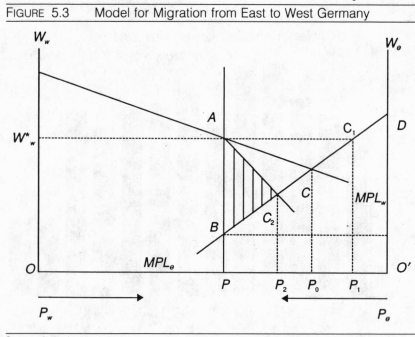

SOURCE: Author's calculations.

trade unions. The West German real wage level would fall from A to C (but, correspondingly, the real wage level of all East Germans would rise from B to C). Let us assume that West German trade unions succeed in maintaining their original real wage level at W^*_w. This outcome is even more likely if we consider that future West German real wages after taxes will probably decrease, because taxes will rise to finance federal transfer payments for the future East German social security system and federal investment expenditures for the East German infrastructure. With an unchanged real wage rate of W^*_w, situation C_1 may take place: massive unemployment in both regions (with or without migration) of the size PP_1, and a total net loss of GDP for both regions equal to the area of BPP_1C_1.

Fortunately, situation C_1 could be disregarded, since in the case of migration, East German emigrants must take into account the considerable risk of unemployment when they search the West German labor market. At this stage we can resort to a model elaborated by Harris and Todaro (1970) for developing countries. This model concerns labor migration from a low-productivity rural sector to a high-productivity urban sector. The main considerations for labor migration are wage differentials, but in the framework of Harris and Todaro the wage differentials must be the expected (and not effective) ones. By applying their model to the German economy, the effective real wage differential is $W^*_w - W_e$, while the probable or expected wage differential is $pW^*w - W_e$, where p represents the probability of finding employment in the West German economy. The coefficient p can be proxied by the ratio of employment (E_w) over the total active population (P_w). In Figure 5.3, AC_2 illustrates the evolution of $pW^*_w - W_e$ where p is assumed to fall increasingly with rising migration. The shaded area ABC_2 represents the shrinking expected wage differential. Migration stops at point C_2, and total migration amounts to PP_2, creating unemployment of the same size in West Germany. The net loss of GDP for the whole territory is the area BPP_2C_2. West German wages remain rigid at W^*_w and East German wages rise from B to C_2.

The above geometrical model represents an oversimplification of the united German labor market. It abstracts from many other determinants of the expected wage differential, which until now has been the single and decisive force for labor migration. There are factors that could enlarge the expected wage differential and others that could attenuate it. Unemployment benefits granted by West Germany to the emigrants for the duration of one year dampen the fall in p, but these have recently been abolished and unemployed East German emigrants receive their proper unemployment benefits from the GDR. In East Germany, existing unemployment of the Stasi and disguised unemployment will also force labor movement. Other elements decrease the expected wage differential. Depending on how real wages are measured in East Germany, they may be higher than generally estimated if we consider more explicitly that certain nontradable goods—such as housing and labor-intensive services—are cheaper in East Germany than in West Germany. A possible fall in the real wage rate of West Germany should not be excluded. In early 1990 existing unemployment in West Germany was 2 million. A rapidly rising unemployment rate could exercise downward pressure on real wages. The federal government could also envisage a premium for remaining (in a similar way as the former "Zitterprämie" granted to the population of West Berlin). Furthermore, the migration may stop at a certain threshold value of a positive expected wage differential to the extent that potential emigrants consider positive nonpecuniary elements such as the value of remaining in their homeland. Finally, life (permanent) income will be the decisive element of migration, and any radical program that shortens the transition period will also decrease the permanent wage differential between West Germany and East Germany.

FIGURE 5.4   East Germany's Monetary Overhang

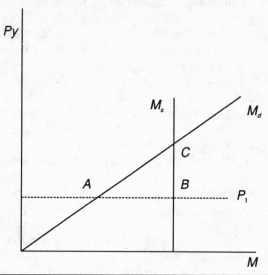

SOURCE: Author's calculations.

Monetary Union and Alternative Arrangements

Like many socialist economies, the GDR faces two monetary issues: the handling of the monetary overhang and the credibility of present and future monetary management. The problem of the monetary union is to solve both issues rapidly and simultaneously.

In Figure 5.4 the money market is represented by the supply (M_s) and demand for money (M_d), where the latter is proportional to nominal income, Py (P being the price level and real income y is assumed to be given). The monetary overhang is measured by the distance AB, the repressed inflation by the distance BC, and P_1 is the artificially low price level. The two extreme solutions for getting rid of the monetary overhang are the equilibrium situations at either point C or point A. Solution C is open inflation (that is, a once-and-for-all increase in the price level), which implies a corresponding fall in the real value of financial assets, M3 in practice. Solution A reduces the nominal quantity of money by the amount AB. There are two possible methods of doing so, either by freezing parts of the money supply or by implementing a currency reform. The freeze of deposits can be accompanied—either simultaneously or subsequently—by the forced conversion of frozen deposits into a government loan or by a voluntary exchange of frozen deposits for private property titles that were formerly collective titles. In both cases, the acquired deposits are withdrawn from circulation. As far as the currency reform is concerned, either a new currency can be created—as was done in 1923 and 1948—or an existing one can be chosen, as was done in the GDR.

It should be noted that a currency reform can also be chosen for the open inflation solution. The currency reform of 1923 is point C, and the reform of 1948 is point A. The essential characteristics of a currency reform lie, in addition to the elimination of the monetary overhang, in signaling the credibility of future monetary policy. The creation of the rentenmark in 1923, backed by mortgage bonds denominated in gold marks, created confidence in future monetary policy, not because the rentenmark issue was linked to the gold standard, but because the maintenance of a fixed exchange-rate system imposed limits for active monetary and fiscal policy. The creation of the deutsche mark in 1949 was somewhat like an "act of God" imposed by the military occupational forces and was combined with the abolishment of a rationing economy. At that moment, the pegging of the exchange rate was without implication for the conduct of monetary policy because of the quasi-worldwide maintenance of exchange controls. It may be that confidence in the new money was an outcome of several factors: lack of democratic bargaining about unemployment and money growth targets, the memory of the great inflation twenty-five years earlier, and the rather quick beneficial results of the market economy.

For the GDR, the German monetary union is analogous to the creation of monetary confidence via the "dollarization" phenomenon. East German monetary sovereignty is exchanged for the West German brand-name capital of the deutsche mark. One could argue, as many German economists did, that the proper adjustment speed should have been more gradual: pegging the ostmark to the deutsche mark and introducing the deutsche mark in a later phase. This would be similar to what was done in early 1957 in the Saarland, which voted to become part of the Federal Republic and converted its French francs into deutsche marks two years later. The GDR, however, has a command economy and a monetary overhang; it is not similar to the Saarland.

In the present debate over the pros and cons of a monetary union, it is often argued that the fiscal burden for the Federal Republic is the maximum possible under the hypothesis of monetary unification. This statement is probably valid, compared with a situation where two independent states are maintained and linked together within a confederation. Under the latter hypothesis, both states would exercise their monetary and fiscal sovereignty. To the extent that the GDR opts fully for a market economy, the so-called transformation could be put forward stepwise. First of all, the present system of relative prices for tradable goods would have to be restructured so that it corresponds to the price structure of Western economies. After this, the money market will determine the general price level, and therefore the level of each individual price. Knowing the general price level, and therefore the price level of tradable goods, the exchange rate can be deduced. It could be set at a level equalizing internal prices of domestic tradables and internal prices of foreign tradables. Or to give some competitive advantage to the GDR, the exchange rate could be fixed at a higher level that would temporarily put the internal prices of domestic tradables under those of foreign tradables. This textbook example suggests that external convertibility may come after implementation of some fundamental price and economic reforms. Furthermore, external convertibility could then imply that the GDR opts for a floating exchange rate instead of pegging to the deutsche mark.

In either case, East Germany would maintain or even enforce its monetary and fiscal sovereignty. Under this hypothesis, it is true that the fiscal burden supported by the Federal Republic for reconstructing the East German economy would be lower. It will be shared by the new East German taxpayers, and the transition period of the transformation process would be far longer. In contrast, a common currency area would constitute a more radical (and thus more credible) solution.

The literature on currency areas is rich and bewildering because of the many criteria a country should meet in establishing a currency area. We shall refer here to one of the first theoretical contributions in this field, written by Robert Mundell in 1961. This particular model seems to fit the situation of both Germanies perfectly. According to this model, countries should join a currency area if there is perfect factor mobility among them. At the moment, there is already perfect labor mobility between the two Germanies. Capital mobility will follow when the last institutional impediments are abolished by East Germany. Factor mobility would avoid unemployment in the member countries of the currency area. If there is unemployment in one country, labor migrates to the other country. If labor is not mobile, a separate currency standard is required. By devaluating its currency, unemployment would be absorbed, provided that wages are not pushed upwards. Furthermore, capital would flow in to sustain the expansion of production.

The Mundell model is valid only when the labor movement does not create unemployment in the other country. However, increased unemployment is the situation that will confront all of Germany in the near future. The final reasons for the rising unemployment rate are twofold: the considerable potential wage differential between the two economies and the definite opposition of West German trade unions to any decline in their real wages. Thus, at first sight, Mundell's model does not seem to apply to either Germany, since unemployment will persist in each currency regime. To erect an economic wall to replace the former Berlin wall to stop the labor inflows would be an economic solution if we abstract from political considerations. Even though some impediments to labor flows will be implemented in the near future in both Germanies (for the GDR, which loses its labor resources, and for the Federal Republic, which increases its unemployed), there seems to be only one option: the currency union. Under any currency regime, labor migration continues. Consequently, one has to reduce the labor productivity differential as quickly as possible.

Furthermore, the temporary maintenance of the East German currency (old or newly created), and its pegging to the DM would not necessarily bring about credibility in the future conduct of East German monetary policy, since the above proposal is often put forward as having the advantages of an adjustable peg. The latter, in turn, is recommended for the competitive advantage a devaluation could produce. Several arguments could be advanced against such a view. First, even though the law of one price for tradables may not hold for small price divergences of a few percentage points, it must hold for more considerable price differences, particularly between East and West Berlin. Second, a more effective way of protecting East German tradable goods would be the temporary imposition of import tariffs, to be negotiated within the framework of the European Community with the hope that they remain transitory. Third, a devaluation may swamp competitive gains if nominal wages are adjusted upwards. Finally, a devaluation may affect the relative prices of tradable and nontradable goods, but this relative price effect may be undesirable to the extent that the "service" sector of the East German economy—housing, transport, handicrafts, etc.—has to be favored in contrast to the present autarkic industrial production pattern.

The possible need for a real appreciation, defined as a fall in the relative price of tradable to nontradable goods (P_T/P_N), is illustrated in Figure 5.5. TT is the equilibrium schedule for the market of tradable goods, NN is the equilibrium schedule for the market of nontradable goods, and MM represents the money market equilibrium for a given outstanding quantity of money. The macroeconomic position of the GDR, as of any other Eastern European country, is situated in the shadowed area of total disequilibrium: excess demand for tradable goods (rightward of TT), excess demand for nontradable goods (leftward of NN), and excess supply of money, namely, the so-called monetary overhang (leftward of MM). Assume that the price level is at P_o, with the specific mix of price levels for tradable and nontradable goods characterized by point A. There are two issues to solve as far as stabilization

Figure 5.5   East Germany's Total Disequilibrium for Goods and
Money Markets

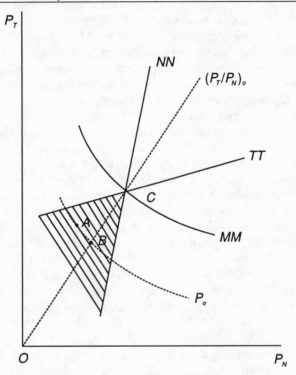

Source: Author's calculations.

policies are concerned: the choice of the real exchange rate and the handling of the monetary overhang.

1. The former development strategy of Eastern European countries not only favored producer goods at the expense of consumer goods, but also fostered the production of tradable goods at the expense of nontradable goods. Even though tradable goods were of rather low quality and limited variety, they were produced nearly autarkically. Consequently, restructuring production will imply a change in the relative price levels of both categories of goods, leading to a real appreciation. One possible way of bringing about the real appreciation is to lower P_T and to increase P_N (point B) so that the general price level P_o remains unchanged.

2. Point B is still a situation of repressed inflation, where the distance AC represents the monetary overhang. Open inflation implies maintaining the outstanding quantity of money (MM) and increasing the price level from B to C (as in Figure 5.4). On the other hand, if it is desired to maintain the price level P_o (including the corresponding nominal wage level), the outstanding quantity of money has to be reduced by the ratio of BC/CO, so that the new equilibrium schedule of the money market coincides with the P_o curve; the TT and NN schedules would shift through point B because they depend only on the relative price P_T/P_N. Case C is that of the Polish economy, and case B that of the East German economy. In the latter case, the technique of eliminating the monetary overhang was conversion of the existing currency.

The most decisive argument for the German monetary union and against all other solutions is precisely its radical, rather than gradual, form. It could be argued that the choice of a radical over a gradual reform program would be a matter of indifference to the extent that the results are identical except for timing. During the structural adjustment process, however, radical programs may have more credibility than gradual ones, since the latter, particularly in democracies, can always be altered, attenuated, or made doubtful, making their final outcome less satisfactory.

Conclusion: German and European Monetary Union

At first glance, German monetary policy seems to be rather contradictory. As far as the European Community is concerned, the Bundesbank was always opposed to acceleration toward a European monetary union (EMU). In contrast, with respect to both Germanies, it (but now the West German government rather than the Bundesbank) preaches the contrary: monetary unification, then economic integration.

There are, however, arguments that can solve this paradox. It should be emphasized that the East Germans want the West German currency in their territory, while the Europeans are opposed to a "deutschemarkization" of their own economies. As a matter of fact, the present European monetary system (EMS) could already be interpreted as a German monetary area. The Bundesbank is concerned only (if at all) with the exchange rate of the deutsche mark with respect to the dollar, while the other countries of the EMS defend their parity with respect to the deutsche mark. If the Bundesbank raises the discount rate, the others follow immediately for fear of devaluation. German monetary policy dictates that of the others. One corollary of this observation would be that the future European monetary union is based on the deutsche mark, but that is precisely the trend that Europeans are strongly opposed to, while it is favored by an overwhelming majority of East Germans.

As already mentioned, the fiscal implications of the German monetary experiment are enormous. There is probably no doubt that the German government will use a mixture of bond and tax financing. Sound fiscal policy could even give preference to budget deficits to the extent that the additional public expenditures are of exceptional nature; only a permanent rise in government expenditures should be financed by taxes. But neither the size nor the time dimension of the future public burden is precisely known. Some sources mention DM 100 billion as additional public outlays; this would correspond to 4 percent of German GDP (the worst budget deficit of the United States in the 1980s was 5 percent). Simultaneously, to the extent that savings and investment are shifted toward East Germany, considerable reduction of the current account is to be expected.

European, as well as German, monetary unification will likely imply fiscal transfers from high-growth to low-growth countries. Since fiscal sovereignty is still maintained, there will be important opposition by the taxpayers of donor countries, as there will be also by West German taxpayers to transfers to East Germany. With respect to the fiscal resistance, there may be a difference in kind rather than degree. National solidarity will make it easier for Germany than for Europe to support the fiscal burden.

In the near future, the pressure on the West German government to rapidly realize the EMU will become stronger. Paradoxically, the attitude of the Bundesbank may also change toward a more optimistic view of a European federal reserve system. Sixty-one plus sixteen is not always necessarily equal to seventy-seven (million inhabitants). The voting power of the Bundesbank will become stronger in the future European central bank, and its dominant weight may more easily assure the ultimate target of European price stability.

Appendix

Consolidated Financial Sector of the German Democratic Republic, December 31, 1989 (billions of ostmarks)

Consolidated balance sheet, Staatsbank

Liabilities		Assets	
		Currency	15.7
Credit to households	26.1	Deposits of households	176.5
Credit to firms	260.4	Deposits of firms	60.4
Claims to nonsocialist		Debt to nonsocialist	
countries	33.4	countries	67.3

Consolidated balance sheet in net terms, Staatsbank

Liabilities		Assets	
		Currency	15.7
		Net deposits of households	150.4
Net credit to firms	200.0	Net debt to nonsocialist	33.9
		countries	

SOURCE: *Der Spiegel*, April 9, 1990.

Comments

DIETER BENDER

With regard to the appropriate speed of German monetary unification, there is dissent among those economists who agree that a European monetary union ought to be the final result of a process of economic integration. The proponents of a gradual approach think that market-oriented internal reforms (private ownership, privatization of state property, market-determined equilibrium prices) and external reforms (convertibility of the ostmark at an exchange rate supporting international price competitiveness) in the German Democratic Republic (GDR) are prerequisites to a future monetary union. On the other hand, supporters of a radical transformation favor an instantaneous monetary unification as the most effective instrument to accelerate the processes of economic transformation and political unification.

Emil Claassen has offered an inspiring chapter by not only concentrating on the economic consequences of monetary unification but also recommending the shock therapy of currency reforms. The virtues of Claassen's presentation lie in applying models of economic theory, thereby providing conclusions that can be traced to underlying assumptions. These results convey the message that the economic risks of monetary unification are relatively low compared with the advantage of accelerating the economic integration and fostering the rapid transformation of the East German economy into a market economy.

I want to dispute Claassen's main arguments by objecting that he underestimates the macroeconomic costs of his radical transformation approach. I have three main objections:

1. Claassen's estimate of the monetary overhang rests on very questionable assumptions, leading to an underestimation of the overhang.

2. The applicability of the neoclassical migration model of Harris and Todaro to the problem of labor market adjustment after currency unification is questionable.

3. More emphasis should have been placed on the problem of how to promote capital mobility from West Germany to East Germany as a substitute for labor mobility from East Germany to West Germany.

My first point can be demonstrated by regarding Claassen's calculation of the monetary overhang in Figure 5.4 of his chapter. Claassen presumes that the East German population's money demand M_d can be derived from the cash-to-income ratio of the West German population and that, therefore, velocities of money are the same in both regions ($V_w = V_E$). We also have to consider, however, the possibility that $V_E > V_w$ because the East Germans have a lower liquidity preference than the West Germans have. This lower liquidity preference is the result of long-lasting experiences of shortages of products without shortages of money holdings under conditions of repressed inflation. If the higher velocity of money is not only a short-term transitory effect of monetary unification but also an indicator of basic differences in behavioral patterns, the price level shock caused by currency reform in the absence of precautionary measures (absorbing part of the overhang by the sale of state property, for example) will be aggravated. The East German money demand will be shown by a graph rotated counterclockwise to the left and above, thereby depicting a monetary disequilibrium larger than *AB*. This monetary disequilibrium will be even larger if the estimated nominal gross domestic product (GDP) of the GDR contains dead stocks of products that will not be purchased with the newly injected DM currency. As a consequence of these uncertainties about the magnitude of the monetary overhang, steps toward privatization of state-owned assets should be taken as concomitant measures to absorb liquidity.

The unemployment effects of monetary unification should have been analyzed by a disequilibrium model of the labor market. This analysis, in my view, is more suitable than the approach of Harris and Todaro shown in Figure 5.3 of Claassen's chapter. Before currency unification, classical unemployment (U_w) is assumed to exist in the West German labor market:

$$U_w = N^s_w (W_w) - N^{dT}_w (W^T_w) - N^{dNT}_w (W^{NT}_w) > 0 \qquad (1)$$

N^S_w: the labor supply in West Germany
N^{dT}_w: the labor demand by West German producers of tradables
N^{dNT}_w: the labor demand by West German producers of nontradables
W^T_w: real wages in the West German tradables production sector
W^{NT}_w: real wages in the West German nontradables production sector.

Disguised unemployment (DU_E) in the East German labor market results from a centrally planned "full employment"–oriented labor allocation (bars denote centrally planned variables):

$$N^S_E (\bar{W}_E, RAT) = \bar{N}^{dT}_E + \bar{N}^{dNT}_E = \bar{N}^d_E$$

$$DU_E = \bar{N}^d_E - N^{dT}_E (W^T_E) - N^{dNT}_E (W^{NT}_E) > 0 \qquad (2)$$

Labor supply N^S_E is demotivated by the degree of rationing of private households on product markets (RAT). At the levels of prevailing sectoral real wages, the demand for labor under profit-maximizing behavior—equating marginal labor productivity with real wages—would be lower than is the case under centrally planned effective employment. Consequently, real wages paid to "fully employed" workers are higher than marginal labor productivity. Furthermore, relative prices in East Germany are distorted, and in comparison with West German market prices, East German prices of tradables are too high $(\bar{P}^T_E > P^T_w)$ and prices of nontradables are too low $(\bar{P}^{NT}_E < P^{NT}_w)$.

Effects of monetary unification

After the establishment of a monetary union, East German nominal wages will be converted into DM at a conversion rate of one to one, and

East German prices of tradables will decrease ($P^T_E = P^T_w$), whereas East German prices of nontradables will rise ($P^{NT}_E \leqq P^{NT}_w$, prices of some basic nontradables will remain subsidized). For the sake of simplicity, we assume that the overall level of workers' real wages in East Germany will not be changed by these effects of monetary unification ($W_E = \bar{W}_E$). Disequilibrium in the West German labor market is changed by the labor migration effect of Harris and Todaro, and the increase in regional unemployment depends on the degree of real wage coherence (as shown by Claassen):

$$U_w = N^S_w (W_w) + \Delta N^S_w (p_w W_w - p_E W_E) - N^{dT}_w (W^T_w) - N^{dNT}_w (W^{NT}_w) \tag{3}$$

$p_w W_w$: expected West German real wage (weighted by the risk of unemployment in the case of migration)
$p_E W_E$: expected East German real wage (weighted by the risk of unemployment in the case of nonmigration).

In the East German labor market, open unemployment will be generated by economic transformation:

$$U_E = N^S_E (W_E) - \Delta N^S_w (p_w W_w - p_E W_E) - N^{dT}_E (W^T_E) - N^{dNT}_E (W^{NT}_E) > 0. \tag{4}$$

Total unemployment in the two labor markets of a unified Germany will be:

$$U_w + U_E = N^S_w (W_w) + N^S_E (W_E) - [N^{dT}_w (W_w) + N^{dNT}_w (W_w)] - (N^{dT}_E (W^T_E, K^T_E) + N^{dNT}_E (W^{NT}_E, K^{NT}_E)). \tag{5}$$

K^T_E: East German capital stock in tradables production
K^{NT}_E: East German capital stock in nontradables production

Therefore, total unemployment will increase by:

$$\Delta U = \Delta N^S_E (RAT = 0) + DU - \Delta N^{dT}_E - \Delta N^{dNT}_E. \tag{6}$$

With respect to this global employment effect, the migration effect of Harris and Todaro, which determines the redistribution of either regional unemployment or regional real wages, is of no relevance. Unemployment will be increased by:

- the greater East German labor supply, stimulated by the removal of rationing ($RAT = 0$) and by enlarged consumption possibilities

- the transformation of disguised unemployment into open unemployment

- a lower demand for labor by the East German producers of tradables, caused by lower prices and, hence, higher real wages:

$$\Delta N^{dT}_E < 0, \text{ if } \Delta K^T_E = 0. \tag{7}$$

The growth in unemployment will be reduced by declining East German real wages in nontradables production (if $\Delta K^{NT}_E = 0$), stimulating output and labor demand. The most efficient strategy of counterbalancing negative employment effects is to promote foreign direct investment that contributes to the growth and modernization of the East German capital stock:

$$\Delta K^T_E > 0, \Delta K^{NT}_E > 0. \tag{8}$$

This investment will raise the marginal productivity of labor in tradables and production of nontradables. These effects of capital mobility can also be depicted by the migration model shown in Figure 5.3 of Claassen's chapter. The East German marginal productivity graph MPL_E will be shifted in an upward direction, and real wages in the GDR will gradually adjust toward the West German real wage level. A reduction of the producitivity and wage gap, as well as an increase in GDP, by means of East German capital imports facilitates a solution that is superior to the unlikely case of depressing real wages in the Federal Republic by means of East German exports of labor. The main problem yet to be resolved is how to substitute capital movement from West to East Germany for labor movements from East to West Germany.

Rapid economic reforms in the GDR and the credibility of a program for transformation to a market economy are the cornerstones of any solution to this problem. I agree with Claassen to the extent that the currency union will have a positive influence on the speed and credibility of these reform processes. Monetary integration alone, however, will not suffice to induce capital flows. Necessary conditions for an effective capital mobility from West to East Germany are privatization of state property, guarantees of private property rights, and an expected profitability of direct investment that is sufficient to cause an eastward reallocation of the growing world capital stock. If these conditions are not met, rapid monetary unification runs the risk of causing too much demand and excessive unemployment.

DANIEL GROS

The proposed European and German monetary unions are implemented in radically different ways. As recognized by Claassen, in the German case the Bundesbank simply extends its authority to the territory of the GDR, whereas in the European case the Bundesbank would have to participate in a system in which it would, at least formally, be only one among twelve equals. Consequently, the Bundesbank takes different positions in these two cases. I do not think, however, that German monetary union (GMU) would necessarily make the position of the Bundesbank inside the European monetary union (EMU) much stronger. At least initially, the increase in size would be offset by the fact that money demand will be less predictable in Germany, which makes the anchor role of the DM less secure.

Moreover, it should not be forgotten, and former Bundesbank president Karl Otto Pöhl has emphasized this several times, that the members of the executive board of the Eurofed should represent not their countries, but rather the general concern for price stability in Europe. This is why he has also favored the principle "one man, one vote."

In the long term, namely, after the transition period, it would be expected, however, that a GMU would increase the power of the Bundesbank, especially since central European countries would be expected to peg their currencies to the DM when several become convertible. If this happens before the Bundesbank is bound into the Eurofed, it will strengthen the Bundesbank's resistance to an EMU: the stronger its role as a leader, the stronger its resistance to making the system more symmetric by creating the Eurofed. As emphasized by Mundell, historically it has always been the case that the country whose currency was at the center of the system opposed the creation of a symmetric monetary union and that, understandably, its resistance increased with the strength of the center country.

I also disagree with the view that there are any commonalities in the field of fiscal transfers. The transfers at the European Community level are big in absolute terms, but they do not represent more than 4–5 percent of the gross domestic product (GDP) of the receiving countries, and a considerable part is in the form of loans. In the German case, the transfers will be on a different scale. Claassen himself mentions a figure of DM 100 billion, which would be 33 percent of estimated East German GDP, but even taking a lower and, I would argue, more realistic figure for the transfers, say DM 60 billion, it would still be 20 percent of East German GDP.

Turning to some potential implications of a German monetary

union, not only for the future EMU, but also for the present European monetary system (EMS), it is often argued, by academic economists at least, that a GMU should lead to a large reduction in the current-account surplus of Germany, that this reduction requires a real appreciation of the DM, and that consequently one should expect tensions inside the EMS.

The reason a reduction in a current-account surplus usually requires a real appreciation can be easily put in the standard tradables-nontradables framework. In this framework an increase in overall demand goes partly toward tradables, thus reducing the external surplus, but it also goes partly toward nontradables, whose supply is not infinitely elastic (or at least much less elastic than that of tradables), thus requiring an increase in the relative price of *nontradables*.

If this standard model is applied to the present case, however, it does not necessarily predict a real appreciation of the DM. A real appreciation of the DM would be required only if West Germans spend more. However, this will not be the case, since they lend or transfer large amounts of purchasing power to East Germans. There is, therefore, no reason why the relative price of, say, French and German nontradables (and hence the real exchange rate of the DM inside the EMS) has to change.

The relative price of East German nontradables (goods that cannot be traded between, say, Germany and France can presumably be considered as nontradables between East and West Germany) may, of course, have to change, but a large jump already occurs through the one-to-one conversion rate for wages, and further adjustments can take place through movements in wages inside the GDR.

One could even argue that the actual or expected increase in taxation in the Federal Republic needed to finance a GMU should lead to a fall in demand in that country, part of which would fall on nontradables and would require a real depreciation of the DM. This might explain why the DM is currently so weak inside the EMS. (The entire group of EMS currencies is strong against the rest of the world because of the current boom in all of Europe.)

In a nationally differentiated tradables framework, there would also be a need for a real appreciation only if East Germans (they are the ones who receive the additional purchasing power) have a high propensity to spend on West German tradables. This does not seem to be the case. With the possible exception of West German investment goods, most of the spending seems to go toward goods that are supplied by other members of the European Community and the newly industrialized countries.

Up to this point a GMU was assumed to represent a demand shock (in the sense that the average savings rate of the aggregate German economy falls, leading to a reduction in the overall German current-account surplus, because before a GMU the Federal Republic had a large surplus and the GDR had a small deficit, and after a GMU the GDR region will have a large deficit), whose effects were discussed implicitly at given factor endowments. Another approach would be to say that the GDR economy opens to trade with the rest of the world, starting out with a very low capital-to-labor ratio. This should lead to capital flows into East Germany. However, given that the German capital market is open to the rest of the world, most of the capital will come from the rest of the world (hence, the lower external surpluses). However, even in this case, a GMU should not necessarily require a change in the relative price of West German exports relative to imports, as long as one remains in the region of factor price equalization.

A last remark on European affairs. It is also often argued that a GMU represents the pure type of country-specific shock that would make it optimal to adjust exchange rates and hence makes an EMU undesirable for the time being. However, this argument is not as convincing as it appears, since, as argued above, a GMU does not necessarily require a real exchange-rate adjustment. German monetary unification does represent, however, a large financial shock, or at least a considerable increase in the variance of the potential money demand error. Since, as is well known, monetary or financial shocks make it desirable to keep exchange rates fixed, it follows that a GMU would make fixed exchange rates more desirable and implies that German monetary unification is no reason not to proceed with EMU.

The Eastern Bloc: Legal Reforms before Monetary and Macroeconomic Policies

It is generally agreed that the communist countries in the process of reform must carry out extensive privatization, establish free prices (exchange rates, in particular), and make tax and legal reforms. The question is, in what sequence?

The point here is that these countries should start with legal reforms, setting a credible agenda to which the government should then more or less adhere (more rather than less). Only when some progress is achieved in this direction should these governments move toward decontrolling prices, selling enterprises, and carrying out other decentralizing policies (Brenner 1990a). The absence of property rights, bankruptcy laws, and, in general, any traditions of the "rule of law"—and familiarity only with the "rule of men" (the powerful bureaucrats among them)—were at the root of much that was inefficient and disastrous in the way that people interacted and managed their lives under the communist regimes. The cure, therefore, should begin by dealing with this problem. How macroeconomic policies depend on progress in legal reforms is the main topic raised in the subsequent sections of this chapter.

It is first shown that, in the Eastern bloc countries, the meanings of "price level," inflationary policies, government deficits, and fiscal policies, all differ from their customary ones in the West, and they all depend on the stage of their legal reforms. Since these reforms are complex, other policies should be kept as simple as possible, in order to enable the fastest transition to reliable calculation of the profitability of enterprises (by eliminating inflationary expectations, in particular) and to prevent the continuance of well-established patterns of corruption in these countries. Simple sales and income taxes are recommended for this reason. The convertibility of currency and lack of controls on exchange rates, in general, are also recommended when looked upon from these perspectives: simplicity and the prevention of recurring procedures, bureaucracy, corruption, and extensive informal activity. As argued, convertibility is not very important unless significant legal reforms are carried out first.

Inflationary Policy and the Price Level

The fact that prices revealed no information on relative scarcity under communist regimes is well known and well documented (Brenner 1990a). Extensive black markets, long waiting lines at stores, years of waiting for apartments, cars, and household appliances, and the lack of heating and light (in Romania) implied that nominal prices and wages had little meaning as indicators of purchasing power and wealth. Calculation of any weighted average based on the quoted numbers had little meaning either. What does it mean that a pound of meat costs only a few pennies, if people cannot find it in the stores or, at best, may get it after staying in line for three hours beginning at five o'clock in the morning? Or, what does it mean to take into account rental values, when people have to wait years (or a lifetime) before finding an apartment (if at all)? The fact that prices do not rise in spite of scarcity and in spite of increases in the money supply—very much as in wartime in Western countries, when price controls and rationing are introduced— means only that the statistical measures concerning price indexes and *real* wages become useless. People in the communist countries were aware of this situation and never paid much attention to the official figures; both Romania and Hungary recently admitted that many of their statistics about both agricultural and industrial output have been nothing but pure fiction for several decades. Thus, not only were the prices used in the computation of indexes completely unreliable but so were the respective weights used in their computation.

A few numerical examples can give some idea how much higher the *true* price level may be in relation to the official one. O'Hearn (1980) summarizes a large number of estimates concerning the size of the second Soviet economy and the prices charged. He found that one-quarter to one-third of the Soviet consumption of fish and alcoholic beverages comes through the illegal economy.[1] The ratio of official to black market prices is 3:14. Neither these weights, nor the higher prices, appear in the official indexes. It is estimated that 80 percent of the muskrats caught are sold privately. State hunters receive up to three rubles per muskrat, whereas poachers get fifteen. Herodotus's *History* sells for ten rubles, whereas the official price is about three rubles (but the book cannot be found in the stores); Dumas's *Three Musketeers* sells for twenty-five rubles, whereas the official price is about two rubles. Prices of records sold in the black market are high, and many of them, just like many books, are not even legally available. For years, Georgian farmers sold their fruits and flowers (during the winter season, Georgia was among the few republics able to produce these) in the open markets rather than to the state (as required) at a token price. The black market exchange rate for the U.S. dollar during 1968 to 1977 was five times higher than the official rate. The official retail prices of new cars, appliances, and clothing do not give any idea of what their cost to buyers may be, as they must pay many bribes (not to calculate the long waiting time) before they get them (Brenner 1990a). Spare parts for cars and for appliances are produced illegally, and the repairs are also made privately. Home repairs, home decorations, and construction of homes in some areas are almost entirely a private affair (and illegal), and the prices do not appear in any official index (Brenner 1990a).

Let us assume, then, that a communist country wishes to abolish rationing and price controls. The result will be a sharp rise in the price level, but the amount will depend on the tightness of the country's monetary policy. However, such a rise does not necessarily mean that, in the specific circumstances described above, standards of living will drop significantly, even if the numerical measures show such a drop. The scarcity of products and the extensive buying on the black market implied that the price level was largely underestimated and that real wages were largely overestimated, since neither took into account the shortages, the higher prices paid in the black market, the increased nominal bribes people paid, the rationing, the long lines, or the years of waiting.

These arguments and other evidence also imply that the fear of the ruble's "overhang" (the term used to describe surplus currency in Soviet-type economies)[2] may be unjustified. The increased money supply of the past few years is probably *already* reflected in both higher black market prices and higher nominal bribes, as well as in less production in both the legal market and the black market (the decrease in production being caused, in part, by the uncertain value of the ruble).[3] If this is the case, people may accept a once-and-for-all inflationary rise in prices without much complaint, because their real standard of living—in contrast to the statistical one—may not be falling at all.

At this point, the difference widens between a Western country restoring itself after a war and a communist one in the process of reform. In the former, the abolishment of controls implies that entry of new firms and increased production of products whose relative price has risen will begin, leading to expectations of increased wealth. This mechanism, however, depends on the existence of well-established laws defining property rights, taxes, and depreciation rates; in the communist countries undergoing reform, these laws are only being discussed (in the USSR) or even when they are enacted, putting them into practice (in Poland) still seems dubious (Brenner 1990a). Thus, whereas the inflationary episode linked with the decontrol of prices is warranted and may turn out to be little more than a statistical artifact, whether such an episode leads to expectations of a better future depends on policies that have nothing to do with the monetary policy.

In fact, unless *credible* and *rapid* steps are being taken to bring about other policies, *prior* to price reforms, the abolished controls may result in much social unrest and may lead to diminished output rather than increased output. A number of reasons can be given for that. Abolishing controls means that the old system for determining prices is no longer in place. If legal reforms do not yet exist, there is no new legal, decentralized method for determining prices, since the legal basis for the new forms of enterprise are not yet in place.[4] Also, the reaction of the many losers toward policies that abolish controls but do *not* have in conjunction with them laws guaranteeing a rapid shift toward a freer economy, can only add to the uncertainty. Unless these people perceive greater opportunities in the near future (possible only through swift legal and constitutional changes), their falling behind may provoke more angry reactions, resentment, and demands for price controls again. Ruthless political demagogues and opportunists will soon exploit these demands. Giving in to such demands, however, can only slow down the rebirth of these countries.

Since it is true that legal reforms are far more complex than monetary ones, carrying them out and learning to obey them should be expected to take longer than carrying out and getting accustomed to a stable monetary policy. That is exactly why these countries should start with legal reforms and be firm about the changes in order to instill public confidence before even starting to decontrol prices. The term "decontrolling prices" is meaningless when the legal framework still does not permit a legal, decentralized method of determining prices to exist.[5] Indeed, many recent Soviet problems in regard to significantly diminished production may be due to the fact that major investment decisions continue to be taken by ministries, while alternative avenues of investment and employment are restricted.[6] In spite of much talk about legal reforms, talk is all it is. Although a few unproductive Soviet units were shut down, no evidence exists at the time of this writing (May 1990) to show that profitable units can expand.[7]

It has been argued that the fear of decontrolling prices in the USSR was based on the fact that Soviet citizens were holding large savings accounts, as well as currency, because they did not fear inflation and expected that they would find more goods in the future. In view of the evidence on the extremely high prices Soviet citizens were willing to pay in the black market (for alcoholic beverages, in particular, during the few years of Gorbachev's misguided experiment with prohibition) and the continuous decline in production, this interpretation of events seems inaccurate. A better one seems to be that most people were holding currency and savings because they had nothing on which to spend them (Desai 1989:5; Birman 1981). If this is the case, the inflation resulting in decontrolling prices and eventual increased production would even be welcome. It is simply not true that people would become "poorer" if latent inflation is allowed to come to the surface. For example, did the rubles make them rich when they could not buy anything with them in the present and did not expect to be able to buy much more in the future? As Oleg Bogomolov, director of the Institute of Economics of the World Socialist System and a member of the USSR congress, put it recently: "There is a decreasing motivation for work. The people will not work for empty rubles. The state pretends to pay wages and the people pretend to work" (Auerbach 1990). We shall come back in a subsequent section to this issue of the lack of any internal convertibility of the ruble.

The rejection of the solution of an inflationary rise may result from either a misunderstanding about what is happening and, therefore, unthinkingly applying some Western notions about the harms of inflation or from the fact that, in spite of all promises, the legal reform toward private property is extremely slow in coming. If the latter is the case, the Soviet policy makers may be right in rejecting decontrol of prices for the moment.

Another reason might be cited for the reluctance to move toward decontrol of prices. The CIA estimates suggest that 50 percent of Soviet savings deposits are held by only 3 percent of the population, and only one out of every eight Soviet citizens has any savings at all (U.S. Central Intelligence Agency 1989:6, fn. 14). What if these 3 percent belong to the powerful Soviet group of bureaucrats and political administrators who have the first opportunity to buy rationed goods at the controlled prices? The reluctance to decontrol prices might reflect the desire to protect their own interests rather than fears about a public outcry. The public might even rejoice if the ruling powers lose part of their wealth, and the effect of inflation is toward increasing equality rather than diminishing it.

It may also be that the Soviet government hopes that, by increasing production first and keeping the money supply tight from then on, prices will increase less when controls are abolished. This strategy does not seem to be a good idea for guiding the country's monetary policy— and at any rate the government was doing just the contrary—because increases in production also depend on the reliability of relative prices (reliability that is already missing when prices are controlled and that diminishes even further when the government pursues an expansionary monetary policy). In conclusion, the best policy option for the USSR, as well as for the other countries in the process of reform, would be to decontrol prices at a time when a legal framework is already at a stage where the establishment of private enterprises is feasible, so that an alternative method of price determination is in place.[8]

Let us reemphasize that when the subject of decontrolling prices in the communist countries undergoing reform is being discussed, we frequently hear about the fear of inflation—the ruble "overhang."[9] As argued above, a once-and-for-all sharp rise in the price level should not be worrisome in these circumstances, since only the latent inflation is allowed to come to the surface and people may not even complain about it. Thus, price reform should not be postponed on these grounds.

Price reform, however, is meaningful *only* if laws exist to allow managers of enterprises and entrepreneurs to set prices afterward, to have the incentive to depart from traditional methods of making decisions in an enterprise, and to produce what they expect to sell.[10] Otherwise, there is no point in decontrolling prices; it is not even clear what these words mean if the legal framework to enable freedom of contract is not in place.[11] To put it differently, there is no point in destroying the old system if a new one is not allowed to replace it.[12]

We now raise the question of how credibility will be restored, how to make people realize that the inflationary episode is a once-in-a-lifetime affair and that from then on the country's monetary authorities can be trusted to pursue inflationary policies no longer, once prices are decontrolled. The answer is simple. At this stage all that was learned from the experience of Western countries since ancient times can be used. The central bank must pursue a tight monetary policy, so that people will eventually learn to trust its decisions.

The Case of Germany

East Germany has an advantage in carrying out macroeconomic reforms. After the West German mark takes over, and if West German laws immediately become the laws of a unified Germany (its tax laws, in particular),[13] the problems mentioned in the first section should be of less concern, as the deutsche mark (DM) has credibility. If we read about fear of inflation in Germany, the fear has to do with a specific problem that differs from that typical of the other countries undergoing reform.[14] Fear of inflation is due to Chancellor Helmut Kohl's pledge to honor an exchange rate of one East German mark for one West German mark, whether for people's wages, holding of currency, pensions, or savings accounts. If the promise is carried out, will the impact necessarily be inflationary? It is not clear.

If output is expected to rise rapidly, the impact may not be inflationary. A number of reasons indicate that there will be a rapid rise in output. Not only did a young and skilled labor force move from East Germany to West Germany (more than 100,000 early in 1990 and 380,000 in 1989),[15] thus diminishing the impact of delays in legal reform in East Germany but the 1986–1990 West German tax reform lead us to expect significant increases in output, even by those who always lived in West Germany. Although the reform left top marginal tax rates at 53 percent, between the range of DM 10,000 (US$6,000) and DM 120,000 (US$72,000), marginal rates were significantly cut (by up to 20 percent). The forecast for growth rates in West Germany was 4 percent in February 1990, and tax revenues were higher than expected.[16] The question is how much the money supply will grow if Chancellor Kohl makes good on his promise.

Here are a few statistics. If the one-to-one exchange rate is chosen, it is estimated that DM 200 billion should be issued to buy up the East German mark (the rate was one-to-three, or less, before July 1990). The plan, however, is to induce the East Germans to buy their apartments and do the conversion gradually, tying up part of the savings for a number of years. Suppose that this would lead to an increase of just DM 80 billion during the first year of the unification. This number equals 19 percent of M1 and 6.5 percent of M3. East Germany's output is supposed to add roughly 15 percent to that of West Germany. If growth rates of the unified Germany turn out to be not more than 4 percent, these numbers would roughly imply a stable price level (using M1 as a guide for making this prediction). Some observers, however, suggest that 15 percent is an optimistic figure, and that East Germany will add less than that during the first years after unification, in which case some increase in the inflation rate should be expected. Bond yields in West Germany went up by 2 percent in the six months ending February 1990. Whether this was because of the expected higher inflation rate or because of expectations of increased borrowing, it is difficult to tell.[17] If the rise is due to the higher inflation rate, the plan should be revised to make the transition either more gradual than planned, with savings tied up for a longer period of time, or the East Germans should be induced to buy up not only their apartments but also newly issued stocks (in order to diminish the rate at which the money supply grows).[18] Meanwhile Chancellor Kohl made good on this promise, and prices on the West German stock market dropped 2.5 percent. Once again, it is difficult to say whether the drop is due to expectations of higher inflation rates or higher interest rates (possibly to both).

Inflationary expectations are linked in the communist countries undergoing reform with speculations about the monetization of the government deficits. Why these expectations are based on different calculations than in the West and how they are linked with the state of the legal reform are some of the issues examined in the next section.

What to Do about Current and Expected Deficits

In 1981–1985 the Soviet Union's deficits hovered around 2 percent of the officially estimated gross national product (GNP). By 1988–1989 they increased to more than 14 percent of the estimated GNP, a consequence not of increased expenditures but of diminished revenues, owing in part to the bad idea of the temporary prohibition of alcoholic beverages.[19] The increased deficits were financed by an increased supply of rubles, while prices were still controlled (Desai 1989:4). Such a practice must stop with the shift toward price reform: the emerging private sector finds it difficult to make its calculations in these countries because of the changing legal and tax structure; expectations of an inflationary policy can only make matters worse. How can these governments eliminate such expectations?

The solutions are linked, just as in the West, not necessarily with balancing the budgets (deficits can persist without inflation) but with providing the information to the public that the government has control over its revenues and expenditures—and assuring it that a mechanism is in place to make people anticipate that, when an unexpected discrepancy occurs and expenditures far exceed revenues, the changes of the difference being monetized remain small. The important issue is how well governments spend their money (Brenner 1990b).

The governments in the process of reform do not yet have such controls, one reason being the lack of advance in legal reform. Let us examine this. Of the annual Soviet budget, 15 percent is spent on subsidizing meat, dairy products, and vegetables (Dobbs 1990), and subsidies to unprofitable enterprises still consume about 30 percent to 40 percent of both the Soviet budget and the budgets of other countries. In the present stage of the legal reforms, the subsidies granted to the state enterprises are not under control. One reason is that the monetary system's role in the communist countries was automatically to lend them credit at zero or low interest rates to buy the inputs they needed to fulfill plans. The consequence was what Kornai (1980, 1982) called a "soft" budget constraint. With the shift toward decontrolling prices and wages, but without introducing either banking reforms or bankruptcy laws, the firms still lacked financial contraints. Thus, the lack of such reforms explains, in part, the persistence of inflationary expectations.[20]

Here we can see once again why decontrolling some, but not all, prices (the partial decontrol in itself being due to the fact that some legal reforms have not yet been instituted) can be harmful rather than useful, implying chaos rather than competition.[21] Unfortunately, this is what some Eastern bloc countries have done. State enterprises were freed from some controls, but the prices of their outputs often remained controlled. As a result, the enterprises were sheltered from competition through cheap credits and tax breaks. Not surprisingly, workers asked for higher wages and got them, knowing that the government would prevent bankruptcy (which would fuel inflationary expectations). Worse still, the enterprises asked for foreign loans and got them.[22]

Other reasons exist for the lack of control over government budgets when reforms do not go hand in hand and when the fundamental legal reforms are being postponed again and again (Brenner 1990a). Soviet Prime Minister Ryzhkov still speaks of five-year plans, and for 1991–1996, he announced that the reform of retail and wholesale prices had been postponed. Also, in 1989 Gorbachev still promised that basic food prices, which include fish, milk, eggs, bread, etc., would stay unchanged for three years. Such a promise implies raising expectations either for further uncontrolled "soft budgets" (and thus inflation whether latent or not), or for diminished production in a wide range of sectors where prices may be decontrolled but whose outputs are used as inputs in the sectors where prices are still being controlled. These are the two possible scenarios when, say, the prices of cattle or tractors are decontrolled, but those of milk and wheat products are not. Let us add to these revised plans the vacillating policies in regard to the Law on Cooperatives and their taxation, as well as the uncertain implications of the land-leasing law and the establishment of a new bureaucracy (the "farm committees") to supervise it, and it is not surprising that outputs did not increase (Brenner 1990a). It is surprising that they did not diminish more.[23]

How can countries escape from this maze and avoid, as much as possible, the consequences of either diminished production or inflationary expectations? Enterprises must become accustomed to budget constraints, which the government can achieve by charging them real interest rates, introducing bankruptcy laws, and being firm about both rather than letting bureaucrats make a case-by-case reevaluation of when enterprises should be allowed to go under and when they should not. Once again, we are back in the realm of the law and its rule.[24] How can bureaucrats calculate whether a state enterprise is potentially profitable after all prices are decontrolled, when, for the time being, the prices of its outputs are controlled, whereas those of its inputs are not? The unavoidable conclusion is that, once significant progress in legal reforms concerning property rights and bankruptcy laws have been made, new businesses should be encouraged to open, even if they compete directly with those owned by the state. Their performance not only puts pressure on state enterprises but also can be used as a source of information for evaluating state enterprises.

Briefly, at this stage of the legal reforms, the communist countries in the process of reform do not seem to have control over the expenditures of state enterprises. This lack of control may be one of the reasons for the persistence of inflationary expectations.

It may be asked whether the other government expenditures are under control. Let us look at the USSR. The official statistics divide expenditures into three main categories: (1) the national economy, (2) social and cultural expenditures, and (3) defense. The statistics show that each, in turn, represented a stable 55–57 percent, 33 percent, and 5 percent of the GNP for 1981–1987 (Desai 1990:4). As Desai (1989) notes, these classifications and the percentages hide more than they reveal. Indeed, even Gorbachev suggested that military expenditures represented 20 percent of the GNP (Desai 1989). Rowen and Wolf (1990), however, suggest that 30 percent of the Soviet GNP, which is about a third of the U.S. GNP, is being spent on the military.[25] Assuming that Gorbachev gave the number for strategic reasons, let us not interpret the 20 percent figure as if it implies a lack of control over these expenditures. Control over the military expenditures may provide the Soviet government with the necessary flexibility to counterbalance unexpected increases in other expenditures during the transition to a less-centralized economy.[26] Such flexibility is necessary not only because the government may be unable to predict for a while how much the state enterprises will cost, but also because the shift toward decontrolling prices brings increased unemployment,[27] with which the government will also have to deal.

Until now we have considered only government expenditures. What about revenues? How do reforms in taxation affect the calculations of the enterprises? Reforms toward privatization in the communist countries also require a complete revision of taxation. The previous ar-

guments about the enormous difficulties involving calculations of profitability, because of the issue of undefined property rights and the
uncertainty of price controls, suggest that the consequences of imposing
taxes on "profits" of private enterprises, cooperatives, and other evolving legal entities can be arbitrary, at best, and can backfire, at worst.
Taxes must thus be kept as *simple* as possible, and their calculation
should be *independent* of the evolving definition of costs and profits. A
uniformly imposed sales tax seems, therefore, an ideal solution. As to
taxes on income, certainly the confiscatory taxation of a marginal rate of
90 percent should be avoided (Brenner 1990a). There is little difference
between a communist economy and a capitalist one, if taxes in the latter
are at 90 percent. Perhaps the German reforms should be emulated.

In order to understand why simplicity is so crucial at this stage, it
may be useful to remind ourselves once again how arbitrary are all the
data that appear on the books of enterprises in the communist countries,
and how unclear the new laws are for the moment, preventing any
meaningful calculation of costs and profits to be used for taxation purposes—not to mention that hardly are some new laws announced when
revisions are being discussed (Brenner 1990a; Milanovic 1990). According to the official statistics, 25–30 percent of the GNP represents "investments," compared with about 6 to 7 percent in the United States
(Ricoeur 1990). Like everything else in Soviet official statistics, little
meaning can be given to these statistics. State enterprises are known to
give exaggerated data, either through lowering the quality of their products or introducing "new" commodities that are new only in name and
allow the enterprises to raise prices. Other data are equally unreliable.
Milanovic (1990:14–15) notes, for example, that:

> In all socialist countries state ownership was (is) a vague cate-
> gory. . . . In some cases, as in Poland, assets of enterprises were
> formally divided into two funds: state fund and enterprise fund. The
> rationale behind the idea was clear. That part of assets acquired
> through state grants should be in principle distinguished from that
> part of assets financed by workers out of their retained earnings. But
> even when financial obligations were imposed only on the first part
> of capital (e.g., paying a prescribed rate of return on the state por-
> tion) the division of capital was essentially done arbitrarily and the
> legal position of the two funds remained unclear. In other cases, like
> Yugoslavia and the Soviet Union, the situation was/is, from the legal
> point of view, even more complicated. Capital assets in Yugoslavia
> were defined to be social property, that is property of all and no-one
> in particular, which were simply given to workers for use. Similar is
> the situation in the Soviet Union where assets are deemed to be "the
> property of all people."

If we combine these aspects with the fact that for the time being prices of raw materials and many other prices are still controlled, it becomes evident that calculating the "profitability" of state enterprises becomes an accounting artifice and that profits and losses are illusionary and can give no information on whether or not the enterprise can survive under a legal system that enables competition. The transition from one legal structure to the other requires complex recalculation,[28] and will take time; only about one hundred large enterprises are expected to change ownership within the next year, even in Poland (which is, with Hungary, at the most advanced stage of its legal reforms) and two hundred in later years (out of a total of seven thousand state enterprises). Governments should, therefore, keep as simple as possible all the rest of the calculations—those involving taxation, in particular.

Let us reemphasize that, since the anticipation of changes in relative prices is already complicated in these countries because of the changing legal structure, the government should do everything in its power not to introduce additional uncertainty by pursuing either an inflationary policy (once the latent inflation is brought to surface) or a complicated tax scheme that is frequently and significantly changing.[29] Everything should be simple, promises should be kept, and mechanisms should be in place to show the public that, if some items in the budget may run out of control (because of eventual unemployment benefits or costs of retraining workers, for example), other items in the budget are flexible enough to rapidly diminish the effects.

Exchange Rate Practices

The socialist countries were socialist only in name (Brenner 1990a). Inequalities within them were probably as great as in Western countries. Ceausescu and his associates had a number of palaces and Swiss bank accounts at their disposal, the Soviet leaders had their dachas and the privileges of better education, better health care, foreign travel, etc., and the privileged bureaucracy used the legal system to maintain its power and obtain benefits (Brenner 1990a). Controls on internal and international economic activity, in particular, have served and (unless significant reforms are made) will continue to serve the bureaucracy—those who are skilled in dealing with such controls and those who have the right political connections. The one characteristic feature of controls on exchange rates, surcharges on imports, taxes on imported goods, licenses, quotas, lists of authorized and unauthorized imports of goods, regulations on foreign investments, tax reimbursements, or bilateral and countervailing agreements[30] is that they all maintain the bureaucracy's grip on the economy. Even if, in some circumstances, arguments can be invented to justify any of these interventions, in the case of the communist countries undergoing reform, these benefits seem small in relation to the large cost that they impose by perpetuating the arbitrariness of decisions within the bureaucratic framework. Diminishing the bureaucracy's grip and legal reform should be the priorities of the countries in the process of reform.

In addition to simplicity and diminished bureaucracy, other reasons can be found for recommending lack of control on exchange rates, such as diminished illegal trade and elimination of the black market. As noted above and discussed in detail elsewhere (Brenner 1990a), illegal transactions in the USSR are all-pervasive. Control of exchange rates would help to maintain these traditions rather than let people learn to live with the law. How will controls work in a society well adjusted to circumventing laws and regulations (Winston 1974:49–65)? In Pakistan, Peru, Turkey, and other countries with well-established traditions of corruption (not dissimilar from the USSR) this is how it worked. Bureaucrats decided to grant an enterprise the right to import machinery at the *fictitious* invoice price rather than at the price it actually paid (entrepreneurs having the incentive to overvalue the merchandise because of the controls). The enterprise then had the right to buy the foreign exchange at the official rate, making a profit on the difference between the over-invoicing and what it actually paid.[31] The consequence of the control, however, was more than over-invoicing. Firms had the incentive to exaggerate the benefits of imports and foreign aid, and they invested in sectors that were import-intensive (trying to depreciate the imported machinery as quickly as possible). They also wasted resources in competing for the access to foreign currency. Moreover, interest groups were created that invented arguments against devaluation and decontrol on the grounds of harm to industrial development and the need to protect both infant industries and those in the "nation's interest" (Brenner 1987:ch. 7). The interest groups were not merely the firms who benefited from over-invoicing; others were the bureaucracy in charge of controlling foreign exchange transactions and the police who enforced the law, up to a point (Brenner 1990a). The impact of such controls turns out to be just the contrary of what these countries in the process of reform now need. Imports are subsidized in those sectors that the government would be most interested in developing locally, and since the machinery is imported from the West, they save on relatively unskilled labor, a resource that they have in abundance.[32] Moreover, the controls maintain the bureaucracy's grip and favor the persistence of the long tradition of bribes, corruption, and investment for getting favors (causing diminished investment in other more necessary areas).[33]

Devaluation and convertibility would prevent all these situations from happening. One does not need to be an expert to imagine far more favorable outcomes when this ingenuity and the willingness to take risks, instead of being invested in innovations to circumvent bad laws and bad regulations, are applied toward other goals.

This policy of lack of control over exchange rates, just like the policy of decontrolling prices, is meaningful only if *other* reforms occur first.[34] Internally, serious progress in legal reform must be made and also latent inflation must be allowed to surface and then be kept under control. Otherwise, convertibility and lack of control over exchange rates cannot work, since there will be very little that these countries can offer to the outside world. It should be noted that for the time being the ruble is not convertible even *inside* the USSR. Why?

There are two main reasons. One reason is that enterprises cannot really buy goods from one another; the exchanges depend on plans and on the ability of the factories to circumvent them (Brenner 1990a). Even if an enterprise (a foreign investor, in particular) had billions of rubles, it could not use them to place orders. Only 5 percent of interenterprise transactions in 1988 were made through contracts (Ricoeur 1990). The rest were made because of orders from "above." The continuing price controls and lack of progress in legal reforms suggest that this practice will continue. How can convertibility be of much use to a foreign investor in such circumstances? How can enterprises that were not planned obtain their resources or sell their outputs within such a rigid, centralized system?

The extensive and unjustified attention to convertibility is probably due to the much-publicized barter exchanges—for example, the US$3 billion PepsiCo Inc. deal, according to which the company received ten tankers and freighters and huge shipments of Stolichnaya vodka and other things in return for its investment. Kaj Harber, who teaches Soviet and Eastern European Law at the University of Uppsala in Stockholm and who has taken part in negotiations for forty-five joint ventures between Soviet and Western companies, points out that, whereas new laws have been introduced, "the new Soviet law decrees that joint ventures need to earn their own hard currency if they are to pay dividends to business partners in hard currency. The easiest way to earn hard currency is to export. But no Western company in its right mind would set up a manufacturing facility in the Soviet Union to produce and export products to the West."[35] The other problem with joint ventures is still that the new laws are either badly written (Brenner 1990a), or that bureaucrats decide on an interpretation that cannot be easily challenged. An example is Stockman's, a Helsinki department store that has been doing business in Moscow for years, shipping orders to Moscow's Western community. It opened a small food store in Moscow, relying on the new laws for joint ventures. For a while it was a big success, but now it remains empty. The reason? According to the regulation, joint ventures can import products only "for their own needs." This regulation was interpreted by some bureaucrats as implying that imports cannot just be resold (Whitney 1990). Thus, whereas there is little doubt that lack of convertibility both prevents foreign investments and maintains the bureaucracy's power, the point made here is that its impact may be small, if significant legal reforms are not made.[36]

We can learn a lesson from successful joint ventures in the Soviet Union. Let us take the case of a factory manufacturing packaging equipment, for example. In spite of the lack of convertibility, lack of infrastructure, and all the rest of the problems that plague the Soviet economy, its success is due to the fact that the responsible ministry has made it a "top project" and "it is instructing everyone to cooperate."[37] This example shows the unreliability of the present system; the arbitrary decision of a few bureaucrats turned this project into a success. The success was due to the traditional Soviet pattern of procedure—the rule of men—and was not due to any fundamental reform.

The second reason for the ruble's lack of internal convertibility is the government's inflationary policy (owing to the monetized deficits). As noted earlier, people produced less and, fearing greater shortages, refused to sell. The Baltic republics began in 1989 to ban the sale of most of their products to "outsiders." In turn, as Goldman (1990) notes, since Leningrad residents were dependent on the Baltic region for food supplies, the authorities there put restrictions on shoppers from other areas. By mid-January 1990, only legal residents could buy food in a Leningrad shop. In retaliation, the city of Novgorod imposed similar restrictions, and apparently other cities followed suit (Moscow among them). Goldman also notes that in 1990:

> Residents of the suburban towns of Solnechnogorsk and Kineshma complain that Moscow suppliers refuse to sell them building materials. Much the same thing happened in Kazakhstan and Uzbekistan, when they imposed bans on "exports" to other Soviet republics. Similarly Azerbaidjan strictly limits what it sells and allows to be shipped to Armenia. . . . Lithuania and Estonia, for example, in order to protect themselves from the continuing collapse of the ruble, have toyed with the idea of introducing their own currencies next year.

Needless to say, making the ruble convertible outside the USSR has little meaning if the money is not even being accepted within the country.

The main reason for not expecting much success from convertibility is that, even independent of inflationary policies, the ruble was (and is) not even internally convertible because of central planning.

The current half-baked policies did not (and will not) provide a solution for dealing with exchange rates. A decree passed on August 19, 1986, giving the exporting enterprises the right to use part of their currency earnings for further imports and using some adjustment coefficients for other enterprises to help them calculate a realistic exchange rate, turned out to lead only to further accounting manipulations, erroneous calculations, and bureaucratic interference. Such regulations implied, as did others, that the same firms should both import and export goods, the hard currency being nontransferable (Ricoeur 1990). According to some Soviet economists, this regulation prevented small and medium-size enterprises from becoming competitive, since they could not get the hard currency needed to import machinery. In order to solve this problem, a new decree was passed on December 2, 1988, making it legal to auction foreign exchange, *but* only Soviet export firms were allowed to take part in the auction (and even they had to pass through the bureaucracy by asking written permission to participate). The bureaucrats had the right to refuse the demand and, not surprisingly, the amounts exchanged through auctions remained minuscule.[38] With such regulations, it is difficult to see when convertibility can be achieved, and calculations by the firms are made even more difficult.[39]

What Should Be Done?

There is no point in talking about convertibility and lack of controls on exchange rates in the countries in the process of reform before the following occur:

1. A definite move is made toward legal reforms to enable a decentralized method of determining most prices. Prices can thus be determined when enterprises are set up, are free to expand (or go bankrupt), and can produce whatever they want;

2. Once such a move is made, the latent inflation should be allowed to surface by decontrol of prices. At this point, controls on exchange rates should be abolished, and convertibility should be permitted.[40]

3. The tax and revenue system of the government is revised, shifting toward the *simplest* possible taxation (a sales tax and a simple income tax), in order to enable enterprises to calculate their profitability and diminish the role of the bureaucracy.[41]

Meanwhile, little evidence exists to show that the USSR is dealing seriously with any of these problems, or that its leaders understand that frequent changes in their plans can only make matters worse. On April 10, 1990, for example, Gorbachev announced that reforms planned for 1992–1993 will be introduced within the next twelve months. Among them are: (1) creation of joint-stock enterprises, (2) liberalization of laws on foreign investment, and (3) initiatives toward making the ruble fully convertible (Dobbs 1990).

These announcements were made after Gorbachev admitted that the Soviet economy had shrunk every month during 1990 by 1.2 percent on average. Ten days later, Gorbachev announced that he was slowing down the pace of change.[42] Under such circumstances, with little progress being made in other reforms, convertibility does not seem to be essential. Moreover, far greater danger exists in Gorbachev's continuously vacillating policies, since they enable the opposition to organize and sabotage his reforms.[43]

We may only guess how nonessential this particular reform might be at this stage, for the available data on the USSR are not reliable, and additional information does not help. As noted, the Central Intelligence Agency (CIA) has painted until now a far more pessimistic outlook of the USSR than the official statistics indicated. A group of seventeen Soviet economists visiting Washington in April 1990 suggested, however, that even the CIA picture was too rosy.[44] They described an economy about half the size the CIA had estimated for years (and with a military budget of not 20 percent, but 40 percent of the GNP), and a living standard less than that of Brazil. How much then can the Soviets sell to foreigners?[45] The fact that Soviet negotiators recently offered the British firm, Rank Xerox, a selection of live falcons, racing camels, and goat horns in return for photocopying machines may suggest how desperate they are (Rank Xerox refused the deal). If this is what the Soviets can sell, what will give their currency credibility? Even gold may not help, since their gold stock may be quickly depleted; at any rate, just how much gold they have is also a matter of speculation.[46] Another reason for the reluctance to move toward convertibility is political; convertibility would reveal to the world officially and without further doubts how far the Soviets have fallen behind the West, and thus show that one of the world's "emperors" had no clothes.[47]

Notes

1. The production of alcoholic beverages during the few years that Gorbachev experimented with prohibition came entirely from the illegal sector, of course.

2. Estimates for the "overhang" vary between 160 billion and 500 billion rubles. See Desai (1989) and Bush (1990). More about the reliability of figures coming from the USSR will appear later in this chapter.

3. To a large extent, however, it may be a result of the changing legal structure, about which the Soviet leaders change their minds almost daily. Desai (1989:5) also notes that "in a rare display of *glasnost* . . . [official sources admitted] that the price index of produce in collective farm markets . . . rose at 2.6 percent in 1981–1985 but much more rapidly at 9.4 percent in 1986." The report of Goskomstat, the state committee for statistics, claimed a nominal increase of 3 percent in gross national product (GNP) for 1989. It mentioned an inflation rate of 2 percent only, but admitted that "taking into account the increase in unsatisfied demand, the scale of inflation in the consumer sector reached 7.5%," as quoted in Bush (1990). What the latter number means, or how it was calculated, is anybody's guess. Other estimates put the inflation rate for 1989 well into double digits, suggesting a severe decline in output.

4. Since a great deal of the production was arranged through bribery and personal contacts, expectations of a shift toward a society where the law will rule may induce fear of continuing with such arrangements. Thus, the traditional methods of "contracting" may be abandoned. Unless an alternative arises, the result may be diminished production.

5. As noted above, the decentralized, *illegal*, one already exists.

6. The resolution of the Council of Ministers on December 29, 1988, prohibited cooperatives from making vodka, weapons, and drugs and from publishing books, making films, establishing schools, dealing in foreign currency, and providing major medical services. See Desai (1990:16).

7. See Desai (1990). She also notes that the more profitable the enterprise is, the higher the rate is at which it is taxed. The less fertile the land is, the higher the price is that the state pays for the products originating from it. Also, for reasons discussed in Brenner (1990a), workers' salaries are still kept rather uniform. All these factors prevent a successful private sector from emerging. The restriction on the growth of cooperatives and private ventures can be achieved not only by restriction of property rights but also by high taxation—actions the Soviets seemed to take.

8. Of course, such a decontrol would enable the establishment of banking institutions that would offer savings accounts at whatever the interest rates would turn out to be.

9. See Shelton (1990), who notes that "Mr. Gorbachev and his advisers decided that . . . reform could not be introduced while such strong inflationary pressures existed." The argument is wrong, as pointed out in the text.

10. Some people recommended selling the apartments in which people were living in order to "absorb" the money surplus. Considering the fact that

apparently a large percentage of urban dwellers share bathrooms and kitchens, how is such a purchase possible without legal reforms? Who can use the kitchens and bathrooms if and when an apartment is bought? Can an additional kitchen and bathroom be built? And if so, by whom?

11. In addition to all the restrictions discussed, it should also be noted that, whereas in Poland factories can employ as many people as they want, in Hungary there is a limit of five hundred, and in Yugoslavia of only twenty, after many years of less than totalitarian regime. See "Survey of Eastern Europe," *The Economist*, August 12, 1989, p. 6.

12. Some may consider as being far from reality the statement that most people would not complain about the inflationary episode, yet a poll taken in Poland on January 21–22, 1990, following the experience of an annual inflation rate of about 700 percent, suggests that people are confident (only farmers and miners are complaining loudly). It was found that 80 percent of Poles would still vote for Solidarity, and communists would get only 1 percent of the votes. See "Bye-bye Queues," *The Economist*, January 27, 1990, p. 48. The poll was taken by *The Economist* and *Los Angeles Times*. What these numbers suggest is that the inflationary episode is being viewed very differently in Poland than it would be in a Western-type economy, where it would be quite unlikely for governments pursuing an inflationary policy to get such overwhelming approval. One reason might be that Poland, perhaps more than the other countries, seems committed to making sweeping legal reforms (although they are now mainly on paper).

13. East Germany was taxing profits at a rate of 90 percent. See Roth (1990).

14. We cannot consider all inflationary episodes as alike, and we must pay attention to the specific circumstances of each country.

15. While West Germany's population had been stagnating or even declining since the mid-1970s, it grew by more than 1 percent in 1989 alone. The immigrants are younger than West Germany's aging population; roughly 40 percent are between 25 and 45 years, compared with 27 percent of the existing West German population. Employment in 1989 increased by 350,000, and unemployment diminished by 210,000. See *Viewpoint*, Economics Department of Commerzbank, D-6000, Frankfurt and Main, no. 1/90.

16. See "German Digestion," *Wall Street Journal*, editorial, February 16, 1990.

17. Information on some of the numbers comes from "D-mark Uber Alles," editorial, *The Economist*, March 3, 1990.

18. Needless to say, the one-to-one exchange should not imply that *wages* in East Germany can be maintained at their previous nominal value when they are eventually paid in West German marks. Since productivity in East Germany is much lower, this would imply bankrupting of factories and loss of jobs, unless the factories are subsidized.

19. Prohibition on drinking and gambling have always had bad consequences, and not only on government budgets. See Brenner and Brenner (1990). In particular, in a country where entertainment alternatives are few, where did Gorbachev expect his people to bury their sorrow and forget for a while their present misery? His arguments sounded exactly like those of the English

moralists of the eighteenth and nineteenth centuries, who also misunderstood the reasons for people's frequent visits to pubs and thought that drinking and gambling were the main reasons for the English workers' lower productivity and, eventually, England's decline. See Brenner and Brenner (1990:ch. 3). Soviet citizens and their government would be far better off if, instead of prohibiting drinking, the government would let gambling and betting businesses flourish (in fact, betting on sports has been legal and popular in the communist countries, and the premiums paid on winning tickets were a sign of the widespread existence of the black markets.)

20. The Hungarians and the Poles have broken up their old banking system, and their central banks have the same roles as in the West. Commercial banks are now in the business of borrowing and lending and may compete (up to a point). Czechoslovakia said it would introduce a similar reform, but announced that the banks may be prevented from competing. Yugoslavia is only now considering revising its banking system. See "Survey of Eastern Europe," *The Economist*, August 12, 1989, p. 7. Thus, transfer of lending functions to banks, based on commercial principles, would be the solution.

21. Wage control in such enterprises is thus critical until there is a shift toward "harder" budget constraints that take into account both the penalties imposed by bankruptcy and a real interest rate.

22. In the USSR a promise was made to end subsidies to 7,500 state enterprises. It was not carried out. See Desai (1989:16). Also see "Eastern Europe's Economies," *The Economist* (January 13, 1990:22).

23. So many rules and regulations exist that the way to get around them is to bribe those who enforce them. Today people are perhaps more afraid of accepting bribes. Thus, the usual mechanism through which business was conducted may have broken down. This may be an additional reason for the diminished output. See Brenner (1990a).

24. Otherwise, we can expect even more haggling, discontent, and struggling for the smaller government outlays that remain, as long as they are politically determined.

25. On a per capita basis, it is even lower, as the population of the USSR is 280 million (if the figures are at all reliable).

26. The West might help to enable Gorbachev to have this flexibility.

27. Among both bureaucrats and in the rest of the labor force. See Brenner (1990a), discussing the magnitude of the problem.

28. The division into two funds has little meaning, since workers know that they will be bailed out whenever they find themselves in financial difficulties—and at a zero interest rate. Milanovic (1990) explains that, because of the vague legal concepts existing when reforms were announced in Hungary, the first impact was to centralize and then sell the enterprises, in order to clear up the issue of ownership.

29. Mistakes in calculations will occur; they are unavoidable in these circumstances. All that the government can do is to diminish the probability that its own actions will be the source of error.

30. See a similar list mentioned in a different context in de Soto (1989).

31. The incentives to do so diminish when there are tariffs, since the importer must pay the tariff also on the "imaginary" import.

32. Also see Winston (1974), making similar arguments in the context of Pakistan.

33. Entrepreneurs are far more ingenious than bureaucrats can imagine. To give just one example, over-invoicing can take endless forms—from misstatement of invoice value and shortages in actual shipment to substitution of old machinery for new (and then blaming Western businessmen for selling products of a shoddy quality). See Winston (1974), who describes Pakistani entrepreneurship diverted to such directions. It should not be forgotten that Soviet managers have had experience in pursuing such strategies for decades.

34. As long as the state enterprises are given credit and can borrow from abroad, putting the emerging private enterprises at a disadvantage (state enterprises can borrow more easily, as the lenders are not afraid of bankruptcy), convertibility can be harmful rather than useful.

35. See "A Slowdown for Soviet Joint Ventures," *New York Times Forum*, April 15, 1990.

36. A better solution than barter could be to exchange debt or rubles for shares in enterprises, after progress in legal reforms is made.

37. See "A Slowdown for Soviet Joint Ventures," *New York Times Forum*, April 15, 1990.

38. Apparently, less than US$1 million is exchanged. See Ricoeur (1990).

39. Which rate should they use to calculate profitability of imports and exports: the black market rate, the one determined at the auction, the one determined by the bureaucracy for some sectors (but nobody knows for how long), or some other rate?

40. The experience of New Zealand and some Latin American countries suggesting that freeing of prices and firms should be preceded by fiscal and monetary stabilization seems irrelevant, since these countries had a legal framework in place that could allow a shift toward a private sector and a decentralized method of determining prices.

41. As far as simplicity is concerned, it may be argued that, although rules are complex in the West and still successful, perhaps rules should not be simple. This argument may be wrong, because we do not know how much better off we would be if laws and regulations were simpler. Rules may not be made simple because too many groups are interested in complexity. See Brenner (1990b).

42. See Michael Parks, "Gorbachev Slows Down Pace of Change: Conservatives See Risk of Upheaval If Reforms Go Ahead," *Los Angeles Times*, as reprinted in *The Gazette*, April 24, 1990.

43. It took ten years for countries in Western Europe to recover from World War II and return to currency convertibility. Meanwhile, they received help and their debts were canceled. In their January meeting this year, Eastern bloc leaders decided that from now on the Council for Mutual Economic Assistance would use world market prices for products and change the accounting system to use convertible currency. Until then, they were calculated in a fictitious

currency (the "transferable ruble"), and prices of goods were negotiated. See Gumbel (1990). Why did the Soviets agree to that? The reason is that the Soviets will benefit because they sell oil and gas, which they can sell in world markets, whereas the Eastern bloc sells to the USSR shoddy machinery that they cannot sell in the West. If Eastern Europe and the Baltic republics paid world prices for Soviet oil and gas, Moscow would earn an estimated US$14.6 billion, increasing annual hard currency income by 40 percent. See Robinson (1990).

44. Relatively reliable figures for the USSR were thought to come from the Central Intelligence Agency's reports and from a series published jointly by the Bank for International Settlements and the Organization for Economic Cooperation and Development. They suggest, for example, that foreign debt increased from US$1.8 billion in 1971 to US$48 billion in 1989, although in a recent speech Prime Minister Ryzhkov gave a higher figure for 1989. Bush (1990) argues that Ryzhkov might have raised the figure for political reasons, to counter a lobby that has argued for massive imports of consumer goods to diminish discontent. We just do not know. Also see Rowen and Wolf (1990).

45. See Paul A. Gigot, "Gorbo Goes out of Fashion in Washington," *Wall Street Journal*, April 12, 1990.

46. The size of Soviet gold production and reserves is a state secret. The CIA estimates production to be about 11 million troy ounces a year and reserves to be about 75 million troy ounces. At US$400 an ounce, that would put them at US$4.4 billion and US$30 billion, respectively. But if the CIA was wrong about other figures, why would we trust this figure? As Morgenstern (1965) and Sayers (1976) showed, even Western countries gave misleading information about gold. Recently, some Soviet commentators have speculated that the cost of producing gold in the USSR is far more than its world price. See Bush (1990). Schroder (1988) argues that, already in 1986, Soviets were selling more gold than they produced, estimating the 1986 sales in the range of US$3 billion to US$4 billion.

47. How can the West help? As noted here, it should accommodate by diminishing military budgets. It may also accept immigrants, who may turn out to be a good export for the Eastern bloc (sending hard currency home), and a good investment for the aging population of the West. Once again, Germany is in a better position than the rest of the Eastern bloc countries. Once East Germans become German citizens, they can work anywhere within the European Community (although it is not yet clear how this or other relations with the European Community will develop). Let us add a last note on the uncertain state of the Soviet economy. According to the official exchange rate, the Soviet GNP equals that of the United States. According to the unofficial exchange rate, however, it is closer to that of Belgium.

Comments

JOHN WILLIAMSON

The central thesis of this fascinating paper is that no reforms can be productive in socialist countries until the legal system has been reformed in order to replace the rule of men with the rule of law. Since there are not many robust generalizations about the sequencing of reform that are yet established in the literature, it is worth considering carefully whether this claim is convincing.

It is useful to start by making a list of the various reforms that have to be sequenced. My list would be as follows:

1. Legal reforms

2. Stabilization, covering fiscal discipline, absorption of any monetary overhang, and the hardening of budget constraints (or perhaps the latter should be a separate entry)

3. Price liberalization

4. Financial liberalization

5. Trade liberalization, covering establishment of a competitive exchange rate, the abolition of quantitative restrictions, nonprohibitive tariffs, and currency convertibility on current account

6. Privatization

7. Deregulation (if not included under item 1 above)

8. Tax reform

Brenner envisages legal reform covering two areas. One is the establishment of property rights—that is, spelling out by law who had the right to determine the use of the various material resources in society. The other is bankruptcy law—that is, establishment of who forfeits command over resources if they are used unproductively. It would be an enormously valuable contribution to the current debate if Brenner could draw on his unusual background (as an economist highly trained in the

Western tradition who has also lived under a socialist regime) in order to spell out explicitly the scope and content of the legal provisions that are needed. Those of us who have lived all our lives in a market economy find it difficult to pin down the nature of the infrastructure of capitalism that we take for granted.

Is it true that these legal reforms need to precede all the other reforms before any of these others can be effective? As bankruptcy laws are an essential part of hardening the budget constraint, stabilization is unlikely to be achieved before legal reform; nevertheless, there seems to be no reason for delaying either fiscal discipline or privatization designed to absorb the monetary overhang. Similarly, prices cannot prudently be decontrolled until enterprises are subject to hard budget constraints and bankruptcy provisions are in place, but price adjustments designed to relieve bottlenecks need not await decontrol. It also seems likely that the efficiency gains expected from price liberalization depend upon a clear assignment of responsibility for taking decisions on pricing policy.

Financial liberalization should certainly not precede institution of the discipline imposed by potential bankruptcy (as the sad story of the U.S. savings and loans has again demonstrated). Perhaps the same can be argued regarding trade liberalization. Neither privatization nor deregulation would seem feasible until the rights and responsibilities of ownership are established. However, I do not perceive any precondition for tax reform. Thus, my preliminary judgment is that, while there are some areas of reform that the government can prudently address even before the legal framework has been sorted out, Brenner has a strong case for arguing the urgency of legal reform.

It should be emphasized that, when Brenner speaks of "lack of control on exchange rates," he is advocating currency convertibility and an absence of quantitative restrictions on trade rather than freely floating exchange rates. It should also be recognized that the prime purpose of convertibility in the Eastern European context is not to attract foreign investors—whose contribution, while doubtless useful, is bound to be marginal (except possibly in Germany)—but rather to enable these countries to replace the hopelessly distorted price systems that they have inherited from the past with the world price structure, which can provide a ready-made indicator of relative scarcities.

Intraregional Convertibility in Eastern Europe: Is It Still an Issue?

The currencies of the Eastern European countries and of the USSR are not convertible, in the sense that they may not be purchased or sold against other currencies at a single exchange rate without restrictions and for all purposes. This implied definition of convertibility is, indeed, an extensive one. It may be argued that some currencies are already partly convertible into some other currencies and under some conditions, as is the case since January 1990 for the Polish zloty. Overall, the starting point is, however, a situation of nonconvertibility. It is generally assumed that these countries should make their currencies convertible and that convertibility is an important part of their transition process toward a market economy, as well as a way of integrating themselves into the world economy (meaning the Western economy).

The focus of this chapter is a particular one. What is generally discussed is the convertibility of the Eastern European currencies into the dominant Western currencies—for instance, the U.S. dollar or the deutsche mark. Should this be achieved, it is assumed that these Eastern currencies would automatically be convertible into *all* other convertible currencies. Would they be convertible among themselves? This question is hardly raised by Western experts, especially by specialists on exchange rate policies, who would consider the issue irrelevant. Why should anyone in any Eastern European country want to hold balances in other Eastern European currencies, except for some limited purposes (such as tourism) for which a limited convertibility exists? The Eastern European experts do not raise the question either. Mostly, they want to find ways to get access to "hard currency," which is their implicit definition of convertibility. The need for convertibility *among* Eastern European currencies seems to have disappeared since the members of the Council for Mutual Economic Assistance (CMEA), regrouping the USSR and six Eastern European countries (along with three developing countries that will not be discussed here), have agreed to shift toward foreign trade conducted in world prices and settled in hard currencies beginning in 1991.

As of May 1990, the picture was the following:

1. Most Eastern European countries have declared that they want to make their currency convertible, implicitly into Western currencies (and the USSR has also stated this as an ultimate long-term aim). Poland claims that it has already achieved such convertibility. All these countries may individually expect Western help in achieving or maintaining convertibility, either already (Poland and Hungary) or in the near future.

2. As for intraregional trade and payments, the usual approach, both in the West and in Eastern Europe, was that trade should be conducted at a minimum level, with a price and payments system "borrowed" from the West. Nobody seems to care for a more or less permanent regulation of intraregional payments, under the assumption that the problems should just disappear along with the withering away of the CMEA.

Although with some reservations, I agree with the few Western experts who suggest a new European Payments Union for Eastern Europe. True, conditions in 1990 there are not comparable with postwar conditions in the West. Helping each Eastern European country in isolation to achieve the convertibility of its currency is not apt to solve all the problems, but there is merit in trying to make Eastern European currencies convertible among themselves in a concerted way. The shift to settlements in hard currencies among these countries is not an adequate response because (1) it cannot be applied to all settlements, and (2) it will inevitably act as a restrictive factor in trade. The second argument may be dismissed by those who consider that reduction of mutual trade should precisely be the aim of Eastern Europe. I challenge this opinion.

The West is understandably mainly interested in the issue of convertibility because the convertibility of Eastern domestic currencies into Western currencies will solve such problems as the repatriation of profits generated by joint ventures and will decrease countertrade demands. Should we be happy with the lack of any concerted monetary policy among the countries of Eastern Europe, with artificial exchange rates between their currencies distorting rational decisions in commercial matters? Can we really adhere to such a stance, while we are advocating a monetary union in the West? Here again, we have to be innovative. A "transferable ruble" cannot be recreated, but other solutions may be devised by looking at the past in Europe and also at the present in many less-developed regions of the world.

Let us first start from an overview of the settlements system in transferable rubles as it operated until 1989 and of the previous attempts to achieve convertibility of the socialist currencies among themselves. Then, let us examine some suggestions for a reform of the intraregional system of settlements, arguing that the absence of a reform would be extremely harmful to the region as a whole. Finally, let us examine the feasibility of schemes drawing on the experience of the past, as well as that of existing monetary unions or regional arrangements in the third world.

The CMEA Settlement System: Trade without Money

It has often been said that CMEA trade was in reality a form of barter. This may be a true statement. The CMEA countries, however, had a formal system of settling their mutual balances. This system took its final form in 1964, with the creation of a "common socialist currency," as it was referred to in CMEA documents—the transferable ruble. The operation of this currency was far from satisfactory, and just at the beginning of glasnost in the USSR, a Soviet author referred to it as a "stillborn child" (Shmelev 1987). Beginning in 1971, numerous attempts have been made to improve this system and all have failed, because the underlying system of trade and economic relations was not substantially modified.

The transferable ruble: a "stillborn child"

Let us first recall the basic features of the intra-CMEA trade system. Bilateral negotiations between countries, at the government level, fix the nature and the quantities of the goods to be traded in the next period, resulting in five-year trade agreements detailed in annual trade protocols. This process involves bargaining, in which each country tries to obtain the greatest quantities of "hard goods," while offering as little as possible of such goods, and tries to sell "soft goods." Hard goods are the goods in short supply within the CMEA region that also may be sold on Western markets in return for hard currency (such as raw materials, energy carriers, and food products). Soft goods are the goods for which supply exceeds demand on the CMEA market and that cannot easily be sold in the West (such as manufactures, especially machinery). Prices used in this trade are not market prices; if they were, the prices for soft goods would have tended to be relatively low, while prices for hard goods would be relatively high. Instead, intra-CMEA prices are, in principle, based on world prices. According to the current regulation, applied since 1975, prices are negotiated each year on the basis of the average world price for a given item over the five previous years. In actual practice, as it is difficult, if not impossible, to identify a "world" price for goods other than commodities (which happen to fall into the category of hard goods), the prices for manufactures are negotiated in bilateral bargaining. The fiction of a world price, however, remains. Each partner tries to document the price he is asking for, or willing to pay, through a reference to capitalist world prices, using catalogs, invoices, etc.

All transactions are expressed in the accounting unit called "transferable ruble" (TR). The TR, created in 1964, replaced the clearing ruble previously used, and it had the same definition. Both units were initially derived from the "devisa-ruble" (the accounting unit used by the Soviet Union to convert its foreign trade figures expressed in various foreign currencies into a like unit linked with the major Western currencies through an arbitrary, and overvalued, exchange rate). The TR, thus, was not anything like the U.S. dollar in Western international trade. Soviet *domestic* currency is not convertible and is not used in international trade. The devisa-ruble is just an accounting unit. The very name of the TR was symbolic of Soviet domination of the CMEA (another reason why the Eastern European countries do not want to refer to it now).

The name "transferable ruble" is misleading. It was never convertible, nor transferable. Intra-CMEA settlements are related to exchanges of goods that are bilateral for the most part. Almost no unallocated free goods are available to buy on the CMEA market outside the network of trade agreements. Multilateral trade has accounted in the past for 1 percent of total CMEA trade, at most. When the TR was introduced, however, it was supposed to allow for multilateral settlements. Country A having a trade surplus with country B was supposed to be able to use this surplus to settle its deficit with a creditor country C. In fact, this scheme never worked. No C country was interested in getting additional TRs, because there was no way to spend them on the acquisition of goods in the CMEA region. Conversely, it is in the interest of any bilateral debtor B to remain in this position, as it means that the country has obtained more goods from its partner than it has sold. Another way of expressing it is to say that the TR is not convertible into goods, thus precluding its transferability. A similar situation occurs in the domestic centrally planned economies—that is, when goods are allocated under an administrative scheme, even when money exists nominally, such money cannot be considered as convertible into goods.

The multilateralization of settlements would have been feasible only if balances in TRs could be spent on purchases in any member country of the CMEA, outside the bilateral quota system, or, alternatively, if these balances could be converted into hard currencies. Both solutions have been contemplated. The first would have amounted to a *commodity convertibility* of the TR, the second, to a *financial convertibility*. Both have failed, because they would have required a complete transformation of the CMEA system into a genuine market, which would, in turn, have required a marketization of the domestic economies.

Indeed, a mechanism existed that ensured settlements among the CMEA countries. Beginning in 1964, it was operated by the International Bank for Economic Cooperation (IBEC). The IBEC acted as an accounting center, recording the transactions in TRs. It also extended credits in TRs, but these credits were totally automatic, as they acknowledged the existence of accounting deficits with the CMEA area as a whole. The debtor country had to pay interest in TRs, in reality increasing its accounting deficit in TRs, as recorded in the bank. The restoration of the balance was, in fact, only achievable through *real* (as distinct from *monetary*) processes, and it implied direct negotiations on a bilateral level between the debtor and each of its creditors, without any interference by the IBEC. Then, could it be said, as some scholars do (Palankai 1990), that the issue of whether or not the CMEA should be dissolved is not relevant, as the CMEA has played no role in trade among its members? I do not think so. The artificial mechanism of the TR had three consequences with distorting effects—fragmentation of intra-CMEA trade, differentiation of exchange rates, and hard currency trade—all of which might have been at least partly avoided if the mechanism had remained totally bilateral.

Fragmentation of intra-CMEA transactions.

- *trade in goods* at international socialist prices. As has been mentioned above, these prices are based upon "world" prices converted into TRs by using the official (commercial) rate of the TR that was initially identical to that of the "devisa-ruble."

- *trade in services* (such as passenger transport, tourism, settlements linked with small manpower movements between CMEA countries, and payments for maintenance of embassies and other organizations in a given country). This "non-commercial" trade had to be separated from the "commercial" trade, because even "derived" world prices could not be applied, owing to the fact that the actual transactions (expenses of tourists, payments of transport fares, etc.) had to be made in the currency and at the *domestic* prices of the country providing the service.

- *transactions linked with the operation of joint ventures or the realization of joint investments.* This is again a different case. A joint investment (for example, the building of a pipeline in the Soviet Union, with contributions by other CMEA countries) involves, apart from supplies of machinery or intermediate goods that may be treated as ordinary trade in goods, a variety of local costs (construction services, utilities, overhead costs, etc.) that cannot be treated as "noncommercial" transactions, because they are not expressed in consumer prices but in wholesale (producer) prices whose absolute and relative levels are dissociated from consumer prices in most countries.

Differentiation of exchange rates.   Each set of transactions thus had to be related to a specific set of *exchange rates* between the transferable ruble and the national or foreign currencies. For trade, no exchange rate was needed between the TR and the domestic currencies, as domestic prices were not used. The official rate of exchange between the TR and the convertible currencies was used in order to calculate the "international socialist prices," taking the world price of a given year for a given commodity in U.S. dollars (or in another currency, but probably dollar prices were most often used) and converting it into TRs at the average official rate of exchange for that given year and then applying (since 1975) the Moscow formula—that is, summing up the TR prices of the five years preceding the settlement year (for instance, 1985–1989 for the year 1990) and calculating the average price. At least, it is supposed that this was the procedure, although it has never been explicitly stated (van Brabant 1989:325). Until 1974, this official exchange rate of the TR was based on the gold parity of the ruble and of the dollar. When all capitalist currencies began to float, the exchange rate of the TR was calculated (and still is) on a monthly basis from a basket of about 13 convertible currencies. The composition and weights of the currency basket were revised every year, and any currency that was used for more than 1 percent of the total settlements of the CMEA countries in convertible currencies was included in the basket.

As for trade in services, the following procedure was used. Such trade ultimately resulted, for each country, in balances in the currencies of its partners, held by the central bank (or foreign trade bank) of that country. These balances were then converted into transferable rubles, using so-called noncommercial special rates corresponding to a purchasing power parity derived from a ratio for consumer prices, based on a basket of consumer items weighed according to the consumption of a diplomatic family. Whereas the procedure applied in the case of commercial transactions required an official and unrealistic exchange rate between the TR and convertible currencies, the procedure for noncommercial transactions yielded an exchange rate between the TR and socialist, nonconvertible currencies that could be considered slightly more realistic, as it took into consideration purchasing power parities (but only in the field of consumer-related goods and services). Thus, an exchange rate existed between the TR and the domestic Soviet ruble, although it was not publicized because it would have revealed the overvaluation of the ruble in relation to the official rate. In the 1970s, this rate amounted to 2.7 rubles for 1 TR, and then it gradually decreased to under 2 rubles for 1 TR.

Finally, for the operation of joint ventures and joint investments, it was necessary to use a variety of ad hoc coefficients for almost each type of cost item. Thus, in the case of the operation of the first bilateral joint venture (the Polish-Hungarian Haldex, created in 1959 in the coal industry), about sixty coefficients existed between the Polish zloty and the Hungarian forint, as documented by the Hungarian economist Sandor Ausch (1972). The multiplicity of these coefficients was acknowledged as very damaging to the expansion of joint ventures among CMEA countries, and it was repeatedly advocated to implement a single exchange rate for these operations, linking each national currency and the TR. To this effect, an agreement was concluded in October 1973 in Karl Marx Stadt in the German Democratic Republic. These "Karl Marx Stadt" rates were actually used only as a reference and were never operational.

All these arrangements were highly cumbersome, and they affected the interests of the countries in various ways. Thus, for countries exporting a large amount of services (especially tourist services), the noncommercial exchange rate, which amounted for all of them (including the Soviet Union) to a "devaluation" of the domestic currency as compared to the official rate, was prejudicial to the exporters of services. It should be noted here that, although data on trade in services were never published, the USSR was in deficit in its invisible trade with the Eastern European countries, so that it benefited from the conversion of "invisible" balances into TRs.

These arrangements explain the "customs war" conducted by Czechoslovakia against its neighbors, and first and foremost against the USSR, in 1988. Arguing that Soviet and other Eastern European tourists were plundering the domestic market because of a favorable exchange rate for the crown in other socialist currencies, and because the country was experiencing losses when converting into TRs its balances in these currencies, Czechoslovakia imposed exorbitant duties on most of the goods exported by tourists. This was followed by other countries, including the USSR itself, which introduced quotas for the export of consumer goods at the end of 1989.

Hard currency trade.   Because the system was cumbersome, in the early 1970s the CMEA countries already decided to conduct part of their trade in convertible currencies and at world prices—exactly what part of their mutual trade (and for what transactions) was never clear. Western experts usually stated that such transactions applied to trade in hard goods above the quantities provided in bilateral agreements. Namely, after the first oil shock, it was thought that some of the Soviet oil sales were paid for in hard currencies (the whole of them in the case of Romania). Thus, the Soviet Union would have earned surpluses in hard currency, but this result was contradicted by the fact that Hungary, the first country to publish its balances with the TR area in hard currency, showed a surplus. This surplus was obviously with the Soviet Union, as acknowledged first by nonofficial sources and, in the course of the 1980s, openly in the Hungarian literature. This surplus was explained by the fact that, while buying a small part of its oil supplies from the USSR in hard currency, Hungary also sold a large part of its food exports to the USSR in hard currency, particularly meat since 1974, when the European Community (EC) closed the Common Market to beef imports from Hungary. Such an arrangement was seen as a form of subsidy to Hungary, and, indeed, it allowed Hungary to achieve an overall surplus in its hard currency trade in the first part of the 1980s. For all that, the share of convertible currency trade in total CMEA trade was never ascertained. Estimates put it in a range of 2 percent in the early 1970s, reaching 10 percent and possibly 15 percent in the beginning of the 1980s, then steadily decreasing, especially from 1986 on, as Hungarian-Soviet trade in hard currencies was reduced.

It should, however, be kept in mind that this trade in hard currencies was always linked with a particular selection of goods traded. The same result may be achieved through a barter-type agreement on goods. For instance, when Hungary is paid for its food supplies to the USSR in additional supplies of oil that Hungary may reexport to the West, this amounts to a payment in hard currency (see Okolicsanyi 1990).

The advocated improvements

Even at a time when CMEA members were not as outspoken about the TR as they are now, the operation of the "collective socialist currency" was acknowledged as unsatisfactory, because it did not bring about the sought-after multilateralization in trade and, therefore, did not contribute to an expansion of mutual trade.

The Integration Program of 1971 that aimed at a combination of the plan and the market in intra-CMEA relations to parallel the orientation of the domestic reforms had very clearly outlined the link between a liberalization of intra-CMEA trade (through gradual reduction in bilateral quotas, allowing for a larger part of trade to be conducted outside quotas) and the reform of the TR system. However, it remained very vague about the second point. The TR was to be strengthened, and its convertibility was advocated—but only in the *domestic* currencies of the CMEA countries.

As all other provisions of the 1971 Integration Program dealt with a shift toward a more "marketized" integration, these provisions were put aside when the energy crisis erupted, and the development of the socialist economic integration from 1974 on was geared to solving the energy problem. This explains, in particular, why a scheme close to the European Payment Union (EPU) scheme failed in 1974.

This scheme was to provide disincentives for structural debtors in TRs. It was decided in 1973, on the basis of a Polish proposal, to experiment with a system of payments in hard currency for a small amount of a debtor's balance (10 percent). This scheme would, it seemed, induce the debtor countries to settle their debts in TRs, and the creditor countries would be less reluctant about keeping a surplus. This scheme has sometimes been mentioned as a system close to the EPU scheme. Discussions about the relevance of the EPU scheme were revived in the socialist literature at that time (largely unnoticed in the West), but the comparison could hardly be sustained, because the scheme operated for only a year and was stopped in view of the hard currency shortages in Eastern Europe. The Soviet Union from 1975 on became by far the largest creditor, and a scheme that would have exclusively benefited the USSR was not politically acceptable. Even if the external conditions had not changed, the scheme was very different from the EPU. It was deliberately narrow, both in scope and in membership (only five countries participating). It was not associated with a move toward convertibility, and no provisions were made to ensure its financing. Each country had to obtain the hard currency needed. Thus, it was much closer to the provisions found in standard bilateral clearing agreements, in which, after a grace period, the debtor has to settle its debt through payments in hard currency for all or part of its balance.

Some excitement was aroused in the Western business and banking community when the Soviet Union announced in 1976 that the IBEC wished to include nonmember countries in the system of settlements in TRs and offered nonmember accounts in TRs or convertible currencies to be held by the bank at a privileged interest rate. Western banks explored how they could use their TR assets in case they decided to enter the scheme. They soon discovered that no opportunity existed for converting these assets into hard currency, for using them for purchases in Eastern Europe, or for financing local expenses in connection with sales of turn-key plants. The 1976 scheme was never applied (Guglielmi and Lavigne 1978). It was also offered to some developing countries, as a way of expanding the scope of the bilateral clearing agreements existing between the CMEA countries and the third world, which at that time reflected over 50 percent of East-South trade. Some countries, such as Colombia, considered entering the system, but they dropped the idea when they realized that, even if their bilateral clearing surpluses with the CMEA countries could be converted into TRs, they would still be unable to convert their assets into goods.

Finally, in 1988, it was decided at the forty-fourth session of the CMEA to reform the organization and set up a "unified market." All the member countries except Romania agreed to work toward "the gradual formation of conditions for the free movement of goods, services, and other production factors among them" (as quoted from the communiqué) and to move toward convertibility of the socialist currencies. It was not clear, however, whether this agreement meant to ensure the convertibility of the domestic currencies among themselves and with the TR or to ensure the convertibility of the socialist domestic currencies with the Western convertible currencies.

For settlements, it was decided to retain the transferable ruble (though acknowledging its drawbacks) and also to introduce a partial convertibility of the domestic currencies in order to use these currencies in bilateral interenterprise cooperation. Several agreements were concluded, to that effect, between the USSR and Czechoslovakia (1988) and later on among Bulgaria, Poland, and Mongolia. According to a Soviet author, such settlements never amounted to more than 0.1 percent of the bilateral trade flows (Sergeev 1989). Such arrangements may probably now be considered obsolete, although it is not clear what may have replaced them—at least for the few "direct links" established at the enterprise level that may still be considered as operational.

At the same time, the standard method of settling trade in transferable rubles was becoming increasingly difficult to manage, as foreign trade reforms developed in almost all Eastern European countries and in the USSR. It happened that in the years 1987 and 1988 the USSR slipped into deficit with its partners after years of surpluses as the result of the fall in oil prices. At the same time foreign trade rights were granted to a growing number of Soviet enterprises that had to earn foreign currency in order to be able to import on their account. Western businessmen soon became aware of the difficulties entailed by the new foreign trade rights. Lacking hard currency to import, the enterprises insisted on countertrade deals or on creating joint ventures.

It is much less known that the same problems appeared in intra-CMEA trade, with a different dimension. The Soviet enterprises (mainly in the machine-building sector) were successful at exporting to their counterparts and earned transferable rubles, so that the Soviet enterprise sector ended with a sizable surplus in TRs (2.5 billion TRs in eighteen months, amounting to about 6 percent of Soviet exports to the six Eastern European countries in 1987 and the first half of 1988). This surplus had two consequences. First, it was necessary to find a way for Soviet enterprises to buy goods in Eastern Europe; otherwise, the new incentives to export provided for in the reform would lose all credibility. Second, it was also necessary to open the Soviet market to the Eastern European firms to allow them to import, at a time when Eastern European governments were already worrying about the overall Soviet deficit.

To achieve both goals, "fairs" in transferable rubles were organized. The first fair was held in Moscow in November 1988, and another was organized in 1989. Actually, to allow for direct transactions between Soviet and Eastern European enterprises, the Soviet Gossnab (the agency responsible for allocating production goods among Soviet enterprises) had to be involved in an intergovernmental framework agreement with the Eastern European agencies, in order to ensure that transactions concluded during the fairs would be included again in the commitments contained in the bilateral trade agreements. This is far from direct relations and convertibility. With all that, the increase in trade transactions generated was minimal. In fact, at the first fair, most of the transactions in TRs were made among Soviet enterprises (also allowed). Just 4 percent of the balances in TRs held by the Soviet enterprises could be used for purchases from Eastern European enterprises in 1988 (Sarafanov 1990). The second fair was slightly more successful, mainly because it included more participants (not only state enterprises but also cooperatives; not only CMEA firms but also firms from the market economies). Transactions could be conducted not only in TRs but also in convertible currencies; and, finally, the "goods convertibility" was more or less achieved as the Gossnab had allowed Soviet enterprises to offer not only their above-the-plan production but also the production manufactured on the basis of state orders (that is, production originally earmarked for the domestic market). Even with these improvements, overall trade in TRs reached less than 30 percent of the TR balances.

It seemed amply demonstrated that the only way to get out of the deadlock was to get rid of the TR. Then, it was questioned whether an attempt should still be made to develop intra-CMEA trade, instead of just letting it decline, with the bulk of East Central European trade shifting to the West.

Collapse of the CMEA and Regulation of Intraregional Trade

The first "post-revolutionary" CMEA meeting, the forty-fifth and perhaps last in the history of the organization, was held in Sofia in January 1990 and was heralded in the West as the beginning of the end. In fact, the only significant decision taken related precisely to the question of intraregional convertibility. It was, however, paradoxically explained:

1. The Eastern European countries insisted that any idea of multilateralism should be abandoned in favor of bilateral links. This insistence is strange, because multilateralism has hardly ever functioned in the CMEA. The bulk of trade was done under bilateral arrangements.

2. The decision was made (which had already in principle been agreed upon between Hungary and the USSR in September 1989) to shift to trade in "world market prices" and in convertible currencies, beginning in 1991. This decision is precisely a step toward multilateralism, unless it may be shown that words do not have their obvious meaning and that trade is not going to be conducted in actual world prices nor in actual convertible currencies. It is necessary to elaborate on this, especially because the Western press, as well as many qualified Western experts in international finance who were not familiar with the idiosyncracies of the CMEA system, took the words for granted.

The shift to settlements in hard currencies and in world prices

These recent decisions of the CMEA have been presented as a Soviet proposal (announced less than a month earlier by Soviet Prime Minister Ryzhkov at a session of the Supreme Soviet), although the Soviet Union has also been said to favor the transferable ruble system and although in the past both Hungarian and Polish experts have advocated such a solution.

What makes clarification difficult is that the new system would clearly be in the interest of the Soviet Union. Just before the January 1990 meeting, the USSR was blamed for having a *deficit* in transferable rubles—that is, for delivering to its partners less than it was getting (of course, at the specific CMEA prices). Calculations made as to the impact of a shift to world prices and hard currency settlements showed that the USSR would then be in *surplus* (by about US$1.5 billion to US$2 billion toward Hungary, while it was in deficit by over 600 million rubles for 1989). The same would occur in trade with Czechoslovakia, and Czechoslovakia was already asking in January for some compensation (*Financial Times*, January 11, 1990). It was said that the Soviet surplus might reach as much as US$11 billion in 1991 (*Wall Street Journal*, January 22, 1990).

Is this situation evidence that, in the traditional system, the Soviet Union was subsidizing its partners? Partly, yes, especially at the time when, in addition, it was maintaining a trade surplus. The effect of relatively low prices of oil (in terms of prices of Eastern European machinery sold to the USSR) was compounded by the free credit extended by the USSR through the sole existence of a surplus in a nonconvertible currency. With the lagged impact of lower world oil prices reacting on intra-CMEA prices, which began to decline slightly in 1986, and with the decrease in the quantities delivered to the six CMEA countries (over 10 percent decrease in 1986–1989), the USSR has been in a deficit position since 1988.

It is not known exactly how the calculations about the gains derived by the USSR from the new system have been made. They have probably taken into account the average world price of oil (with assumptions as to its evolution). They have also included estimates of the value of Eastern European manufactured goods usually sold to the Soviet Union when the Soviet Union would have to pay for these goods at a realistic price reflecting their low competitiveness on the Western market and not at the inflated TR price. Have these calculations also included volume effects? Soviet supplies of oil are not likely to increase because of difficulties in domestic production. A further decrease in Soviet deliveries was publicized at the beginning of 1990. The USSR announced a decrease in its supplies of fuel to Poland (by one-third for the first three months of 1990), to Czechoslovakia (by 20 percent in January), and to Bulgaria (by an undisclosed amount in January) (*Financial Times*, February 14, 1990). Though fuel supplies to Romania increased in January 1990, this increase was meant as an emergency aid measure rather than as a new basis for trade. As for Soviet imports, the forecast is ambiguous. On the one hand, the Soviet Union might want to buy the same amount of Eastern European goods with a large discount, as these goods (especially machinery) fit into the obsolete Soviet production system, which cannot be revamped with Western machinery at short notice. On the other hand, the Soviet

Union might use its accrued surpluses in hard currency from Eastern Europe to import more from the West; in this case, the volume of trade would shrink on the import side.

All these speculations take for granted that the new system will, indeed, be implemented in a straightforward form—trade at world prices and payments in actual hard currencies. This is not about to happen.

As far as prices are concerned, it has been shown that in the past, world prices were a reference in intra-CMEA trade only for commodities. Thus it would be possible to apply world prices for Soviet sales of oil, gas, and raw materials and for Soviet imports of food (even, in this case, with some convention as to the actual reference prices chosen, but this is a field in which the CMEA countries have long experience). In no case could the world prices serve as a reference for prices of manufactured goods. In the past, these prices were already agreed bilaterally on the intergovernmental level. The difference might now be that the prices would be contracted on the enterprise level. This change would not be easy, especially when exchange rate considerations are taken into account.

All the countries under review have shifted to new exchange rates in the 1980s (and Hungary, even earlier, in 1976). Their aim was to set up "realistic exchange rates" to enable the planners to make the right decisions in regard to foreign trade, to enable the exporting enterprises to be paid for their exports according to their earnings in foreign currency converted into domestic currency, and ultimately to enable the domestic price system to be connected with world prices. The setting up of realistic exchange rates was also regarded as a way of preparing for the convertibility of the domestic currency. In all cases, initial calculations of these realistic exchange rates were derived from ratios of the domestic value of the weighted export basket of the country (in the dollar area and the ruble area) to the value of the same basket in foreign currency (dollar or ruble), thus expressing how much domestic currency was needed on average to earn one unit of foreign currency. Eastern European economists rightly often stressed that the marginal rate would be a more significant measure (that is, the additional domestic cost of earning one unit of foreign currency), but in actual practice the average cost approach prevailed.

Such realistic exchange rates always amounted to a strong devaluation of the domestic currency in relation to the official exchange rate of the monetary unit used as an accounting currency (the devisa-ruble, forint, zloty, etc.). In the case of the Eastern European countries, it also amounted to a strong implicit devaluation of the devisa-ruble (and, hence, of the TR, whose exchange rate may be considered approximately identical to that of the devisa-ruble).

Prior to introducing these realistic exchange rates as their new official commercial rates, all Eastern European countries had applied them—without publishing them—in their planning practice and as incentives for their exporters, often differentiating them according to the nature of the goods exchanged. This procedure was particularly highlighted in the case of the Soviet Union. In 1988 the USSR used 6,000 or more "differentiated currency coefficients." This use amounted to multiplying the official rate (in rubles per unit of foreign currency) by coefficients ranging from 0.3 to 6.[1] The Soviet Union is now the only country not to have shifted to new "realistic" commercial rates. The country did not even succeed in unifying the coefficients, which should have been replaced with a single coefficient at the beginning of 1990 that is equal to 2 in relation to the convertible currencies (meaning, for instance, that beginning in January 1990, US$1 should have been worth 1.24 rubles, instead of 0.62 ruble at the official rate at the end of 1989).

What matters here is that the recomputation of the exchange rate in all the Eastern European countries was done by each country, without any coordination and without any direct influence of the market. The only country that shifted in late 1989 to a determination of the exchange rate through market mechanisms (and only in regard to convertible currencies) was Poland. The Mazowiecki government undertook, beginning in September 1989, to devalue the zloty in order to bring it to the level of the black market rate and to be able to introduce internal convertibility of the zloty.

As a result of these procedures, the exchange rates of the domestic Eastern European currencies in relation to the dollar and to the ruble yielded widely divergent ruble/dollar cross-rates, whereas, in the past, with fixed official exchange rates in all the CMEA countries pegged to the devisa-ruble, the cross-rates were identical to the official Soviet exchange rate of the ruble against the dollar. Thus, in 1989, the cross-rates were on average as follows[2] (in rubles per U.S. dollar):

Romania	1.6
Bulgaria	1.9
Czechoslovakia	2.3
Hungary	2.6
Poland	3.6 (end of 1989)

This dispersion of the cross-rates is not apt to facilitate negotiations on prices. The ex-CMEA countries are in a precarious position. Price reforms and marketization of the domestic economies are underway everywhere, as well as stabilization programs, monitored or not by the International Monetary Fund (IMF). The exchange rates are *bound to fluctuate widely* in the coming period. Thus, despite the principal decision taken at the Sofia meeting of the CMEA, the actual solutions are much more conservative and closer to the former mechanisms than generally believed. In the first months of 1990, several countries reached bilateral agreements with the Soviet Union concerning the gradual shift to the new system:

- A Bulgarian-Soviet agreement in January 1990 provides for cuts of about 15 percent in mutual trade for that year, along with a gradual introduction of hard currency settlements beginning in 1991. For three years, both the TR and the U.S. dollar would be used in the transactions, without any further details as to the actual mechanism to be applied (Engelbrekt 1990).

- In March, a Polish-Soviet agreement was reached on the volume of trade for 1990 and on the principle of settlements using hard currency for accounting, beginning in 1991. The case of Poland is specific, as it is the only country still indebted to the USSR both in TR (over 5 billion) and in U.S. dollars (1.5 billion), with both debts rescheduled. Poland is now arguing that it has repaid its debt to the USSR through its past contributions to joint CMEA investments in the Soviet Union (Stefanowski 1990).

- The Soviet-Hungarian agreement was reached in March after Hungary had suspended, in January 1990, the export licenses granted to Hungarian enterprises to sell to the USSR and had then renewed them on a case-by-case basis, in order to "divert" as few goods as possible to the CMEA market and to prevent the export to the USSR of goods salable to the West. Overall, trade with the USSR was to decrease by one-third in 1990, on account of both the Hungarian sales of machinery and the Soviet oil deliveries. What is remarkable in this agreement is that it provides for a settlement in dollars of the Soviet debt in TRs. Beginning in 1991, this debt will be reimbursed at a rate of 0.92 dollar to one ruble. Should the Hungarian ruble/dollar cross-rate be applied, Hungary would receive only 0.40 dollar for each ruble of the Soviet debt; should the official TR/dollar rate be retained, it would yield 1.52 dollars for one TR. It appears that both parties have struck a fifty/fifty deal by deriving a rate of exchange that is the average of the two cross-rates. As for the future, the significance of the settlements in dollars remains obscure; the Hungarian comments seem to suggest that this might be a clearing in dollars close to the Finnish-Soviet mechanism, rather than an actual settlement in dollars.

The Eastern European countries clearly seem in disarray about the present situation. They would obviously like to benefit from the advantages of both systems. It has often been said that the ambition of communist workers was to have a level of consumption equal to the West, with a labor intensity according to Eastern European standards. Here, the ideal pattern would be a set of relative prices as in the TR price-fixing system, with settlements in dollars, in order to take advantage of the present terms of trade. Unfortunately, since 1988, any solution is unfavorable to Eastern Europe. Pricing and accounting in TRs yield nonconvertible surpluses for the countries in Eastern Europe; pricing and accounting in dollars yield convertible surpluses for the USSR. Why not just try and get rid of the Soviet trade altogether? This is precisely what Western advisers suggest.

The Western views

Overall, in the West the dominant view is that it should assist the integration of Eastern Europe into the world economy and not try to revive any regional union. The Soviet case is increasingly disjoined from Eastern Europe, both because of the permanent features of the Soviet economy (size, resource endowment) and because of the growing uncertainties about the future of Soviet reform.

It is necessary to answer two questions: (1) What exactly is "the West"?, and (2) What is advocated in the short term?

The "West" is taken here as the international organizations that may influence present or future domestic or international policies of Eastern Europe and the experts and consultants who advise them. In most cases, the institutions do not care for a deep understanding of the intricacies of the former mechanisms, whose irrationality and perversity seem obvious to them. They apply standard representations of how a market economy should work. From this point of view, they generally consider that trade within the ex-CMEA should be downgraded to a minimum level, on the basis of the following arguments that are also put forward by the new governments of East Central Europe:

1. The present pattern of trade is obsolete. It is based on Soviet deliveries of energy and raw materials that are needed because the area is consuming large quantities of such goods under the "Stalinist" mode of development imposed on Eastern Europe

after World War II. It is better to cut this trade down to a minimum level in order to force structural changes that may hurt but that should adapt the Eastern European economies to the requirements of the Western markets. Even if it is necessary to close the plants that manufacture goods especially for the Soviet market, this measure will be beneficial in the long term as it will compel the enterprises to become more competitive.

2. Trade among Eastern European countries and between them and the USSR is not "natural." The prewar situation is referred to, ignoring the fact that the USSR was discriminated against and that in East Central Europe a network of trade and payment accords centered on Nazi Germany.

3. Surpluses in nonconvertible trade have a negative impact on the domestic economy because they increase inflationary pressures. This situation was of particular concern to the IMF in its negotiations with Hungary and Poland. In both cases, the mechanisms of clearing in transferable rubles implied that the exporting enterprises were not paid by the Soviet importer but by the central bank (Hungary) or the Foreign Trade Bank (Poland) in domestic currency. As exports were greater than imports, a net creation of money occurred, while fighting inflation was considered one of the most pressing aims in domestic economic policy.

4. Such surpluses may represent a hidden diversion of convertible currency to the Soviet Union in all cases where a given item paid for in TRs by the USSR has been manufactured with materials imported from the West by the Eastern European country and paid for in hard currency. Poland and Hungary had repeatedly made this point in their discussions with the USSR, and the IMF experts have been sensitive to it, though it could be argued that exports from the USSR represented savings in hard currency and were gains in hard currency every time the given commodities (in fact, oil) were reexported (either as crude oil or in a processed form).

The Western institutions do not widely publicize their views. Those of the IMF are best known through information provided by the Eastern European countries, for which this is a way to back their own positions. The European Commission is in a somewhat difficult position. On the one hand, as the aid program to Eastern Europe promotes marketization and privatization and is backed by trade measures facilitating access to the European market, it is logical for the commission to support a movement toward a closer relationship with Western Europe and away from intraregional trade. On the other hand, the commission does not want to encourage wishful thinking about a quick integration of Eastern Europe into the European Economic Community (EEC), though agreeing to offer association schemes. This was clearly expressed in a speech by Jacques Delors, president of the commission, a few days after the Sofia meeting of the CMEA at the European Parliament in Strasbourg:

> In the economic field, apart from the EFTA [European Free Trade Association], we have the CMEA which could, provided it was deeply reformed, prove to be useful, if only for providing outlets to goods which are not apt, due to their quality, to compete on world markets. Apparently the officials participating in the Sofia meeting have understood this, despite their reservations as to this organization. Should the CMEA countries indeed decide for a reform and should they express such a wish, the Community would obviously be ready to provide them with its expertise in the field of economic cooperation [January 17, 1990. Translation from the official French text].

The Economic Commission for Europe (ECE) of the United Nations is the only significant Western institution that has expressed some views about the suitability of a new scheme comparable to the postwar European Payments Union.[3] The quoted source proposes a new EPU-scheme only for countries in the process of reform, as a transition to a full-fledged reform of the domestic economy and to a new pattern of international economic relations. The system could be monitored by the Bank for International Settlements (BIS), and the heart of it might be the European currency unit (ECU). Such an arrangement would clearly designate the scheme for assistance from Western Europe (or from the Group of Twenty-Four). Would it be a workable scheme?

A New Monetary Union in the European CMEA Area?

As the opponents of this idea often present it in a simplified way, some initial caveats are necessary. What is suggested here is not that the CMEA countries should seek intraregional convertibility rather than general convertibility of their currencies, nor that a monetary union or arrangement among them should revive the old TR system. What is suggested is to look for a possible regional arrangement among the European CMEA countries, of which a monetary arrangement would be a part.

The arguments against a monetary arrangement

These arguments are rather difficult to express coherently. Up to May 1990, no serious discussion of any proposal had taken place. The only spelled-out scheme, that of Jozef van Brabant (1990), summarized in Economic Commission for Europe (1990), has not yet been addressed in Eastern Europe or in the West. In fact, there is a global rejection of the idea of a monetary arrangement as such. There are several reasons for this rejection.

The political context.   The political argument is very strong when it is assumed that the Soviet Union should be part of the scheme.

Eastern Europe has a fear of the USSR. This country is no longer looked on as a superpower, dominating or exploiting the Eastern bloc, but as an unstable country that is not really engaged in reform. Thus, it seems dangerous to associate with the USSR in the transition period. Western views are mixed. In the West, the idea of the USSR as a superpower has not yet totally been abandoned, and security arguments are invoked when it comes to discussing the feasibility of a scheme that includes the USSR. On the other side, to exclude it from a regional scheme may also be seen as a potential threat to international security. This thinking leads to support for status quo—the acknowledgment of the dissolution of the CMEA with no replacement scheme at all.

Since the ultimate aim of several Central European countries (Hungary, Poland, Czechoslovakia) is membership in the EEC, any new regional arrangement is seen as dangerous because it might be taken as a pretext to delay the granting of this membership. Any hint of a revival of the previous "bloc autarky" must be resolutely avoided. This belief leads to a straightforward conclusion that intraregional convertibility within the ex-CMEA area is no longer an issue.

Finally, each Eastern European country is very sensitive to sovereignty issues. Even if the USSR is not to be a member of a new arrangement, nonmembership would imply a loss in sovereignty if compulsory provisions were applied to exchange rate matters, for instance, and this situation is not readily accepted politically. For this reason, even the idea of a limited regional grouping (including Poland, Hungary, and Czechoslovakia), which has gained some credibility in 1990 (Palankai 1990), is still questioned.

The economic arguments.   Apart from extreme views, it is generally understood both in the West and in Eastern Europe that a reasonable amount of trade should be maintained within the ex-CMEA area. In any case, the reorientation of trade to the West will take time, even with such favorable conditions as the lifting of quantitative restrictions by the EEC and the United States, the granting of generalized preferences, etc. Several reasons explain this delay:

- There is no large supply response in the short term to the domestic adjustments either for the domestic market or for exports.

- Integration in the world market requires structural adaptation (greater productivity, sectoral industrial restructuring, and modernizing). In the meantime, the same types of goods are to be manufactured, and these goods are not adapted to the world market.

- A large part of Eastern and Central European industry is still geared to the Soviet market, both as a supplier and a buyer. To disrupt these links would entail bankruptcies of firms selling to the Soviets and domestic disorganization of supplies.

Thus, as a transition, trade with the USSR and also among Eastern European countries should remain as a significant share of total trade. The present shares (as of 1989) range from 40 percent to 70 percent of total trade, and amount on average to 50 percent. It could not, even if there was an open aim, be brought down to, say, 20 percent of total trade (which would still be much more than the trade among developing countries belonging to regional groupings) without great harm to the national economies.

True, CMEA trade is shrinking. According to Soviet data for 1989, trade with the European CMEA countries decreased overall, with Soviet imports growing by 1.7 percent and Soviet exports decreasing by 3.3 percent.[4] And it decreased still more in 1990. But in the long term and even in the medium term, a revival of CMEA trade may be expected. For instance, gas sales of the Soviet Union might increase even beyond the offsetting of the likely decrease in oil sales, because East Central Europe, despite its drive toward self-sufficiency, will be strongly pressed by Western Europe to shift away from coal as the main source of energy, for ecological reasons. Among the Eastern European countries, assuming that they develop into genuine markets, a great potential exists for trade in specialized manufactures, as well as for trade in modern services.

Even with a sustained trade potential, it does not follow, according to the dominant views, that a monetary arrangement would make any sense, for two main reasons: (1) The Soviet Union cannot be included in such an arrangement for political reasons, as stated above; if it is not included, special arrangements within the East Central European zone would not be useful as there are no large imbalances in mutual trade. (2) Once the national currencies become really convertible into Western currencies and once the domestic economies are marketized, the problem will solve itself.

These arguments are not sustainable. Past and present experiences of market economies, as well as the specifics of Eastern Europe, plead for a monetary arrangement, not necessarily in the form of a new EPU.

Desirability of a new monetary arrangement

It may be useful to revert to the standard analysis of regional monetary integration, which is defined loosely as "any arrangements under which the effects of the existence of separate currencies merely approach, more or less, the effects of the existence of a single one" (Kafka 1969). Regional integration may serve three main purposes: (1) promotion of intra-regional trade, (2) economizing on international reserves, and (3) progress toward multilateralization.

Are past experiences relevant?   The recourse to past experiences is appealing, but may be misleading. The EPU comes to mind immediately. As the main advocate of such a borrowing, Jozef van Brabant (1990), explains, the conditions are not exactly comparable, though an analogy may be found between the state of the Western economies devastated after World War II and the state of the Eastern European countries devastated by over forty years of distorted growth strategy and wrong economic decisions. The EPU was created to promote intraregional trade among Western European countries, but this trade was halted by the bilateral arrangements set up between these countries and by the famous "dollar gap." Unlike the Eastern European countries, Western European nations were market economies, and the domestic markets, even if still regulated through war-type controls (such as rationing and administrative allocation of essential goods), were already functioning on the basis of market rules. A second very important difference was that Western Europe accounted for more than 50 percent of world trade, while the share for Eastern Europe *and* the USSR was under 8 percent at the end of the 1980s. What is the most relevant, if anything, in the postwar experience to the East Central European countries is the role played by the Organization for European Economic Cooperation, which was later transformed into the Organization for Economic Cooperation and Development (OECD), in removing the quantitative restrictions in intraregional trade and in preparing the ground for the European Coal and Steel Community to be created in 1952 and the Common Market in 1957 (see Yeager 1966).

If, following van Brabant, it is agreed that the main task faced now by the countries of East Central Europe is to revamp their economic relations "on the basis of rational economic decisions" (van Brabant 1990:18), any new scheme must be preceded by the marketization of the domestic economies, to allow for a "goods convertibility" of the domestic currencies and to create adequate conditions for their "monetary" convertibility, at least for current account transactions. But then we are faced with an argument currently used in regard to monetary unions in the developing world—that these unions have never worked satisfactorily, though many of them have been started. There is only one exception, but it is not conclusive.

In a study prepared in 1979, in view of the then proposed Preferential Trade Area of Eastern and Southern African States, an IMF paper looked at improvements in payments arrangements that would promote intraregional trade (Anjaria, Eken, and Laker 1982). In 1980 intraregional trade among the seventeen countries concerned amounted to 4.1 percent of their total trade (in 1974 to 6.4 percent). Three countries accounted for two-thirds of intraregional trade (Kenya, Uganda, and Tanzania). Trade flows were imbalanced, with a few countries being major net exporters (Kenya, particularly); most of the trade took place with the industrial countries of Western Europe and North America. The study concluded that, as a large part of the intraregional flows were unbalanced, a clearing facility would not be able to restore the balance as it might have done if deficits with one or more countries were offset by surpluses with others. The low level of intraregional trade could not allow for big savings in hard currency after the clearing arrangement was finalized. The use of the regional currencies would not be stimulated either, unless the traders became confident in these currencies. Nevertheless, the report concluded that a new clearing facility would be useful "as a means of promoting intraregional contacts and cooperation"; "also, the formation of more flexible links among groups of developing countries following the establishment of a regional clearing facility could . . . usher in a further stage in the post-independence evolution of these countries' financial and economic relationships" (Anjaria, Eken, and Laker 1982:2–3). However, the scheme was never operational. The authors of the IMF paper probably anticipated that: "Finally, establishment of a clearing arrangement to support agreements in other economic fields would signal a willingness to maintain a certain degree of openness toward regional partners. Such a stance, however, could not be sustained over the long term in the absence of (1) appropriate policies to overcome present financial difficulties and to promote economic growth, and (2) a high degree of political commitment" (Anjaria, Eken, and Laker 1982:3). The last sentence might easily be applied to Eastern Europe.

The only success story in monetary arrangements among developing countries is that of the French franc zone, which comprises France, twelve African states, and the Comores. Of these twelve states, eleven are members of monetary unions: the West African Monetary Union (Benin, Burkina Faso, Ivory Coast, Niger, Senegal, and Togo) and the members of the Bank of Central African States (Cameroon, Central African Republic, Chad, Congo, and Gabon). Each of these unions has its CFA franc (meaning, in the first case, *franc de la communauté financière africaine* and, in the second case, *franc de la coopération financière en Afrique centrale*). Though all are small in population, none having more than 10 million inhabitants, these countries have different levels of per capita income and different political choices. The French zone is obviously a sequel of colonialism, explaining why Madagascar and Mauritania stepped out in 1973, while Mali walked out in 1962 and came back in 1967 but maintained its own central bank. The monetary unions were set up in 1972 and 1973 (along with an Africanization of the monetary institutions). The principles of the French franc area are the following: the currencies of the zone are convertible among themselves and into other currencies for residents and nonresidents; the African francs are pegged to the French franc with a fixed and unchanged rate; the foreign exchange reserves are pooled and deposited into four central banks (BCEAO—Banque Centrale des Etats de l'Afrique de l'Ouest, BEAC—Banque des Etats de l'Afrique Centrale, plus the Central Bank of Mali and the Central Bank of the Republic of Comores). These foreign reserves are kept in French francs; France guarantees the convertibility of the African currencies.

What was the impact of this regime? Trade among the countries of the zone increased from 3.7 percent of their total import trade in 1963 to 6.4 percent in 1972, but from then on has remained stable. These countries had a growth rate that was not worse (for the Sahelian countries) or was better (for the others) than that of comparable African countries. None of these countries experienced hyperinflation. The existence of the "operations account" (exchange reserves) helped to solve the debt problems of some of these countries.

This example is not significant from the point of view of Eastern Europe. First, it has worked because it was consistently supported by France, which in exchange could maintain its privileged trade links with the countries of the grouping. The only country that might be thought to play a comparable role would be the USSR. Indeed, a Hungarian economist, Kalman Pecsi (1989) has in the past advocated a comparable solution, with the Eastern European currencies being pegged to a convertible Soviet ruble. Apart from the political impossibility of such a scheme, however, the Soviet Union would not be in a position to bear such a burden.

Second, the French franc is on the verge of collapse. Because of its attractiveness as the only really convertible African currency, the CFA franc is gradually being removed from circulation in the context of the growing deterioration of the African economies. It is hoarded by nonmember countries as reserve money whose convertibility is guaranteed, at increasing costs to France. The nonconvertibility of the CFA franc is now widely expected, and this would mean the collapse of the French franc area as well.

A specific approach to the needs of East Central Europe.   Before any progress can be made on the monetary front, several conditions are to be met, as already noted. Each country (including the USSR) has to stabilize its economy (in particular, to eliminate the monetary "overhang" that plagues most of them) and allow market rules to operate in domestic trade. Such action requires the lifting of the remaining planning controls and the introduction of competition at home between producers, which, in turn, calls for a dismantling of the administrative monopolies (but not necessarily the dismantling of all big enterprises). These changes do not require immediate privatization, which at any rate would be impossible on short notice.

Steps have to be taken toward a liberalization of foreign trade, allowing the domestic enterprises to choose their partners. This action has already been taken in Hungary and Poland (but not nearly completed), and the process has just begun elsewhere. Obviously, an essential part of the liberalization process is the introduction of internal convertibility, by which the resident economic agents (including the joint ventures and the foreign enterprises that have invested in the country) can have access to foreign currency on a domestic foreign exchange market (as is now the case in Poland).

Once these conditions are met, could it not be said that ipso facto the problem is solved because all payments among the ex-socialist countries can now be made in convertible currencies? I do not believe so. First, these conditions cannot be met immediately in all countries. Second, intraregional trade flows must be encouraged because, even with an internal convertibility, trade cannot immediately be diverted to the West. The high cost of procuring hard currency on a free market will keep many enterprises out of this market. The existing industrial structure at the same time commits many enterprises to produce for the intraregional market, but this market will be closed to them if, to enter it, they can no longer count on intergovernmental agreements and have to earn hard currency.

In this instance, the provisions to be implemented in 1991, as has been seen, preclude direct settlements in hard currency in interenterprise relations. The solution not explicitly spelled out, but apparently sought, is a set of bilateral arrangements of a clearing type that would restore the previous situation.

A feasible scheme would be a multilateral monetary arrangement providing for settlements in the domestic currencies, with a commitment to make these currencies gradually fully convertible (for residents and nonresidents) within the area and outside the area. Such a monetary arrangement would have to be part of a trade arrangement (a free trade area or, better, a customs union). It would include provisions for monitoring the exchange rates of the domestic currencies—helping to reduce the differences in the cross-rates mentioned above.

Technically the regional payments union could function on the basis of credits granted by each central bank in its own currency. Each currency would have an official exchange rate against the chosen unit of account (let us assume that it would be the ECU). One would need a financial institution to manage the accounts and to consolidate the members' debts and claims into an overall net balance. Since the financial institutions of the CMEA are now discredited, as is the CMEA itself, this task should be performed by a nonregional agency. One option would be to use the Bank for International Settlements; another would be to create an agency specifically for this purpose, with Western participation in management as well as in the funding of the necessary stabilization fund. As was the case for the EPU, beyond a given quota the debtor countries would have to settle their debts in hard currencies, with a credit whose share in the total debt would be gradually reduced so that, in the end, all would be settled in hard currencies. Among Western European countries the process lasted nine years.

Such a payments arrangement must be supplemented with a program for trade liberalization. The Eastern European countries are not yet ready to liberalize their mutual trade. The most market-oriented countries claim that their enterprises engage in trade on the basis of their own decisions, but limitations still remain, especially for regional trade, and will not be lifted at once, particularly for trade with the less market-oriented partners. Here, the experience of the Organization for European Economic Cooperation is instructive; it ensured a gradual shift toward quota-free trade among its members.

Since a main obstacle would be the lack of political goodwill, the impulse should come from the outside. The monetary arrangement should be granted some help from the West—for example, in the form of an Exchange Reserve Fund in hard currency managed by a Central European organization but with some control by a Western institution (for instance, by the new European Bank for Reconstruction and Development). The latter choice would allow for financial involvement by the Soviet Union—a price it would pay to avoid being marginalized in the new European architecture.

The interest of the West in participating in such an arrangement would be to help the economic reconstruction of Eastern Europe while ensuring an organized transition to increased links with the West and to allow many questions pertaining to relations with the European Community to be solved not only on a case-by-case basis but also in a multilateral way.

A final note is desirable. In this chapter, I have referred to Eastern Europe or East Central Europe (a term now politically preferred to "Eastern Europe") as comprising the six CMEA members: Bulgaria, Czechoslovakia, the German Democratic Republic, Hungary, Poland, and Romania. Although Bulgaria and Romania have not yet advanced on the reform path as decisively as Hungary, Poland, and Czechoslovakia, they ought not to be classified as nonreforming countries. In any case, the problems of the area will have to be solved as a whole. The German case is different. It is not correct to say that the reunification will automatically solve all the problems. Germany (East and West) has committed itself to honor its long-term contracts with the CMEA countries, and particularly with the Soviet Union (Jackson and Donovan 1990). This might strengthen the monetary arrangement that I would recommend, through a stronger involvement of West Germany, and would also induce other Western European countries to participate actively in this solution in order not to leave the field too open for Germany.[5]

Notes

1. See Lavigne (1989) for a survey of the Soviet sources on the matter.

2. Quoted from Il'in (1990), except for the Polish rate; see Economic Commission for Europe (1990).

3. "Lessons from History: A New EPU as a Bridge-Gap," in Economic Commission for Europe (1990: 3–74 to 3–76).

4. *Ekonomika i Zhizn'* (formerly *Ekonomicheskaia Gazeta*), supplement to no. 15, April 1990.

5. This chapter was written in mid-1990. At the beginning of 1991, the situation may be characterized as follows. The Gulf crisis and war made the transition to the new system of pricing and settlements among the ex-CMEA members still more difficult, since the increase in oil prices gave the Soviet

Union a large terms-of-trade advantage. However, it was also obvious in the second half of 1990 that the Soviet Union would not substantially benefit from this new situation, because of the fall in oil production and exports, and indeed the expected decrease in Soviet supplies was perceived in Eastern Europe as a greater threat than the increase in prices. Mainly because of the decrease in Soviet exports and the corresponding decrease in imports, the volume of intra-CMEA trade fell by an estimated 20 percent in 1990 and is expected to decrease still more in 1991.

The transition to the new system of settlements as of January 1, 1991, was acknowledged as a reality in the beginning of this year, while steps were taken to definitively dismantle the CMEA and replace it with a loose consultative body. However, the new system was not actually operating, not just because of transitional arrangements between the USSR and Eastern Europe and among Eastern European countries. On the enterprise level, there was an overall reluctance of Eastern European firms to use hard currency for purchases from CMEA partners, and a surge in barter and compensation deals, often arranged through specialized Western firms (in particular Austrian) because of the lack of the former intergovernment framework for such deals. This leads to the conclusion that the question of intraregional settlements is by no means resolved and should give more credibility to the solutions we advocate for strengthening trade links within the CMEA region.

Since January 1991, the Czechoslovak currency (the crown) has become almost convertible internally, with some restrictions. The convertibility of the Hungarian forint is expected for 1992 (it was announced in May 1991). In November 1990 the USSR introduced a new commercial rate for the devisa ruble—1.8 per US$1—which does not reflect the much deeper depreciation of the ruble shown by the black market rates (30 to 35 rubles per US$1).

The CMEA was officially dissolved at the forty-sixth session of the organization, held in Budapest on June 28, 1991. A small information agency among the former CMEA members might be created in the future. In 1990, trade volume between East Central Europe and the USSR fell by 15–20 percent, and the collapse of trade is expected to be still greater in 1991. By mid-1991, East Central European countries were gradually moving toward arrangements with the Soviet Union and/or the republics, mainly Russia, providing for payments accounted in convertible currencies and settled partly in clearing. Part of mutual trade was expected to be settled in national currencies, which will in practice take place through barter-like arrangements. The East Central European countries were increasingly pressing the developed countries to make Western assistance to the USSR at least partly conditional on a resumption of Soviet imports from East Central Europe.

PART THREE

DEVELOPING COUNTRIES

BIJAN B. AGHEVLI AND
PETER J. MONTIEL   CHAPTER EIGHT

Exchange Rate Policies
in Developing Countries

This chapter provides a broad overview of the evolution of exchange rate regimes and movements of exchange rates in developing countries since the late 1970s. It also considers a number of analytical issues per-. tinent to the formulation of exchange rate policy in these countries. It would be useful to note at the outset that, since the collapse of the Bretton Woods system in the early 1970s, the process of exchange rate determination in most developing countries has been fundamentally different from that in the industrial countries. With the increasing openness of capital markets in the industrial countries, exchange rates of major currencies have been largely determined by market forces, notwithstanding periodic interventions by the major central banks. By contrast, in most developing countries the exchange rate has continued to be regarded as an instrument of policy, with the rate being set by the monetary authorities. Although the exchange rate may in some cases be adjusted frequently, in the vast majority of developing countries the official exchange rate is not directly influenced by market forces, at least in the short term. Consequently, exchange rate policy plays an important role in the process of external adjustment in the developing countries.

This chapter is organized into two parts. The first part describes the exchange rate arrangements of the developing countries, examines the evolution of these arrangements, and reviews developments of exchange rates in various groups of countries. The focus is on the pattern of exchange rate arrangements adopted by these countries and on the actual movements of nominal and real effective exchange rate indexes in various groupings of countries. The examination reveals a number of common patterns in the movements of exchange rate indexes in these countries. The second part considers a number of policy issues, including the effects of exchange rate adjustments on the economy, the implications of real exchange rate rules for financial stability, and the relationship between financial discipline and the exchange rate regime. A final section presents a brief summary of the main findings.

Recent Exchange Rate Arrangements

As indicated above, the vast majority of developing countries maintain an official parity for their currencies. This parity is expressed in terms of an intervention currency and represents the rate at which the central bank will exchange domestic currency for foreign currency with private individuals. However, not all categories of economic transactions are eligible for such exchanges at par value. Frequently, different official exchange rates apply to different types of imports, and some categories of imports are not eligible to receive foreign exchange at the official rate. Similarly, exporters are often legally required to surrender the proceeds of their foreign sales to the central bank, which compensates them in domestic currency at an exchange rate that may vary across categories of exports. Similar restrictions and multiple exchange rate practices may also apply to other current account transactions, such as private debt service, profit repatriations, and other remittances. With regard to the capital account, private individuals are frequently prevented from lending abroad and are subject to surrender requirements on their foreign borrowing.

Foreign exchange control practices of the type described above obviously give rise to various forms of evasion, prominent among which are the existence of black markets for foreign exchange. In such markets, the supply of foreign exchange from illegal exports, under-invoicing of exports, over-invoicing of imports, and unreported receipts from tourism satisfy the demand of individuals to hold their financial wealth in the form of foreign exchange, as well as to finance illegal imports (such as smuggling). Black markets are typically run by private vendors. High black market rates, substantially over the official exchange rate in some cases, reflect both the scarcity value of foreign exchange and the risk attached to such transactions.

Parallel exchange markets are given legal recognition in some developing countries. In such cases, banks and foreign exchange houses tend to dominate the market, although the central bank may intervene in the market to affect the exchange rate premium. Under dual arrangements, certain favored categories of foreign exchange receipts from exports and tourism are permitted to be sold in the free market, while less-favored importers are required to acquire foreign exchange in that market.

Although foreign exchange controls and dual exchange markets are common in developing countries and dual markets may have important macroeconomic implications, the majority of foreign exchange transactions continue to flow through the official market. For this reason, and because information on the parallel market is difficult to obtain for most developing countries, we confine our attention in the remainder of the chapter to the official exchange market.

Evolution of Exchange Rate Regimes

Since the mid-1970s, a significant shift has occurred in the exchange rate regimes adopted by developing countries. This shift has basically taken the form of a movement away from a fixed parity with a single currency toward either pegging to a composite of currencies or adopting a more flexible arrangement under which the domestic currency is adjusted more frequently.

The patterns of exchange arrangements of developing countries for the period 1976–1989 are presented in Table 8.1. It can be observed that the proportion of developing countries choosing to retain single currency pegs has steadily declined from 63 percent in 1976 to 38 percent in 1989.[1] The proportion of countries pegging their currency to the U.S. dollar declined from 43 percent to 24 percent during this same period. The shift away from pegging to the U.S. dollar reflects the high variability of exchange rates between the U.S. dollar and the currencies of other major industrial countries during the 1980s. The proportion of countries pegging to the pound sterling declined even more dramatically—in fact, by 1989, no country pegged to this currency. By contrast, the French franc held its ground, as those countries pegging to the French franc represented a stable 11–12 percent of all developing countries throughout the period 1976–1989. This pattern reflected the maintenance of the currency union arrangement among the fourteen African countries in the CFA franc zone that have had strong and longstanding ties with France.

A number of countries have chosen to peg their currencies to the special drawing right (SDR) as a convenient method of approximating

TABLE 8.1   Exchange Rate Arrangements of Developing Countries, 1976–1989 (percentage of total number of countries)

Classification	1976	1979	1983	1989
Pegged arrangements	86.0	75.2	71.7	66.4
To a single currency	62.6	52.1	43.5	38.2
U.S. dollar	43.0	35.0	29.0	23.7
French franc	12.1	12.0	10.5	10.7
Pound sterling	2.8	2.6	0.8	0.0
Other currency	4.7	2.5	3.2	3.8
To composite	23.4	23.1	28.2	28.2
SDR	10.3	11.1	11.3	5.3
Other (currency basket)	13.1	12.0	16.9	22.9
Flexible arrangements	14.0	24.8	28.2	33.6
Adjusting to indicators	5.6	3.4	4.0	3.8
Other[a]	8.4	21.4	24.2	29.8
Total	100.0	100.0	100.0	100.0
Number of countries	107	117	124	131

NOTE: Data are based on mid-year classifications, except for 1989, which is based on year-end classifications. Democratic Kampuchea, for which no information is available, is excluded.
a. Includes the following categories: (1) flexibility limited vis-à-vis single currency, (2) managed floating, and (3) independently floating.
SOURCES: International Monetary Fund, Annual Report (1982), Report on Exchange Arrangements and Exchange Restrictions (1983), and International Financial Statistics (April 1990).

the relative importance of the major currencies in international transactions. The proportion of developing countries opting for the SDR peg averaged about 10 percent of the total during 1976–1983, but the SDR lost substantial ground after 1983, with only 5 percent opting for the SDR peg. By contrast, the share of countries opting to peg to a trade-weighted basket of currencies rose sharply, particularly during the 1980s, from 13 percent in 1976 to 23 percent in 1989.

The decision by an increasing number of developing countries to switch their pegging arrangement from a single currency to a composite basket of currencies has been prompted partly by the desire to shield their economies from the undesirable effects of fluctuations in the real exchange rates of major currencies that have taken place since the advent of generalized floating in 1973. These fluctuations have introduced an exogenous source of variability in the real effective exchange rates of developing countries, engendering various problems for these countries, ranging from uncertainty about the profitability of investment in traded goods sectors to the management of public finances, external debt, and foreign exchange reserves.

Developing countries have also relied increasingly on more flexible arrangements, under which the exchange rate is adjusted frequently. Such arrangements are often officially described as "managed floating" or "independently floating." These terms, however, do not accurately reflect the arrangements in place, as the exchange rate is ultimately set by the authorities, although adjusted more frequently than in the case of an adjustable peg. For the purpose of this discussion, these arrangements are described as "flexible." The pattern of the increase in flexible arrangements is evident in Table 8.1. During 1976–1989, the proportion of countries relying on flexible arrangements more than doubled to one-third of the total. At the same time, the proportion of countries pegging to a single currency fell from 63 percent to 38 percent. It is clear that the generalization that developing countries peg to a single currency (although, perhaps, true a decade and half ago) is no longer valid. Indeed, the tendency toward adopting more flexible exchange rate arrangements appears to be strengthening.

The increase in the use of more flexible arrangements in developing countries can be attributed to a number of factors. First, many developing countries have experienced a sharp acceleration in their domestic rates of inflation during the 1980s. This acceleration was particularly pronounced in the countries of the Western Hemisphere, for which the average rate of inflation rose from 25 percent in the late 1970s to nearly 300 percent in the late 1980s, and it was also evident in some of the developing countries in Africa and Europe. The countries experiencing high rates of inflation inevitably were forced to depreciate their currencies rapidly to avoid a deterioration in their external competitiveness. In fact, in many of these countries, the exchange rate and domestic inflation were linked systematically.

A second factor was the uncertainty associated with the fluctuations in the exchange rates of the major currencies. As indicated earlier, a number of countries have adopted a basket peg in order to reduce the fluctuations in the value of their currencies in terms of other currencies. However, some countries have been reluctant to adopt a basket peg arrangement as it would entail frequent adjustments of the exchange rate in relation to the intervention currency, according to a preannounced formula. These countries were particularly reluctant to follow the short-term movements of major currencies, as they were considered to be transitory. Given the political stigma attached to devaluation under a pegged value, an increasing number of countries have found it expedient to adopt a more flexible arrangement. By adjusting their exchange rates on the basis of an undisclosed basket of currencies, some of these countries have been able to take advantage of the fluctuations in major currencies to camouflage an effective depreciation of their exchange rate whenever such a depreciation was desirable. In this context, an interesting question is to what extent such removal of political constraints on devaluation may undermine financial discipline and thus contribute to the generation of inflation. This point will be discussed in a subsequent section of the chapter.

These factors suggest a need to manage nominal exchange rates more flexibly in order to avoid unintended movements in real effective exchange rates. In addition, during the past decade, developing countries have been subjected to a number of external shocks, including a slowdown in the growth of industrial countries, high international interest rates, and a drying-up of external sources of funds because of the international debt crisis. Certain groups of developing countries have also experienced adverse movements in their terms of trade. Adjustment to these shocks has led many of the developing countries to seek to depreciate their real effective exchange rates through a more active use of the nominal exchange rate as a policy tool.

Before assessing the behavior of exchange rates in developing countries, it is useful to examine the relationship between the geographical location and the type of exchange rate arrangement maintained by these countries over the decade of the 1980s. For this purpose, the developing countries have been divided into three broad categories that differ somewhat from the official classification used in Table 8.1. The pegged rate category, under which the exchange rate is pegged to a single currency or a composite of currencies, is retained but the flexible rate classification is divided into two categories: managed rates and crawling rates. Under the managed rate category, the rate is adjusted frequently on the basis of undisclosed indicators, but such adjustments are relatively moderate and do not exhibit a strong secular trend. Clearly, the countries adopting a managed exchange rate arrangement have only low or moderate rates of inflation. Under the crawling peg arrangement, the nominal exchange rate depreciates rapidly, along with a relatively high rate of inflation.

As is evident from Table 8.1, the composition of exchange rate arrangements among developing countries shifted mainly during the years 1976 to 1982 and remained relatively stable in the following years. Table 8.2 provides a list of countries that maintained, for the most part, a single exchange rate arrangement throughout the period 1983–1989. As can be observed, with only a few exceptions, countries in Africa adopted a pegged regime. The fourteen countries in the CFA franc zone maintained a fixed parity to the French franc, while other countries pegged to the U.S. dollar, the SDR, or a basket of currencies. All the Middle Eastern countries in the sample also operated under a pegged regime. The developing countries in Europe (including the centrally planned economies, such as Hungary, Romania, and Yugoslavia), as well as countries in the Western Hemisphere, adopted either a pegged or a crawling exchange rate arrangement, depending on their rate of inflation.

TABLE 8.2	Geographical Distribution of Exchange Rate Arrangements for Developing Countries, 1983–1989				
Exchange rate arrangement	Africa	Asia	Europe	Middle East	Western Hemisphere
Pegged U.S. dollar	Ethiopia Liberia Sudan			Egypt Saudi Arabia	Bahamas Barbados El Salvador Guatemala Haiti Honduras Nicaragua Panama Paraguay Surinam Trinidad and Tobago Venezuela
French franc	Burkina Faso Cameroon Central African Republic Congo Côte d'Ivoire Gabon Mali Niger Senegal Togo				
SDR	Burundi Rwanda	Myanmar		Jordan	
Basket of currencies	Algeria Madagascar Malawi Mauritania Mauritius Tunisia Zimbabwe	China Fiji Nepal	Hungary Malta Romania	Cyprus Kuwait	
Crawling peg	Nigeria Tanzania Zaire Zambia		Turkey Yugoslavia		Argentina Brazil Chile Colombia Costa Rica Ecuador Jamaica Mexico Peru Uruguay

(continued)

TABLE 8.2   *(continued)*

Exchange rate arrangement	Africa	Asia	Europe	Middle East	Western Hemisphere
Managed floating	Kenya Morocco South Africa	Bangladesh India Indonesia Korea Malaysia Pakistan Philippines Singapore Sri Lanka Thailand Western Samoa			

Source: Same as Table 8.1.

Not surprisingly, all of the countries in the Western Hemisphere that adopted a pegged regime (primarily, small Caribbean economies) fixed their rate to the U.S. dollar. Countries in the Asian region behaved unlike those elsewhere, overwhelmingly adopting managed exchange rate arrangements. No Asian countries in the sample pegged to a single currency.[2]

Movements of Exchange Rate Indexes

In this section, indexes of nominal and real effective exchange rates are defined and their behavior examined for various groupings of developing countries since the late 1970s. In policy-related work on exchange rates, extensive use is made of effective exchange rate indexes. The real exchange rate is operationally defined as the ratio of foreign prices to domestic prices, adjusted for exchange rates. Using a log-linear formulation, the real effective exchange rate (re) is defined as the nominal effective exchange rate (ne) as adjusted for relative prices (rp).

$$re = ne - rp \qquad (1)$$

The relative price index is defined as the difference between the foreign price (fp) and domestic price (dp); fp is measured as the weighted average of the price index in each of the i countries with which the home country trades, $fp(i)$, with the bilateral trade weights given by $w(i)$. Therefore:

$$rp = fp - dp \qquad (2)$$

$$fp = \sum_{i=1}^{n} w(i) \cdot fp(i) \tag{3}$$

Similarly, the nominal effective exchange rate is defined as:

$$ne = \sum_{i=1}^{n} w(i) \cdot e(i) \tag{4}$$

where $e(i)$ is the bilateral exchange rate expressed as units of foreign currency per unit of domestic currency (that is, an increase corresponds to an appreciation of the domestic currency).

A number of choices are available for selecting the price indexes to be used. These include the consumer price index, the wholesale price index, and the gross national product (GNP) deflator. This study uses the consumer price index, which is readily available in the developing countries.[3] In this specification, the real exchange rate measures the relative purchasing power of the country's currency. It should be noted that, although it would be preferable, from a theoretical standpoint, to define the real exchange rate as the ratio of the price of traded to non-traded goods, separate price indexes for traded and nontraded goods are not generally available for the developing countries. However, if it is assumed that the price of traded goods moves broadly in line with foreign prices (that is, if the foreign real exchange rate is relatively constant), it can be shown that the ratio of the price of traded goods to nontraded goods would move in line with relative consumer prices.[4]

It should also be noted that movements in the real exchange rate can result from a host of supply and demand shocks that could alter equilibrium relative prices.[5] In addition to such shocks, any monetary-induced change in the domestic price level that is not accompanied by an adjustment in the nominal exchange rate would also alter the real exchange rate. Notwithstanding the difficulties in identifying the effects of real shocks on equilibrium relative prices and the real exchange rate, it is useful to examine the movements of these indexes with a view to discerning any apparent patterns among developing countries.

The indexes for relative prices (rp), the nominal effective exchange rate (ne), the real effective exchange rate (re), and the terms of trade (tt), were calculated for developed and developing countries, as well as for geographical groupings of developing countries—Africa, Asia, Europe, the Middle East, and the Western Hemisphere.[6] Movements of these indexes are given in Table 8.3 for the three periods 1978–1981, 1982–1985, and 1986–1989, as well as for the entire period 1978–1989. They are also depicted for the period as a whole in Figures 8.1 and 8.2.[7]

TABLE 8.3   Trend Movements of Relative Prices, Nominal and Real
Effective Exchange Rates, and Terms of Trade for
Different Regions, 1978–1989 (cumulative percentage
changes)

Region	Indicator	1978–81	1982–85	1986–89	1978–89
Industrial countries	rp	−4.9	−7.1	−1.8	−13.7
	ne	−5.9	−9.2	1.5	−13.6
	re	−1.1	−2.1	3.3	0.1
	tt	−7.0	2.3	9.8	5.1
Developing countries	rp	−20.1	−30.9	−54.8	−105.8
	ne	−15.6	−34.1	−74.7	−124.4
	re	4.5	−3.2	−19.9	−18.6
	tt	−12.4	2.1	−21.0	−31.4
Africa	rp	−19.2	−21.8	−26.6	−67.6
	ne	−8.3	−32.2	−56.4	−96.9
	re	10.8	−10.4	−29.8	−29.4
	tt	−22.4	9.1	−27.8	−41.0
Asia	rp	−5.9	−8.2	−6.2	−20.2
	ne	−12.8	−8.1	−27.4	−48.2
	re	−6.9	0.1	−21.2	−28.0
	tt	−7.0	8.4	−5.3	−3.9
Europe	rp	−27.6	−30.1	−85.0	−142.8
	ne	−27.9	−38.1	−90.1	−156.0
	re	−0.2	−8.0	−5.1	−13.3
	tt	−19.7	1.7	2.7	−15.2
Middle East	rp	−16.8	−33.5	−49.1	−99.4
	ne	−19.7	−19.2	−65.5	−104.4
	re	−3.0	14.3	−16.4	−5.1
	tt	20.7	−7.8	−58.9	−46.1
Western Hemisphere	rp	−31.9	−58.9	−126.4	−217.2
	ne	−22.8	−62.8	−136.6	−222.3
	re	9.0	−3.9	−10.3	−5.1
	tt	−18.8	−6.9	−7.1	−32.9

NOTE: rp = relative prices; ne = nominal effective exchange rates; re = real effective exhange rates; and tt = terms of trade.
SOURCE: Authors' calculations.

Comparing first the experience of the developing countries to that of the developed countries, a number of significant differences can be identified by inspection of Figure 8.1. The developing countries recorded a substantially larger deterioration in their relative prices than the developed countries did (over 100 percent, compared with 10 percent) during 1978–1989, reflecting the higher inflation rate of most developing countries relative to that of industrial countries (which account for the largest share of trade of most developing countries). Concomitantly, the nominal exchange rate depreciated substantially in the developing countries, particularly after 1985, when many of these countries devalued their

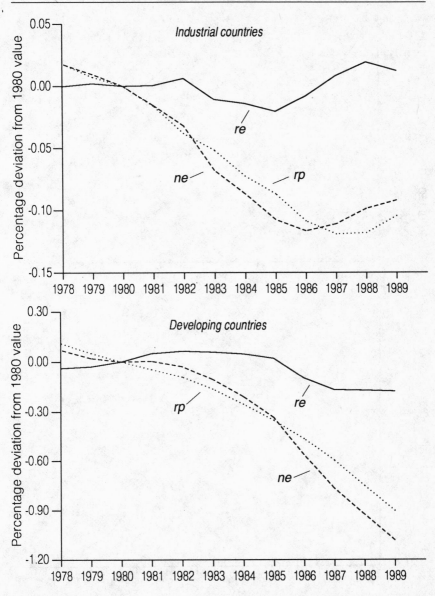

FIGURE 8.1   Industrial and Developing Countries: Movements of
Real and Nominal Effective Exchange Rates and
Relative Prices, 1978–1989

SOURCE: Authors' calculations.

FIGURE 8.2 Regions of the World: Movements of Real and Nominal
Effective Exchange Rates and Relative Prices,
1978–1989

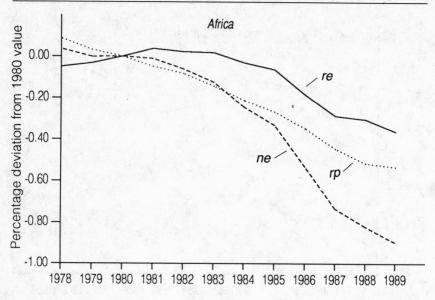

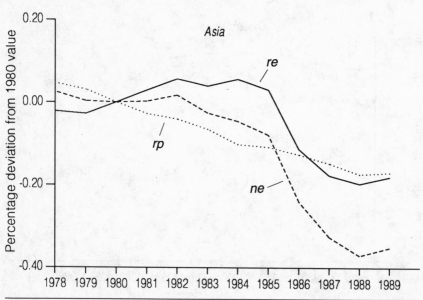

(continued)

FIGURE 8.2 (continued)

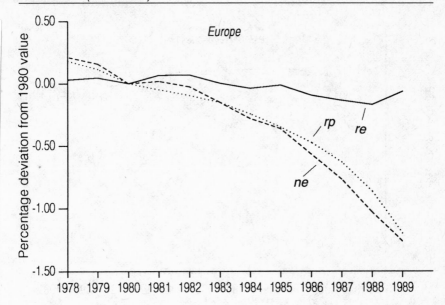

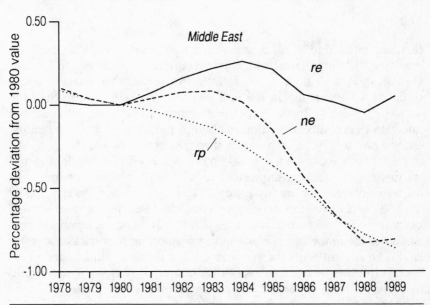

(continued)

FIGURE 8.2 (*continued*)

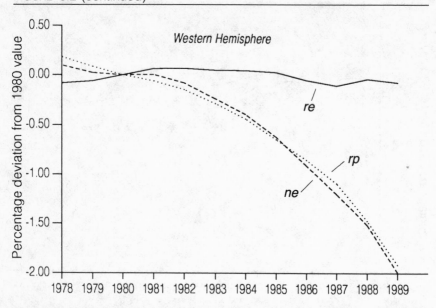

SOURCE: Authors' calculations.

currency relative to the U.S. dollar at a time when the dollar itself depreciated sharply against other major currencies. Consequently, notwithstanding their high inflation rates, the developing countries had a significant depreciation in the real exchange rate (19 percent over the period 1978–1989). In the developed countries, the nominal exchange rate also depreciated over time, although moderately, but the real exchange rate remained quite stable throughout this period.

The above movements of real exchange rates in the developing and the developed countries are consistent with the observed movements of the terms of trade for the two groups. The terms of trade deteriorated by over 30 percent for the developing countries, but they improved by 5 percent for the developed countries (Table 8.3).[8] The substantial depreciation of the real exchange rate in the developing countries as a group is also consistent with the requirements of external adjustment in response to other adverse shocks—for example, slower growth of world markets for their exports, higher international interest rates, and the debt crisis.

A review of the experiences of various geographical groupings of the developing countries reveals a number of common trends. As is evident in Figure 8.2, relative prices in all country groups deteriorated rapidly during the period 1978–1989, except in the case of Asian countries with relatively low rates of inflation. The rise in relative prices followed a similar pattern in all groups (except Asia), accelerating throughout the period, particularly after 1985. All groups also recorded a depreciation in the nominal exchange rate, with the pace of depreciation accelerating sharply during the period 1985–1987. This acceleration reflected both the increasing willingness of countries to undertake exchange rate adjustments and the precipitous fall of the U.S. dollar, which was the intervention currency for most developing countries.

For all of the geographical regions, except the Middle East, the sharp depreciation of the nominal exchange rate in the period after 1985 more than offset the deterioration in relative prices, resulting in the depreciation of their real exchange rates. The low inflation regions (Asia and Africa) experienced the largest depreciation in their real exchange rate. The movements of the real exchange rate to 1985, however, varied across the groups. In the case of the Asia and Europe, the real exchange rate was relatively stable during 1978–1985. In the case of Africa and the Western Hemisphere, real exchange rates appreciated during 1978– 1981, but depreciated subsequently. The initial appreciation of the real exchange rate in these groups was attributable to the reluctance of these countries to depreciate their currency in line with their relatively high domestic inflation. In the case of the Western Hemisphere, the initial appreciation of the real exchange rate was associated with a substantial outflow of capital that contributed to the widespread debt crisis in the early 1980s. In the case of the Middle East, the real exchange rate appreciated sharply during 1980–1985, owing to the significant improvement in the terms of trade of these countries.

Next, exchange rate developments are reviewed for the three groups of countries that maintained a single exchange rate arrangement (pegged, managed, or crawling peg) throughout the period 1982– 1989.The exchange rate indexes for these groups are provided in Table 8.4 and are depicted in Figure 8.3. In the case of the group with pegged exchange rates, the nominal exchange rate appreciated initially but depreciated sharply after 1985, reflecting both the weakening of the U.S. dollar (to which the currencies of many of the countries in this group were pegged) and more frequent devaluations. This pattern was mirrored in the movements of the real exchange rate, despite a rise in the average rate of inflation for this group. For the whole period, the real exchange rate depreciated by about 11 percent. This depreciation masked great differences among the subgroups that were using different pegging arrangements. The real exchange rate depreciated for countries pegging to a composite basket of currencies (32 percent), to the

TABLE 8.4   Trend Movements of Relative Prices, Nominal and Real
Effective Exchange Rates, and Terms of Trade for
Groups of Countries, According to Their Exchange Rate
Arrangements, 1982–1989 (cumulative percentage
change)

Exchange rate arrangement	Indicator	1982–85	1986–89	1982–89
Pegged arrangement	rp	4.2	−19.8	−15.6
	ne	9.0	−35.6	−26.6
	re	4.7	−15.8	−11.1
	tt	5.0	−22.9	−17.9
To U.S. dollar	rp	3.7	−64.7	−60.9
	ne	19.5	−76.1	−56.6
	re	15.8	−11.4	4.3
	tt	−2.7	−16.3	−19.0
To French franc	rp	5.2	18.4	23.6
	ne	−1.5	15.8	14.3
	re	−6.7	−2.6	−9.3
	rt	8.2	−45.7	−37.6
To SDR	rp	4.7	−2.2	2.5
	ne	19.8	−20.1	−0.3
	re	15.1	−17.9	−2.9
	tt	17.8	−18.1	−0.3
To basket of currencies	rp	4.1	0.9	4.9
	ne	1.1	−28.0	−26.9
	re	−3.0	−28.9	−31.9
	tt	8.3	−16.5	−8.3
Managed arrangement	rp	−11.9	−4.3	−16.2
	ne	−19.2	−29.9	−49.0
	re	−7.3	−25.5	−32.8
	tt	8.3	−3.7	4.6
Crawling peg arrangement	rp	−126.4	−187.0	−313.4
	ne	−148.7	−205.2	−353.9
	re	−22.3	−18.1	−40.4
	tt	−10.5	−6.8	−17.3

NOTE: rp = relative prices; ne = nominal effective exchange rates; re = real effective exchange rates; and tt = terms of trade.
SOURCE: Authors' calculations.

French franc (9 percent), and to the SDR (3 percent), but it appreciated for countries pegging to the U.S. dollar (4 percent).

In the case of the group with managed exchange arrangements, relatively low domestic inflation, together with the flexible exchange rate policy, led to a significant depreciation of the real exchange rate (33 percent). For the group with crawling peg exchange arrangements, the depreciation of the real exchange rate was even greater (40 percent), as the depreciation of the nominal exchange rate more than offset the substantial deterioration in relative prices. Thus, there seems to be a loose link between the degree of exchange rate flexibility and the observed improvement in external competitiveness.

Although it is not possible to identify, and much less quantify, the effects of various real factors on the real exchange rate, it would be interesting to examine the bilateral relationship between this variable and the terms of trade in different groups of the developing countries. As already indicated, the significant depreciation of the real exchange rate for the aggregate group of developing countries during 1978–1989 is consistent with the deterioration in the terms of trade for this group. A comparison of the movements of the real exchange rate and terms of trade for the geographical regions, however, reveals a mixed pattern. The African countries, which had the greatest deterioration in their terms of trade, also recorded the most depreciation in the real exchange rate. Both the Middle East and the Western Hemisphere countries undertook only a small real depreciation, although they experienced a substantial deterioration in their terms of trade. By contrast, Asian countries recorded a large depreciation in the real exchange rate, in spite of only a modest deterioration in the terms of trade. This experience is consistent with the outward orientation of the Asian countries that aggressively pursued export-led growth.

A comparison of the movements of real exchange rates and terms of trade for the three groups of countries that were using different exchange rate arrangements reveals a clear pattern. The group with pegged arrangements witnessed the largest deterioration in the terms of trade (18 percent), yet recorded only a moderate depreciation in the real exchange rate. By contrast, the group with managed arrangements which recorded a significant improvement in its terms of trade, achieved a substantial depreciation in the real exchange rate. The group with crawling peg arrangements recorded great real exchange rate depreciation and terms of trade deterioration. Thus, it appears that the group with pegged arrangements has been least successful in adjusting the real exchange rate in response to terms of trade shocks. However, even if this conclusion would be warranted on the basis of such casual empiricism, the question would be whether the inability of the group with pegged arrangements to adjust the real exchange rate was inherent to the pegged rate regime or resulted from lack of adherence to the financial discipline required by this regime. In this context, it is interesting to note that, if domestic inflation for the group had not exceeded foreign inflation, the real exchange rate would have depreciated 23 percent.

FIGURE 8.3 Movements of Real and Nominal Effective Exchange
Rates and Relative Prices for Countries with Pegged,
Managed, or Crawling Peg Exchange Rates,
1978–1989

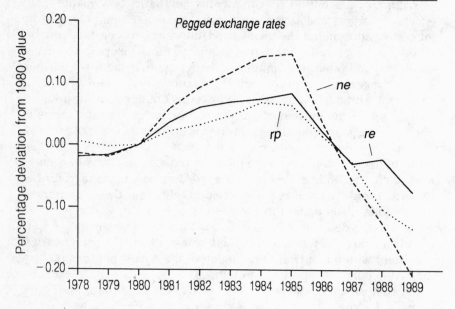

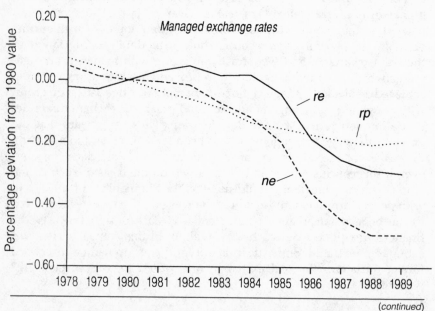

(continued)

Figure 8.3   (*continued*)

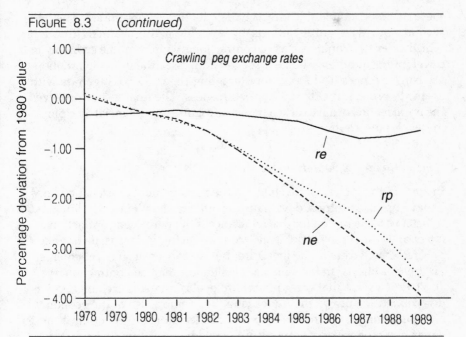

Note: RE = real effective exchange rates; NE = nominal effective exchange rates; and RP = relative prices.
Source: Authors' calculations.

Some Policy Issues

The exchange rate instrument has become an important component of adjustment programs in the developing countries. In many of these countries, unfavorable external shocks and overly expansionary financial policies have led to overvaluation of the domestic currency. In such cases, nominal devaluations have been used to realign relative prices—that is, the real exchange rate—in one action, in preference to undergoing a prolonged period of costly deflation.

In spite of the increased use of the exchange rate as an instrument of external adjustment, exchange rate management has remained a controversial issue in developing countries. Over the last decade or so, a consensus has emerged that "getting the exchange rate right" (that is, avoiding prolonged periods of overvaluation of the domestic currency) is of prime importance for achieving a stable macroeconomic environment conducive to sustained growth.[9] Nevertheless, devaluation is regarded as having potential adverse effects on domestic output and inflation.

In the remainder of the chapter some of the arguments concerning these macroeconomic side effects of devaluation are examined. The first section addresses output effects by examining the channels through which a devaluation may exert a contractionary effect on the economy in developing countries. The next section addresses the possible inflationary consequences of the policy of targeting the real exchange rate with a view to protecting external competitiveness. The final section analyzes the implications of a fixed exchange rate regime for "financial discipline" in developing countries.

Contractionary devaluation

In spite of the increased flexibility in the management of exchange rates in developing countries, devaluation is often undertaken only with great reluctance. One reason for this reluctance is the perceived contractionary effect of devaluation on domestic economic activity. This issue has been debated extensively in the literature, but no consensus has yet emerged on the conditions under which a devaluation may be contractionary.[10]

To the extent that the equilibrium level of the real exchange rate is determined mainly by the underlying "fundamentals" of the economy, a devaluation would have no long-run effects on the economy,[11] and any contractionary effects on output would be transitory. Existing work, however, has tended to focus on impact effects, thus overlooking the possibility that a small and short-lived contraction in output may well be offset by a significant expansion over the longer term.[12]

With regard to impact effects, the arguments for a potential contractionary effect of devaluation involve both the demand and supply sides of the economy. In examining these effects, it is important to distinguish between traded and nontraded goods, since the factors affecting the demand for these two types of goods are generally quite different. For traded goods, whose prices in foreign currency are determined abroad, a devaluation increases the domestic price at which they can be sold. Thus, devaluation would increase the incentives for production of traded goods, unless the marginal cost of producing such goods rises in the same proportion.

The effect of devaluation on demand for nontraded goods is less clear. Demand for such goods emanates from domestic private consumption, private investment, and public sector spending. A devaluation may reduce private consumption of nontraded goods through a number of channels. These include: (1) the fall in the real value of income and wealth associated with both the rise in domestic prices and in the real value of external liabilities of the private sector, (2) the fall in private disposable income associated with the increase in the real value of ad valorem trade taxes, (3) a possible redistribution of income from those with high marginal propensities to spend to those with low propensities to spend, and (4) the rise in the domestic real interest rate associated with the decline in the real money supply. Similarly, private investment could fall, owing to the rise in the price of imported capital and intermediate goods as well as to the rise in interest rates. As for the public sector, if the government is a net external debtor, devaluation would increase the domestic real cost of debt servicing, requiring cutbacks in other government spending.

These contractionary effects may be offset by a number of countervailing factors. To the extent that the private sector may be a net international creditor, a devaluation would weaken (and possibly reverse) the above-mentioned wealth effect of devaluation. The wealth effect would be further weakened if some of the private sector's domestic assets are indexed to the price level. Furthermore, the effect of devaluation on trade taxes may be partly offset by a reduction in the real value of other taxes emanating from the increase in the price level and the presence of lags in tax collection.[13] It may also be asked what effect devaluation would have on domestic real interest rates. Although an anticipated future devaluation may cause nominal rates to rise in order to compensate holders of domestic assets for the anticipated capital loss, a devaluation may actually lower nominal rates if it has been previously anticipated. The effect of devaluation on nominal interest rates would also depend on the extent to which such rates are market-determined and on the degree of capital mobility. The conditions favoring increased nominal interest rates are: (1) domestic interest rates are market-determined, (2) traded goods have a large share in the domestic price index, (3) capital mobility is low, and (4) the demand for money is relatively interest-inelastic. Even if these conditions are satisfied, however, the real interest rate need not increase if the associated increase in the expected rate of inflation exceeds the rise in the nominal interest rates. Mitigating factors are also at work with regard to effects of devaluation on private investment. The increase in the price of imported capital and intermediate goods, for example, would not be inimical to investment in the traded goods sector, where output prices would rise in the same proportion. Moreover, as the real wage is likely to fall on impact, this may itself induce an increase in capacity expansion.

An important effect of devaluation is the induced shift in the composition of domestic demand from traded to nontraded goods. To the extent that the fall in domestic demand for traded goods can largely be replaced by foreign demand, this shift results in a net increase in the total demand for domestic production. This "substitution effect" has long formed the basis for the conventional view that devaluation fosters an expansion in domestic output.

This discussion suggests that devaluation would increase the demand for traded goods, but it would have an ambiguous effect on the demand for nontraded goods. On the supply side, devaluation is likely to raise the domestic costs of production for both sectors, owing to the associated rise in the domestic price of imported inputs and in the nominal wage. The price of imported inputs is likely to increase by the same proportion as the devaluation. The response of the nominal wage, however, is more complex, depending on the extent and nature of indexation, on whether the devaluation was previously anticipated, and on the elasticities of aggregate labor demand and supply. Although production costs may rise, as long as the increase in the nominal wage is not excessive, the net demand and supply effects are likely to favor production of traded goods. However, the impact effects of devaluation on output of nontraded goods are ambiguous.

The presence of distortions may affect the likely effects of devaluation on output. For example, the contractionary effects of a devaluation-induced rise in the domestic price level would be weaker in the presence of quantitative restrictions on imports, to the extent that the domestic price of such goods would already reflect their scarcity value. Moreover, quantitative restrictions on imports of capital and intermediate goods undertaken for balance of payments reasons may be eased in conjunction with devaluation, reducing domestic production costs. It is also possible, however, that the lifting of restrictions would shift demand from domestic to foreign goods. Thus, the effects of devaluation on output would be greatly influenced by the nature of the initial distortions and by any specific changes in restrictions that may accompany the devaluation.

On balance, no clear analytical case can be made for presuming that devaluation would lead to a contraction of domestic output on impact. Effects of devaluation on the output of nontraded goods are ambiguous and will depend on the circumstances of the particular case, while the effects on the output of traded goods are likely to be positive. Simulation exercises, as well as recent empirical work, suggest that dynamic effects may be important—that is, short-term effects in a contractionary direction may be reversed over the longer term.[14] In any event, if the real exchange rate becomes substantially overvalued, the alternative to devaluation is to keep domestic inflation significantly below that of trading partners over a prolonged period. Such a slowdown in inflation would inevitably require contractionary financial policies that would entail their own output costs.

Real exchange rate rules

The move toward greater exchange rate flexibility in developing countries reflects, in part, an increased concern with protecting competitiveness in response to a number of adverse external and domestic shocks over the past two decades. It is well known, however, that competitiveness depends on the value of the real, rather than the nominal, exchange rate. Consequently, an important motivating factor behind the movement toward greater flexibility of nominal exchange rates has been assurance that the real exchange rate would be sustained at a competitive level.

Since the real exchange rate is an endogenous macroeconomic variable, it cannot be directly controlled by the authorities. Policy makers have at their disposal several policy instruments—such as the level and composition of government spending and taxation—to achieve desired values of the real exchange rate. However, in recent years, an increasing number of developing countries have relied on arrangements under which the nominal exchange rate is adjusted in line with inflation in order to maintain purchasing power parity (PPP). Since such arrangements entail the pursuit of a real target with a nominal instrument, they could have disquieting implications for macroeconomic stability. In particular, the adoption of a real exchange target may leave a small open economy without a nominal anchor for the domestic price level, creating the possibility that shocks to domestic inflation may become permanent and, under some circumstances, lead to hyperinflation. To the extent that the supply of money in an open economy can be augmented from external sources, an explosive price pattern can emerge, even under a nonaccommodative credit policy. For example, if the authorities seek to achieve an overly depreciated real exchange rate by devaluing the nominal rate, domestic prices would rise—thus increasing the demand for money and inducing capital inflows to clear the money market. The more flexible domestic wages and prices are, the more quickly a new equilibrium can be restored and the need to devalue again will come sooner. With nothing to pin down the domestic price level, the attempt to depreciate the real exchange rate further through nominal devaluations would merely result in an acceleration of inflation.

The experience of several countries in Latin America with high inflation raises concerns regarding the advisability of real exchange rate rules. All of these countries have experienced extremely high rates of inflation in the past decade. Their inflation has had a "plateau" character—that is, periods of fairly stable, but high, inflation that give way by discrete jumps to periods of yet higher, but again fairly stable, inflation. In some cases, such jumps have been associated with discrete devaluations, followed by crawling pegs based on PPP rules. In all of these countries, recent stabilization attempts have featured a fixed nominal exchange rate to provide a nominal anchor. It should be noted, however, that crawling pegs based on PPP are not invariably associated with near-hyperinflation.

Analytical work on the consequences of real exchange rate rules for price stability has been surprisingly limited. Adams and Gros (1986) have examined the issue by using a sequence of simple analytical models with different assumptions concerning commodity composition, price-wage stickiness, capital mobility, etc. They concluded that (1) the monetary authorities might lose control of inflation if they set the nominal exchange rate according to a real exchange rate rule, and (2) if they do try to control inflation, they are likely to lose control over some other macroeconomic target. They also argued that if the real exchange rate target is overdepreciated relative to the equilibrium real exchange rate, inflation is likely to be higher.

Lizondo (1989) constructed a model in which the steady-state real exchange rate is a function not only of the real variables mentioned above but also of the domestic rate of inflation. He found that the domestic rate of inflation determines the magnitude of the government's real revenue from the inflation tax and that this, in turn, affects the steady-state value of private wealth and expenditure—and thereby, the equilibrium real exchange rate. Each real exchange rate target is thus associated with a steady-state domestic inflation rate, other things being equal. However, the associated rate of inflation is not necessarily unique, not all real exchange rate targets are feasible, and not all real exchange rate rules will move the economy to the chosen target, even if that target is feasible.

The analyses by both Adams and Gros and Lizondo suggest that real exchange rate rules have potentially dangerous consequences for price stability. This potential would exist even if the target real exchange rate is at its steady-state equilibrium value, but the real threat of hyperinflation is particularly eminent if the target real exchange rate is overdepreciated. In view of the frequency and severity of both external and internal shocks to which developing countries are likely to be subjected, as well as the limited quantitative knowledge about the determination of equilibrium real exchange rates, the pursuit of real exchange rate targets in these countries appears to be risky.

Financial discipline and the exchange rate regime

Proponents of fixed exchange rates in developing countries often argue that the adoption of an official parity prevents the monetary authorities from permitting excessive growth of the money supply, thereby imposing a degree of financial discipline that would be absent if a country's currency floated freely and the domestic inflation rate was free to deviate permanently from that of its trading partners. Advocates of greater flexibility, for their part, maintain that financial discipline, if absent, is unlikely to be enforced by the adoption of a fixed exchange rate. Instead, the announcement of an exchange rate target would merely result in a succession of financial crises followed by devaluations, introducing a high degree of instability into the behavior of the real exchange rate. In turn, macroeconomic uncertainty and disruption of trade and investment flows would result.

This section attempts to evaluate these arguments from the perspective of recent developments in macroeconomic theory. The following two questions are addressed: (1) What is the nature of the constraints that are imposed on domestic macroeconomic policies by the maintenance of a fixed exchange rate? (2) Are there valid reasons for the monetary authorities to precommit to an exchange rate target, and under what conditions can such a commitment be made credible?

Financial constraints imposed by a fixed exchange rate. The conditions under which a small open economy can maintain a fixed exchange rate have been studied intensively in recent years. These conditions were a primary concern of the literature on balance of payments crises that had its inception with the work of Krugman (1979). Consider a small open economy that maintains a fixed exchange rate for both commercial and financial transactions, and suppose that both domestic goods and securities are close substitutes for their foreign counterparts. Under these conditions, the law of one price implies that the domestic inflation rate is equal to the world inflation rate plus the rate of depreciation of the domestic currency. Under a fixed regime, the latter rate is an exogenous, policy-determined variable that can be taken for simplicity to be zero. Assuming a unitary income elasticity of money demand, the rate of growth of domestic money is determined by the rate of growth of real output plus the rate of world inflation.

Suppose also that the monetary authorities require that some minimum fraction of the domestic money supply must be backed by foreign exchange reserves in order to defend the fixed parity. If foreign exchange reserves would fall below this critical value, the fixed parity would be abandoned and the domestic currency would float. It follows then that the rate of growth of domestic credit cannot permanently exceed the rate of growth of nominal income. This is true because, if domestic credit grows faster than the demand for money for an extended period of time, domestically created money would gradually replace foreign exchange reserves in the central bank's balance sheet, and the reserve threshold of the authorities would soon be breached.[15]

According to the literature, maintaining the viability of a fixed exchange rate requires that the underlying rate of growth of domestic credit should not exceed a specified upper bound. The upper bound in question is based on the rate of growth of the demand for money (which depends on the world rate of inflation), the policy-determined rate of depreciation of the domestic currency, the rate of growth of real income, and the income elasticity of demand for money. The permissible rate of growth of domestic credit would be greater (that is, the degree of financial discipline imposed by the requirements of exchange rate viability would be less binding) for (1) a higher rate of world inflation, (2) a higher rate of growth of real income, and (3) a greater income elasticity of demand for money.

It should be pointed out that financial discipline is imposed only on the long-term rate of growth of credit. Transitory episodes of rapid credit expansion are not incompatible with the maintenance of the official parity, as long as these events are perceived to be reversible. The duration of such periods of rapid credit expansion—and thus the effective degree of discipline—depends both on the initial stock of reserves and on the reserve threshold of the authorities. The larger the initial stock of reserves is, relative to the target, the longer excessive credit growth can be sustained and the weaker is the amount of discipline imposed by the fixed regime.

The financial discipline imposed on the authorities may be weakened in the presence of capital mobility. Access to capital markets enables the central bank to replenish reserves and to sustain the exchange rate parity by financing intervention through foreign borrowing. Thus, the reserve threshold would not be binding, as long as the central bank could finance any shortfall in reserves by convincing its external creditors that a policy reversal is soon coming. Under such circumstances, large and persistent deviations from the "upper-bound" growth rate of credit can be sustained, considerably weakening the amount of financial discipline.

It thus becomes relevant to inquire as to the conditions under which foreign financing would continue to be available to the authorities.[16] To address this question, it is appropriate to consider the consolidated accounts of the financial and nonfinancial public sectors, since from the standpoint of the country's external creditors, the resources of both sectors are available to service debt. In brief, external creditors would be willing to lend to the domestic public sector as long as that sector is perceived to be financially solvent. The solvency requirement ultimately sets the financial conditions under which a fixed exchange rate is viable, and it therefore captures the financial discipline imposed on the economy.

The public sector will be solvent if the present value of its anticipated future debt-service payments (amortization plus interest) is at least equal to the face value of its existing debt. The resources available to service debt, in turn, consist of the stream of future primary surpluses of the public sector and future seignorage revenue. Thus, external financing will be available as long as the present value of anticipated future primary surpluses plus seignorage revenue is at least as great as the face value of the public sector's net debt.

The role of a fixed exchange rate in the context of solvency is that, by setting the economy's steady-state inflation rate equal to that of its trading partners, it limits the future seignorage revenue available to the public sector. Given the initial stock of debt and the solvency requirements, this limit on seignorage puts a lower bound on the present value of the stream of future primary surpluses of the public sector. If the exchange rate floated, smaller surpluses could be accommodated by printing money and accepting a higher domestic rate of inflation, as long as the economy is on the "right" (that is, the inelastic) side of the inflation-tax Laffer curve. If the solvency condition is violated with a fixed exchange rate, the authorities would not be able to borrow, and the exchange rate could be sustained only as long as the reserves of the authorities themselves were not depleted. In the absence of a policy correction, a speculative attack would soon ensue—much as predicted in the literature on the balance-of-payments crisis—and the fixed rate could no longer be defended.

In summary, in a world of capital mobility, a fixed exchange rate requires a developing country to be able to maintain fiscal discipline, in the sense that its primary surpluses must satisfy an intertemporal budget constraint. This constraint will be less, if the public sector's initial net debt is smaller and the seignorage revenues are greater. The latter depend on the world inflation rate, the growth of domestic output, and the income elasticity of the demand for money.

Credibility of an announced exchange rate target.   The "financial discipline" referred to in this discussion is associated with an exchange rate that is fixed permanently rather than adjusted periodically. Recurrent devaluations would enable the government to wipe out periodically the part of its debt denominated in domestic currency, thereby easing its solvency constraint. Thus, fixing the exchange rate would not necessarily impose financial discipline, if the government maintained the option of periodically adjusting the exchange rate. The issue, then, is whether the incentive structure under a fixed-rate regime is conducive to the adoption of an immutable exchange rate peg (with attendant financial discipline) or to periodic exchange rate adjustments.

Recent developments in the literature on time consistency would seem to suggest that the latter possibility is more likely to be the case.

Suppose that inflation has a social cost, but that positive inflation "surprises" (that is, inflation rates higher than anticipated levels) also have socially beneficial effects. These surprises may include, for example, increasing the level of domestic output or raising the revenue from the inflation tax. Suppose also that domestic and foreign goods are such close substitutes that movements in the domestic price level depend on changes in the exchange rate. The authorities could then use the exchange rate as an instrument to alter the rate of inflation in pursuit of socially desirable objectives. Well-informed private agents would, of course, be aware that the authorities are formulating their exchange rate policy in this fashion. Would a stable-price equilibrium (with no devaluation) tend to emerge in this setting?

The answer depends on the characteristics of the government's social welfare function (see Barro and Gordon 1983). To the extent that the private sector expects prices to be stable, an unexpected increase in the price level would increase social welfare at the margin. The authorities would then have an incentive to engineer an inflation "surprise"—say, through a devaluation. However, since private agents would be aware of this incentive, they would not expect stable prices but would expect inflationary policies to be pursued. If the social cost of an increase in inflation increased initially with higher rates of inflation, the economy would then settle at an inflation rate so high that the cost of a marginal increase in "surprise" inflation would be equal to its benefits. Only in such a high-inflation equilibrium would the authorities fail to have an incentive to deviate from the expected inflation path. Of course, since inflation is assumed to affect social welfare adversely, this outcome would be inferior to an outcome of stable prices.

The point here is that the nature of the incentives for the authorities makes it unlikely that a stable price equilibrium would emerge, even when policy makers are maximizing welfare. As long as a marginal deviation from stable prices appears to be beneficial, the private sector will expect the authorities to try to produce inflation surprises. This expectation in itself increases the cost of a policy of stable prices because, if such a policy is pursued, it would produce *negative* inflation surprises. Thus, high inflation, with recurrent devaluations, is likely to emerge under these circumstances.

The solution to the problem would be for the authorities to convince the private sector that they would forgo the incentives to inflate—in other words, they would precommit to a policy of price stability. This policy would facilitate the maintenance of a fixed exchange rate, because it would eliminate costly private expectations of inflation. The problem with this solution, however, is that the authorities might find it difficult to make their commitment credible. Unless they could find a way to do so, disbelief on the part of the private sector might result in worse economic outcomes than a high-inflation equilibrium. Thus, policy makers would find it desirable to precommit to fixing the exchange rate indefinitely, if they could do so convincingly.

An obvious way to make the fixed exchange rate regime credible is for the authorities to surrender their power to alter the exchange rate. This could be achieved, for example, by a constitutional amendment that sets the value of the currency or by membership in a currency union where the exchange rate could be altered only by international agreement.[17] In either case, the authorities would be "tying their hands" by forgoing the use of a policy instrument.[18] It should be noted, however, that although such arrangements might make it costly to alter the exchange rate, they do not make it impossible. Obviously, the constitution could be altered or the country could withdraw from a currency union. Clearly, the commitment of the authorities to forgo the use of devaluation to engineer inflationary surprises will be all the more credible as the cost of using it rises.

The preceding discussion raises the issues of how great the cost of breaking a commitment to a fixed rate should be and how this cost should be imposed. In general, it is not desirable to make the cost inordinately high, as that would, in effect, fix the exchange rate permanently. It may sometimes be socially optimal to alter the exchange rate in response to exogenous shocks. Thus, although it would be desirable for policy makers to attach a higher cost to inflation than that perceived by society as a whole, this cost should not be so great that the exchange rate is never moved. An optimal solution would be to adopt rigid exchange rate rules, according to which the exchange rate could be moved only in response to well-specified exogenous shocks.

Exchange rate rules that are contingent on the specific state of the economy are difficult to design and to enforce. Rogoff (1985) has suggested that an alternative way for inducing the authorities to behave as if they attach a higher cost to inflation than society does as a whole is through the appointment of a financially conservative central banker. This approach illustrates a commitment to price stability that is greater than would appear warranted by the social costs of inflation, but it retains the flexibility of responding to exogenous shocks in extreme cases.

This analysis has obvious implications for the formulation of exchange rate policy in adjustment programs of developing countries. As a preferred option, exchange rate policy in such programs should seek to replicate the government's rules for exchange rate management. Devaluation should be undertaken only in response to significant exogenous shocks (but not to ratify expansionary domestic policies). In this context, a period of unsustainable fiscal deficits should be countered by fiscal overcorrection rather than by fiscal correction accompanied by devaluation.

If such government rules for exchange rate adjustment prove difficult to implement or are insufficiently transparent to the domestic private sector, credibility problems may persist in countries adopting adjustment programs. In this case, a second-best alternative would be to grant considerable autonomy to a central bank that is regarded as conservative in its management of monetary policy, although this alternative may entail some reluctance to devalue the currency, even in the face of exogenous shocks that would optimally require a devaluation. The international economic institutions may have a role to play in supporting such financially conservative policies. In other words, a commitment to the target of a nominal exchange rate may have its credibility enhanced by support from the international financial organizations.

Summary and Conclusions

After the collapse of the Bretton Woods system, the vast majority of the developing countries continued to maintain a pegged exchange rate regime, under which the official exchange rate was fixed either to a single currency or to some currency composite. The existence of a plethora of restrictions and controls on both current and capital accounts in these countries have often given rise to the emergence of parallel foreign exchange markets. In some cases, such parallel markets have played an important role in the allocation of foreign exchange. In most cases, however, the official foreign exchange market has remained the dominant market.[19]

The conduct of policy in the developing countries with regard to the official exchange rate has undergone a marked evolution over the past decade and a half. Fluctuations in exchange rates of major currencies, as well as an upsurge of inflation within the developing countries themselves, have required greater flexibility in the conduct of exchange rate management in these countries. Moreover, during the same period, external shocks—including a slowdown in the growth of industrial countries, an increase in international interest rates, the debt crisis, and adverse terms of trade developments—have induced many developing countries to seek to depreciate their real effective exchange rates as central components of adjustment programs. The combination of all these factors has resulted in an evolution of exchange rate regimes in developing countries toward more flexible arrangements and more frequent use of the exchange rate as a policy tool, even in those countries that have retained a single currency peg.

As a result of greater exchange rate flexibility, developing countries as a group have recorded substantial depreciation in their real effective exchange rates over the past decade and a half, in spite of a significant deterioration in their relative price performance. For the group as a whole, the real exchange rate appreciated during 1978–1982, stabilized up to about 1985, and depreciated substantially through 1989, despite a significant acceleration in inflation during the last period. The depreciation of the real exchange rate was widespread among subgroups of developing countries, but the groups experiencing low to moderate inflation were more successful in improving their external competitiveness.

In spite of increased exchange rate flexibility, developing countries have continued to show reluctance to undertake discrete adjustments in their exchange rates, partly out of concern for possible adverse consequences on domestic economic activity. Although, in principle, adverse consequences cannot be ruled out in the short term, it is unlikely that any contractionary effects on output would exceed those resulting from the alternative policy of restricting aggregate demand aimed at realigning relative prices through a prolonged period of deflation. In fact, devaluation would obviate the need for fiscal overcorrection and allow a more gradual adjustment of the fundamentals to their equilibrium levels.

A more serious concern relates to the pursuit of targets for real exchange rates through linking exchange rate adjustments to domestic inflation. Such targeting may push an economy toward hyperinflation, particularly in a world characterized by real shocks of uncertain duration and with uncertain effects on the equilibrium real exchange rate. The conclusion would seem to be that the nominal exchange rate should retain a role as nominal anchor—that is, some burden of the adjustment to an equilibrium real exchange rate must be borne by the domestic price level. This conclusion is strengthened when credibility issues are taken into account. Unless the private sector becomes convinced that the government has incentives to resist repeated devaluations, an undesirably high level of domestic inflation may well emerge. A number of developing countries, particularly in Latin America, seem to have recently been caught in a vicious cycle of this kind.

In view of the above considerations, a relevant question is whether the recent pursuit of exchange rate flexibility in developing countries has gone too far. Given the severe problems associated with the overvaluation of the currency in many developing countries in the past, it is difficult to take a strong position in support of greater rigidity of nominal exchange rates. Nevertheless, a case can be made that the burden of external adjustment must be shared by both the exchange rate and financial policies. Although exchange rate changes may facilitate the process of adjustment to external shocks, governments may find it desirable to establish a reputation for financial responsibility. An effective means for establishing such a reputation would be to eschew use of the exchange rate to ratify the effects of previous expansionary policies, except where a credible commitment can be made to forgo excessively expansionary policies in the future.

Notes

The authors are grateful to Delano Villanueva for his substantial contribution to the first part of the chapter, to Mohsin S. Khan and J. Peter Neary for helpful comments, and to Ravina Malkani for valuable research assistance. The views expressed, however, are those of the authors and do not necessarily reflect those of the International Monetary Fund.

1. The proportion of countries adopting various exchange rate regimes is also affected by the increase in the number of countries included in the sample over this period, but this effect does not significantly change the observed patterns.

2. For a more detailed assessment of the experiences of Asian countries with various exchange rate policies, see Aghevli (1981).

3. See Wickham (1985) and Mussa (1986) for a discussion of relative merits of various price indexes.

4. To see this, assume that the domestic price level is a weighted average of prices of traded goods (tp) and nontraded goods (np), with the relative weights of these goods in the domestic price index given by u and $(1-u)$. That is:

$$dp = u \cdot np + (1-u)\, tp$$

Assuming $fp = tp$, it follows that:

$$rp = ft - dp = u(tp - np)$$

5. Models of real exchange rate determination in developing countries are presented in Edwards (1989a), as well as Khan and Montiel (1987).

6. For each of these variables, the group value is the simple average of country values.

7. The variables re, ne, and rp in Figures 8.1 and 8.2 are as defined in the text.

8. This discussion of the relationship between the real effective exchange rate and the terms of trade adopts the standard presumption that a terms of trade deterioration is associated with a depreciation of the equilibrium real exchange rate. As J. Peter Neary has remarked, however, this need not be so. For an analysis of the issue, see Corden and Neary (1982).

9. See, for example, Fischer (1986). This consensus reflects a convergence of views on a narrower issue—that is, the trade balance in most developing

countries is, indeed, responsive to the level of the real exchange rate over a policy-relevant time period, contrary to the developing country version of "elasticity pessimism."

10. For a recent survey of the analytical issues involved, see Lizondo and Montiel (1989a), on which the discussion in this section relies heavily.

11. These statements must be made with caution, however, because it is possible to construct models in which nominal devaluations have long-term real effects. See Obstfeld (1986), as well as Lizondo and Montiel (1989b).

12. This issue has only recently been analyzed by the use of simulation models. A recent example is Haque, Montiel, and Symanski (1990).

13. The real value of taxes could fall because of lags in collection and, in the case of specific taxes, because of failure to adjust the base to inflation. See Aghevli and Khan (1977), Olivera (1967), and Tanzi (1977).

14. For some recent empirical work, see Edwards (1986a). A simulation study, using a model that incorporates many of the channels described above, is described in Haque, Montiel, and Symanski (1990).

15. The insights of the literature on the balance of payments crisis are that, with well-informed agents, the threshold will be reached suddenly by means of a speculative attack and that the timing of the attack can be determined analytically. See Krugman (1979) and Obstfeld (1984).

16. This issue has been related to the question of exchange rate viability by Buiter (1986).

17. The CFA franc zone is an example of such an arrangement.

18. Giavazzi and Pagano (1986) see this as one of the advantages of the European Monetary System.

19. This may be an overstatement in countries where illegal trade is important.

Comments

J. PETER NEARY

This chapter presents a useful review of the exchange rate experience of developing countries since 1976, as well as an informal and sensible discussion of the policy issues that arise in the choice of exchange rate regime. As the authors note, exchange rates of the larger developed countries have been dominated by market forces during this period and have exhibited significant fluctuations occasioned by volatile international capital movements. By contrast, most developing countries have viewed their exchange rate as an instrument of economic policy, in many cases pegging it to some external standard. In this comment, I note some reservations about their statistical evidence, elaborate on their discussion of the effects of terms-of-trade changes, and end with some remarks about policy.

The authors point out that the proportion of developing countries in their sample that adopted pegged exchange rates declined between 1976 and 1989. However, since their sample size is not constant, this exaggerates the trend toward more flexible regimes. As shown in Table 8.1, the actual number of countries with pegged arrangements fell only by five between 1976 and 1989 (from 92 to 87). It would be of interest to examine this further. Does the change reflect continuity in policy by those countries in the 1976 sample or does it reflect a disproportionate tendency to adopt pegged arrangements by countries that entered the sample between 1976 and 1989? This qualification to the authors' conclusions does not negate the principal lessons they draw from Table 8.1: the decline in the importance of pegging to a single currency (from 67 to 50 countries), in favor of an increased tendency to peg to a composite (from 25 to 37 countries) or to adopt flexible arrangements (from 15 to 44 countries). These findings highlight the need to amend textbook models of a small open economy in one important respect: in a world of floating rates between major trading blocs, the "rest of the world" should be disaggregated and a fixed rate with a single currency makes sense only if it is the dominant currency in which foreign trade is invoiced.

Highly managed exchange rates, implying that international capital movements into and out of these countries have been heavily regulated, raise the issue of what set of models is appropriate in trying to understand the experience of these developing countries. One way of interpreting the present chapter's contribution is that it argues implicitly for the continued relevance to developing countries of the types of models used in international macroeconomics in the 1950s. These were characterized by fixed but adjustable exchange rates, the effective absence of private international capital flows, and sticky domestic wages and prices (with the implication that contractionary policies have high output costs).

In such an environment, the choice of exchange rate regime is an important determinant of the real exchange rate and of macroeconomic performance, in general. Hence, considerable interest attaches to the empirical results, which find a "loose link" between the degree of exchange rate flexibility and the observed improvement in external competitiveness. A more formal statistical analysis (even if only a simple analysis of variance) would be needed, however, to establish this link convincingly. This is especially true because the strongest link between changes in the real and nominal exchange rates (with average depreciations of 40 percent and almost 400 percent, respectively) is found for countries with crawling exchange rates. However, since these countries are mostly those with high inflation, it is likely that the nominal exchange rate changes merely accommodated the loss of control over domestic monetary and fiscal policy, and they should not be seen as an independent cause of the real exchange rate depreciation.

In explaining why the relationship between the nominal and real exchange rates varies so much between countries, the authors note that changes in the terms of trade are a major independent influence on the real exchange rate. Although this is certainly true, the sign of the influence is not predictable on theoretical grounds, contrary to the impression given in the chapter. To see the equilibrium effects of changes in the terms of trade on the real exchange rate, consider the equilibrium condition in the market for nontraded goods, which requires that excess demand be zero:[1]

$$E_N(p_N, p_X, p_M) = 0. \tag{1}$$

Here, p_N, p_X, and p_M are the domestic prices of the nontraded, export, and import goods, respectively. Equation (1) may be totally differentiated to give:

$$\phi_N \hat{p}_N + \phi_X \hat{p}_X + \phi_M \hat{p}_M = 0, \tag{2}$$

where a circumflex over a variable denotes a proportional rate of change and ϕ_i is the (uncompensated) elasticity of excess demand for the nontraded good with respect to the price of good i. The own-price elasticity ϕ_N must be negative (since a change in the price of the nontraded good has no income effects in general equilibrium); and the three elasticities must sum to zero (since excess demand is homogeneous of degree zero in nominal variables). Hence:

$$-\phi_N = \phi_X + \phi_M > 0. \tag{3}$$

Thus, the nontraded good must be a general equilibrium substitute for at least one of the other goods, although it may be a general equilibrium complement for one of them (that is, either ϕ_X or ϕ_M may be negative).

I will now derive the effect of changes in the terms of trade on the real exchange rate. The terms of trade are defined as the relative price of exports to imports, p_X/p_M, while the real exchange rate is the relative price of traded goods to nontraded goods, p_T/p_N. The price index for traded goods, in turn, is a weighted average of the prices of exports and imports, or, in differential form:

$$\hat{p}_T = \theta_X \hat{p}_X + \theta_M \hat{p}_M. \tag{4}$$

Combining equations (2) and (4), and using equation (3) to simplify, yields:

$$(-\phi_N)(\hat{p}_T - \hat{p}_N) = (\phi_M \theta_X - \phi_X \theta_M)(\hat{p}_X - \hat{p}_M). \tag{5}$$

Recalling that ϕ_N is negative, equation (5) shows that the "normal" outcome, whereby a deterioration in the terms of trade (a fall in p_X/p_M) leads to a real depreciation (a rise in p_T/p_N), requires that the expression in parentheses on the right-hand side be negative. In fact, however, the sign of this expression is ambiguous. Without quantitative information on the ϕ_i and θ_i parameters, all that can be said is:

> A deterioration in the terms of trade leads to (1) an equilibrium real depreciation if the nontraded and the importable goods are general equilibrium complements and (2) to an equilibrium real appreciation if the nontraded and the exportable goods are general equilibrium complements. If all three goods are general equilibrium substitutes, the outcome is indeterminate.

By contrast, the effect of changes in world prices on domestic nominal prices is more predictable. This effect may be obtained by noting that the change in the domestic price of either an importable or exportable good equals the sum of the change in its world price and the change in the nominal exchange rate, e (defined as the domestic price of foreign exchange): $\hat{p}_i = \hat{p}_i^* + \hat{e}$. Substituting into equation (2) and manipulating leads to:

$$\hat{p}_N = \phi_X' \hat{p}_X^* + \phi_M' \hat{p}_M^* + \hat{e}, \tag{6}$$

where the weights ϕ_i' (which equal $-\phi_i/\phi_N$) sum to unity. This shows that the impact of changes in world prices on prices of nontraded goods depends both on what world prices have changed and on the nominal exchange rate policy adopted. Taking the case closest to that considered in the chapter, we may conclude that:

> A fall in the world price of exports (with no change in the world price of imports) leads in equilibrium to a fall in prices of nontraded

goods *or* to a nominal depreciation (a rise in *e*) *or* to some combination of the two, if and only if, the nontraded good and the exportable good are general equilibrium substitutes.

How plausible is the case of general equilibrium complementarity between nontraded and exportable goods, that, as equation (5) shows, leads to the opposite effect of a change in the terms of trade on the real exchange rate from that assumed by Aghevli and Montiel? Little systematic evidence on the issue of complementarity in demand is available. On the supply side, however, it is easy to construct plausible examples of production structures that exhibit this property. A number of such examples may be found in Corden and Neary (1982). An even simpler example may be constructed by adapting a model developed by Gruen and Corden (1970) in a different context. Suppose that all three sectors use labor but that only the import-competing and export sectors use capital. Suppose also that, of the latter two, the export sector uses capital relatively intensively. In that case, a rise in the price of the exportable good lowers real wages (by the usual Stolper-Samuelson mechanism) and thus encourages more production of the nontraded good. Thus, the nontraded and the exportable goods are general equilibrium complements in production, since the output of both is encouraged.

This indeterminate relationship between the terms of trade and the real exchange rate (even in full equilibrium) shows that the mixed empirical findings of Aghevli and Montiel are not surprising. Although, on average, all the developing countries in their sample experienced a significant real depreciation and a terms of trade deterioration during 1978–1989, Table 8.4 shows that the opposite association was exhibited during 1982–1989 by those countries whose currencies were pegged to the U.S. dollar (they experienced a terms of trade deterioration but a real appreciation) and also by those that adopted managed arrangements (they experienced a terms of trade improvement but a real depreciation). Clearly, a more detailed analysis is needed before the links between the terms of trade and the real exchange rate can be summarized in any simple fashion.

Turning finally to policy issues, the second half of the paper departs somewhat from current International Monetary Fund orthodoxy in questioning the advisability of greater exchange rate flexibility in developing countries. The authors are surely correct in stressing that a nominal depreciation is no substitute for bringing domestic monetary and fiscal policies under control. However, in admitting the existence of "exogenous shocks that would optimally require a devaluation," they are allowing more scope for discretionary exchange rate policy than they may intend. In particular, such exogenous shocks need not be external in origin. Domestic shocks that could justify a devaluation include exogenous wage increases or a program of trade liberalization. The authors are thus closer than they realize to advocating a crawling peg arrangement, providing that it is accompanied by a credible commitment to avoid overexpansionary monetary and fiscal policies.

Note

1. The analysis to follow draws on and extends that of Dornbusch (1974) and Neary (1988).

Capital and Current
Account Liberalization and
Real Exchange Rates
in Developing Countries

Although economic liberalization has become a central component of most structural adjustment programs in the developing countries, the outcome of these reforms has not always been successful.[1] In fact, in many countries, liberalization policies are reversed after a short period of time. Several new cross-country studies have found that historically the success of liberalization episodes has been closely linked to the behavior of the real exchange rate. For example, in a summary of a recently completed study on the liberalization experiences of nineteen countries, Michaely (1991:119) states that:

> The *long term* performance of the real rate of foreign exchange clearly differentiates "liberalizers" from "nonliberalizers" . . . [L]iberalizers have tended to be *persistent in maintaining a more-or-less* given level of the real exchange rate over the long-run; whereas "nonliberalizers" have tended to let this rate suffer from spasms.

In their recent evaluation of the experiences in the Southern Cone (Argentina, Chile, and Uruguay) with liberalization policies, Corbo and de Melo (1987) point out that the behavior of the real exchange rate—and more specifically, the persistent real exchange rate appreciation that developed in all three countries—was one of the main causes of the

243

less-than-successful outcome of these reforms in the early 1980s. More recently, Edwards (1989b) has shown that real exchange rate behavior is at the heart of the explanation of why only a few of the countries that have received World Bank structural adjustment loans (SALs) have succeeded in liberalizing their economies. Also, Edwards (1989c) found that real exchange rate volatility has negatively affected economic performance, including growth, in a score of developing countries.

In spite of the obvious importance of real exchange rate behavior in liberalization attempts, only a few studies have formally investigated the process for determination of real exchange rates in these countries. Moreover, few researchers have attempted to assess the impact on the real exchange rate of policies aimed at liberalizing the capital and current accounts of the balance of payments.

The purpose of this chapter is twofold. First, a simple intertemporal framework is developed for analyzing the effect on the real exchange rate of different structural adjustment and liberalization policies. Second, some of the existing empirical studies on the subject are surveyed. The empirical review deals with some published material and with a number of unpublished papers. It focuses on multicountry studies, as well as on publications analyzing the behavior of real exchange rates in four Latin American countries (Argentina, Chile, Colombia, and Uruguay).

These four countries form a particularly interesting group because, during the past twenty or thirty years, all of them have experienced major changes in their structure of controls on international trade. For example, Argentina's modern economic history is plagued with liberalization attempts, mostly unsuccessful, that have resulted in wide swings in the structure of incentives, drastic variations in real exchange rates, and periodic crises in the balance of payments.[2] Chile, on the other hand, represents the boldest modern attempt of a developing country to liberalize the external sector. Starting in 1975, the Chilean authorities embarked on an ambitious liberalization program that resulted in reduction of import tariffs from an average exceeding 100 percent to a flat 10 percent and in elimination of many of the controls on capital movements.[3] The case of Colombia is rather different. In 1967, the economic authorities decided to move away from a policy that tightly controlled and restricted the external sector, and it adopted a crawling peg exchange rate regime that allowed the government to avoid real exchange rate misalignment, open up the external sector, and encourage exports.[4] In Uruguay, it is interesting that, in the late 1970s the government completely eliminated capital controls, while still maintaining significant restrictions on trade in goods. This sequencing of reform—contradicting conventional wisdom—generated large inflows of capital into the country and, according to some interpretations, put pressure on the real exchange rate.[5]

Finally, the closing section of the chapter discusses some of the most important policy implications of both the theoretical and the empirical results. In particular, the analysis shows how real exchange rate movements affect the sequencing of economic liberalization policies.

Analytical Framework for Economic Liberalization and Equilibrium Real Exchange Rates

This section presents a simple analytical framework for investigating how different economic liberalization measures affect the path of equilibrium real exchange rates in a small developing economy, starting with a real model that ignores the role of monetary variables. However, the role of monetary and macroeconomic factors is discussed briefly, dealing with the misalignment of real exchange rates. The analysis is maintained at a simple level, and most technicalities are relegated to the appendix at the end of this chapter.

Consider a small open economy with three production sectors: importables (M), exportables (X), and nontradables (N). Outputs of X, M, and N are produced by many competitive firms. The three factors of production are labor, natural resources, and capital. Consumers in this economy consume all three goods produced.[6] It is further assumed that the country is small within the context of the world economy and, thus, that it faces given world prices of importables and exportables.

To the extent that the discussion focuses on analyzing the role of capital movements and capital controls, it is necessary to incorporate an intertemporal dimension to the model. The simplest method for doing this is to consider the existence of two periods—the present (period one) and the future (period two). Consequently, all economic agents in this economy face an intertemporal budget constraint that restricts the present value of income to being equal to the present value of expenditures. In a particular period, however, aggregate income can exceed (or fall short of) expenditure, so that, in any period, the current account of the balance of payments can be in deficit (or surplus). The intertemporal nature of the model permits us to focus on decisions as to savings and investment and to define the current account as the difference between savings and investment. Although the current account balance can be different from zero in any period, the intertemporal budget constraint requires the discounted sum of the current account in both periods to add up to zero. The nontradable goods sector, however, is assumed to be permanently (in every period) in equilibrium. The formal setup of the model is described in the appendix.

It is assumed that, as is the case in most developing countries, the external sector of the economy is subject to two kinds of distortions. First, imports are subject to a tariff equal to t; the domestic price of importables (p) in each period is equal to the world price (p^*) plus the tariff ($p^i = p^{*i} + t^i$). Second, capital controls exist in the form of a tax on foreign borrowing (σ). Consequently, the domestic real interest rate (r) is equal to the world rate (r^*) plus this tax ($r = r^* + \sigma$).

In this particular model, two real exchange rates are present in each period (i): the relative price of exportables to nontradables ($1/q^i$) and the relative price of importables to nontradables (p^i/q^i). In order to simplify the exposition, let us focus on the inverse of the real exchange rate for exports (q^i). The equilibrium (exportable) real exchange rate in a particular period is defined as the relative price of nontradables that (for given values of other variables, such as world prices, technology, tariffs, and taxes) equilibrates the external and internal sectors simultaneously. In this context, internal equilibrium means that the nontradable goods market clears in the current period and is expected to be in equilibrium in the future, and that the rate of unemployment does not differ from its "natural" level.[7] External equilibrium, in contrast, means that the current account balance in the present period and the balances expected in the future satisfy the *intertemporal* budget constraint that states that the discounted value of the current account balances must be equal to zero. In other words, external equilibrium means that the current account balances (current and future) are compatible with long-term sustainable capital flows.

Four implications follow from this definition of equilibrium real exchange rates. First, the equilibrium real exchange rate is not an immutable number. When there are changes in any of the other variables that affect the country's internal and external equilibriums, changes also take place in the equilibrium real exchange rate. For example, the real exchange rate required to attain equilibrium when the world price of the country's main export is low is not the same as the one required when that price is high. In a sense, then, the equilibrium real exchange rate is itself a function of a number of variables, including import tariffs, export taxes, real interest rates, capital controls, etc. These immediate determinants of the equilibrium real exchange rate are called real exchange rate "fundamentals."

Second, there is not a single equilibrium real exchange rate. Rather, there is a path of equilibrium real exchange rates through time.

Third, the path of equilibrium real exchange rates is affected not only by the current values of the fundamental determinants but also by

FIGURE 9.1   Initial Equilibrium in the Economy

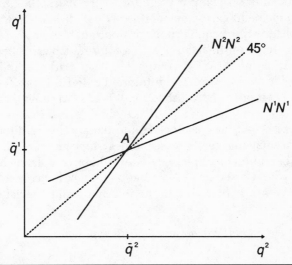

SOURCE: Author's calculations.

their expected future values. To the extent that possibilities exist for intertemporal substitution of consumption through foreign borrowing and lending and for intertemporal substitution of production through investment, expected future events—such as an anticipated change in the international terms of trade—will affect the current and expected future values of the equilibrium real exchange rate.

Finally, in analyzing the interaction between fundamentals and equilibrium real exchange rates, it is important to distinguish between permanent and temporary changes in the fundamentals. For example, a temporary worsening of the terms of trade will affect the equilibrium real exchange rate very differently from a permanent worsening. This distinction between temporary and permanent is especially important in the case of import tariffs.

The initial equilibrium in the economy is illustrated in Figure 9.1, where $\bar{q}^1$ is the equilibrium real exchange rate in period one (present) and $\bar{q}^2$ is the equilibrium real exchange rate in period two (future). Schedule N^1N^1 depicts the combination of prices of nontradables in period one (q^1) and in period two (q^2) that is compatible with market equilibrium for nontradables in the first period. The intuition behind the positive slope of N^1N^1 is that an increase in the price of N in period two will affect the discount factor of consumption, making consumption in that period relatively more expensive. As a result, there will be a substitution of expenditure away from period two and toward period one. This substitution will put pressure on the market for N in period one, and an incipient excess demand for N will develop in that period. The reestablishment of equilibrium for nontradables in period one will require an increase in the relative price of nontradables. Schedule N^2N^2 depicts the locus of q^1 and q^2 compatible with market equilibrium for nontradables in period two. The intuition behind this positive slope is analogous to that of the N^1N^1 schedule. It is easy to show that the N^2N^2 schedule is steeper than the N^1N^1 schedule (see Edwards 1989a). It should be noted that the existence of intertemporal substitution in consumption is what makes these schedules slope upward. If no intertemporal substitution takes place, N^1N^1 would be completely horizontal, while N^2N^2 would be vertical. A similar result would occur if this country had no access to borrowing in the international financial market.

Capital account liberalization and equilibrium real exchange rates

Consider next a liberalization program that consists of relaxing the extent of capital controls or of reducing the tax on foreign borrowing (σ). This policy will result in capital inflows in period one and will affect the market for nontradables by means of a substitution effect and an income effect.

In terms of Figure 9.2, the effects of a capital account liberalization on the equilibrium real exchange rates will be captured by shifts of both the N^1N^1 and N^2N^2 schedules. Let us first concentrate on N^1N^1. A reduction in σ will generate a drop in the domestic rate of interest r ($= r^* + \sigma$) and thus will induce intertemporal substitution in consumption from period two into period one. Part of the increased consumption in period one will fall on nontradables, generating an incipient excess demand in that market. This demand will require an increase in q^1 to maintain equilibrium for nontradables in period one. In terms of Figure 9.2, this intertemporal substitution effect will generate an upward shift of the N^1N^1 schedule. In addition to the substitution effect, this liberalization program will also have an income effect. To the extent that the reduction of this distortion increases welfare, a positive income effect will result that will put additional pressure on the price of N in period one and will further shift the N^1N^1 schedule upward.[8]

The effect on the market for nontradables in period two is somewhat similar. The reduction in σ generates, through intertemporal substitution, a reduction in that period's expenditure, creating an incipient excess supply for nontradables. This excess supply will require a reduction in q^2 to reestablish equilibrium. In Figure 9.2, this phenomenon is also

FIGURE 9.2   Effect of Liberalization of the Capital Account on
Equilibrium Real Exchange Rates

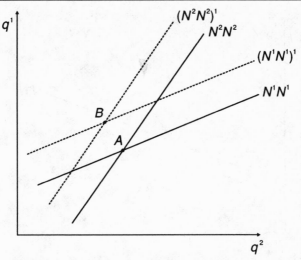

SOURCE: Author's calculations.

reflected by an upward shift of N^2N^2. In this case, however, the income effect will work in the opposite direction. As welfare increases, demand for all goods will increase in every period. If the income effect dominates the intertemporal substitution effect, the N^2N^2 schedule could shift downward rather than upward. In the rest of the exposition, it will be assumed that intertemporal substitution dominates and that N^2N^2 shifts upward.

As Figure 9.2 shows, liberalization of the capital account will result in an equilibrium real exchange rate appreciation in period one and an equilibrium real exchange rate depreciation in period two.

Trade liberalization and the equilibrium real exchange rate

In contrast to the elimination of the tax on capital just analyzed, the effect of trade liberalization on the path of equilibrium real exchange rates will depend on whether the tariff reduction is temporary or permanent. In this section, the effect of a temporary trade reform on the path of equilibrium real exchange rates is discussed first and then the case of a permanent tariff reduction is dealt with briefly. Throughout the analysis, it is assumed that all three goods (importables, exportables,

FIGURE 9.3   Effect of a Temporary Reduction in Import Tariffs on
Equilibrium Real Exchange Rates

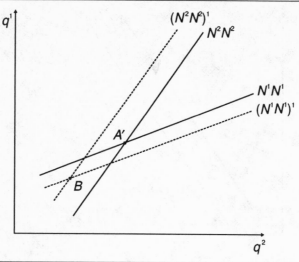

SOURCE: Author's calculations.

and nontradables) are substitutes in consumption, so that all cross-demand elasticities are positive.

A temporary reduction in import tariffs in period one will shift both the N^1N^1 and N^2N^2 schedules, generating a new vector of equilibrium relative prices of nontradables (Figure 9.3). As with the case of capital account liberalization, both substitution and income effects will occur. Two types of substitution effects will result, however: *intertemporal* substitution (which was discussed in the first section) and *intratemporal* substitution, stemming from the change in relative prices in period one.

Let us first consider the effects of the tariff reform on N^2N^2. A temporary reduction in import tariffs implies that the price of imports in period one will decline, making present consumption as a whole relatively less expensive. Consequently, by means of the intertemporal substitution effect, consumers will move expenditure away from period two and substitute it in period one. The result will be a reduction in the demand for all goods in period two (including nontradables) and in a lower q^2. As a result, the N^2N^2 curve will tend to shift to the left. This movement in the N^2N^2 curve is a reflection of the degree of intertemporal substitutability in consumption. It will be greater or smaller according to whether the cross-elasticity of expenditure in periods one and two is large or small. In the extreme case of no intertemporal substitution, the N^2N^2 schedule will be vertical and will not shift as a result of a temporary tariff liberalization. The income effect will tend to operate in the opposite direction. As long as the reduction in distortions will increase welfare, expenditures will increase for all goods in every period. However, the assumption that the substitution effect dominates is sufficient for N^2N^2 to shift to the left.

A temporary reduction in import tariffs will also affect the N^1N^1 schedule. In this case, however, there will also be an *intratemporal* effect, related to the change in relative prices within period one. The lower domestic price of M in period one, resulting from the lower tariff, will generate an increase in the quantity of M demanded in that period. Under the assumption of substitutability, there will be, owing to this effect, a reduction in the demand for N that will put downward pressure on its price. As before, the income effect will work in the opposite direction, putting upward pressure on q^1. However, if it is assumed that the substitution effect dominates, the N^1N^1 schedule will shift downward. Thus, a tariff reduction will result in a decline of q^1 and q^2, or in a real exchange rate depreciation. It should be noted, however, that it is not possible to know a priori whether the N^1N^1 schedule or the N^2N^2 schedule will shift more. This fact gives rise to the possibility of some interesting equilibrium paths for the real exchange rates that will be characterized by drastic swings in the equilibrium real exchange rate.

The case of a permanent trade reform can be handled by using the same apparatus. In this case, however, intratemporal substitution effects will occur in both periods. It is easy to show that, under the maintained assumption that the three goods are substitutes in consumption, a trade liberalization will require an equilibrium real exchange rate depreciation in both periods. If, however, the less plausible case is considered, where two of the goods are complementary, a trade reform can generate either an appreciation or depreciation of the real exchange rate (Edwards 1989a).

To sum up, it has been found that, while a capital account liberalization will require an equilibrium real exchange rate appreciation in the present period, a trade reform will call for a real exchange rate depreciation. Indeed, this movement of the real exchange rate in opposite directions has been at the heart of most discussions of the appropriate sequencing of economic reforms. For example, such authors as McKinnon (1982) and Dornbusch (1983) have argued that, since capital liberalization tends to frustrate the depreciation required to sustain trade reform, the capital account should be opened up after the current account has been fully liberalized.

Role of monetary factors

Since the outlined model deals with a real economy, the discussion up to this point has dealt exclusively with the *real* determinants of the *equilibrium* real exchange rate and has concentrated on trade and capital controls. Monetary factors, however, do play a role in the short-term, and even medium-term behavior of real exchange rates. More specifically, macroeconomic developments—including credit creation and fiscal behavior—will usually have an impact on the dynamics of the real exchange rate, often generating situations where the actual real exchange rate departs from its long-term equilibrium value. This type of situation, which is known as real exchange rate misalignment, will result when the macroeconomic policies being pursued are inconsistent with the chosen nominal exchange rate. Although a model will not be developed to deal formally with these questions, the remainder of this section discusses effects of macroeconomic and monetary factors on the dynamics of real exchange rates.

Perhaps the case of a "high" fiscal deficit under fixed nominal rates is the clearest example of inconsistency between macroeconomic and exchange rate policies. In most developing countries, fiscal imbalances are partially or wholly financed by money creation. The inflation required to finance a final deficit equal to a fraction (δ) of gross domestic product (GDP) can be calculated as shown in the equation:

$$\pi = \delta/\lambda \tag{1}$$

where π is the rate of inflation tax required to finance the government deficit and λ is the ratio of high-powered money to GDP. If, for example, a country has a fiscal deficit of 8 percent of GDP and its stock of high-powered money represents 20 percent of GDP, the required rate of inflation will be 40 percent a year. If the required rate of inflation is as high as in this example, there will generally be an inconsistency between the fiscal deficit and the maintenance of a fixed nominal exchange rate. Since the domestic price of nontradables increases at a rate approximately equal to the rate of inflation and the domestic price of tradables grows at approximately the rate of world inflation, the real exchange rate in this case will experience a growing appreciation. This type of situation, of course, will not be sustainable and will eventually result in a serious balance of payments crisis.

The monetary sector plays another important role in the dynamic behavior of the real exchange rate. Generally speaking, changes in the quantity of money (and resulting changes in domestic prices) will be the main channel through which changes in the fundamentals will actually affect the real exchange rate. Consider, for example, the case of a liberalization of the capital account. As was shown in the first section, this policy will result in an equilibrium real exchange rate appreciation. In the case of an economy with a fixed exchange rate, this change in the real exchange rate will actually take place by means of a higher price of nontradables that is induced by a short-term excess supply of domestic money. This price rise, in turn, will take place through the monetization of the capital flows by the central bank (see Neary and van Wijnbergen 1986).

The nominal exchange rate is the other important short-term determinant of the real exchange rate. More specifically, a very important policy question is whether a nominal devaluation will have an impact on the real exchange rate. From a theoretical point of view, nominal devaluations should have no lasting effect on the real exchange rate. However, as has been pointed out by a number of authors, if a country starts from a situation of real exchange rate overvaluation, a nominal devaluation is a powerful and useful tool to help reestablish equilibrium real exchange rate. The extent to which a nominal devaluation will affect the real exchange rate in the short term is, of course, an empirical matter.

Results of the theoretical analysis

The theoretical analysis presented here gives clear results in terms of the relationship between liberalization policies and equilibrium real exchange rates. According to the theory, a relaxation of capital controls will result in increased foreign borrowing—under the assumption of a well-functioning domestic capital market—and will also result in an equilibrium appreciation of the real exchange rate. In contrast, a trade liberalization reform will have an ambiguous effect on the equilibrium real exchange rate. Depending on the strength of different forces, the reduction in tariffs can generate a real exchange rate appreciation or depreciation. Which effect finally dominates is an empirical question.

In spite of the advances in the theoretical analyses on the relationship between liberalization policies and equilibrium real exchange rates, only a few empirical studies on the subject exist. The next section presents a review of the existing literature on the relationship between external sector reforms and the real exchange rate in the developing countries. This review focuses on three important questions: (1) What do the data say about the effect of trade reforms on the real exchange rate? (In other words, how has the limited existing empirical evidence helped to solve the theoretical ambiguity discussed above?) (2) As the theory suggests, have capital account liberalizations had a negative effect on the equilibrium real exchange rate? (3) What are the findings of these studies regarding the effects of variables different from external sector restrictions on the real exchange rate?

Effects of Liberalization Policies on Real Exchange Rates

This section selectively reviews the empirical literature on the effects of liberalization policies on the real exchange rate. The focus is first on cross-country evidence, followed by discussion of empirical research relating to four Latin American countries: Argentina, Chile, Colombia, and Uruguay.

Cross-country evidence

In a series of recent papers, Edwards (1988b, 1989a) has investigated real exchange rate determination for a group of twelve developing countries. An important aim of these studies has been to establish the effects of liberalization policies on real exchange rates. Naturally, this aim can be satisfied properly only within the context of a general model that explicitly incorporates the role of other variables in the evolution of the real exchange rate. An important characteristic of this research is that it postulates that, while in the short term the real exchange rate is affected by both monetary and real variables, in the long term only real variables—the so-called fundamentals—will affect the real exchange rate.

Edwards (1988b) argues that, at the very general level, the dynamic behavior of real exchange rates can be captured by the following equation:

$$\Delta \log e_t = \theta \{\log e_t^* - \log e_{t-1}\} - \lambda \{Z_t - Z_t^*\} \qquad (2)$$
$$+ \phi \{\log E_t - \log E_{t-1}\}$$

where e is the actual real exchange rate, e^* is the equilibrium real exchange rate (in turn, a function of the fundamentals, including impediments to international trade, capital controls, and the like), Z_t is an index of macroeconomic policies (that is, the rate of growth of domestic credit), Z_t^* is the sustainable level of macroeconomic policies (that is, rate of increase of demand for domestic money), E_t is the nominal exchange rate, and θ, λ, and ϕ are positive parameters that capture the most important dynamic aspects of the adjustment process. According to equation (2), the actual dynamics of real exchange rates respond to the three forces. First, there will be an autonomous tendency for the actual exchange rate to correct existing misalignments, given by the partial adjustment term $\theta\{\log e_t^* - \log e_{t-1}\}$. The speed of adjustment is captured by parameter θ. The smaller θ is (that is, the closer it is to zero), the slower will be the speed at which real exchange rate disequilibrium will be corrected. Theoretically, the value of θ will depend on a number of institutional factors, including the existence of wage indexation rules that will influence its level.

The second determinant of real exchange rate movements is related to macroeconomic policies and is given by $-\lambda[Z_t - Z_t^*]$. This term states that, if the macroeconomic policies are not sustainable in the medium to longer term and are inconsistent with a pegged exchange rate (that is, $Z_t > Z_t^*$), there will be pressures toward a real appreciation. Moreover, if macroeconomic disequilibrium or λ is large enough, these forces can easily dominate the self-correcting term, generating an increasing degree of overvaluation through time.

The third determinant of movements of real exchange rates is related to changes in the nominal exchange rate (that is, to nominal devaluations) and is given by the term $\phi\{\log E_t - \log E_{t-1}\}$. A nominal devaluation will have a positive effect on the real exchange rate on *impact*, generating a short-term real depreciation, the actual magnitude of which will depend on parameter ϕ. As said before, a key feature of this formulation is that, although nominal devaluations will have an effect on the real exchange rate in the *short term*, this effect will not necessarily persist through time. In fact, whether the nominal devaluation will have any impact over the medium to longer term will depend on the two other two terms of equation (2), or, more precisely, on the initial conditions, captured by $(\log e^* - \log e)$, and on the accompanying macroeconomic policies, captured by $[Z_t - Z_t^*]$.

According to the model presented earlier and developed in the Appendix, the most important *fundamentals* in determining the behavior of equilibrium real exchange rates are: (1) import tariffs, (2) capital controls (or the resulting capital flows), (3) external terms of trade, and (4) the level and composition of government consumption. In the regression analysis, however, a proxy for technological progress was included in order to capture the possible role of the so-called Ricardo-Balassa effect on the equilibrium real exchange rate.

In the dynamics equation (2), the term $-\lambda\{Z_t - Z_t^*\}$ measures the role of macroeconomic policies in real exchange rate behavior. According to the discussion, with other things given, if macroeconomic policies are inconsistent, the real exchange rate will become overvalued. The following components of $\{Z_t - Z_t^*\}$ were used in the estimation: (1) excess supply for domestic credit (*EXCRE*), measured as the rate of growth of domestic credit minus the lagged rate of growth of real GDP—that is, $EXCRE_t = \{d\log \text{ domestic credit}_t - d\log GDP_{t-1}\}$, (2) the ratio of fiscal deficit to lagged high-powered money (*DEH*) as a measure of fiscal policies, and (3) the rate of growth of domestic credit (*DPDC*).

The following equation was estimated on pooled data for twelve countries:

$$\Delta\log e_t = \gamma_1 \log(TOT)_t + \gamma_2 \log(GCGDP)_t$$
$$\gamma_3 \log(TARIFFS)_t + \gamma_5 (KAPFLO)_t + \gamma_6 \log(TECHPRO)_t \qquad (3)$$
$$- \theta \log e_{t-1} - \lambda EXCRE_t + \phi NOMDEV_t + u_t$$

using the following notation:

e:	bilateral real exchange rate, defined as $E\ WPI^{US}/CPI$
TOT:	external terms of trade, defined as (P_X^*/P_M^*)
NGCGDP:	ratio of government consumption of nontradables to GDP
TARIFFS:	rate of import tariffs
TECHPRO:	measure of technological progress
KAPFLO:	capital inflows (if negative, denotes capital outflows)
OTHER:	other fundamentals, such as the investment/GDP ratio
NOMDEV:	nominal devaluation
u:	error term.

In this formulation, lagged capital flows are used as a measure of capital controls, under the assumption that, as discussed in the first section of this chapter, a low level of these controls will encourage larger capital flows. Thus, according to the theory presented, the coefficient of *KAPFLO* would be expected to be negative.

A serious problem faced in estimating this model is the lack of reliable time series for trade impediments and tariffs. This problem was dealt with by relying on two proxies: (1) the implicit tariff rate, computed as the ratio of tariff revenues to imports, and (2) the premium in the parallel market for foreign exchange. The latter is supposed to capture the overall extent of external controls in the country, and it was referred to as "exchange controls" (*EXCONT*).

Table 9.1 contains results obtained by Edwards (1989a) for this formulation, using pooled data for 1962–1985 for twelve countries (Brazil, Colombia, El Salvador, Greece, India, Israel, Malaysia, the Philippines, South Africa, Sri Lanka, Thailand, and Yugoslavia). The results obtained are quite satisfactory. All monetary variables have the expected sign and are significant, and the real variables are highly significant as a group, as reflected by the value of the χ^2 statistics reported at the bottom of the

TABLE 9.1   Real Exchange Rate Determination in Developing
Countries

Dependent variable	Real exchange rate	Real equilibrium exchange rate
Estimation procedure:	Ordinary least squares	Instrumental variable
Monetary variables		
EXCRE	−0.076	—
	(−3.404)	
DEH	−0.027	
	(−2.016)	
DPDC	—	−0.055
		(−2.128)
NOMDEV	0.620	0.536
	(11.130)	(8.439)
Real variables		
Log TOT	−0.054	−0.043
	(−1.748)	(−2.371)
Log EXCONT	—	−0.255
		(−2.682)
Tariffs	−0.396	—
	(−0.682)	
KAPFLO$_{-1}$	−0.195	−0.231
	(−1.948)	(−1.406)
Log NGCGDP	−0.101	0.054
	(−0.982)	(1.712)
Growth	0.496	0.997
	(1.512)	(2.257)
Lagged dependent variables		
Log e_{t-1}	−0.051	−0.261
	(−4.579)	(−8.947)
N	225	226
χ^2	53.4	52.1

NOTES: Dash indicates that the variable was not included in the regression equation. χ^2 is a chi-square test for the joint significance of the real variables.
SOURCE: Author's calculations.

table. In terms of the variables related to liberalization, the coefficient of capital flows is negative, as expected, indicating that a change in controls that induces capital inflows will cause the real exchange rate to appreciate. It should be noted, however, that the estimated coefficients are barely significant. With respect to the effects of controls on commodity trade (tariffs), although the theory is ambiguous, the results indicate that, independently of the proxy used, a rise in import impediments will generate an *appreciation* of the real exchange rate. Naturally, this means that a trade liberalization reform will require a real exchange rate depreciation. In fact, the opposite directions in which the real exchange rate reacts to a capital account and trade reform will have important consequences in discussions on the sequencing of liberalization reforms.

As discussed in the preceding section, an important implication of the theory of equilibrium exchange rates is that the reaction of the real exchange rate to liberalization will depend on whether these policies are temporary or permanent. In order to investigate this issue, Edwards (1989a) used the technique of Beveridge and Nelson (1981) to decompose the *KAPFLO* and the *EXCONT* series into a permanent and a temporary component. He found that, although permanent *EXCONT* increases had a significantly negative effect (for example, appreciated) on the real exchange rate, a temporary increase in this variable had an insignificant positive effect. Regarding capital flows, however, the results were not conclusive.

Country-specific studies on liberalization and real exchange rates in Latin America

Some of the estimating country-specific evidence on the relationship between liberalization and real exchange rates in four Latin American countries is discussed here. A number of papers, both published and unpublished, are reviewed.

Argentina.   Carlos Diaz-Alejandro (1970, 1976) provided early and illuminating studies on the behavior of the external sector in Argentina. In a 1982 paper, he used data for almost fifty years of Argentinian history (1928–1976) to analyze how changes in protectionism and terms of trade affected the real exchange rate in that country. Using an index of protectionism (*PROT*), he found the following results from the estimation of an ordinary least squares regression:

$$et = -24.52 - 0.58 \sum_{i=0}^{4} TOT_{t-i} - 0.15\ PROT_t \qquad (4)$$
$$(-2.19)\quad (1.54)\qquad\qquad (-2.09)$$

As can be seen, these results indicate that, as was the case in the cross-country studies reported above, an increase in protectionism will tend to result in an *appreciation* of the real exchange rate. However, a serious limitation of these estimates (and one acknowledged by Diaz Alejandro) is that a number of variables, including capital flows and monetary variables, are omitted.

Most studies of the recent behavior of the Argentinian economy have argued that the substantial real exchange rate appreciation, with concomitant losses in competitiveness, that took place in Argentina in the late 1970s was at the center of the collapse of the liberalization reforms attempted by Martinez de Hoz, the economics minister.[9] There is less agreement, however, on what the forces were behind this real exchange rate appreciation. Although some authors have focused on the exchange rate and domestic credit policies, others have emphasized the role of domestic financial liberalization.[10] In a recent unpublished paper, Cottani and García (1989) developed a small econometric model to analyze how different factors have affected real exchange rate dynamics in that country. They then used their results to conduct some counterfactual historical simulations, arguing that, under a set of "reasonable" policies, most of the overvaluation of the real exchange rate in Argentina under Martinez de Hoz could have been avoided. Although counterfactual history is risky, the simulations by Cottani and García lead us to wonder what would have been the outcome of the liberalization reforms of Martinez de Hoz if these more reasonable policies on exchange rates had been pursued.

The model by Cottani and García is basically static, focusing on five basic building blocks: the market for nontradable goods, the trade account, capital flows, exchange rate policy, and monetary markets. In constructing their model, the authors paid particular attention to the mechanism through which changes in real exchange rate fundamentals are transmitted into changes in the real exchange rate. In doing this, they emphasized the relation between the different accounts of the balance of payments and monetary equilibrium. For example, in their model, a reduction in import tariffs results, with other things given, in a trade deficit and a reduction in the stock of international reserves and of high-powered money. In turn, this result puts negative pressure on prices of nontradable goods and, therefore, works its way toward a real depreciation. This means that, in their model, both the transmission channel and the nature of the effect on trade reform differ from what was postulated in the general equilibrium model presented in this chapter where the transmission mechanism was strictly real, and the effects of a tariff reform on the real exchange rate were ambiguous. Regarding capital account liberalization, their model also differs from the analytical framework presented in this chapter, where a liberalization of the capital account affected the equilibrium real exchange rate through changes in the consumption rate of interest. In their model, an increase in capital inflows will generate a real appreciation through an increase in the stock of domestic money.

In their empirical estimation, Cottani and García tried to determine the roles played by three basic factors in the real appreciation of the peso during 1976–1981: (1) the relaxation of capital controls that resulted in massive inflows of capital into the country, (2) the reduction of the level of export taxes, and (3) the inconsistency between domestic credit policy and the nominal exchange rate policy.[11] By estimating a two-equation system, consisting of a real exchange rate and a trade account equation, Cottani and García provided support for the theoretical view that the opening of the capital account contributes to generating a real exchange rate appreciation. They also found that in Argentina the liberalization of the export sector and the inconsistency of the domestic and nominal exchange rate policies also resulted in an appreciation of the real exchange rate. These three factors account for about two-thirds of the observed real exchange rate variability, with each individual element contributing approximately an equal share to the overall explanation of the phenomenon. Interestingly enough, the estimates by Cottani and García provide some support for the hypothesis that changes in real exchange rate fundamentals do affect the real exchange rate through a monetary channel (for example, the monetary impact of the accumulation or decrease of international reserves).

In what is perhaps the most interesting part of their analysis, Cottani and García used their estimated equations to perform a set of counterfactual estimations. The most revealing of them computed the hypothetical path of the real exchange rate under the assumptions that: (1) imports are liberalized at the same time as exports, (2) domestic credit policy is consistent with the devaluation policy, (3) nominal devaluation is set at 2 percent a quarter, starting in 1981, and (4) there is a reduced inflow of capital. Interestingly, they found that, under this scenario, the real exchange rate in Argentina would not have experienced an overvaluation and would have remained at a level approximately equal to that achieved in 1970.

Uruguay. Although Uruguay has experienced extensive economic changes during the past fifty years or so, relatively few studies on this country have been made available in the English language.[12] In "The Determinants of the Real Exchange Rate in Post-War Uruguay," Edgardo Favaro and Pablo Spiller (1989) have analyzed empirically the dynamics of real exchange rate behavior in Uruguay. Two main features of this country make this study particularly important for the purposes of the survey presented in this chapter. First, in the mid-1970s Uruguay eliminated all controls on capital mobility, while still maintaining severe restrictions on international trade in goods. Thus, Uruguay is one of the few countries where the sequencing of liberalization has been characterized by a complete liberalization of capital account restrictions that have preceded even the most basic liberalization measures in relation to trade. Second, because of Uruguay's geographical characteristics (being a small country located between Argentina and Brazil), nontradable goods in Uruguay conform to a peculiar market. In fact, Favaro and Spiller argue that, properly speaking, Uruguay does not have non-tradable goods, because its consumers can (and do) purchase non-tradables from Argentina. This peculiar feature of the country implies that economic developments in Argentina greatly affect the dynamics of the real exchange rate in Uruguay. Along these lines, Favaro and Spiller developed a model of the determination of real exchange rates in Uruguay, where the spread between the official and parallel nominal exchange rate in Argentina plays a fundamental role in the determination of the real exchange rate in Uruguay. The reason for this is that, although prices of Argentinian and Uruguayan nontradables are linked by means of the foreign exchange rate in the parallel market, prices of each country's tradables are related to the world price of tradables through the official commercial rate.

As in the model presented in this chapter and fully developed in the appendix, the model by Favaro and Spiller (1989) assumes that the equilibrium real exchange rate depends on import tariffs, terms of trade, capital inflows, the composition of government expenditures, and real income. Since the observable variable on which they focus in their empirical work is the observed real exchange rate, they also assume that it is a function of domestic credit creation, expected inflation, and the nominal exchange rate.

Favaro and Spiller estimated several variants of their model, using ordinary least squares estimation for the period 1950–1984. In terms of the variables of interest for the survey in this chapter, they found that, as suggested by the intertemporal model in the preceding section, an increase in the magnitude of capital inflows in Uruguay during this period resulted in a real exchange rate appreciation. The coefficients for the capital inflows variable was significant in most cases, its value ranging from -0.005 to -0.019. (In these equations, all variables—except capital inflows, the rate of devaluation, and a proxy for the exchange gap—are measured in logs.) With respect to import tariffs, the results of the model by Favaro and Spiller are in line with the findings for other countries reported earlier. They found that a raising of the level of import tariffs in Uruguay resulted in a real exchange rate appreciation. Although the coefficient of the tariffs was not always significant, its estimated value ranged from -0.121 to -0.348.

Their empirical results also support the regional implications of the model, indicating that changes in Argentina's real exchange rate have had a positive and significant impact on Uruguay's real exchange rate.

This effect became particularly strong after 1973. In a regression restricted to the period 1974–1984, the coefficient of the log of the real exchange rate in Argentina was significantly positive—the estimated coefficient being 0.621, with a t-statistic of 3.60. This result contrasts with the estimate for the complete 1950–1984 period, where the coefficient of the log of Argentina's real exchange rate turned out to be 0.189, with a t-statistic of 1.79. These results, however, should be looked at cautiously, since the 1974–1984 regression had only eleven observations. Favaro and Spiller also found that increases in government expenditure had a small negative effect on the real exchange rate and that, with all other things given, nominal devaluations had a positive effect on the real exchange rate that lasted for at least two years.

Using their estimated equations, Favaro and Spiller performed a number of counterfactual simulations, trying to determine whether alternative policies could have prevented the pronounced real exchange rate appreciation of the late 1970s and early 1980s. They found that both a more stable Argentinian real exchange rate and reduced capital inflows could have contributed significantly toward reducing the importance of the episode of real exchange rate appreciation that many observers indicate as the main cause of the collapse of the Uruguayan reforms of the early 1980s (Corbo and de Melo 1987). The finding regarding the positive effect of capital account restrictions on the real exchange rate provides some support to the view that capital controls should be maintained until the remainder of the sectors—and, in particular, the trade account—are fully liberalized (see the concluding remarks of this chapter).

Colombia. In many ways, Colombia represents a special case within the Latin American economies. More than twenty years ago, the Colombian authorities decided to open up their external sector and to make an effort to insulate their economy as much as possible from shocks in the terms of trade stemming from fluctuations in coffee prices. As a method for achieving these objectives, in 1967 Colombia abandoned any attempt to fix the exchange rate and adopted a crawling peg exchange rate regime characterized by frequent minidevaluations. Although the Colombian experience with a crawling peg regime has been analyzed by a number of authors, including Wiesner (1978) and Urrutia (1981), only a few studies have used formal econometric techniques to inquire how different variables have affected the dynamics of Colombia's real exchange rates. An exception is the study by Edwards (1986b), who used a four-equation econometric model to investigate how changes in the terms of trade, among other variables, affected Colombia's real exchange rate behavior.

For the purposes of the present survey, a more interesting study is that of García-García (1989), who investigates the role of capital mobility in the process of determination of the real exchange rate in Colombia. He focuses on four elements: (1) the conduct of monetary policy, (2) the extent of capital mobility, (3) the behavior of the market for nontradables, and (4) the determinants of the nominal exchange rate policy, with special emphasis on the rules followed by the Colombian authorities in determining the crawling peg exchange rate. As in the theoretical framework developed in this chapter, García-García's model predicts that increases in import tariffs, a capital account liberalization, and an improvement in the terms of trade will all lead to an appreciation of the real exchange rate. In addition to these real "fundamentals" of real exchange rate behavior, García-García incorporates two macroeconomic variables as short-term determinants of the real exchange rate: (1) an indicator of the excess supply of money, and (2) nominal devaluations. In that regard, García-García's model for the dynamics of the real exchange rate is very similar to that reviewed in this chapter for cross-country studies.

In the empirical application of his model, García-García estimated four behavioral relationships: (1) a demand-for-money equation, (2) an equation for domestic interest rates; (3) an equation for real exchange rates, and (4) a reaction function to explain the conduct of exchange rate policy in the period after 1967. The most interesting results are obtained from the equations for the interest rate and the real exchange rate. With respect to the former, García-García found that, contrary to what could be thought a priori, interest rates in Colombia have been quite responsive to changes in factors pertaining to an open economy, such as world interest rates and expected rates of devaluations. This result indicates that the effectiveness of capital controls in Colombia has been rather limited, failing to isolate the domestic rate of interest from the gyrations of world financial markets and from devaluation policies. Regarding real exchange rates, the empirical results obtained by García-García are highly satisfactory, providing ample support for his specific model, as well as more generally for the theory of real exchange rate determination outlined in this chapter. As predicted by García-García's model, a capital account liberalization that results in higher capital inflows will generate a real exchange rate appreciation, and a relaxation in import tariffs (export taxes) will result in a real exchange rate depreciation (or appreciation). An important difference between García-García's paper and other contributions to this general literature is that García-García introduced explicitly in his regression analysis both import tariffs and export taxes. The coefficient of import tariffs ranged from -0.80 to -0.88, and it was always significant. The estimated coefficient of export taxes ranged between 0.29 and 0.34, with the t-statistic ranging from 1.73 to 2.07.

For Colombia, where coffee greatly dominates legal exports, it is particularly interesting to determine the role played by changes in the terms of trade in the real exchange rate. As predicted by Dutch-disease models,[13] the empirical results obtained by García-García indicate that an increase in the price of coffee will have a strong effect on the real exchange rate. In fact, the estimated coefficient of the log of terms of trade turned out to be approximately −0.85, indicating that an improvement of 10 percent in the terms of trade will result in a real exchange rate appreciation of 8 percent. Moreover, as the absolute value of this coefficient is as large as that of import tariffs, any attempt to use commercial policy to ameliorate the effects of fluctuations in the terms of trade on the real exchange rate would require significant swings in trade controls, generating a score of inefficiency costs.[14] Finally, García-García's results also indicate that inconsistent monetary policies resulting in an excess supply of domestic money will tend to generate a situation of real exchange rate overvaluation and eventually a crisis in the balance of payments.

Chile. Beginning in 1973, Chile embarked on an ambitious program aimed at greatly reducing the importance of the public sector and at reducing government controls. The cornerstones of this program were a trade liberalization reform, financial liberalization, an aggressive privatization program, and a reform of the social security system. Also, starting in 1979, many of the controls on capital mobility were relaxed. In 1982 the reform process suffered a serious setback, when a drastic financial and production crisis took place.[15] Real output declined by almost 15 percent, unemployment soared past 25 percent, most banks ran into serious financial difficulties, and some of the liberalization reforms were partially reversed. At that point, Chile had the highest foreign debt per capita in the world, and debt service became a major burden.

The interpretation of this interesting period of Chile's economic history has generated considerable controversy. Different analysts have tried to determine the role of policy mistakes—and, in particular, of the fixed exchange rate policy followed from 1979 to 1982—in determining the nature and magnitude of the 1982 crisis. Most of the discussion has centered on trying to explain the causes behind the explosive increase in foreign indebtedness and behind the 30 percent real appreciation that took place between 1979 and 1982. Basically, there have been two interpretations of the causes of this appreciation of the real exchange rate during this period. On the one hand, a group of analysts, of which Corbo and de Melo (1987) are perhaps the most forceful representatives, have mainly ascribed the appreciation to nominal forces, including the adoption in June 1979 of a fixed (to the U.S. dollar) nominal exchange rate, at a time when nominal wages were indexed to past inflation. An alternative view, based on the reaction of the equilibrium real exchange rate to changes in fundamentals, has been put forward by de la Cuadra (1981), Edwards (1986c), Harberger (1985), and Hachette (1989). According to these authors, the liberalization of capital controls in Chile in 1979 generated a massive inflow of foreign funds and, along the lines of the theoretical model presented in this chapter, provoked a major appreciation of the real exchange rate. What is particularly important about this interpretation is that, to the extent that the 1979–1981 appreciation was driven by massive capital inflows stemming from the liberalization of capital controls, this liberalization was a short-term real equilibrium phenomenon and did not represent a classical case of exchange rate overvaluation.

In an effort to estimate the role of capital inflows in the process of determination of the real exchange rate in Chile, Edwards (1986c) applied ordinary least squares estimation to quarterly data for the period 1977–1982 to estimate a simple real exchange rate equation that included as explanatory variables net capital flows lagged one quarter ($KF1$), the log of the terms of trade lagged one period ($TT1$), lagged real growth as a proxy for technological progress ($G1$), a devaluation dummy (D), and the lagged log of the real exchange rate ($e1$). The estimated coefficient of the capital flows variable was equal to -0.076, with a t-statistic of -3.521, confirming the hypothesis that in Chile, as in other countries, there has been a negative relationship between capital inflows and the real exchange rate.

In the Chilean debate, the question of causality became particularly important. Supporters of the view that the 1979–1981 real appreciation was a real phenomenon argued that the capital inflows had preceded the decline in the real exchange rate. Others, favoring the view that a situation of overvaluation had developed, argued that the real appreciation took place first and that its effect on interest rates helped to generate the massive capital inflows observed in Chile in the late 1970s and early 1980s. In a perceptive article, Morande (1988) tackled this issue by using time series for 1975–1982 to test Granger-causality between capital inflows and real exchange rate behavior. In his analysis, Morande also extends the scope of explanation of the behavior of real exchange rates by estimating VARs for real exchange rates, capital inflows, interest rate differentials, and terms of trade (unfortunately, the lack of time series precluded him from incorporating import restrictions). Morande's results confirmed the view that the capital account liberalization in Chile generated an important real exchange rate appreciation. Technically speaking, he concluded: "Capital inflow is . . . an a priori causal variable of the real exchange rate under most possible scenarios." Regarding nominal policies and the behavior of the real exchange rate during Chile's liberalization, he said: "The use of nominal exchange rate policy for stabilization purposes . . . was not necessarily the reason for the observed real appreciation of the peso and loss of international competitiveness of Chilean products."

In his contribution to the Chilean debate, Hachette (1989) addressed two key issues. First, how can the rapid accumulation of foreign debt by the private sector since 1979 be explained? More specifically, he asked whether capital inflows were at an "abnormal" level. Second, he inquired about the effects of the significant increase in capital inflows during this period. After analyzing the most important factors behind the demand and supply of foreign funds, Hachette concluded that, until 1980–1981—when the accumulation of private debt by the private sector almost tripled—the rate of capital flow into Chile cannot be termed as abnormal. For these two crucial years, he claimed that increases in perceived wealth and, consequently, in the permanent income fueled extremely rapid increases in the demand for foreign credit. Although Hachette did not present econometric results, he argued convincingly that one of the most important consequences of the opening up of the capital account in Chile was the generation of a substantial real exchange rate appreciation.

Implications of the Theoretical Analysis

The theoretical analysis and the review of empirical studies presented in this chapter have a number of important implications. First, it was found that, as suggested by the theory, the short-term movements of the real exchange rate have responded to both real and monetary forces. Second, the review of the empirical literature indicates that, as implied by the model presented in the first section of this chapter, the liberalization of the capital account in circumstances of a liberalized (that is, nonrepressed) domestic capital market, has resulted in an equilibrium real exchange appreciation. Third, all the country studies reviewed indicate that a trade liberalization will result in (or require) an equilibrium real exchange rate depreciation. These results are particularly interesting, because they provide evidence that helps to clarify theoretical ambiguities. However, an important limitation of most of the empirical studies reviewed is that they have not taken into account explicitly the intertemporal dimensions of the interaction between trade reform and real exchange rates. Only a few studies have distinguished between temporal and permanent liberalization measures. There is little doubt that a future improvement in the understanding of real exchange rate behavior in the midst of structural reforms will require progress in this area of research.

The analysis presented in this chapter has important policy implications for the sequencing of economic reform. In particular, the fact that the real exchange rate will move in opposite directions, depending on whether there is a trade or capital liberalization, has a direct bearing on the issue of *competition of instruments*. The basic point here is that the attainment of a particular target may require some variables, such as the real exchange rate, to move in a particular direction, while the attainment of other objectives will require those variables to move in the opposite direction. This problem is, in part, related to the problem of policy assignment discussed by Tinbergen and Mundell in the 1960s. However, the current problem has a broader scope, stemming from intertemporal and credibility considerations.

Jeffrey Sachs (1987, 1988) has recently stressed in a forceful way the issue of competition of instruments within the context of the sequencing of structural reforms and stabilization programs. His main point is that countries such as Japan embarked on fundamental structural reforms geared toward liberalizing markets only after they had stabilized the economy. Based on this historical experience, Sachs has argued that, analytically, when discussing issues related to sequencing, one of the most important considerations has to do with the competition of instruments.[16] Naturally, this problem is not only present when discussing the sequencing of stabilization and liberalization programs but also when evaluating the appropriate order of a liberalization program.

Of course, in terms of the stylized model, real exchange rate behavior represents an important sphere in which competition of instruments is reflected. From the perspective of sequencing, the present analysis tends to support Ronald McKinnon's view (1973, 1982) that the liberalization of the capital account should not occur until the trade account reform is already consolidated. McKinnon argued that capital account restrictions should be relaxed only after trade and other industrial sector distortions had been dismantled. He based his argument on the fact that capital inflows will result in a real exchange rate appreciation that, in turn, removes protection from the tradable goods sector at a time when, owing to the tariff reductions, a real exchange rate depreciation is needed.[17] According to McKinnon: "Unusually large capital inflows of foreign capital . . . inhibit the exchange rate to depreciate sufficiently . . ." (1973:160). This problem is compounded by the fact that these flows are not sustainable in the long term. Consequently, McKinnon argued, a structural reform of the trade account should "deliberately avoid an unusual or extraordinary injection of foreign capital" (1973:161).

Appendix

An Intertemporal Model of Equilibrium Real Exchange Rates

This appendix presents a *minimal* fully optimizing model of equilibrium real exchange rates. The model is partially based on Edwards (1989a), and it captures the main features of the analytical framework discussed in the first section of the chapter. The equilibrium real exchange rate is defined as that relative price of tradable goods to nontradable goods that, for given sustainable (equilibrium) values of other relevant variables (such as taxes, international prices, and technology) results in the simultaneous attainment of *internal* and *external* equilibrium. *Internal equilibrium* means that the market for nontradable goods clears in the current period and is expected to be in equilibrium in future periods. In this definition of the equilibrium real exchange rate, it is implicit that this equilibrium takes place with unemployment at the "natural" level. *External equilibrium*, on the other hand, is attained when the intertemporal budget constraint that the discounted sum of a country's current account must be equal to zero is satisfied. In other words, external equilibrium means that the current account balances (current and future) are compatible with long-term sustainable capital flows.

Implications of the definition of the equilibrium real exchange rate

A number of important implications follow from this definition of the equilibrium real exchange rate. First, the equilibrium real exchange rate is not an immutable number. When there are changes in any of the other variables that affect the country's internal or external equilibrium, there will also be changes in the equilibrium real exchange rate. For example, the real exchange rate required to attain equilibrium will not be the same with a very low world price of the country's main export as with a very high price of that good. In a sense, then, the equilibrium real exchange rate is itself a function of a number of variables, including import tariffs, export taxes, real interest rates, capital controls, etc. These immediate determinants of the equilibrium real exchange rate are the real exchange rate "fundamentals." Second, the equilibrium real exchange rate will not only be affected by current fundamentals but also by the expected future evolution of these variables. If intertemporal substitution of consumption is possible by means of borrowing and lending and intertemporal substitution in production is possible through investment, expected future events (such as an expected change in the international terms of trade, for example) will affect the current value of the equilibrium real exchange rate. In particular, the behavior of the equilibrium real exchange rate will depend on whether changes in fundamentals are perceived as being permanent or temporary. If there is perfect international borrowing, a temporary disturbance to, say, the terms of trade, will affect the complete future path of equilibrium real exchange rates. However, if there is rationing in the international credit market, intertemporal substitution of consumption will be cut and temporary disturbances will tend to affect the equilibrium real exchange rate in the short term only. In this case, a distinction between short-term and long-term equilibrium real exchange rates becomes useful.

Description of the sample small economy

Although the analytical framework is general and can accommodate many goods and factors, it is useful to think about this small sample economy as being comprised of a large number of profit-maximizing firms that produce three goods—exportables (X), importables (M), and nontradables (N)—using constant returns to scale technology, under perfect competition. It is assumed that factors exist besides tradable goods, so that factor-price equalization does not hold. One way to think about this is by assuming that each sector uses capital, labor, and natural resources.

It is assumed that there are two periods only—the present (period one) and the future (period two)—and that there is perfect foresight. Residents of this small country can borrow or lend internationally. However, there are taxes on foreign borrowing, and the domestic (real) interest rate exceeds the world interest rate. The intertemporal constraint states that at the end of period two the country has paid its debts. The importation of M is subject to specific import tariffs in both periods one and two. In the model the current account is equal to savings minus investment in each period. Consumers maximize intertemporal utility and consume all three goods.

The government consumes both tradables and nontradables. Government expenditure is financed through nondistortionary taxes, proceeds from import tariffs, proceeds from the taxation of foreign borrowing by the private sector, and borrowing from abroad. As in the case of the private sector, the government is subject to an intertemporal constraint—that is, the discounted value of government expenditure (including foreign debt service) must equal the discounted value of income from taxation.

In addition to the private sector and government budget constraints, internal equilibrium requires that the market for nontradables should clear *in each period*—that is, the quantity of nontradables supplied must equal the sum of the demands by the private and public sectors for these goods. The model is completely real; with no money or other nominal assets.

Equations for the model

The general model is given by equations (A1) through (A9), where the world price of exportables has been taken as the numeraire:

$$R(1,p,q,V,K) + \delta\tilde{R}(1,\tilde{p},\tilde{q};\tilde{V},K+I)$$
$$- I(\delta) - T - \delta\tilde{T} = E\{\pi(1,p,q),\delta\tilde{\pi}\,(1,\tilde{p},\tilde{q}),W\} \tag{A1}$$

$$G_X + p^*G_M + qG_N + \delta^*(\tilde{G}_X + \tilde{p}^*\tilde{G}_M + \tilde{q}\tilde{G}_N) = \tau(E_P - R_P)$$
$$+ \delta^*\tilde{\tau}(E_{\tilde{P}} - \tilde{R}_{\tilde{P}}) + b(NCA) + T + \delta^*\tilde{T} \tag{A2}$$

$$R_q = E_q + G_N \tag{A3}$$
$$\tilde{R}_{\tilde{q}} = E_{\tilde{q}} + \tilde{G}_N \tag{A4}$$

$$p = p^* + \tau \tag{A5}$$
$$\tilde{p} = \tilde{p}^* + \tilde{\tau} \tag{A6}$$
$$\delta\tilde{R}_K = 1 \tag{A7}$$
$$P_T^* = \gamma P_M^* + (1-\gamma)P_X^*;\ \tilde{P}_T^* = \gamma\tilde{P}_M^* + (1-\gamma)\tilde{P}_X^*;\ (P_X^* = \tilde{P}_X^* = 1) \tag{A8}$$

$$RER = (P_T^*/P_N);\ R\tilde{E}R = (\tilde{P}_T^*/\tilde{P}_N) \tag{A9}$$

Table 9.2 contains the notation used.

Equation (A1) is the intertemporal budget constraint for the private sector and states that the present value of income valued at domestic prices must equal the present value of private expenditure. Given the assumption of a tax on foreign borrowing, the discount factor used in (A1) is the domestic factor δ, which is smaller than the world discount factor δ^*.

Equation (A2) is the intertemporal budget constraint of the government. It states that the discounted value of government expenditure must equal the present value of government income from taxation. NCA, which is equal to $(\tilde{R} - \tilde{\pi}E_{\tilde{\pi}})$, in (A2) is the current account surplus of the private sector in period two, and $b(NCA)$ is the discounted value of taxes on foreign borrowing paid by the private sector. It should be noted that the use of the world discount factor δ^* in (A2) reflects the

TABLE 9.2   Notation Used in the Model of Equilibrium Real Exchange
Rates

Symbols	Definitions
$R(\ )$, $\tilde{R}(\ )$	Revenue functions in periods one and two. Their partial derivatives with respect to each price are equal to the supply functions.
p; $\tilde{p}$	Domestic relative price of importables in periods one and two.
q, $\tilde{q}$	Relative price of nontradables in periods one and two.
V, $\tilde{V}$	Vector of factors of production, excluding capital.
K	Capital stock in period one.
$I(\ )$	Investment in period one.
δ^*	World discount factor, equal to $(1+r^*)^{-1}$, where r^* is world real interest rate in terms of exportables.
δ	Domestic discount factor, equal to $(1+r)^{-1}$. Since there is a tax on foreign borrowing, $\delta < \delta^*$.
$b = (\delta^* - \delta)$	Discounted value of tax payments per unit borrowed from abroad.
p^*, $\tilde{p}^*$	World relative price of imports in periods one and two.
τ, $\tilde{\tau}$	Import tariffs in periods one and two.
T, $(\tilde{T})$	Lump sum tax in periods one and two.
G_X, G_M, G_N; $\tilde{G}_X$, $\tilde{G}_M$, $\tilde{G}_N$	Quantities of goods X, M, and N consumed by government in periods one and two.
$E(\ )$	Intertemporal expenditure function.
$\pi(1,p,q)$; $\tilde{\pi}(\ )$	Exact price indexes for periods one and two. Under assumptions of homotheticity and separability, these correspond to unit expenditure functions.
W	Total welfare.
NCA	Noninterest current account of the private sector in period two.
P_M^*, P_X^*; $\tilde{P}_M^*$, $\tilde{P}_X^*$	Nominal world prices of M and X in periods one and two. It is assumed that $P_X^* = \tilde{P}_X^* = 1$.
P_N, $\tilde{P}_N$	Nominal price of nontradables in periods one and two.
P_T^*, $\tilde{P}_T^*$	World prices of tradables, computed as an index of the prices of X and M in periods one and two.
RER, $R\tilde{E}R$	Definition of the real exchange rate in periods one and two.

SOURCE: Author's calculations.

assumption that in this model the government is not subject to the tax on foreign borrowing.

Equations (A3) and (A4) are the equilibrium conditions for the market for nontradables in periods one and two. In each of these periods, the quantity supplied of N (R_q and $\tilde{R}_{\tilde{q}}$) must equal the sum of the quantity demanded by the private sector (E_q and $E_{\bar{q}}$) and by the government. Given the assumptions about preference (separability and homotheticity), the demand for N by the private sector in period one can be written as:

$$E_q = \pi_q E_\pi \tag{A10}$$

Equations (A5) and (A6) specify the relation between domestic prices of importable goods, world prices of imports, and tariffs. Equation (A7) describes investment decisions and states that profit-maximizing firms will add to the capital stock until Tobin's q equals unity. This expression assumes that the stock of capital is made up of the numeraire goods.

This model distinguishes between the real exchange rate for exportables ($1/q$) and the real exchange rate for importables (p/q). Since the relative price of X and M can change, it is really not possible to consider a tradable goods composite. It is still possible, however, to *compute* how an index of prices for tradables would evolve through time. Equation (A8) is the definition of the price index for tradables, where γ and $(1-\gamma)$ are the weights of importables and exportables. Equation (A9) defines the real exchange rate index as the domestic relative price of tradables to nontradables. Equations (A1) through (A9) fully describe the intertemporal and intratemporal (external and internal) equilibrium in this economy.

This model has an equilibrium path for the real exchange rate. The vector of equilibrium real exchange rates ($RER,\bar{RER}$) is composed of those real exchange rates that satisfy equations (A1) through (A9) for given values of the other fundamental variables. It should be noted that, since no rigidities, externalities, or market failures are assumed, the equilibrium real exchange rates imply the existence of full employment (see, however, Edwards 1989a). From straightforward manipulation of equations (A3) and (A4), it is possible to derive the slopes of schedules N^1N^1 and N^2N^2 presented in the chapter. Use of these equations in combination with the rest of a model allows us to formally carry out the diagrammatical analysis of the main test.

From the inspection of equations (A1) through (A9), it is apparent that exogenous shocks in, say, the international terms of trade, will affect the vector of equilibrium relative prices and real exchange rates through two interrelated channels. The first one is related to the *intratemporal* effects on resource allocation and decisions regarding consumption and production. For example, as a result of a temporary worsening of the terms of trade, a tendency will arise to produce more and consume less of M in that period. This tendency, along with the income effect resulting from the worsening of the terms of trade, will generate an incipient disequilibrium in the market for nontradables that will have to be resolved by a change in relative prices and in the equilibrium real exchange rate. In fact, if it is assumed that there is no foreign borrowing, these intratemporal effects will be the only relevant ones. However, with capital mobility and investment, as in the current model, there is an additional *intertemporal* channel through which changes in exogenous variables will affect the vector of equilibrium real exchange rates. For example, in the case of a worsening of the terms of trade, the consumption discount factor ($\tilde{\pi}\delta/\pi$) will be affected, altering the intertemporal allocation of consumption. Also, in that case, the investment equilibrium condition (A7) will be altered, affecting future output.

Naturally, without specifying the functional forms of the expenditure, revenue, and other functions in equations (A1) through (A9), it is not possible to write the vector of equilibrium relative prices of nontradables, nor the equilibrium real exchange rates, in an explicit form. It is possible, however, to write them implicitly as functions of all the sustainable levels of all exogenous variables (contemporaneous and anticipated) in the system:

$$RER = h(p^*, \tilde{p}^*, \tau, \tilde{\tau}, \delta, \delta^*, V, T, \tilde{T}, G_X, \tilde{G}_X \ldots) \qquad (A11)$$

$$R\tilde{E}R = \hbar(p^*, \tilde{p}^*, \tau, \tilde{\tau}, \delta, \delta^*, \tilde{V}, T, \tilde{T}, G_X, \tilde{G}_X \ldots) \qquad (A12)$$

A crucial question is related to how the equilibrium vectors of relative prices and real exchange rates will change in response to different types of disturbances—that is, what are the most plausible signs of the partial derivatives of *RER* and *RĒR* with respect to their determinants? The actual discussion of these effects is beyond the scope of this chapter and can be found in Edwards (1989a,b,c).

Summary and conclusions

The main conclusions from the manipulation of the model can be summarized as follows:

1. With low initial tariffs, the imposition of import tariffs (either temporarily or permanently) will usually generate an *equilibrium real appreciation* in both current and future periods. A sufficient condition is that there is net substitutability in demand among all three goods: *X*, *M*, and *N*. If initial tariffs are high, in order for this result to hold, it is necessary, in addition, that income

effects be dominated by substitution effects. If, however, there is complementarity in consumption, it is possible that the imposition of import tariffs will generate a real equilibrium depreciation.

2. If the income effect associated with a deterioration in the terms of trade dominates the substitution effect, a worsening in the terms of trade will result in an *equilibrium real depreciation.*

3. Generally, it is not possible to know how the effect of import tariffs and terms of trade shocks on the equilibrium real exchange rate will be distributed through time.

4. It is crucially important to distinguish between permanent and temporary shocks when analyzing the reaction of the equilibrium real exchange rate.

5. A relaxation of exchange controls will always result in an equilibrium real appreciation in period one. Moreover, in that period it will be observed that there are simultaneously a real appreciation and an increase in borrowing from abroad.

6. A transfer from the rest of the world (or an exogenously generated capital inflow, for that matter) will always result in an equilibrium real appreciation.

7. The effect of an increase in government consumption on the equilibrium real exchange rates will depend on the composition of this new consumption. If it falls fully on nontradables, there is a strong presumption that the real exchange rate will experience an equilibrium real appreciation. If it falls fully on tradables, there will be an equilibrium real depreciation.

Notes

Some of the material has drawn on a report written for the World Bank in June 1989. I am indebted to Miguel Savastano for helpful comments, and I gratefully thank the Rockefeller Foundation for financial support.

    1. The Baker and Brady plans designed to deal with the debt crisis consider trade liberalization as the cornerstone of the reforms needed in the developing countries. A large number of World Bank Structural Adjustment Loans (SALs) have included a trade liberalization component. See Halevi (1989).

2. For early episodes, for example, see Diaz-Alejandro (1970). For more recent history, see Dornbusch and de Pablo (1989) and Cottani and García (1989).

3. On the Chilean liberalization episode, see, for example, Edwards and Cox-Edwards (1987) and Hachette (1989).

4. On the evolution of Colombia's external sector, see Diaz-Alejandro (1976), Thomas (1985), and García-García (1989).

5. On Uruguay, see Corbo and de Melo (1987) and Favaro and Spiller (1989).

6. Formally, consumers in this economy maximize a time-separable intertemporal utility function, where each subutility function depends on that period's consumption of X, M, and N. See the Appendix to this chapter.

7. See the Appendix at the end of this chapter for a formal discussion.

8. Since more than one distortion exists, we cannot really know whether a reduction in σ will enhance welfare. This is, however, the most plausible outcome.

9. For a discussion on period one and the role of the real exchange rate, see, for example, Calvo (1986).

10. See Corbo and de Melo (1987), Dornbusch and de Pablo (1989), and Calvo (1986).

11. Beginning in January 1979, the Argentinian authorities adopted a preannounced devaluation scheme that came to be known as the *tablita* (see Calvo 1986).

12. For a comparative study of Uruguay's liberalization reforms in the 1970s, see Corbo and de Melo (1987).

13. The role of changes in the terms of trade on the behavior of the equilibrium real exchange rate is also captured by the model presented in the appendix to this chapter.

14. Actually, how to avoid coffee-induced changes in real exchange rates continues to be one of the most serious problems of macroeconomic management in Colombia.

15. These developments were partially the result of the world recession and debt crisis. See Edwards and Cox-Edwards (1987).

16. Sachs (1988) specifically points out that "the instruments of stabilization may well compete with the instruments of liberalization."

17. The fact that capital inflows result in a real exchange rate appreciation has been investigated extensively within the context of the Dutch-disease effects of foreign aid. See, for example, van Wijnbergen (1984).

Growth Collapses, Real Exchange Rate Misalignments, and Exchange Rate Policy in Developing Countries

This chapter is based on the results of a multicountry study of twenty-one countries undertaken for the World Bank and entitled, "The Political Economy of Poverty, Equity, and Growth." The countries were classified into three categories in terms of their resource endowments, based on the three-factor, n-good model of an open economy developed by Krueger (1977) and Leamer (1987). Countries were classified as: (1) labor abundant and land scarce, (2) land abundant and labor scarce, and (3) in an intermediate category, in terms of where their endowment ratio in the late 1950s lay in the Leamer endowment triangle with respect to the aggregate endowment point of the noncommunist countries. This classification and the countries in the sample are listed in Table 10.1. This classification by resource endowment was useful in identifying alternative stylized development paths for the countries and in linking the evolution of factor prices on these paths to the political economy of the countries concerned.[1]

The most common exchange rate policy in these twenty-one countries is some form of managed exchange rate, with exchange controls of varying degrees of severity and effectiveness. Some of the countries, however, have maintained a form of colonial currency-board system, with almost 100 percent backing of the domestic currency by foreign assets. Nigeria and Ghana were part of the West African Currency Board System, established in 1912, but both countries abandoned this system

Table 10.1   Growth Instability in Twenty-one Developing Countries, 1950–1985

Countries by category	Trade orientation	Growth rate of GDP	Standard deviation	Coefficient of variation	Cyclical growth	Period of growth collapse
Labor-abundant						
Hong Kong	SO	8.9[a]	4.47	50.20		
Singapore	SO	8.3[b]	4.20	50.60		
Malta	MI	5.6[c]	5.74	102.50	Cycl.	
Land-abundant						
Malaysia	MO	6.9[a]	2.73	39.60		
Thailand	MO	6.7	2.99	44.70		
Brazil	MO	6.6	3.88	58.80		1980s
Mexico	MI	5.7	3.13	55.00		1980s
Turkey	SI–MO	5.6	6.57	117.40	Cycl.	1980s
Costa Rica	MO–MI	5.0	4.45	89.10		1981
Colombia	MO–MI	4.7	1.95	41.60		
Nigeria	MI–SI	3.7	10.00	270.20	Cycl.	1976 on
Ghana	SI	1.3[d]	5.13	394.70	Cycl.	1980s
Uruguay	SI–MO	1.1[e]	4.28	388.90	Cycl.	1980s
Intermediate						
Egypt	n.a.–MI	5.4	3.10	57.30		
Indonesia	MO–MI	5.3[f]	3.64	68.70		1960s
Sri Lanka	SI–MI	4.7	3.26	69.40		
Malawi	n.a.–MO	4.3[g]	5.62	130.80	Cycl.	
Peru	SI	4.1	3.96	96.50	Cycl.	1980s
Jamaica	MO–MI	3.3	4.38	132.70	Cycl.	1973 on
Mauritius	n.a.–MO	2.9	6.93	238.98	Cycl.	
Madagascar	MI–SI	2.0[h]	3.48	174.14	Cycl.	1978 on

n.a. = not available; MI = moderately inward; MO = moderately outward; SI = strongly inward; SO = strongly outward.
a. 1960–85.
b. 1960–86.
c. 1950–84.
d. 1966–86.
e. 1955–84.
f. 1952–85.
g. 1954–86.
h. 1950–86.

(continued)

upon the establishment of independent central banks after they attained political independence. Two of the countries—Singapore and Hong Kong (except for the period 1972–1983)—have maintained a type of currency-board system. In addition, despite monetary independence, some countries have for a substantial length of time maintained currency convertibility, underwritten by Gladstonian fiscal and monetary rectitude—notably Mexico (which, until Echeverría, maintained a fixed parity and full convertibility with the U.S. dollar), Indonesia (after Sukarno), Malta, Malaysia (until recently), and Thailand.

TABLE 10.1   *(continued)*

Country	Average annual growth rate of consumer prices (%)			
	1950–73	1973–80	1965–80	1980–85
Labor-abundant				
Hong Kong	n.a.	n.a.	8.1	7.9
Singapore	2.5[i]	6.0	4.8	3.2
Malta	2.6	7.7	n.a.	3.0
Land-abundant				
Malaysia	1.7	6.3	4.9	4.6
Thailand	3.0[j]	11.1	6.8	4.9
Brazil	26.0[k]	43.5	31.6	148.9
Mexico	5.3	20.7	13.2	60.7
Turkey	8.8[j]	39.0	20.8	38.6
Costa Rica	2.8	12.3	11.2	34.8
Colombia	9.7	24.1	17.5	22.3
Nigeria	4.1[j]	18.8	14.5	18.7
Ghana	5.8	54.3	22.8	55.5
Uruguay	45.9[l]	62.8	57.7	44.8
Intermediate				
Egypt	2.0	12.1	7.5	14.3
Indonesia	36.4[m]	19.3	34.3	9.7
Sri Lanka	2.4	9.8	9.5	12.0
Malawi	5.4[l]	11.0	7.3	13.1
Peru	10.0	41.1	20.5	102.1
Jamaica	4.6[j]	22.0	12.6	16.6
Mauritius	3.7[n]	18.2	11.8	9.1
Madagascar	3.6[k]	10.8	7.7	20.0

n.a. = not available.
i. 1960–73.
j. 1955–73.
k. 1964–73.
l. 1968–73.
m. 1964–73.
n. 1963–73.

(continued)

Many of these countries suffered growth collapses in the 1970s and 1980s. The first section of this chapter identifies these countries and the periods of their growth collapses and then seeks the causes of these growth collapses. The second section considers whether trade orientation is a sufficient explanation and finds this wanting. In the third section, the proximate cause of growth collapses is found to be unsustainable fiscal deficits and inflation that lead to misalignment of real exchange rates. The types of such misalignments that can arise (and their costs) from exogenous shocks—in capital flows or in terms of trade—are analyzed. Illustrations come from the sample of countries. The extreme fragility of predictions about the necessary movements in

TABLE 10.1   *(continued)*

Country	Central government surplus or deficit as % of GDP			Manufactured exports as % of total exports	
	1960	1972	1985	1960	1985
Labor-abundant					
Hong Kong	n.a.	n.a.	n.a.	80	92
Singapore	−0.4(1963)	1.3	2.1	26	58
Malta	−0.9	−4.7	−4.0	n.a.	
Land-abundant					
Malaysia	1.9	−9.2	−7.4	6	27
Thailand	0.1	−4.3	−5.5	2	35
Brazil	−2.1	−0.3	0.9	3	41
Mexico	−1.7(1966)	−3.0	−8.7	12	28
Turkey	−1.9(1967)	−2.2	−7.4	3	54
Costa Rica	−3.1	−4.3	−1.2	5	30
Colombia	−0.4	−2.5	−1.1	2	18
Nigeria	−2.3(1965)	−1.1	−3.1	3	0
Ghana	−6.4(1965)	−5.7	−2.2	10	5
Uruguay	−3.8(1965)	−2.5	−2.2	29	37
Intermediate					
Egypt	−1.9	n.a.	−10.1	12	10
Indonesia	−0.7	−2.4	−0.3	0	11
Sri Lanka	−6.8	−7.7	−9.5	0	27
Malawi	0.3(1964)	−5.6	−8.0	n.a.	5
Peru	1.8	−1.1	−2.3	1	11
Jamaica	−1.0	−4.1	−17.8	5	12
Mauritius	−2.2(1966)	−3.1	−5.0	n.a.	31
Madagascar	−1.9(1965)	−2.5	n.a.	6	9

n.a. = not available.
SOURCE: Author's calculations.

the real exchange rate to maintain smooth adjustment is emphasized, because it casts doubt on the desirability of maintaining discretionary exchange rate regimes in developing countries. Automatic mechanisms for exchange rate adjustment, such as those in a floating exchange rate or in a currency-board system of genuine fixed exchange rates, are emphasized. In turn, these mechanisms point to the importance of a fiscal and monetary constitution as an essential part of an efficient economic framework for promoting growth.

Dimensions of Growth Instability

The stability in growth performance of the twenty-one countries has varied considerably. Annual growth rates of real gross domestic product

(GDP) have been extremely volatile. To give some idea of their comparative performance, Table 10.1 classifies the countries into three groups. The first group consists of countries whose growth has been relatively *steady*, where steadiness is measured by the standard deviation of annual percentage rates of growth of less than 4 in the period 1950–1985. The second group consists of countries with *cyclical growth*, as based on figures showing the growth performance for each country in the appendix to the synthesis of the multicountry study on which this chapter is based. It appears that countries in this group have clear cycles of growth performance, with a standard deviation in annual growth rates greater than 4.[2] The third group includes countries that will also be in one of the other two categories but that have at some period suffered a *growth collapse*.

The "growth collapse" countries were identified by means of the judgments of the authors of the country studies on turning points. Since there is no rigorous way to establish the sustainable long-run growth rate of an economy, relying on the economic historian's judgment on the occurrence of a growth collapse is unavoidable.

The resulting classification is given in Table 10.1, which has two striking features. The first is that a majority of the countries in the intermediate factor-endowment group have a cyclical growth performance, as do most of the relatively poor performers (in terms of average growth performance) in the land-abundant group. Perhaps these countries have not diversified into exports of manufactures and are still specialized in production of primary commodities whose world prices are known to be unstable. From the data on the share of manufactures in exports of the sample of countries in 1985 (shown in Table 10.1), it is clear that any such inference is insecure. Thus, Malaysia and Thailand have similar shares of nonmanufactured exports, as compared with Uruguay, and yet have experienced relatively steady growth.

The second noteworthy feature is that over half of the land-abundant countries have suffered growth collapses (seven out of ten). None of the labor-abundant countries and only Jamaica, Peru, and Madagascar in the intermediate group have suffered growth collapses (excluding Indonesia's growth collapse under Sukarno).

Causes of Growth Collapses

Most of the growth collapses, moreover, occurred in the 1970s and 1980s. This is not surprising. The economies of most of these countries (despite attempts at autarky in some) are relatively open, and their economic fortunes are linked to that of the world economy. Until 1973, the world economy went through what has been called its "Golden Age" of tranquil expansion. Since the first rise in oil prices in 1973, however, the world economy has been buffeted by gyrating primary commodity prices, a second rise in oil prices in 1979, followed by a large fall, and large fluctuations in capital flows and their associated real interest rates. This turbulent world economic environment involved similar external shocks for many developing countries, but their performance diverged sharply.

Trade orientation

A summary of the extent of the shocks associated with the high oil prices, commodity prices, and interest rate changes in the early and late 1970s, as well as of the ways in which the various countries dealt with them, is provided by a system of accounting for the sources of balance of payments disturbances and adjustments, conducted by Balassa (1984). His results for the countries in this study are summarized in Table 10.2.[3]

Balassa's own conclusions are based on a classification of countries as "outward looking" and "inward looking." He concludes that outward-looking countries, despite greater shocks in both periods, performed better because they chose output-increasing policies of export promotion and import substitution, whereas the inward-oriented countries adjusted to the 1974–1976 shock by borrowing at (often negative) real interest rates to cover their balance of payments deficits, but then had to take extreme deflationary measures in 1979–1981, as their increased indebtedness and the rising world interest rates limited further borrowing. Hence, he concludes that economic growth rates were substantially higher in outward-oriented than inward-oriented countries.

Without doubt, there is a great deal of truth in these conclusions, but they raise the question of why some countries were inward-oriented and others were outward-oriented. Also, insufficient weight is placed in this explanation on the underlying fiscal pressures that are most likely, in the face of exogenous shocks, to lead to growth collapses. Furthermore, no explanation is provided of exactly what it is about outward and inward orientation that makes efficient adjustment in the face of exogenous shocks so different. Also, there is the uncomfortable fact that some inward-looking countries, such as India (which is not one of the sample countries), fared much better in terms of the stability of their growth performance, compared with, for example, an outward-oriented country like Brazil that suffered a growth collapse.

Table 10.1 also shows the classification of the twenty-one developing countries by inward and outward trade orientation, as given in the

TABLE 10.2   External Shocks and Adjustment in Thirteen Developing Countries, 1974–1981

Countries ranked by severity of external shock in 1974–76	Period	External shock (balance of payments deficit) as % of GDP	Policy responses as % of external shock			GDP growth
			Additional foreign borrowing	Income from export promotion	Income from import substitution	
1. Singapore	1974–76	20.2	87.1	−3.9	−34.0	50.6
	1979–81	34.4	36.6	89.7	−53.3	29.3
2. Jamaica	1974–76	13.6	7.3	−9.9	38.4	64.2
	1979–81	35.5	44.2	−24.7	21.2	61.3
3. Turkey	1974–76	7.5	120.2	−3.9	−11.2	−5.2
	1979–81	6.4	−11.0	10.9	52.1	48.0
4. Egypt	1974–76	7.4	296.6	−25.2	−177.7	6.3
	1979–81	6.9	47.9	−20.1	34.8	37.5
5. Uruguay	1974–76	6.6	61.6	30.3	29.7	−21.6
	1979–81	10.3	98.9	4.3	71.4	−74.8
6. Thailand	1974–76	4.5	8.2	30.3	52.1	9.4
	1979–81	7.2	78.7	39.7	−38.3	19.9
7. Mauritius	1974–76	4.2	147.1	47.1	176.5	−264.7
	1975–81	17.9	57.8	1.4	42.2	−2.0
8. Brazil	1974–76	3.9	82.6	12.4	19.8	−14.8
	1979–81	4.2	−33.5	38.4	46.2	109.0
9. Peru	1974–76	3.6	199.2	−39.8	−54.9	−4.5
	1979–81	1.3	−459.1	400.7	−74.5	32.9
10. Mexico	1974–76	1.6	177.6	−59	−19.3	0.8
	1979–81	1.9	315.4	562.4	−904.5	−73.3
11. Colombia	1974–76	0.9	142.7	2.1	−406	−4.2
	1979–81	5.0	149.1	53.0	−102.3	0.2
12. Indonesia	1974–76	−19.3	−90.3	16.0	−23.9	−1.8
	1979–81	−7.4	−118.6	16.5	7.3	−5.2
13. Nigeria	1974–76	−53.8	−60.6	−3.8	−34.4	−1.2
	1979–81	−4.1	−227.7	−28.5	27.7	128.5

SOURCE: Bela Balassa, "Adjustment Policies in Developing Countries: A Reassessment," *World Development* 12, no. 9 (September 1984).

World Development Report for 1987.[4] Of the ten countries that suffered growth collapses in the 1970s and/or 1980s (that is, excluding Indonesia), only Ghana and Peru were strongly inward-oriented, while Nigeria moved to being a strongly inward-oriented country from a moderately inward-oriented country between 1973 and 1983. Costa Rica and Jamaica were moderately outward-oriented before 1973 and became moderately inward-oriented subsequently. Mexico was moderately inward-oriented and Brazil was moderately outward-oriented, while Uruguay moved from being strongly inward-oriented to being moderately outward-oriented. Clearly, neither their placement in the outward-inward orientation categories nor the movements between them can provide an explanation in itself for the growth collapses in this sample of twenty-one countries.

Inflation and fiscal deficits

A more significant relationship can be seen between the acceleration of inflation and growth collapses. Except for Uruguay, where there was a deceleration in its high inflation rate in the 1980s when growth collapsed, all the other growth collapse countries recorded an acceleration in their inflation rates. One significant difference, even among the growth collapse countries, is that the Latin American countries (Brazil, Mexico, Costa Rica, Uruguay, and Peru) had a much higher average inflation rate than the former British colonies in the group (Nigeria and Jamaica), except for Ghana.

When comparing the data on inflation rates and growth of the money supply across these countries, it is clear that there is a positive relationship, but it is not tight. This is not surprising, as the inflationary impact of any increase in the money supply will depend on changes in money demand. These depend on two counteracting influences.[5] It is well known that population and real income growth will increase the demand for money. At the same time, inflation acts as a tax on money holdings, and as with any other tax, holders of money will, ceteris paribus, seek to economize on their money holdings, causing the demand for money to be lower in an inflationary than in a noninflationary economy. In a hyperinflation, of course, there will be a shrinkage in the demand for real money balances.

A useful classification of inflationary experiences has been provided by Harberger.[6] He divides countries into categories of chronic and acute inflation. Countries with chronic inflation are those where consumer prices have risen by more than 20 percent over an extended period, while countries with acute inflation are those where inflation has run over 80 percent a year for three or more years. Harberger also shows that in countries with chronic inflation, because the positive elements in the demand for money have not been swamped by the negative effects of inflation tax, the growth of the money supply can be expected to be higher than the growth in the price level. By contrast, in countries with acute inflation the demand for real money balances shrinks, and the inflation rate is higher than the rate of the growth of money. Use of this latter and theoretically more relevant criterion, together with Harberger's more arbitrary cut-off points, results in Table 10.3. This shows the countries in this sample that fall into these two categories (during the

TABLE 10.3   Developing Countries with Chronic or Acute Inflation or Growth Collapse, 1964–1985

| | | Average annual % increase | | |
| | | Consumer | Money | Growth |
Country	Period	prices	supply	collapse
Chronic inflation				
Turkey	1965–80	20.8	27.4	No
	1980–85	37.1	51.9	No
Brazil	1965–80	31.6	43.4	No
Colombia	1980–85	22.5	27.2	No
Ghana	1965–80	22.8	25.9	No
Uruguay	1965–80	57.7	65.3	No
Indonesia	1965–80	34.3	54.9	No
Peru	1965–80	20.5	25.9	No
Acute inflation				
Turkey	1980	110.2	54.2	Yes
Brazil	1964	91.4	86.1	No
	1980–87	158.6	141.2	Yes
Peru	1980–85	98.6	102.5	Yes
Mexico	1980–85	62.6	61.4	Yes
Costa Rica	1980–85	36.4	31.1	Yes
Ghana	1980–85	57.0	41.4	Yes
Uruguay	1967–68	125.3	87.0	No
	1980–85	44.6	44.2	Yes
Growth collapse without chronic or acute inflation				
Nigeria	1965–80	14.5	28.5	Yes
	1980–85	11.4	10.5	Yes
Jamaica	1965–80	12.6	17.3	Yes
	1980–85	18.3	26.5	Yes
Madagascar	1965–80	7.7	12.0	Yes
	1980–85	19.4	13.1	Yes

SOURCES: World Bank, *World Development Report 1987*, Table 1; International Monetary Fund, *International Financial Statistics Yearbook*, 1988, Table 25.

1965–1980 and 1980–1985 periods), as well as their inflation rates and growth rates of the money supply in the relevant periods.[7]

Table 10.3 shows clearly that cases of acute inflation are associated with growth collapses. By contrast, chronic inflation does not necessarily lead to a growth collapse. This is just a reflection of the well-known argument that a moderate, steady, anticipated inflation is unlikely to have any real effects on growth performance.

The fairly firm connection between increased money and acute inflation with growth collapses in the latter group, raises the question of what the reasons are for this monetary expansion. In his study, Harberger (1987) found that "the bulk of the cases in which countries initially pursuing fixed exchange rate policies are ultimately forced to devalue their currencies, have their roots in fiscal deficits financed by recourse to the banking system." Unfortunately, the available data on fiscal deficits (particularly for Latin American countries) is imperfect (Lal and Wolf 1986). What is required is a measure of the whole public sector's borrowing requirement. As in most third world countries, the public sector extends well beyond the fiscal published figures of the central government's deficit. These data, therefore, are highly imperfect indicators both of the size of the public sector's borrowing requirement and of trends in it.

An alternative path in line with Harberger is to consider the connection between inflation and government borrowing from the banking system. Table 10.4 shows the net change in the government's debt to banks, expressed as a ratio of the same year's GDP, for the acute inflation countries in this sample that have suffered a growth collapse. The link between increasing public indebtedness, rises in money supply, and accelerating inflation in the growth collapse countries is clear.

Exogenous shocks and misalignment of real exchange rates

If deficit financing induced the acute inflation associated with most of the growth collapses in these sample countries, there are still two countries with chronic inflation (Jamaica and Nigeria) that have suffered growth collapses. Their problems are associated with the mishandling of the rents accruing from booms in income from natural resources, and the associated problems encapsulated by the generic term, the Dutch disease. These problems, as well as the consequences of inflationary outcomes in the countries with chronic inflation, are best discussed within the analytical framework of the so-called Australian or dependent economy model of an open economy.

Such a model is depicted in Figure 10.1,[8] where PP is the production possibility curve for the economy of a country that produces (with given stocks of two factors of production—capital and labor) and consumes three goods. One good is an importable good, and the second is an exportable good. Domestic prices of both goods are set by given world prices and the nominal exchange rate. These two goods can be combined into a Hicksian composite commodity at the given world prices into a composite tradable group. The third good is a nontradable good whose domestic price is set by domestic demand and supply. The initial equilibrium of the economy is at A, where the highest attainable community indifference curve is tangential to the production possibility curve. The slope of the common tangent measures the *real exchange rate*, defined as *the relative price of nontradable to tradable goods*.[9]

TABLE 10.4   Changes in Ratio of Public Debt to GDP in Countries
with Chronic or Acute Inflation, 1965–1986

| | | Percentage change | | |
Country	Year	Public debt/GDP ratio in preceding year (% of GDP)	Consumer prices	Nominal money
Turkey	1978	4.1[a]	45.3	34.1
	1979	0.8	58.7	54.8
	1980	1.0	110.2	54.2
	1981	1.0	36.6	37.3
	1982	0.5	30.8	27.5
	1983	−0.4	32.9	41.1
Mexico	1981	−0.7[a]	27.9	36.8
	1982	1.0	58.9	41.5
	1983	7.3	101.8	44.1
	1984	−3.2	65.5	53.2
	1985	−4.3	57.7	53.7
Brazil	1979	0.5[b]	52.7	46.2
	1980	0.7	82.8	76.0
	1981	0.9	105.6	65.1
	1982	−0.7	97.8	82.0
	1983	1.2	142.1	95.0
	1984	0.2	197.0	141.1
	1985	2.9	226.9	274.6
Costa Rica	1981	2.0[a]	37.1	38.8
	1982	6.3	90.1	70.4
	1983	−10.1	32.6	45.3
Ghana	1965	1.8[b]	26.4	24.1
	1966	1.5	13.3	−0.3
	1967	6.8	−8.5	−4.3
	1975	2.9	29.8	36.6
	1976	6.4	56.1	46.1
	1977	−1.3	116.5	50.9
	1978	−0.1	73.1	74.1
	1979	−3.9	54.4	30.3
Uruguay	1980	0.4[b]	63.5	34.9
	1981	−0.5	34.0	33.9
	1982	5.9	19.0	1.0
	1983	7.6	49.2	45.8
	1984	12.6	55.3	24.0
	1985	−7.3	72.2	71.8
Peru	1980	−1.3[b]	59.2	71.1
	1981	0.4	75.4	43.4
	1982	−1.5	64.4	33.7
	1983	7.6	111.2	75.4
	1984	−2.5	110.2	97.3
	1985	−5.0	163.4	204.6
	1986	n.a.	77.9	175.6

n.a. = not available.
a. One-year lag.
b. No lag.
SOURCE: International Monetary Fund, *International Financial Statistics Yearbook*, 1988.

FIGURE 10.1   Three-Good Model of an Open Economy

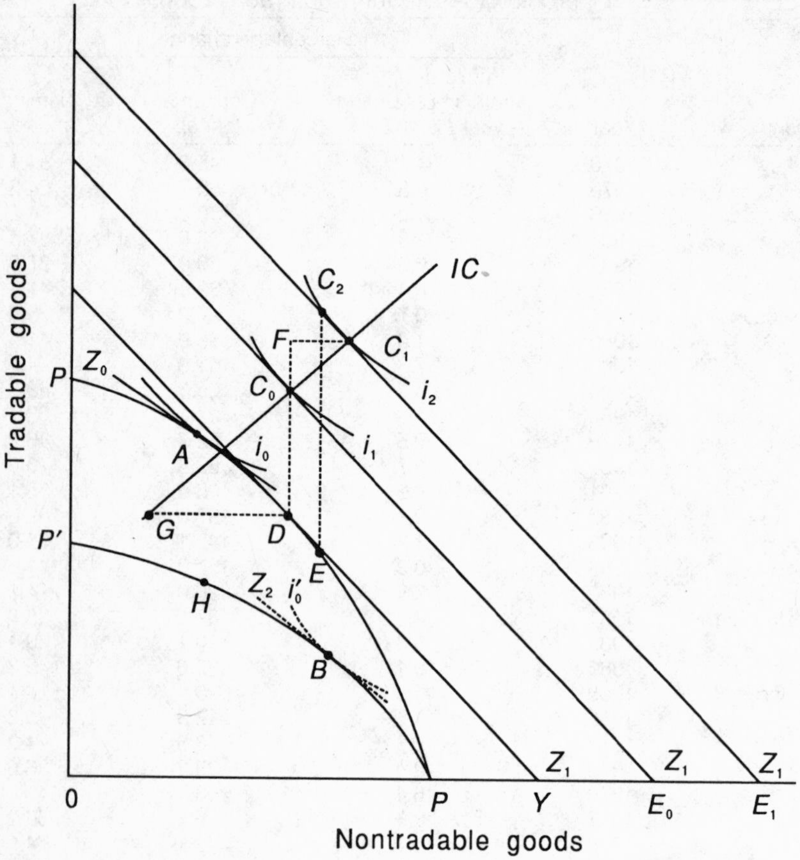

SOURCE: Author's calculations.

Foreign exchange windfalls and fiscal expansion.   Now suppose that there is
a large inflow of capital from either aid inflows (for example, in Sri
Lanka after the United National Party's victory or in Egypt since the
Camp David accord with the United States), commercial bank borrowing or other private inflows of capital (Mexico in the 1970s, Brazil, and
Uruguay), foreign remittances by workers abroad (Turkey, Egypt, and
Sri Lanka), or rents from natural resources (bauxite or alumina in Jamaica, oil in Nigeria and Indonesia). The new equilibrium that maintains both internal and external balance is given by the production point
D) and the consumption point C_0 vertically above it (as the demand and
supply of nontradable goods must be equal for internal balance). The
trade deficit C_0D (equal to the excess demand for the tradable good) is

exactly equal to the capital inflow that, in turn, is exactly equal to the excess of domestic expenditure (OE_0 over domestic output) OY measured in terms of the nontradable good. In this equilibrium adjustment to the capital inflows, the real exchange will have appreciated from Z_0 to Z_1 (the slope of the tangent at D being greater than that at A or Z_0). There will be no further adjustment problem.

Suppose, however, as is common in most developing countries, the government maintains exchange control and does not sterilize the effects of the foreign exchange inflows because it does not use a notion of high-powered money in its budgetary planning. With the rise in its foreign exchange reserves, given the time lag between the receipt of foreign exchange and its subsequent spending by private or public agencies, the government is advised to use these foreign exchange reserves for development purposes by running a budget deficit equivalent to E_0E_1, in terms of the nontradable good. Otherwise, it can decide to use the windfall for expanding public expenditure and to run a budget deficit (for example, in Mexico after the first rise in oil prices in 1973, Sri Lanka in the late 1970s, Jamaica in the mid-1970s, and Nigeria). With production still at point D, consumption shifts to C_1 along the income consumption curve IC (for the real exchange rate Z_1). There is now a secondary trade deficit of C_0F as well as excess demand for the nontradable good of C_1F. This excess demand will lead to a rise in the price of the nontradable good (a further real exchange rate appreciation) until the nontradable goods market clears with consumption at C_2 (on the unchanged real income indifference curve i_2), vertically above the new production point E. The final excess demand for tradables will be C_2E, leading to an unsustainable balance of payments deficit of C_2E minus the capital inflow of C_0D.

The ensuing loss of reserves (including the use of any international credit the government might be able to muster) must entail some adjustment. A necessary part of this adjustment must be a reversal of the excess absorption E_0E_1, as well as a reversal of the excess exchange rate appreciation (from the slope of the production point at E-slope of the consumption indifference curve at C_2) to the new postcapital inflow equilibrium exchange rate Z_1.

If prices of nontradable goods are flexible, this latter "switching" effect will occur automatically because, with the reduction in expenditure to OE_0, excess supply appears for the nontradable good, putting downward pressure on its price. If, however, because of labor market rigidities or slowness of price adjustments, this downward movement of the price of nontradable goods is sluggish, the requisite real exchange rate depreciation will not occur. In that case, a devaluation of the nominal exchange rate that raises the domestic price of tradable goods relative to nontradable goods will be required to implement the switching of expenditure entailed by a real exchange rate depreciation.

It is this inability to devalue in a "hard-money" monetary system (such as the West African franc zone, or in the currency-board systems operated by Singapore and Hong Kong) that is considered to be one of its main weaknesses. However, this weakness is essentially based on the assumed *downward rigidity of prices of nontradable goods*. As shown by the movements in both directions in the real exchange rates for the two clear-cut, hard-money economies (Singapore and Hong Kong), even in these predominantly industrial economies this assumption is not necessarily valid. However, in some countries (Jamaica and Nigeria), where the capital windfall was used in large part to expand public employment, the implicit money wage adjustment that is required for such automatic expenditure-switching may be resisted. Explicit depreciation of the *nominal* exchange rate will then be necessary to allow the equilibrium real wage to be established (assuming that while nominal wages are rigid downward, real wages are not).

To see more clearly the consequences of any downward rigidity in the prices of the nontradable goods in the adjustment process, consider another type of stochastic disturbance that affected many of the countries in this sample in the late 1970s. Let us assume that the economy is in internal and external balance, with equilibrium capital inflows of C_0D, at the production point D, consumption point C_0, and equilibrium real exchange rate Z_1.

Let us assume further that there is a sudden contraction or cessation of this inflow (as in commercial loans to Mexico, Uruguay, and Brazil, or in natural resource rents in Jamaica and Nigeria). With domestic expenditure unchanged at OE_0, the balance of payments deficit of C_0D is unsustainable. Suppose the government reduces expenditure to the sustainable level OY, but because of sluggishness in movements in the price of nontradable goods, the real exchange rate remains at Z_1. An expenditure level OY and a real exchange rate at Z_1 will still leave an excess demand for tradables (not drawn) and a trade deficit. With the unchanged real exchange rate Z_1, the government will have to reduce expenditure further until the economy is at the production and consumption point G (on the Z_1 income consumption curve IC) that is horizontally to the left of D. At G there will not be a balance of payments deficit, but there will be excess supply and hence unemployment in the nontradable goods industry, of GD. There will have been a fall in output below its potential (as happened in many of the Latin American debtor countries). However, this fall in output is entirely due to the misalignment of the real exchange rate, and it could be cured swiftly by a depreciation of the nominal exchange rate or more slowly as the excess supply and unemployment in the nontradable goods industry leads to a fall in the price of nontradable goods.

The cost of this real exchange rate misalignment in this case is the forgone output of GD. Alternatively, the government may maintain real expenditure at the level of OY but may seek to control the accompanying trade deficit through import controls. This policy will lead to the dead-weight and rent-seeking costs associated with this type of intervention[10] and will once again place the economy within its production possibility frontier PP.

Terms of trade changes. We have examined the likely effects on output and growth of alternative forms of adjustment to two types of "shocks"—one external (an increase or decrease in capital flows) and the other internal (an excessive fiscal expansion that may be associated with these windfalls). There is a third type of shock—namely, a change in the external terms of trade—that has also affected various countries in the sample. Some have suffered from a positive shock, as the terms of trade of some of their primary product exports—notably, oil for Indonesia, Nigeria, and Mexico in the 1970s—have risen markedly, while most of the others have seen a fall or cycles in their terms of trade.

The effects of such changes in the terms of trade on instability and growth can also be analyzed by references to Figure 10.1. Suppose there is a deterioration in the terms of trade, with the foreign currency price of importables rising and the price of exportables and the nominal exchange rate unchanged. The production possibility curve will shift inward to PP', as the relative price of exportables falls in terms of *importables (assumed to be the numeraire for the tradable goods)*, and hence at any point on the initial PP curve the quantity of exportables produced by the given allocation of resources can be exchanged for fewer importables. Thus, the overall quantity of tradable goods, measured in terms of the numeraire (importables) falls, and the PP curve shifts to PP'. Simultaneously, the community indifference curve will twist upward. With the rise in the price of importables, consumers can obtain only the same quantity of tradables at a higher cost in terms of the numeraire (the domestic price of importables).

Whether the new equilibrium point on PP', where the highest attainable new indifference curve is tangential to the shrunken production possibility curve, implies a rise or fall in the *real exchange rate* will depend (assuming perfect factor mobility among the three goods industries) purely on the relative factor intensities in producing the three goods. This can be seen from Figure 10.2, which depicts the factor price frontier for given product prices for the three goods. Assuming that the

FIGURE 10.2   Three-Good Model of Prices, Wage Rates, and Rental Rates

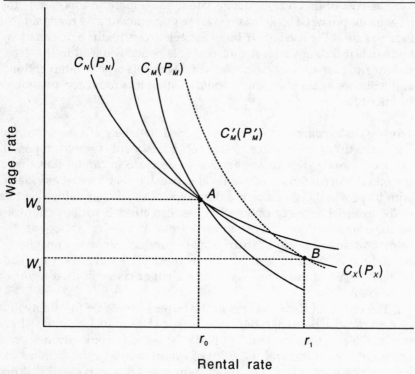

NOTE: k_i—capital-labor ratio in industry producing good
$i = X$—exportables
    M—importables
    N—nontradables
P'—money price of good i
w—wage rise
r—rental rate

Terms of trade	I	II	III
(P_M/P_X) Improvement	If $k_M > k_X > k_N$	$k_M > k_N > k_X$	$k_X > k_M > k_N$
$(P_M/P_X) \downarrow$ Deterioration	$w \uparrow r \downarrow P_N \uparrow$	$w \uparrow r \downarrow P_N$	$w \downarrow r \uparrow P_N \downarrow$
$P_M \uparrow$ P_X	$W \downarrow r \uparrow P_N \downarrow$	$W \downarrow r \uparrow P_N \uparrow$	$W \uparrow r \downarrow P_N \uparrow$

The slope of the iso-cost curve shows the capital-labor ratio at the relevant wage-rental ratio.

SOURCE: Author.

nontradable good is the most labor-intensive (least capital-intensive) of the three goods, its factor price curve will, therefore, have a lower slope at each wage-rental ratio than the other two industries, of which importables are assumed to be the most capital-intensive. A rise in the price of importables shifts the C_M curve outward but leaves the C_X curve unchanged (as the price of exportables P_X has not changed). The new wage-rental equilibrium is given by the point B, with a lower wage and a higher rental rate. For this equilibrium to be sustainable, the C_N curve must also pass through this point—that is, the C_N curve must shift downward, or the price of the nontradable good (P_N) must fall and the real exchange rate must depreciate. The converse would be the case if the nontradable good was less labor-intensive than the exportable good. The various changes in the factor prices, together with the possible combinations of factor intensities, are set out in the note to Figure 10.2.

Suppose the new equilibrium point at B in Figure 10.2 implies a fall in the real exchange rate that in turn implies that nontradable goods are more labor-intensive than exportables. In the type of hard-money economy discussed in the first section (assuming that wages and prices are flexible), the economy would move smoothly from A to B. With the shift in the production possibility curve, and hence an excess of expenditure over the reduced output at the initial consumption and production point A, there will be a balance of payments deficit accompanying the deterioration in the terms of trade. The resulting loss of reserves will lead (in a currency-board type of hard-money system) to an equivalent reduction in the domestic money supply—reducing the demand for all goods. The fall in the demand for tradables will directly improve the balance of trade, because the disabsorption will be equivalent to a shift in the expenditure line from OY to the line passing through B (with the slope of Z_1). In addition, given the factor intensity assumptions, the real exchange rate will also change (to Z_2), with the price of nontradable goods falling to maintain internal and external balance on the shrunken production possibility curve PP'. There would be an unavoidable fall in total output because of the decline in real income associated with the worsening terms of trade, but there would be no further adjustment effect on output or growth. Moreover, if this movement in the terms of trade is reversed, as has been the case for many primary product exporting countries, then with rational expectations and no public policy shocks, the economy would return to its original equilibrium at A. There should be no effects on long-term growth from these stochastic environmental shocks.

However, as in the case with declining capital inflows, if the government seeks to maintain expenditure at OY through fiscal policy, then again there will be a balance of payments crisis that will require disabsorption. It is uncertain whether a devaluation will also be necessary. This can be seen as follows. For the case where nontradable goods are the most labor-intensive of the three goods, we know from Figure 10.2 that the equilibrium real exchange rate falls from Z_1 to Z_2. With the decline in the terms of trade, say, the immediate effect (in Figure 10.1) is to shift the production point from A to H, vertically below it on the shrunken production possibility curve PP'. However, the implicit producer prices at H, given by the slope of the production curve, will imply a lower relative price of nontradable goods than that given by the unchanged real exchange rate Z_1. They will still represent an implicitly lower real exchange rate (slope at H) than the new equilibrium exchange rate Z_2 (slope at B) that, in itself, is lower than the original real exchange rate Z_1 (slope at D). Therefore, in the final equilibrium, there will be a real exchange rate appreciation relative to Z_2, implicit at H, but a real exchange rate depreciation relative to Z_1 (slope at D).

We also know from the previous case, where we examined a pure fiscal expansion (the move from OE_0 to OE_1) that, ceteris paribus, a fiscal expansion will involve a real exchange rate appreciation. The question, therefore, is whether the appreciation following from this latter source is greater than that required to establish the new equilibrium exchange rate Z_2. In general, nothing can be said on this issue. Hence, in dealing with a balance of payments crisis caused by a decline in the terms of trade and an unsustainable budget deficit, theory does not reveal whether the required deflation of expenditure should be accompanied by an appreciation or depreciation of nominal and real exchange rates.

The data on economic indicators accompanying the country profiles in the appendix to the synthesis of the multicountry study on which this chapter is based show the real exchange rate[11] and wage series for the countries in the sample. During the 1970s, when most of these countries (except Indonesia and Nigeria) were affected by a negative external shock amounting to a deterioration in the terms of trade, their real exchange rate and real wage movements would have been determined by the relative factor intensities of their exportable goods.[12] Table 10.5 summarizes the direction of the movements in the real exchange rate and wage rate for these countries during the aftermath of the two oil shocks (after 1973 and after 1979), and it also shows the implied factor intensities that can be deduced from the three-good models depicted by Figure 10.2. Without any data on the actual factor intensities of the three types of "aggregates," it is impossible to test the model in any meaningful way. However, the implied factor intensities were judged by the authors of the country studies to be in agreement with their expectations, based on their in-depth studies of the various countries.

Thus it can be concluded that there will be equilibrium fluctuations in real wages and in real exchange rates (caused by exogenous shocks) depending on the relative factor intensity of exportables relative to nontradable goods and importables. A rise in the real exchange rate (and in the real wage) after a country suffers an unfavorable external shock

TABLE 10.5   Factor Intensities and Price and Wage Rate Movements in Twenty Developing Countries, 1973–1986

Implied factor intensities	Country	Price and wage movements	
		1973–78	1979–86
$k_N > k_x$	Hong Kong	$P_N \uparrow\ w \downarrow$	$P_N \uparrow\ w \downarrow$
$k_N > k_x$	Singapore	$P_N \uparrow\ w \downarrow$	$P_N \uparrow\ w \downarrow$
$k_x > k_N > k_M$	Malaysia	$P_N \uparrow\ w \uparrow$	
$k_N > k_x$	Thailand	$P_N \uparrow\ w \downarrow$	$P_N \uparrow\ w -$
$k_x > k_N$ and then $k_N > k_x$	Turkey	$P_N \uparrow\ w -$	$P_N \uparrow\ w \downarrow$
$k_x > k_N > k_M$	Brazil	$P_N \uparrow\ w \uparrow$	$P_N \uparrow\ w \uparrow$
$k_x > k_N > k_M$	Mexico	$P_N \uparrow\ w \uparrow$	$P_N \uparrow\ w \uparrow$
$k_M > k_x > k_N$	Costa Rica	$P_N \downarrow\ w \downarrow$	$P_N \downarrow\ w \downarrow$
$k_M > k_x > k_N$	Colombia	$P \downarrow\ w \downarrow$	$P_N \downarrow\ w \downarrow$
$k_N > k_x$	Ghana	$P_N \uparrow\ w \downarrow$	$P_N \uparrow\ w \downarrow$
$k_x > k_N$	Uruguay	$P_N \uparrow\ w -$	$P_N \uparrow\ w \uparrow$
$k_x > k_M > k_N$	Egypt	$P_N \uparrow\ w \uparrow$	$P_N \uparrow\ w \uparrow$
$k_M > k_x > k_N$	Indonesia	$P_N \uparrow\ w \downarrow$	$P_N \uparrow\ w -$
$k_N > k_x$	Sri Lanka	$P_N \uparrow\ w -$	$P_N \uparrow\ w \downarrow$
$k_M > k_x > k_N$	Malawi	$P_N \downarrow\ w$ n.a.	$P_N \downarrow\ w -$
$k_x > k_N$	Peru	$P_N \uparrow\ w$ n.a.	$P_N \uparrow\ w$ n.a.
$k_x > k_N$	Nigeria	$P_N \uparrow\ w -$	$P_N \uparrow\ w^a$
$k_N > k_x$	Jamaica	$P_N \uparrow\ w \downarrow$	$P_N \uparrow\ w \downarrow$
$k_N > k_x$	Mauritius	$P_N \uparrow\ w \downarrow$	$P_N \uparrow\ w \downarrow$
$k_N > k_x$	Madagascar	$P_N \uparrow\ w \downarrow$	$P_N \uparrow\ w \downarrow$

n.a. = not available; k = capital-labor ratio; x = exportables; M = importables; N = nontradables; P = money price of goods; w = wage rise; $\uparrow$ = deterioration; $\downarrow$ = improvement.
a. 1979–81.
SOURCE: Author's calculations.

cannot in itself be taken as a sign of any misalignment of exchange rates or of failures of labor market policy that could lead to a growth collapse. To establish any exchange rate based on information on relative factor intensities, the requisite equilibrium movement in the real exchange rate would have to be determined. Only then can it be established whether the actual real exchange rate movement is excessive. If it is, it will usually be because of an inappropriate change in fiscal and trade policy following the external shock.[13]

Costs, Consequences, and Lessons

In recent work, Edwards (1988a, 1988b) has attempted to formulate and estimate a model, based on the structure depicted by Figure 10.1, of misalignment of real exchange rates from their equilibrium values for twelve developing countries, including five in this sample (Brazil, Colombia, Malaysia, Sri Lanka, and Thailand). He then performed a statistical test to determine whether real exchange rate misalignment (as defined with reference to a model with a changing equilibrium real exchange rate) was inversely related to growth performance. He found that it was.[14] Furthermore, he found that lack of fiscal discipline was the main source of real exchange rate disequilibrium.

The first conclusion, therefore, is that many of the facile prescriptions offered about the proper real exchange rate in the face of crises in the balance of payments induced by terms of trade are incorrect. Thus the common prescription that a decline in the terms of trade requires a depreciation of the real exchange rate is not generally valid.[15] Second, in the face of some exogenous shock, it is impossible to deduce whether the exchange rate is misaligned by merely observing the movements in the real exchange rate. Third, it will, therefore, be difficult also for governments to determine the correct direction or the magnitude of the required nominal exchange rate movement in the face of exogenous shocks. However, since a nominal depreciation is required only if price changes of nontradable goods are sluggish (when there is a decline in the equilibrium exchange rate), it is in cases where balance of payments deficits have been generated largely by fiscal expansion that there will be a presumptive need for devaluations. Given all these uncertainies,[16] it may be best to adopt a flexible exchange rate if there are nominal wage rigidities or there is sluggishness in price movements of nontradables.[17]

More important here, however, is the fourth conclusion—that, in reversing unsustainable fiscal expansions, output losses may occur. These fiscal expansions, in turn, were based on unsustainable increases in either "big push" investment programs (Mexico, Brazil, and Turkey) or in social expenditures (Costa Rica and Uruguay). This is a conclusion that is supported by these country studies and seems to be the major explanation for the growth collapses, including those in the nonchronic and acute inflation countries (Jamaica and Nigeria). These latter countries suffered from the Dutch disease. They used the windfalls from rising natural resource rents to expand the public sector, in the form of unproductive government employees and in the growth of inefficient and unproductive parastatal enterprises engaged in production or trade. However, as the contrasting experience of Indonesia demonstrates, infection with the Dutch disease need not lead to a prolonged debilitating illness. The crucial difference in Indonesia was the tight control over the growth of public expenditure that, by contrast, exploded in both Jamaica and Nigeria. Secondly, after the Pertamina crisis, Indonesia reined in its public investments in heavy industry, whereas both Jamaica and Nigeria used large shares of their windfalls to promote inefficient and unproductive import-substituting industries on familiar structuralist grounds.

It is also worth noting that the oil boom in Nigeria was not the country's first windfall. As Bevan, Collier, and Gunning (1990:part 3, section 5) emphasize, Nigeria also experienced the boom associated with the rise in commodity prices during the Korean war. Government reserves rose because of the increased revenue from trade taxes. But, according to Bevan et al., "the policy response was largely passive, resulting in reserve accumulation. . . . This was so because the marketing boards, in keeping with their stabilization role did not adjust producer prices for export crops in line with world prices. The resulting accumulation was unintentional to the extent that the boards did not foresee the boom's magnitude. . . . Adjustment during the [following] downturn was still semi-automatic (as it had been before the war) because an independent monetary policy was impossible."

This example underlines the importance of the fifth conclusion—namely, the need for an *implicit or explicit* monetary and fiscal constitution under which the government operates. As emphasized by Bevan, Collier, and Gunning (1990), a major reason for the Indonesian government's more successful management of the oil boom was that "by that time the Indonesian government had constrained its own policy choices by its commitment to convertibility and budget balance." Hence, insofar as monetary independence has historically been associated with the easing of the budget constraint on governments, a rethinking of monetary and fiscal arrangements must form an essential part of the design of an economic framework that prevents the growth process from being attenuated by growth collapses induced by public policy when countries have to cope with the unavoidable volatility of a changing world economic environment.

Notes

My chapter is based on the draft synthesis of a multicountry study, "The Political Economy of Poverty, Equity, and Growth," directed by Deepak Lal and Hla Myint for the World Bank, Washington, D.C. The synthesis was based on the following nine country studies:

Malawi and Madagascar, by Frederick Pryor

Egypt and Turkey, by Bent Hansen

Sri Lanka and Malaysia, by Henry Bruton

Indonesia and Nigeria, by David Bevan, Paul Collier, and Jan Gunning

Thailand and Ghana, by Oey A. Meesook, Douglas Rimmer, and Gus Edgren

Brazil and Mexico, by Angus Maddison and Associates

Costa Rica and Uruguay, by Simon Rottenberg, Claudio Gonzales-Vega, and Edgardo Favaro

Colombia and Peru, by Antonio Urdinola, Mauricio Carrizosa Serrano, and Richard Webb

Five small economies: Hong Kong, Singapore, Malta, Jamaica, and Mauritius, by Ronald Findlay and Stanislaw Wellisz

1. See Lal (1989a) for an application of the Leamer framework to Latin America.

2. Recently, a more sophisticated technique for distinguishing between the permanent and cyclical elements of time series has been developed by Beveridge and Nelson (1981) and Nelson and Plosser (1982). It includes a measure of stochastic (rather than the conventional, purely deterministic) element in the steady-state growth trend of a time series, so that it can shift up or down. The cyclical fluctuations around this shifting growth path are then estimated, and they will typically yield a small cyclical component in the time series. This method has not been used, as it would not markedly change the qualitative judgments sought. For an application to Colombia, see Cuddington and Urzua (1989). The seminal contributors to the techniques are Beveridge and Nelson (1981) and Nelson and Plosser (1982). A useful description of the technique and its uses is provided by Stock and Watson (1988).

3. See Balassa (1984) and A. Fishlow's comments on Balassa's approach. Most people should agree with the broad heuristic dimensions of at least the different directions in which countries responded to these shocks.

4. See Figure 5.1 in *World Development Report 1987*. The few countries not listed—that is, Egypt, Jamaica, Malawi, Malta, and Mauritius—have been assigned to the relevant categories on the basis of the authors' judgment in the country studies.

5. For the clearest statement on the topic see Harberger (1987).

6. Harberger (1987) has analyzed the inflation and growth experience of a number of developing and developed countries. He found that fiscal imbalances are a major cause of what he terms "chronic" and "acute" inflation.

7. Thus, countries are included in the acute inflation group whose inflation rate is higher than 20 percent but less than 80 percent a year but whose rate of growth of money was less than the growth in prices.

8. The following account is based on Lal (1989b), which also provides detailed references to the relevant literature. Also see Lal (1987:273–300). These two references are revised versions of Lal (1984).

9. Latin Americans define their real exchange rate as the inverse of the usual definition—namely, the relative price of tradable to nontradable goods.

10. A graphic illustration of the rent seeking associated with import controls is provided by Rimmer for Ghana. Discussing the growth of corruption under the import control regime in the 1970s, Rimmer notes: "As in 1964–65, the quantity of import licenses became a specially notorious area for the appropriation of administratively generated rents. Kept women could be kept by the issue of licenses, so that aspirants to this status 'paraded the corridors of power

offering themselves for libidinal pleasures in return for favours'" (Rimmer 1990: ch.7, p. 6).

11. It should be noted that these real exchange rates are surrogates for the relative price of nontraded to tradable goods that we need. They have been derived by Wood (1988:2) by adjusting the normal exchange rate of each country "by the difference between its own inflation rate and the weighted average inflation rate of the industrial countries, measuring inflation by the rate of increase of the implicit GNP deflector." The relationship between the "purchasing power parity real exchange rate" and the real exchange rate defined as the relative price of nontraded to tradable goods is discussed in Lal (1985).

12. Lal (1986) provides an algebraic model and econometric test of the model for a land-abundant country.

13. For an explicit exercise in this vein, see Lal (1985).

14. The estimated equation in Edwards (1988a:46) was:

$$\text{Growth of real GDP} = 0.052 - 1.050 \text{ misalignment}$$
$$(18.440) \ (-1.929) \ R^2 = 0.27$$

where the figures in parentheses are t statistics.

15. The same confusion surrounds the required movements in the exchange rate in trade liberalization. The correct answers are derived in Corden and Neary (1982). Also see Edwards and van Wijnbergen (1987).

16. There are further problems concerning the dynamic path of the real exchange rate and other variables that depend on the relative speed of adjustments in the relevant markets, and that can lead to overshooting or undershooting from their relevant equilibrium values. See Lal (1989b) for a diagrammatic account within the same framework.

17. See Lal (1980, 1987). Also see Edwards (1988a) for an alternative view.

Comments

APOSTOLOS CONDOS

It is a pleasure to read this chapter for its clear line of reasoning and substance. If I find a fault, it is with the articulation between its empirical and theoretical arguments. It is not tight enough to be entirely self-contained. It certainly makes us look forward to the publication of the World Bank study, "The Political Economy of Poverty, Equity, and Growth," on which Deepak Lal's chapter is based.

The line of reasoning

The focus of the chapter is the search for proximate causes of growth collapses in the 1970s and 1980s among the sample countries. The inward or outward trade orientation of countries with such experiences is not found to be adequate as a proximate cause. Unsustainable fiscal deficits and inflation do better as explanations, as does the associated real exchange rate misalignment since most countries studied are (or were) under some kind of managed exchange rate regime. Acute and accelerating inflation ensuing from larger fiscal deficits, supported by increasing public debt as a proportion of GDP, is an even better explanation, but two countries in the sample that had different inflation histories did suffer growth collapses. Here the explanation involves mismanaged foreign exchange windfalls from capital inflows of various origins or excessive fiscal expansion under favorable terms of trade. In any case, inability or unwillingness of governments to adjust downward as soon as the situation required certainly contributed to the magnitude of the eventual adjustment effort.

These trade hypotheses are consonant, in broad outline, with the data presented in Tables 10.3 and 10.4 and are also easy to handle within the standard dependent-economy Australian model and its policy implications. They are also consistent with the "conventional widsom" on this subject.

In the case of a foreign exchange windfall in the form, say, of aid flows, and starting from an equilibrium position (real expenditures equal output), it would be expected that an increase in expenditures equal to the windfall would lead to a new equilibrium position (as long as the windfall continues) that will be associated with an increased (appreciated) equilibrium real exchange rate. Even without excessive fiscal expansion, if the capital inflow should cease, disabsorption will be needed on the way to the old equilibrium, and if prices of nontradables are flexible, the real exchange rate will depreciate by the force of the market mechanism. A devaluation, however, would be necessary, if prices of nontradables are inflexible downward. In the framework of this two-good model, no doubt exists about the direction of nominal exchange rate intervention, if it should be needed.

Unsustainable fiscal expansion in this framework implies both a trade deficit beyond the level that can be supported by capital inflows and a further appreciation of the real exchange rate that is necessary for internal equilibrium. When the crunch comes, the policy implications with respect to the exchange rate are the same as those just previously mentioned, together with a devaluation needed to compensate for high prices of nontradables and to prevent underutilization of resources that disabsorption at an unchanged real exchange rate would bring about, if it is to be strong enough to eliminate the trade deficit.

The implications of a nominal exchange rate policy in the case of a shock in the terms of trade, however, are more difficult to analyze because a three-commodity framework is required (as a minimum). Therefore, if the structure of the economy is not fully known, even the direction of intervention cannot be known.

The basic point is that the factor intensity structure among the exportable, importable, and nontradable goods industries will determine whether market-led adjustment will be associated with a higher or lower equilibrium real exchange rate. Because of this, if fiscal policy in the face of an adverse shock attempts to maintain real expenditure at the preshock level, disabsorption eventually becomes inevitable. However, devaluation becomes advisable only if the contribution of fiscal expansion to real exchange rate appreciation is smaller than the depreciation needed to return to the preshock full equilibrium (and, of course, if the market cannot do it).

The latter point is illustrated by comparing the real exchange rates at four positions of the economy: (1) original (preshock) equilibrium, (2) postshock short-term equilibrium on the reduced production possibility curve before adjustment in the market for nontradables, (3) sustainable equilibrium with capital inflows in the preshock situation, and (4) postshock long-term equilibrium. The gist of the argument is that, while the real exchange rate (RER) in position (2) is less than the real exchange rate in position (4) (implying appreciation along the path toward equilibrium), and the real exchange rate in position (3) is greater than the real exchange rate in position (4) (implying depreciation along the path toward equilibrium), theory offers no guidance in general, whether RER (3) − RER (4) is greater or less than RER (4) − RER (2). (If RER (3) − RER 4 is greater than RER (4) − RER (2), then it is desirable to devalue). In other words, it is difficult to know whether, when the economy is coming down from an unsustainable level of expenditures to the reduced production possibility frontier, it will arrive to the right or to the left of the long-term equilibrium point (4).

The fundamental conclusion of this line of reasoning is that discretionary exchange rate regimes, together with undisciplined budget procedures, are the main sources of trouble. It follows that either freely floating exchange rates or "specie-flow" mechanisms, on the one hand, and fiscal commitment to budget balance, on the other, are necessary ingredients of an efficient framework for growth.

Some questions

If this summary does not misinterpret Deepak Lal's reasoning, the only possible critical discussion would be about the correspondence of specific country realities with the theoretical model. I do not have the required country knowledge to venture in this direction. Alternatively, one could invoke structuralist-interventionist reasons in the monetary-fiscal areas to question the validity of the general framework of the analysis presented. I cannot do that, either, for the simple reason that I find Deepak Lal's approach entirely convincing in its major thrust and conclusions. Instead, I will raise some questions about points that need to be clarified.

1. What is the significance of the three-factor n-good model for the content of this chapter (as opposed to its significance for the World Bank study)? The three-group classification of countries appears extraneous to the main discussion that is based at a certain point on a two-factor three-good frame of reference.

2. The first striking feature of Table 10.1—the cyclical growth experience—relates to the majority of countries in the two more numerous groups and to one country out of three in the labor-abundant group. The second noteworthy feature is the occurrence of growth collapse in the majority of the land-abundant countries in the sample, in three or four out of eight in the intermediate group, but in none of the three labor-abundant countries. It is not easy to understand the attempted stylization of outcomes. The contrasts seem weak, and the comparison groups are unbalanced. What is the significance of endowment proportions for those outcomes?

3. With reference to Table 10.5, the text suggests that P_N and W changes are equilibrium movements, so that factor intensity rankings are *deduced* for each country. If independent evidence on factor intensities is brought into the picture (and the shock in each country identified), then the direction of change in P_N and W can be deduced. Did the study use the endowment proportions to arrive, one way or another, at factor intensities? If so, why are factor intensities in Table 10.5 *deduced*, instead of being compared with the theoretical expectations given P_N and W movements or, alternatively, changes in P_N and W data compared with their theoretical expectations? In any case, if data and theoretical values disagree, would the author suspect the heavy hand of intervention? Would he reject the model or would he reject the data?

4. The greater the excess of fiscal expansion is over and above the sustainable level, the greater the likelihood is that a devaluation will be needed, with a concave-to-the-origin production possi-

bility frontier and substitution in consumption of nontradable for tradable goods. Does not this consideration extenuate somewhat the generally valid criticism that actual real exchange rate movements do not reveal much about exchange rate misalignment? What about the place of devaluation in structural adjustment programs?

5. The major cause of growth collapse (and, in every case, output loss) was found to be reversing unsustainable fiscal expansion that had taken place in the direction of "white elephants" and expansion of the public sector. Would Deepak Lal recommend resumption of capital flows to developing countries without the strong conditionality of a fiscal and monetary constitution guaranteeing a balanced budget and convertibility?

6. It is relatively easy to monitor a government's fiscal and monetary behavior, but what guarantees are needed to avoid "white elephants"? What framework is best for lending to both governments and the private sector? Is it conceivably possible for bank lending to be directed to the private sector without some form of government guarantees, and if not, is there an alternative to direct foreign investment, with all its internal reform presuppositions, if repetition of earlier experience is to be avoided?

A technical slip

Discussing the production possibility curve, in the section "Terms of trade changes," with regard to the inward shift after an unfavorable shock in the terms of trade, the author correctly indicates that, at a higher price of the importable, the maximum quantity of tradables (measured in terms of importables) for every quantity of nontradable goods will be smaller. Therefore, the new production possibility curve, starting at the same maximum quantity of nontradable goods, will arrive at a lower level on the tradable axis. But he further notes that the extent of the shift depends on the relative elasticities of substitution in production and the proportion in which resources are deployed in the tradable and nontradable goods industries. These intersectoral adjustments, however, have nothing to do with the production possibility curve, which is a strictly technological construct. I presume, also, that the "upward" shift in the community indifference curve in the same section is really downward and to the right.

Exchange Rate Policy in Countries with Hyperinflation: The Case of Argentina

Exchange rate policies in countries with hyperinflation deserve special consideration because the external sector plays a unique role. High inflation implies that the stock of foreign exchange held by residents usually becomes the target of runs against domestically produced nominal assets. When runs are not the cause of sharp devaluations, erratic inflation and portfolio shifts dominate the short-term dynamics of either market exchange rates or exchange rate policies.

This chapter first discusses foreign exchange policy, emphasizing the portfolio and liquidity services of foreign exchange. Exports and imports and the current account of the balance of payments play a minor role in the theoretical analysis. Important changes in terms of trade will be mentioned, in order to understand specific aspects of stabilization efforts in Argentina.

Fundamental simplifying assumptions are: (1) Foreign assets can be held by domestic residents and by the government. (2) The balance of payments is always in equilibrium, and trade in goods, services, and foreign assets with the rest of the world does not modify the available stock of foreign currency. (3) At all times, government and private agents can trade domestic assets against foreign assets.

The second section summarizes recent economic developments in Argentina, providing the background information for both the analysis in the third section and the model discussed in the appendix to this chapter. The fourth section contains the concluding remarks.

Recent Economic Developments in Argentina

Beginning in 1985, Argentina experimented with several stabilization plans to reduce inflation. The first was the Austral Plan and the second was the Primavera Plan. Neither of these plans worked, and the economy headed into hyperinflation in mid-1989. To stop the hyperinflation, a new administration introduced another plan that did not work. Inflation decreased for a few months, but it then accelerated toward the end of 1989 and the beginning of 1990. A summary of these plans is presented in this section, as based on Fernández (1990a, 1990b), to provide the background information that supports the theoretical analysis of the next section.

The Austral Plan

The Austral Plan relied on three basic measures. First, prices of public sector enterprises were increased to reduce their cash flow deficit. Second, most prices (public and private) were frozen at the level prevailing on June 14, 1985. For some sectors, however, prices were frozen at the level of some weeks before June 14, because in anticipation of price controls, several firms (if not all) had increased prices to survive the price freeze. Third, the president promised in a public speech that, from June 14 on, the central bank would not print any money to finance public sector operations. A few days after the announcement, the plan was accepted by the International Monetary Fund (IMF). It essentially respected the monetary and fiscal targets of the standby agreement reached in the previous weeks. Even more, it was said that the plan set more ambitious targets than those agreed upon with the IMF. Besides freezing prices and salaries, as well as freezing prices of public services (after upward adjustments), the Austral Plan included control of exchange and of the banking system, with a regulating scheme for the main financial activities. Foreign trade regulations and the general level of protection were left without major modifications.

Before the Austral Plan, economic conditions were very disturbing, with accelerating inflation that arrived at a monthly rate of 30 percent and with fear that the process would lead to hyperinflation. Although this process was foreseen by the public as a serious hyperinflation risk, price increases were more the result of anticipation of price control by private agents than of a fiscal and monetary overflow.

The prevailing high inflation rates and the anticipation of the government's policies affected expectations. High expected inflation spread across the economy in high nominal interest rates, indexation schemes, and all types of contracts with deferred payments. If a sudden stabilization were to have occurred, unanticipated lower inflation would have caused unexpected transfers among economic agents. To take into account unanticipated lower inflation, the Austral Plan took legal measures to adjust contracts by a schedule that contemplated the difference between the old expected inflation and the new expected inflation supposedly generated by the stabilization plan. This action alone did not have any direct implication for the working or dynamics of the stabilization program. It just tended to avoid unexpected wealth transfers under the assumption that the plan would be successful.

Although high real interest rates and concentration on short-term maturities reflected lack of credibility, the Austral Plan started with favorable public opinion. The popular support of the plan can be interpreted in two ways: (1) The public accepted the stabilization plan as a reasonable approach to stop inflation, or (2) the public accepted the plan anyway, approving the decision of the government to give serious consideration to the problem of inflation. (Before the Austral Plan, the monthly rate of inflation more than doubled from December 1983 to June 1985, reaching 42 percent in the latter month.)

Mass media (often directly controlled by the government) advertised the Austral Plan as producing a favorable effect on general expectations, so that an abrupt fall in prices and free interest rates occurred. The favorable impact of the government's advertisement did not last, nor did the favorable public opinion. The lack of fiscal discipline—together with unsound monetary management—caused an acceleration of inflation in 1986–1987 to an average level close to 10 percent a month. Interest rates for loans denominated in australes increased to reflect expected inflation, and domestic interest rates for operations in U.S. dollars reflected an important element of country risk.

Interest rates for operations in U.S. dollars were about four times the London interbank offered rate (LIBOR). The high rates reflected the poor credit assessment by foreign creditors, who, because of the impossibility of collecting any payments, lacked any alternative other than restructuring most of Argentina's external debt. For the first time during the twentieth century, Argentina decided to ignore the effect of debt restructuring on its reputation.

The consequences of the Austral Plan lasted for several years. Credibility in the government's announcements was already low and became even lower. The public felt that populist democracy had failed again. Most importantly, the economic standard of living of low-income people—to whom populist governments are said to pay special attention—deteriorated or remained at the level of the preceding decade. Although the Austral Plan was presented and discussed in the media as a "new" approach to stabilization, there was hardly anything new. It followed the traditional income-policy approach. The only exception was the public commitment of a populist president to put a stop to monetary expenditure for financing public sector operations. For the first time in Argentina's history, a populist president sounded like his archenemies, the monetarists.

The traditional approach to stabilization in Argentina was fiscal discipline plus price controls, and the traditional result was increasing inflation after a short period of stabilization. The Austral Plan confirmed this tradition, since, after a few months, inflation accelerated again, reaching a monthly rate of two digits at the beginning of 1988. Those who elaborated the plan and were managing it believed that stabilization was a necessary precondition for a reform of the public sector that would allow for sound and permanent monetary and fiscal policy. Others were doubtful about the real possibility of this approach, and they believed that the transformation of public sector enterprises and the institutional behavior of local and provincial governments were prerequisites to stabilization. The failure of Argentina's Austral Plan seemed to confirm their interpretation. President Raúl Alfonsín, who resigned five months before the constitutional date for the change of governments, acknowledged his failure to take the necessary actions to reform the public sector.

President Alfonsín's promise to stop monetary expenditure to finance public sector operations was not honored. The Banco Hipotecario Nacional (National Mortgage Bank) spent almost US$5 billion in concessional loans related to the political campaign. Another US$2 billion was granted to countries with poor credit rating (such as Cuba, Nicaragua, and African countries), presumably to support the Argentine chancellor as a secretary to the United Nations General Assembly. The loans were granted in domestic currency to be used in purchasing domestic goods. These two operations alone more than doubled the monetary base.

As fiscal discipline was not achieved with the Austral Plan, deficits forced the government to borrow from various sources to balance the budget. One source of financing was monetary creation by the central bank. To sterilize part of the monetary expenditure, the central bank increased reserve requirements and paid competitive interest rates on reserves. This disguised borrowing eventually resulted in the dominant force behind the hyperinflation of mid-1989, a subject to be discussed later. First, let us discuss some complementary policy actions attempting to rescue the Austral Plan from total failure.

During 1987, the government undertook policy actions to complement the Austral Plan. Some policies were a repetition of previous policies, but others were new. Repeated policies were a new price freeze, plus discretionary authorizations to increase prices up to 10 percent for some items. Authorizations were granted for items that did not violate special price schedules elaborated by the secretary of commerce.

Price controls did not work, and the authorities decided to take more direct action to stop inflation. Somehow they imagined that increasing the supply of foodstuffs would stop inflation. As one way of increasing it, they imported chicken—spending government money in a deficit-ridden country to import several tons of chicken. Unfortunately, they imported the wrong kind of chicken. Argentineans refused to eat chickens fed with anything but corn from the pampas. Even with a gradual decrease in prices of chickens, consumers did not want them—especially when the chickens started to smell bad. Spoiled chicken was the final outcome of the government's stabilization strategy. They imported too many chickens for the taste and freezing capacity of Argentina. Inflation did not fall, nor did the long-term relative price of chicken. In the short-term, the demand for chicken fell because people reduced consumption of chicken in restaurants and other places. They were afraid of consuming a spoiled chicken disguised as a special dish or delicacy. Many domestic chicken producers went into bankruptcy, reducing the supply of the kind of chickens that people would have liked to consume.

The government also determined a wage policy in an attempt to keep salaries in line with price inflation. In October 1987 the authorities increased the minimum wage by 75 percent (from 200 to 300 australes per month) and increased by 12 percent general wages in the private and public sector, as well as pensions. However, the average real wage decreased, leading to angry complaints by labor union leaders, who called several strikes. Toward mid-1988, a general strike by workers in public sector utilities ended with a severe disorder in Plaza de Mayo and several acts of vandalism in downtown Buenos Aires. Next, labor union leaders were asking for the resignation of the economic minister.

As in previous stabilization plans, the government did not reduce public spending and tried to balance the fiscal budget by borrowing and by increasing the tax burden. Since borrowing in the capital market meant a severe crowding-out and high real interest rates, the government opted for "forced borrowing." This measure implied that the government obtained from taxpayers a mandatory loan equivalent to 40 percent of the last period's revenue from the income tax and the net assets tax. First introduced in 1985–86 as an emergency measure, forced borrowing was reintroduced in 1987, again affecting government credibility and its reputation.

The government increased the fiscal burden by raising the tax on imports, cigarettes, and checking accounts. This last specific measure—a true innovation in fiscal policy—taxed current accounts each time the account was debited. To avoid tax evasion, check endorsements were restricted. The tax was paid by holders of current accounts, and commercial banks acted as a withholding agent for the government. Fiscal experts cannot understand the rationale for such a checking account tax, but the secretary of the treasury, who proposed it, claimed to have a good explanation as follows: "Well-known neutral taxes are very high in Argentina; therefore, there is much evasion and tax exemption. So, tax revenue is low in relation to the level of taxes. But black market operations, exempted operations, and evaders, all use checks; therefore, taxing checks increases revenues and improves the neutrality of the system." The flaw in this explanation is that all checks are taxed, and people who do pay their taxes also use checks. The explanation would be correct only if tax evaders were more intensive users of checks than regular taxpayers.

A new element in the economic policy undertaken during 1987 was the liberalization of the exchange market. It was not a full liberalization because there were two markets: the official market for commercial operations and the financial market for everything else. The recognition of a financial market ended with several years of ineffective restrictions to stop capital flight. Together with the liberalization of exchange markets, there was an announcement of commercial policy. Import restrictions would gradually be eliminated, in an effort to improve resource allocation instead of forcing entrepreneurs to keep prices low. There were two commercial policy measures. First, nontariff restrictions were replaced by a system based on indifference tariffs that, supposedly, would eliminate redundant protection. Second, temporary admission was granted to all kinds of inputs. These measures were weak in relation to the level needed for effective protection, but they were in the right direction. Another favorable event was an improvement in Argentina's terms of trade that was used to launch another economic plan known as the Primavera plan.

The Primavera Plan and hyperinflation

"Primavera" means "spring season" in Spanish, and that was the name given by the media to the economic plan introduced months before the spring of 1988. Argentina's favorable terms of trade were mostly due to the drought conditions in the Northern Hemisphere that increased the international price of some agricultural commodities. The Primavera Plan allowed the government to realize a profit in exchange operations.

The proceeds from exports were obtained at a low commercial exchange rate and were sold at a higher rate in the financial market. During several months, the spread between the financial rate and the commercial rate exceeded 20 percent. To sell dollars in the financial market, the central bank fixed a minimum value above which it would sell foreign exchange, although not in unlimited amounts. The amount, however, was large enough to affect the price of the dollar in the short term.

Although not explicitly stated, another intention of the government was to influence inflationary expectations affecting the path of the dollar in the free market. Several other measures attempt to affect inflation. First, there was a price agreement with trade unions to keep the rate of inflation on the order of 3–4 percent a month in September and the following months. On the other hand, as a part of the agreement, the government offered to decrease the value-added tax by 3 percent.

Second, government and trade union representatives created a price commission to follow up prices and costs, as well as public sector finances. At the beginning of August, there was a 30 percent increase in prices of public sector utilities. This increase was thought to be large enough to guarantee the balancing of the budget of public enterprises.

Third, collective agreements with labor unions would set the path for nominal wages, and employees of the central government administration received a salary increase of 25 percent.

Fourth, commercial policy measures included the intention to reduce tax on exports for 500 products and to eliminate nontariff restrictions on 3,000 products. Nontariff restrictions were introduced during the Malvinas war (1982) and later with a special provision (1983) and were never removed during President Alfonsín's administration.

Fifth, all reserve requirements for different kinds of deposits were replaced by two special government obligations, denominated A–1241 and A–1242 by the central bank resolutions that created them. Although the denomination of "reserve requirements" gives a first approximation to the idea, a word of caution is necessary. A large part of reserve requirements were not "reserves" because banks could not cash them. They were special bonds (or nondisposable deposits in the central bank) that substituted for reserve requirements. These two government obligation bonds were remunerated at the average deposit rate of commercial banks, plus 0.5 percent monthly. This meant that a large part of commercial bank assets were held in a bond that, on average, would pay whatever interest rate the commercial banks were willing to pay to depositors. For example, if depositors were afraid of a devaluation, they would try to cash in their deposits to buy dollars. Bankers, to avoid a decrease in deposits, would increase the deposit rate, so that it, in turn, would imply a higher interest on these two bonds. If the expectation of a fiscal deficit generated the expectation of a devaluation, it would occur even with fiscal surplus. An overall deficit would also occur because interest accruals on most of the domestic debt were indexed to panics.

Although some measures under the Primavera Plan were in the right direction—especially the exchange rate liberalization and the commercial policy—the plan did not succeed. Fiscal reform was not realized, and the perverse dynamics of the remuneration of most of the domestic debt drove the system to accelerate inflation. Inflation had decreased from 27.6 percent in August to 5.7 percent in December 1988, but in February 1989—the turning point into hyperinflation—the monthly inflation rate was 9.6 percent and kept increasing to reach a peak of 196.6 percent in July 1989.

In a general evaluation of the period 1984–1988, Fernández and Mantel (1988) concluded that price controls of the sort introduced with income policies and heterodox policies delayed the adjustment path to steady-state equilibrium. Firms, anticipating price controls in oligopolistic markets, set prices higher than they would have done otherwise to protect themselves from the government's political incentive to fix prices lower than long-term marginal costs. With the positive probability of a stabilization failure, firms may be temporarily better off with "nonoptimal" higher prices. It may be that, if stabilization fails, the higher price will cushion the firm, for a while at least, from "authorized prices" lower than long-term marginal costs.

A similar argument can be presented for nominal and real interest rates. The conclusions of Fernández and Mantel had three important implications. First, given that delaying the adjustment might imply that the real interest rate can remain for a longer period at higher values than the long-term natural rate, it is doubtful that price controls can help to avoid the recessionary effects usually associated with stabilization. Second, higher real interest rates introduced by a stabilization plan with price controls suggest the existence of short-term economic wealth transfers across sectors that should be carefully evaluated before justifying the "social advantage" of price controls. Third, price controls with fiscal lags imply an important delay in the adjustment of the global deficit, since its size depends on the magnitudes of the real rate of interest and the rate of inflation.

Although the economic plan failed, the authorities insisted on price controls even after the monthly rates of inflation were well above 10 percent. Of course, price controls were totally ineffective, and high inflation accelerated even more. When the authorities abandoned the idea of heterodox economic policy making and gradually moved to more orthodox measures, such as reduction of public sector deficit and sound monetary management, it was too late. The strong credibility available at the beginning of the Austral Plan was gone, and the side effects of orthodox measures without credibility imposed a significant political cost. The lack of credibility and the fear of repudiation of the government debt increased interest rates to levels never before seen in Argentina. Government borrowing in the domestic financial system, at the beginning of 1988, took place at annual effective rates larger than 30 percent for operations adjusted to the U.S. dollar—that is, four times the LIBOR.

Structural reform of the public sector was never given a serious consideration by the political authorities. There were timid attempts at deregulation and privatization, and when they tried to be more effective in structural reform, it was too late. They awoke in the middle of hyperinflation. The severity of hyperinflation and the danger of social unrest forced the elected government to accept an immediate transfer of power. A new administration took over on July 9, 1989, to insist on price controls. The announcements of the new administration were a mixture of heterodox and orthodox doctrines. On the one hand, the idea of having an income policy was heterodox and was always present from the beginning. On the other hand, the rhetoric and the appointment of high-ranking officials tended to be orthodox.

The preliminary figures for 1989 indicated that the overall deficit was decreased 1.6 percent of GDP from 1988 to 1989. A further reduction was expected for 1990, according to budgetary projections. The evidence available does not support the hypothesis of a fiscally ridden high-inflation process toward the end of 1989. During the months following the hyperinflation of June–July 1989, the central bank did not issue any significant amount of money to cover operating expenses of the public sector. Most of the monetary expenditure of that period was generated by purchases of foreign exchange by the central bank (some of it used to pay international organizations). Part of the monetary expenditure was sterilized by issuing certificates of deposit or short-term central bank debt.

This new debt was issued at very high nominal rates. Given the fixed exchange rate of 650 australes per U.S. dollar up to the end of 1990, in the period from July to October 1989 the average yield of financial assets was more than 15 percent monthly in U.S. dollars. This did not seem to trouble bankers or depositors because most of the money was lent to the government, and it remunerated average reserve requirements of about 80 percent of private bank deposits. All indexed debt created by Resolution A–1388 that became due in the second half of 1989 was reprogrammed with a new bond denominated "BOCON."

FIGURE 11.1   Nondollar Share of the Argentine Government Debt,
November 1986–December 1989

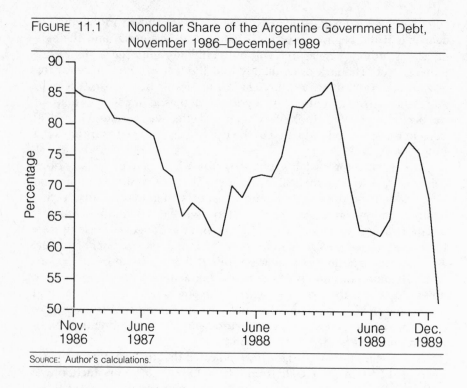

SOURCE: Author's calculations.

Even the most naïve of depositors knew that the situation could not last long, and at a given point of time they would consider it reasonable to convert austral deposits to U.S. dollars. In a few months, some smart depositors in Argentina could realize a gain that would take almost a decade to obtain in the world financial market. Of course, not all could realize such a gain. The attempt of many investors to capitalize such a gain promoted a run on the financial system leading to hyperinflation. That is the simplest and most reasonable explanation of the hyperinflations of 1989—the one beginning in February and the other starting in October but aborted in January 1990.

Figure 11.1 illustrates the portfolio shifts in Argentina from 1987 to 1989. Government debt was of three types: nonindexed debt yielding a nominal interest rate, indexed debt (adjusted to price indexes with certain lags), and debt adjusted by the price of the U.S. dollar. The data used in Figure 11.1 do not include external bonds or external debt. The portfolio shifts registered in Figure 11.1 as two sharp decreases in the nondollar debt share of the government predict correctly the two periods of hyperinflation: one in mid-1989 and the other at the end of 1989.

Analysis of Exchange Rate Policy

A topic in exchange rate theory that deserves special attention in high-inflation environments is what Sargent and Wallace (1981) have denominated "unpleasant monetarist arithmetic." It deals with the policy dilemma of financing deficits by printing money or by printing bonds. Sargent and Wallace ask what would happen if the government decided to decrease the share of the deficit financed by using money creation. This would tend to decrease further the devaluation of domestic currency. However, if the government is expected to shift to full money creation later, lower money creation means faster transitory accumulation of debt and higher money creation in the future. Anticipation of higher money creation in the future implies higher inflation and devaluation in the present. With a positive constant real interest rate, a higher debt means higher interest payments in the steady state. If the economy is on the left side of the Laffer curve, an increase in the stock of debt implies a higher inflation tax in the steady state. However, if the economy is on the right side of the Laffer curve, a higher debt will require a lower inflation; and the proposition of Sargent and Wallace would not hold.

When the assumption of a constant interest rate for different levels of government debt is replaced by the assumption that higher debt is associated with higher real interest rates, higher inflation is obtained on both sides of the Laffer curve. This can be verified by means of this set of relationships extracted from the model presented in the appendix to this chapter.

The government financial policy dilemma is represented by the following steady-state relationships:

$$\alpha.b.r = m.\epsilon \tag{1}$$

$$(1-\alpha).b.r = s \tag{2}$$

The first equation represents the share α of the quasi-fiscal deficit (that is, the deficit generated just by the real interest rate r on government debt b) that is financed by the devaluation-inflation tax $(m.\epsilon)$, where m is the real stock of money and ϵ is the rate of devaluation. The second equation shows the share $(1-\alpha)$ of the quasi-fiscal deficit that is paid with the primary surplus s.

Let $\Phi(\epsilon) = m/b$ be the proportion of real money yielding no interest to the stock of real government debt with $d(\Phi)/d\epsilon < 0$. This is a simplifying assumption that (as shown below) will permit the normalization of debt service and inflation revenue in terms of the stock of debt. This, in

FIGURE 11.2   Relationships of the Real Interest Rate and the
               Devaluation Rate

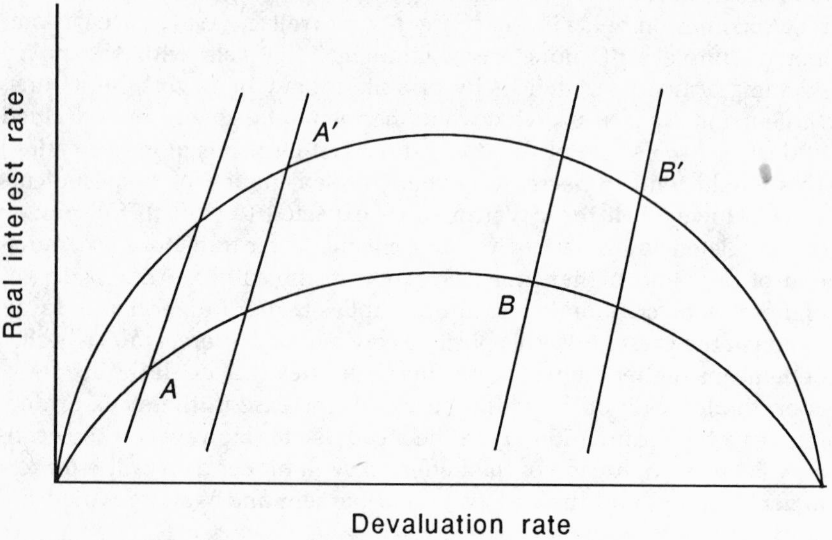

Devaluation rate

SOURCE: Author's calculations.

turn, allows the representation of the Laffer curve in the real interest
and inflation space. In the particular case of Argentina, m corresponds
to the definition of real M1, and b can be considered bonds and deposits
yielding interest. Deposits are government obligations because of the
high reserve requirements remunerated at competitive rates by the Cen-
tral Bank. Let $b = b(r,\epsilon)$ with $db/dr > 0$ and $db/d\epsilon < 0$. We substitute this
relationship in equations (1) and (2) to obtain:

$$r = (1/\alpha).\Phi(\epsilon).\epsilon \tag{3}$$

$$b(r,\epsilon).r = s/(1-\alpha) \tag{4}$$

Let us assume that $\epsilon.\Phi(\epsilon)$ is increasing in $\epsilon < \epsilon'$ and decreasing in ϵ
for $\epsilon > \epsilon'$. This implies that if the stock of bonds $b(.)$ is a constant or
independent of ϵ and r (as in most of the literature on inflation tax), the
graph of seigniorage revenue against the inflation-devaluation rate
would have the usual Laffer curve property. Figure 11.2 illustrates relationships (3), with a curve, and (4), with a positively sloped line.
Fernández (1990b) shows, in a model where the dynamics are explicitly
specified, that the line representing (4) must cut from below the line

representing (3) to obtain a saddle point equilibrium. Otherwise, the system is unstable.

A decrease in α implies an upward shift in (3) and a rightward shift in (4) and, as shown by Figure 11.2, we obtain a solution with greater devaluation, irrespective whether the economy is on the left side or on the right side of the Laffer curve (see points A' and B').

This analysis reveals that the crowding-out effect on the service of government debt caused by increased borrowing produces greater devaluation. Alternatively, just printing money to pay for debt services produces less depreciation of the domestic currency.

Conclusions

This chapter emphasizes the well-known result that exchange rate policy in high-inflation economies must be coordinated with policies that attempt to find a solution to the fiscal disarray—in particular, policies attempting to finance the fiscal deficit. Policy makers frequently believe that, with high inflation, anything is better than just printing money to finance the deficit. In particular, they tend to think that, by decreasing the share of the deficit financed by printing money, the devaluation of the domestic currency can be reduced. As we show next, this idea turns out to be false.

This analysis teaches us that the crowding-out effect on the service of government debt caused by increased borrowing produces greater devaluation. The impact of higher borrowing on the stock of debt and on real interest requires more inflation-devaluation to pay for it than the alternative of not borrowing. If the government decides just to print money to pay for debt service, less inflation is produced than by the alternative of paying a lower share but on a higher total debt that has been increased by borrowing.

The former analysis is related to the "unpleasant monetarist arithmetic" of Sargent and Wallace (1981) that, as originally formulated, is true only if the economy is on the left side of the Laffer curve. In the method formulated in this chapter, it is true on both sides of the Laffer curve.

Appendix

A Theoretical Framework for Exchange Rate Policy during High Inflation

In Fernández (1990b) I have analyzed the empirical evidence during high inflation in Argentina. A negative association was found between inflation and the real quantity of money, defined as M1 (currency plus demand deposits), and a positive association was found between real M1 and the real interest rate. A principal reason for a positive association between the real interest rate and M1 is the complementarity between time deposits and M1 in producing liquidity services. This can be formalized either by using a standard cash-in-advance constraint of the Clower type, where money and deposits (bonds) are needed to buy goods, or by using M1 jointly with other deposits to save shopping time. Brock (1989) follows this latter approach, but he assumes substitutability.

Basic assumptions

Let us assume four assets: (1) money yielding no interest (M), (2) a bond (B) that represents all government obligations, including high reserve requirements yielding a competitive interest rate, (3) foreign assets (E) in the form of U.S. dollars "under the mattress" plus deposits in foreign banks yielding liquidity services, and (4) a pure foreign bond (Z) that does not yield liquidity services. Let P be the general price level, and total real wealth ($a \equiv A/P$) is:

$$A/P = M/P + B/P + E/P + Z/P \qquad (A1)$$

All variables are time-dependent, but time-subscripts are omitted to simplify the notation.

The lifetime utility of the representative consumer is given by:

$$\int_0^\infty u(c)exp(-\delta t)dt \qquad (A2)$$

where $u(.)$ is increasing, twice-continuously differentiable, and strictly concave, c denotes consumption, and $\delta > 0$ is a constant subjective discount rate.

Following Calvo and Végh (1990) and Walsh (1984), let us assume that the consumer is subject to a liquidity-in-advance constraint that requires the use of money (foreign and domestic) and interest-bearing deposits (most of them government bonds in Argentina) to purchase goods. Therefore:

$$c \leq g(m,b,e) \tag{A3}$$

where m, b, and e denote the real stock of money, bonds, and foreign assets held by domestic residents. The partial differentiation of g is as follows: $g_m > 0$, $g_b > 0$, $g_e > 0$, $g_{mm} < 0$, $g_{bb} < 0$, $g_{ee} < 0$, $g_{mb} > 0$, $g_{me} > 0$, and $g_{be} > 0$.

Defining nonfinancial real income as y, interest on bonds as i, interest on foreign assets yielding liquidity as r^* (international inflation being assumed to be equal to zero), interest on the pure foreign bond as ζ, and government lump-sum net subsidies as τ, the consumer's flow constraint can be written as:

$$\dot{a} = y + \tau - c + a.\zeta + b.(i - \pi - \zeta) + \\ e.(r^* + \epsilon - \pi - \zeta) + z.(\epsilon - \pi) - m.(\zeta + \pi) \tag{A4}$$

where $\dot{a} = da/dt$, π is the rate of inflation, and ϵ is the rate of devaluation of the domestic currency.

The consumer's optimization problem consists of maximizing equation (A2), subject to equations (A1), (A3), and (A4). As in Calvo and Végh (1990), output will always be demand-determined, so that the consumer is not subject to quantity constraints, and the analysis will be restricted to equilibrium paths where equation (A3) holds with equality to assure the existence of positive financial assets. For simplicity, let us assume current account equilibrium at all times, so that the budget constraints of the representative consumer is a good representation of the budget constraints for the whole economy. Steady-state equilibrium and the first-order conditions for a maximum imply the following relationships:

$$g_m / g_e = [\zeta + \epsilon] / [\zeta - r^*] \tag{A5}$$

$$g_b / g_e = [\zeta - (i - \epsilon)] / [\zeta - r^*] \tag{A6}$$

where r is the domestic real interest rate defined by $i - \epsilon$. Equations (A5) and (A6) state that the ratio of marginal products of assets producing liquidity services must equal the ratio of their corresponding opportunity costs. With δ and r^* constant and exogenously given, equations (A5), (A6), and (A3) (holding with equality) implicitly define the demand for money, the demand for bonds, and the demand for foreign assets yielding liquidity services.

The sign for the arguments of the explicit form depends on the relative sizes of the partial differentials of the liquidity constraint. Asset functions consistent with the empirical finding discussed in previous sections require the following conditions: $g_e^2 g_{mm} g_{bb} > g^2_{mb}$; $g_e g_{mb} - g_b g_{em} > g_m g_{be} - (g_b/g_e)g_{ee}g_m$; and $g_e g_{mb} - g_m g_{eb} > g_b g_{me} - (g_m/g_e)g_{ee}g_b$ that are assumed to be met. Therefore, the demand functions representing equilibrium in assets markets are:

$$M/P = L(r,\epsilon,c), \quad L_r > 0, \ L_\epsilon < 0, \ L_c > 0 \tag{A7}$$

$$B/P = b(r,\epsilon,c), \quad b_r > 0, \ b_\epsilon < 0, \ b_c > 0 \tag{A8}$$

$$f.E/P = e(r,\epsilon,c), \quad e_r < 0, \ e_\epsilon > 0, \ e_c > 0 \tag{A9}$$

where the real stock of foreign assets yielding liquidity is redefined as $f.(E/P)$, to distinguish the physical stock of foreign assets from the real exchange rate $(E/P = e)$.

Foreign assets not yielding liquidity are held only by private agents. For simplicity, let us assume a fixed stock of these assets in the hands of domestic residents. The government will be assumed "honest," as in Auernheimer (1974), and will not permit price jumps. If a change of policy occurs, the government will accommodate all once-and-for-all portfolio shifts of private agents modifying its physical holdings of foreign assets. This means that the government (secretary of commerce) enforces a path for prices (and inflation) and that the central bank keeps a crawling peg or an indexation scheme to maintain a constant real exchange rate, by setting ϵ equal to π at all times.

The economy produces a fixed amount of aggregate output that, together with real earnings of foreign assets held by private agents and government, gives a fixed amount of real income. For simplicity, consumption, which will always equal fixed real income, will be ignored in assets functions.

Comparative results

To get results that could be easily compared with previous studies of hyperinflation, the demand for money is redefined as follows:

$$\Phi(\epsilon).b(\epsilon,r) \equiv L(r,\epsilon), \quad \Phi_\epsilon < 0. \tag{A10}$$

Also, it is assumed that $\epsilon.\Phi(\epsilon)$ is increasing in $\epsilon < \epsilon'$ and decreasing in ϵ for $\epsilon > \epsilon'$. This implies that, if the stock of bonds $b(.)$ is a constant or is independent of ϵ and r (as in most of the literature on inflation tax), the graph of seigniorage revenue against the inflation rate would have the usual Laffer curve property.

Let T be revenue generated by net lump-sum taxes and by earnings of the government's foreign assets. The budget constraint is:

$$b.i + \dot{f}e_0 = T + \dot{m} + m.\pi + \dot{b} + b.\pi \qquad \text{(A11)}$$

where $\dot{f}e_0$ is the change in the government's foreign assets evaluated at the constant real exchange rate e_0; and $\dot{m}$ and $\dot{b}$ are the change in real money and bonds, respectively. Equation (A11) states that the current interest deficit and changes in the government's foreign assets are financed by current revenues, by printing money, or by printing bonds.

At each moment of time, the government sets a fiscal policy modifying lump-sum taxes or subsidies, so that the following relationship holds:

$$T = s + \dot{f}e_0 + \Phi.b.(\epsilon - \pi) \qquad \text{(A12)}$$

where s represents a constant primary surplus (that is, a surplus definition that excludes interest accruals from government spending). Fiscal policy represented by equation (A12) means that neither the primary surplus nor the financial policy to be described below will be affected by flow changes in the government's foreign assets or by changes in the real exchange rate. It should be noted that in the steady state $\dot{f}=0$, and the second term in the right-hand side of (A12) vanishes. Outside of the steady state, the fiscal policy sterilizes the transitory impact on the budget of gradual changes in the stock of foreign assets and changes in the real exchange rate.

Using $i = r + \epsilon$, (A11), (A12), and the differentiation of (A8) and (A10), the budget constraint can be written as:

$$b.r - s = (b.\Phi_\epsilon + (1+\Phi)b_\epsilon)\,\dot{\epsilon} + (1+\Phi)b_r\dot{r} + \Phi.b.\epsilon \qquad \text{(A13)}$$

The term $b.r$ is sometimes denominated the quasi-fiscal deficit when most of the debt has the form of remunerated reserve requirements. In Argentina, for the period under analysis, most of the domestic debt was central bank debt, with different types of obligations, the most important of which were remunerated reserve requirements. Other domestic government debt existed, and some of it was adjusted for different types of indexes. For simplicity, let us assume that all debt is remunerated with competitive, market-determined, nominal interest rates.

Financial policy

Given the budget constraint (A13), financial policy is undetermined. The reason is that, to finance the deficit, the government can print money, can print bonds, or can print both. It has frequently been claimed that a driving force to hyperinflation was the expected monetary expenditure by part of the central bank to pay for the quasi-fiscal deficit. Without making an a priori judgment of this statement, we will introduce a financial policy that will allow us to analyze that type of conjecture.

We will incorporate a financial policy similar to one previously introduced by Blanchard and Fischer (1989) and also used by Fernández (1990b), stating that a fraction of real interest accruals is financed by the seigniorage of the central bank. The part that is not paid by seigniorage would be paid either with the primary surplus or through borrowing. Using α to split the financing of the deficit, we will represent this sort of assumption with the following two relationships to split the right-hand side of equation (A13):

$$\alpha.b.r = (b.\Phi_\epsilon + \Phi.b_\epsilon + b_\epsilon)\dot{\epsilon} + \Phi.b.\epsilon \qquad (A14)$$

$$(1-\alpha).b.r - s = (1+\Phi)b_r\dot{r} \qquad (A15)$$

Equation (A14), which in a steady-state equilibrium corresponds to equation (1) in the chapter text, will be understood as the fraction of quasi-fiscal deficit financed with inflation-devaluation, while equation (A15), which in steady state corresponds to equation (2) in the chapter text, is the fraction financed with the primary surplus (s). It should be noted that the right-hand side of equation (A14), outside of the steady state, is not strictly seigniorage nor is the right-hand side of equation (A15) strictly borrowing. The terms in (A13) have been grouped, not on the basis of the demand for money and the demand for bonds, but on a policy assumption of netting the effects of devaluation and real interest on the government budget constraint.

Let us define $\beta \equiv -b/[b\Phi_\epsilon + (1+\Phi)b_\epsilon]$ and $\Gamma \equiv 1/[(1+\Phi)b_r]$, and the reduced form of the system is:

$$\dot{\epsilon} = \beta.[\Phi\epsilon - \alpha.r] \qquad (A16)$$

$$\dot{r} = \Gamma.((1-\alpha).b.r - s) \qquad (A17)$$

Equations (A16) and (A17) give a solution path for ϵ and r. With P given at $t=0$, equations (A7), (A8), and (A9) must solve the rest of the system as follows. The assumption of an "honest" government implies that immediately after the announcement of a new policy at $t = 0$, the government steps into the assets market and trades money and bonds against foreign assets to avoid a once-and-for-all change in E. As the economy moves along the trajectory for ϵ and r, determined by (A16) and (A17), equations (A7), (A8), and (A9) set the path for nominal money, nominal bonds, and the real stock of foreign assets in private hands.

Straightforward computations in the system given by (A16) and (A17) show that the system is either unstable or has a unique solution with a saddle-point equilibrium. Divergent equilibrium paths can be ruled out by arguments similar to those of Obstfeld and Rogoff (1983, 1986). A saddle point requires that the line representing equation (A17) cuts from below the Laffer curve, representing (A16) (see Figure 11.2). Saddle points are possible on any side of the Laffer curve. This result contrasts with the previous literature on rational expectations where the right-hand side of the Laffer curve is usually associated with multiple solutions.

Comments

Juan L. Cariaga

Without a doubt, Argentina has been one of the most discussed cases in the literature on hyperinflation in recent years. This is true not only because the problem has proved intractable but also because a number of heterodox measures have been tried that have not achieved the results intended (Machinea and Fanelli 1988:148). From the outset, some economists predicted that the program launched in 1985 was intended to avoid hyperinflation rather than to remove inflation altogether (Canavese and Di Tella 1988:153). Others, such as Heymann, remarked later that the program had focused on the problems resulting from the transition to disinflation, while the following steps were left undefined (Heymann 1990:13). The truth is that, throughout this process, appearing in its several stages under the name of "Plan Austral" and "Plan Primavera" (Kiguel and Leviatan 1990:41), the program centered primarily on measures to freeze prices and wages (without strengthening tax administration or broadening the tax base) in conjunction with active central bank borrowing to curb inflation. In its various stages, the program employed fixed exchange rate policies, a crawling peg policy and even an experimental foreign exchange auction that produced disastrous effects in the form of a major loss of international reserves.

In this interesting chapter, Fernández does not perform a detailed analysis of exchange rate policies in their role of complementing the heterodox measures of the Argentine program. Instead, he focuses on what he calls foreign exchange policy, emphasizing portfolio and liquidity services of foreign exchange. This is a careful theoretical approach wherein he concludes, inter alia, that the crowding-out effect in servicing government debt by means of increased borrowing produces greater devaluation. He uses a mathematical model to construct a Laffer curve by means of optimizing the lifetime utility function of a representative consumer, giving total real wealth, a liquidity-in-advance constraint (that requires the use of money and interest-bearing deposits), and the consumer's flow constraint. Then, by process of transformation, he develops two equations that allow him to find a solution for ϵ (the rate of devaluation) and r (the real interest rate).

According to Fernández, as the economy moves along the trajectory for ϵ and r, the demand functions representing equilibrium in the assets market set the path for money (in nominal terms), bonds (in nominal terms), and the real stock of foreign assets in private hands. Fernández states that a unique solution in saddle points is possible on any side of the Laffer curve constructed with the equations, and he goes on to say that an increase in the primary surplus or a reduction in the deficit works independently of whichever side of the Laffer curve is considered. Thus, the impact of higher borrowing on the stock of debt and on the real rate of interest requires more inflation to pay for it than the alternative of not borrowing. In other words, the alternative of just printing money to pay for debt service produces less inflation than the alternative of paying what he calls "a lower share but on a higher total debt that has been increased by borrowing."

There can be no doubt that Fernández's generalization is very interesting. Among other things, it serves to explain a posteriori what happened in Argentina when the financial authorities made exaggerated use of borrowing for this purpose. Having said that, I would simply add the following comments:

1. In summarizing the situation in Argentina, Fernández claims that the available evidence so far does not support the hypothesis of a fiscally ridden process of high inflation toward the end of 1989. It seems to me that, apart from temporary expenditure cuts and very short-lived primary surpluses, Argentina never

had a lasting fiscal equilibrium. Nor were there dramatic adjustments in the budget or changes in the tax base. According to Heymann (1990:17) "independently of the particular views on the detailed behavior of price dynamics, it is generally agreed that the crucial reason why inflation accelerated again after the Austral [Plan] was the lack of a sustainable fiscal correction." Kiguel and Leviatan (1990:38) assert that: "sustainability of the fiscal adjustment, (was) a property lacking not only in the Austral Plan, but also in all the stabilization programs over the past 30 years in Argentina."

2. In discussing the assumptions made in the model, Fernández postulates that the consumer is subject to a liquidity-in-advance constraint that requires the use of money and interest-bearing deposits in order to purchase goods. As I understand it, this assumption was introduced as a guarantee that the consumer will use money for all his transactions. (During high hyperinflation, the consumer might refuse to use it all; hyperinflation also drives the economy to primitive arrangements for transactions.)

3. Finally, Fernández states that these conclusions are achieved when the assumption of a constant interest rate for different levels of government debt is replaced by the assumption of interest rate increasing with real government debt. Of course, this might be true when one thinks of the Argentine case where the financial authorities had to pay highly competitive rates (sometimes pegged to the U.S. dollar) for their borrowings. One question must be asked. How useful is this model in explaining circumstances in which borrowing is not subject to this constraint, in devising other means of borrowing from the public, or in explaining the alternatives for solving the problem of debt-related hyperinflation in Argentina?

Note

The views presented are those of the author and do not necessarily reflect the views of the Inter-American Development Bank.

Unification of Official and Black Market Exchange Rates in Sub-Saharan Africa

In the 1980s and continuing into the 1990s, unifying official and black market exchange rates has been one of the prominent macroeconomic issues in anglophone Sub-Saharan Africa. The interpretation of the unification experience results in three main conclusions in this chapter. First, the black market premium on foreign exchange is an implicit tax on exports, so that unification will lead to resource allocation benefits in terms of higher exports. Second, the revenues from this implicit tax on exports, usually hidden in the fiscal accounts, reduce the need for inflationary finance (that is, printing money) to finance the fiscal deficit. Third, there is therefore a trade-off between the resource allocation benefits and the inflation costs of unification.

In many instances in Sub-Saharan Africa, black market exchange rates in the 1980s attained levels several hundred percent greater than official rates, resulting in inequity through import license rents and a heavy tax on exports. Recent reforms have thus emphasized the unification of official and black market exchange rates, often with the explicit goal of reducing black markets and minimizing black market premiums on foreign exchange (Quirk, Christensen, Huh, and Sasabi 1987). This chapter shows that such policy advice, based on the argument that multiple exchange rates misallocate resources through their tax-subsidy effects, sometimes overlooks an important consideration—that, when multiple rates become an important source of hidden fiscal revenues, the widened deficit resulting from unification leads to higher inflation. In Sierra Leone and Zambia, attempts to unify official and black market exchange rates caused inflation to surge. The welfare and political costs of inflation are high, undermining the credibility of reform and leading to policy reversals. Therefore, a balance needs to be struck between the resource allocation benefits and the inflation costs of unification. This chapter provides a framework to evaluate this trade-off and illustrates it by citing the recent experience of Ghana, Nigeria, and Sierra Leone.

While a dual official–black market exchange rate regime is conceptually similar to multiple exchange rates, a few important features should be highlighted. First, the fiscal effect from a dual regime arises because the government's foreign exchange transactions are at an official rate that reflects a lower price of foreign exchange (dollars) than a market-clearing rate, rather than because foreign exchange is bought and sold at multiple official rates (see Dornbusch 1985, 1986). The fiscal effects of unification therefore depend on whether the government on balance sells dollars (for example, Nigeria) to the private sector or buys dollars (for example, Ghana and Sierra Leone). In the net seller case, unification would eliminate the subsidy on foreign exchange to the private sector, improving the deficit. In the net buyer case, a substantial loss of revenues from exports could result, worsening the deficit. The chapter concentrates on the net buyer case, which is more common, with exceptions being noted in the case study on Nigeria.

Second, the tax revenues from exports through the premium are not obvious in the fiscal accounts. Rather, these revenues are implicit in enabling less money to be printed to cover the gap between spending and revenues than would be necessary if these hidden tax revenues were not forthcoming. In effect, the premium is a tax instrument, so that there is a trade-off between this tax on exports and inflation (the tax on domestic money) in financing the fiscal deficit.

Third, unlike other tax rates (for example, an import tariff of 30 percent), the premium cannot be fixed arbitrarily but is determined endogenously by the general equilibrium of prices of assets and goods in the economy. Identifying the determinants of the premium is therefore an important step in examining the effects of unification.

Real Exchange Rates, Inflation, and the Black Market Premium

This section develops a framework for viewing the country experiences with unification presented in the next section.[1] The basic idea is simple. The fiscal deficit is financed partly by the revenues from the black market premium that serves as a tax on exporters, and partly by printing money. The amount of revenue from the premium is proportional to its size or to the wedge between the official and black market exchange rates.

Upon unification of the official and black market rates, this wedge is obliterated, so that the related revenues vanish. Therefore, unless real government spending is simultaneously lowered or other compensating sources of tax revenue are raised, the fiscal deficit will widen. Given the time-consuming nature of fiscal reform and the limited choice of tax instruments available, the most likely outcome is that this additional deficit will be monetized, raising inflation. In short, unification results in the loss of a tax instrument that, in the absence of accompanying fiscal reform, is compensated for by increased reliance on printing money or the "inflation tax."

The framework in this section is developed in six stages. First, the nature of the exchange rate regime is discussed. Second, the demand for the domestic money function is developed in a currency substitution context (Calvo and Rodriguez 1977). Throughout, "dollars" signifies foreign money and "pesos" signifies domestic money. Third, the exchange rate regime and the demand-for-money function are integrated with the monetary financing of the fiscal deficit in presenting the trade-off between the black market premium and inflation—the main focus of this chapter. Fourth, the real exchange rate is briefly discussed. Fifth, the short-term dynamics of corrective fiscal and exchange rate policy are discussed, and lastly, the determinants of the premium are summarized.

Exchange rate regime

The official foreign exchange market is rationed through import licenses and capital controls. The government issues import licenses according to expected export earning collection (some exports are smuggled) after subtracting its own requirements for official imports and foreign debt service. As a result, reserves remain constant in dollar terms (that is, there is no net official accumulation of dollars). All official foreign exchange transactions, including the issuance of import licenses, take place at the official exchange rate e (pesos per dollar) that depreciates at a rate chosen by the government and denoted $\dot{e}/e$.

As a result of rationing, the marginal cost of foreign exchange is determined in a black market where the currency floats freely. The black market rate b (pesos per dollar) is at a premium relative to the official rate ($b \geq e$). Domestic prices adjust fully to the black market rate with all imports, even those obtained through import licenses, converted from dollars into pesos at the rate b. Consequently, there are close links between inflation and currency depreciation in the black market, with b adjusting to equilibrate demand and supply in the foreign exchange market as a whole.

The pricing of imports at their marginal cost b is precisely what gives rise to the phenomenon of rents associated with import licenses sold at the official exchange rate e. Rents are merely the difference between b and e. For importers, the official exchange rate is completely infra-marginal.

Exporters either smuggle their exports out (earning b) or surrender them to the authorities at e. They incur *private costs* of smuggling, con-sisting of bribes paid to various officials. *Social costs* of smuggling are ignored for three reasons: (1) the issue has already been widely re-searched, (2) the focus here is on the tax and inflation trade-off effects associated with the black market premium, and (3) smugglers use more or less the same means of export as the authorities, with the exception of having to bribe various officials along the way.

The marginal cost of smuggling increases with the volume of exports smuggled. At the margin, exporters equate the returns between the official and black markets. Consequently, the marginal return for ex-porters is determined by the official exchange rate e. In contrast, e is completely inframarginal for importers. This difference gives rise simul-taneously to import license rents, on the one hand, and to the black market premium serving as a tax on exports, on the other.

The marginal return to exporters in a dual official–black market exchange rate regime could be a source of confusion. It is argued by some that the marginal return is a weighted average of b and e, with the weights dependent on the share of exports through each market. Such an argument is valid if (and only if) the share of exports through each market is predetermined and known ex ante by the exporters. Suppose the government sets up a scheme whereby 40 percent of export dollars must be surrendered at rate e, but 60 percent can be sold freely. In these circumstances, the marginal return on exports would be $(0.6b + 0.4e)$. Such a scheme is inherently contrary to the notion of an export-smuggling function. In its absence, and given smuggling with costs as described above, the marginal return to exporters is e.

Demand for money

Domestic residents hold two noninterest-bearing assets—pesos (M) and dollars (F)—in their portfolios. Private sector financial wealth is given by $W \equiv (M + bF)$, with dollars being converted into pesos at the relevant rate b. The desired shares of M and F in W are determined by portfolio balance considerations. Let λ be the desired fraction of pesos (that is,

$M = \lambda W$); λ depends on the expected differential rate of return between pesos and dollars. In the absence of interest rates, this is just the expected black market rate of depreciation. Assuming perfect foresight, so that the expected rate of depreciation in the black market equals the actual rate ($\dot{b}/b$), and assuming instantaneous clearing in the asset market, the result is:

$$M = \lambda \, (\dot{b}/b) \, . \, [M + bF] \text{ and } \lambda' < 0, \tag{1}$$

that is, the desired share of pesos goes down as the rate of currency depreciation and domestic inflation go up.

Financing of the fiscal deficit

For simplicity, let us assume that the government spends only for imported goods and makes interest payments on foreign debt, whose stock remains constant. The government buys dollars from exporters at the rate e, the export proceeds thus raised representing officially declared exports, with the balance of exports being smuggled. After setting aside the dollars required for its own needs, the government returns the remainder of the exports to the private sector through import licenses, also at rate e. The dollars retained by the government are partly paid for by tax receipts that are also fixed in dollars and partly by printing pesos to cover the deficit. The existence of a black market premium that taxes exporters then raises the issue of a trade-off between inflation (printing pesos) and the premium in financing the deficit. The rationing scheme in the exchange rate regime thus amounts to a redistribution within the private sector through import licenses, coupled with an implicit tax transfer to the government.

Letting g and t denote government spending and taxes, respectively, in dollars, the peso deficit $e(g - t)$ is financed by printing pesos. Since official reserves are fixed in dollars (see the section "Exchange rate regime"), it follows that the change in the stock of pesos in private portfolios is given by:

$$\dot{M} = e(g - t). \tag{2}$$

Thus, $\dot{M}$ depends both on the budget and on official exchange rate policy. Budget equation (2) can be rewritten as $\dot{M}/e = (g - t)$. Multiplying and dividing by M/b and rearranging gives:

$$(\dot{M}/M)(M/b)(b/e) = (g - t). \tag{3}$$

Equation (3) simply says that the proceeds from seigniorage or the inflation tax must equal the deficit $(g - t)$. The expression $(\dot{M}/M)$ on the left-hand side is the growth rate of nominal money that may be interpreted as the rate of the inflation tax, while (M/b) may be regarded as the base of the tax, being the real money stock. It may be recalled from the portfolio balance equation (1) that M/b in equilibrium is the demand for money given by the functional form in (1). The demand for pesos depends on financial wealth, the expected depreciation in the black market, and the fraction $\lambda(.)$. The last expression on the left-hand side of equation (3) is b/e—that is, the black market premium (strictly, the premium plus one). Letting $\phi \equiv b/e$ denote the black market premium, equation (3) can be rearranged to give:

$$g/\phi = t/\phi + (\dot{M}/M)(M/b). \tag{4}$$

Suppose $g = \$100$, $b = 4$ pesos per dollar, and $e = 3$ pesos per dollar. Then $g/\phi = \$75$. But the government actually spends \$100. The balance of \$25 represents the implicit tax on exporters. It is given by $g - g/\phi = g((b - e)/b)$. It arises precisely because the government is able to command dollars at 3 pesos per dollar rather than the marginal cost of 4 pesos per dollar. As a result, it prints less money, relying less on inflation than it would have to if $b = e$. Incorporating this hidden tax on exporters, budget equation (4) can be unraveled to give the complete fiscal accounts:

$$g = t/\phi + (\dot{M}/M)(M/b) + g(1 - 1/\phi) \tag{5}$$

where the tax on exporters through the premium is shown explicitly as the last term on the right-hand side of equation (5). If $\phi > 2$ (that is, the black market premium exceeds 100 percent, as has been common in Africa in recent times) the implicit tax on exporters finances upward of 50 percent of government spending on imports and foreign interest payments.

Exports and home goods: real exchange rate

We abstract from capital and assume that exports are produced by domestic labor alone. Home or nontraded goods (nontradables) are produced by using labor and intermediate imports (oil).[2] In Africa, home goods would include commerce (for example, the distribution and marketing of imported consumer goods and protected manufacturing that thrives on cheap imports as a result of import licenses).

The goal here is merely to make the point that the relative price of exports, indicating the marginal incentive to produce exports, varies inversely with the black market premium. This follows from the facts that (1) the premium is an implicit tax on exports, as discussed earlier, and (2) home goods include intermediate imports that are priced at their marginal cost—the black market rate. Consequently, the relative price of exports to home goods is inversely related to the premium. Therefore, in order to stimulate exports, the premium must be lowered.

It is worth noting that the capacity to import is eventually a function of the volume of exports. Taxing exports through the premium and thereby creating disincentives to produce exports ultimately lowers the ability to import intermediate goods, leading to the phenomenon of "import compression" and its deleterious effects on capacity utilization and unemployment that are noted in many African countries. This stark reality lends an urgency to the conflict between the allocative goal of stimulating exports through exchange rate unification and the financing of the fiscal deficit with a limited choice of tax instruments. Fiscal and exchange rate reforms need to be coordinated, rather than implemented in isolation.

Short-term dynamics of corrective policy

This discussion examines, in a short-term stabilizaton context, the dynamics of corrective fiscal policy and exchange rate rules whose goal is to lower the black market premium. In view of the short time-horizon, it is assumed that the stock of dollars (F) is given. Nevertheless, changes in the desired level of F will be reflected in movements in the premium. The dynamics are presented in the context of a simple monetary model consisting of equations (1) and (2) above. Defining $m \equiv M/e$ and recalling that $\phi \equiv b/e$, these equations can be manipulated to yield:

$$m = \frac{\lambda(\dot{\phi}/\phi + \pi)}{1 - \lambda(\dot{\phi}/\phi + \pi)} \phi F \qquad (6)$$

$$\dot{m} = (g-t) - m\pi \qquad (7)$$

where $\pi \equiv \dot{e}/e > 0$ is the chosen rate of crawl. The steady-state solution is:

$$\phi^* = \frac{g-t}{F} \frac{1-\lambda(\pi)}{\lambda(\pi).\lambda} \qquad (8)$$

$$m^* = (g-t)/\pi. \tag{9}$$

Figure 12.1a summarizes the dynamics in ($\phi - m$) space. The vertical line MM denotes the financing of the deficit. Along this line, the deficit is matched by the inflation tax ($g-t = m\pi$). The upward-sloping line PP represents portfolio balance. An increase in m increases the desirability of dollars and raises the premium ϕ. E_0 is the unique steady-state equilibrium (m^*, ϕ^*). It is shown in the appendix to this chapter that the steady-state solution is saddle-point stable, with the saddle path SS positively sloped but flatter than PP.

Consider an unanticipated, one-shot maxi-devaluation, after which the chosen rate of crawl π is maintained. Following this, m jumps from m^* to m_0 (see Figure 12.1a) and the premium falls to ϕ_0 so that the point E_1 on SS is attained. This is mirrored in Figure 12.1b, where $\dot{m}$ jumps from zero to $\dot{m} = A > 0$. Since monetary dynamics have remained basically unaltered, the premium returns to its predevaluation level along SS. The one-shot devaluation, in the absence of more fundamental reforms, has had only temporary salutary effects.

In contrast, a permanent reduction in real government spending g permanently lowers the premium, as can be seen from Figure 12.1c. In this case, MM shifts to the left to $M'M'$ owing to the lower steady-state requirement of seigniorage to finance the smaller deficit. The premium drops immediately to B and adjusts to its new equilibrium value, corresponding to E_2 along the trajectory $S'S'$. The reason is that with π held constant, m becomes relatively scarce in the new equilibrium, lowering ϕ.

Lastly, consider an increase in the rate of crawl π. In Figure 12.1d, the line MM shifts to the left to $M'M'$ because, with a given deficit, a smaller monetary base is now needed to generate the same seigniorage. This alone would have the effect of lowering the premium. However, a rise in the rate of crawl implies an increase in steady-state inflation—and hence, the differential rate of return between dollars and domestic money. This makes dollars relatively more attractive, causing the PP curve showing portfolio balance to shift upward. This portfolio effect exerts upward pressure on the premium. If domestic money demand is highly inflation-sensitive (such that the prevailing rate of inflation exceeds the seigniorage-maximizing rate, for instance) the steady-state premium could actually rise. This corresponds to the case in Figure 12.1d where PP shifts to $P''P''$ and E_4 is the new equilibrium. However, if money demand is less inflation-sensitive, so that PP shifts to $P'P'$ and E_3 is attained, the premium would fall. Without further information on the inflation elasticity of domestic money demand, therefore, the effect on the premium of an increase in the rate of crawl is ambiguous.

Two policy conclusions emerge from the above: (1) A credible reduction in real government spending will always lower the premium.
(2) If unification is desirable, nominal exchange rates rules in isolation
may not work. In the absence of fiscal reform, one-shot devaluations are
eventually ineffectual. Accelerated crawls could produce the exact opposite of the intended results, raising the premium instead of lowering
it, if domestic money demand is highly inflation-sensitive.

Overnight floats and inflation

Embedded in equation (5) is the trade-off between inflation and the
premium, to be discussed here. Recall that the government chooses the
official rate of depreciation $\dot{e}/e$. Assume that this is given and the system
is in steady state. By definition, $\dot{M}/M = \dot{b}/b = \dot{e}/e$ (that is, inflation equals
the growth rate of money and the rate of depreciation in the black
market, so that the real domestic money stock and premium are con-
stant at their steady-state values). Letting $\pi \equiv \dot{e}/e$ denote the steady-state
rate of inflation, equation (5) can be rewritten as:

$$g = t/\phi + (M/b) . \pi + g(1 - 1/\phi). \tag{10}$$

Suppose now that there is an unanticipated overnight float of the currency. The government abandons rationing and lets the market determine the rate of exchange and currency depreciation. All official
transactions are now at the market exchange rate, so that the premium
vanishes. In other words, $b = e$ and $\phi = 1$. It follows from equation (10)
that the implicit tax on exporters $g(1-1/\phi)$ vanishes, since $\phi = 1$ now.
The government's net revenue loss is $(g-t)(1-1/\phi) > 0$, where the calculation is at the steady-state value of the premium prior to the float.
The size of the loss, as well as the deficit, depends on this value. Clearly,
if the government cannot maintain the real value of the revenues (assuming that t is fixed in dollars), the effect will be even greater. Letting
π^* denote the new steady-state level of inflation following the float,
equation (10) leads to:

$$g = t + (M/u)^*\pi^* \tag{11}$$

where u is the unified rate and $(M/u)^*$ is the new steady-state real money
stock. Comparing equations (10) and (11), it is readily seen that $(M/u)^*\pi^*$
$> (M/b).\pi$ since ϕ in (10) is greater than unity. In other words, the
burden of the inflation tax has gone up to compensate for the loss of
revenues from the premium. What will guarantee that $\pi^* > \pi$ (that is,
that the rate of inflation itself goes up)? Recalling the money demand

FIGURE 12.1   Dynamics of the Exchange Rate and Fiscal Policies

a. Maxi-devaluation

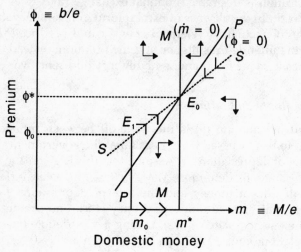

b. Money supply dynamics

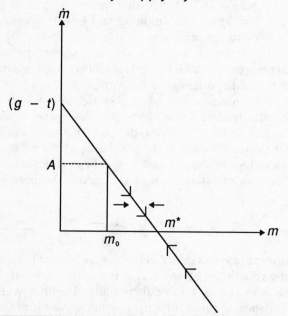

(continued)

FIGURE 12.1 *(continued)*

c. Reduction in real government spending

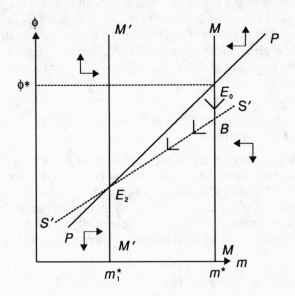

d. Increase in rate of crawl

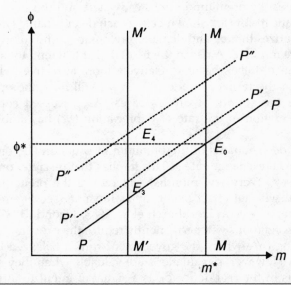

function in (1), this would depend on the inflation elasticity of domestic money demand measured at the prefloat inflation rate π. Since the product of the real money stock and rate of inflation must go up in the new steady state, it follows that inflation itself will rise if money inflation elasticity is less than one, but it will fall if this elasticity exceeds one. If the elasticity is less than one, then inflation is guaranteed to rise. The magnitude of the jump in inflation will be higher, the larger the premium preceding the float and the greater the dollar component of the government deficit.

Determinants of the premium

From the above discussion, it is seen that the premium depends on the following parameters: demand for domestic money as captured by equation (1)—that is, $\lambda(.)$, $\dot{b}/b$ and W; the financing of the deficit and rate of inflation—that is, g, t, $\dot{e}/e$; and the terms of trade, or the ratio of the price of exports to that of imports, denoted p_x.[3] This steady-stage dependence can be summarized (for a technical discussion, see Pinto 1991) as:

$$\phi^* = \phi(g, \quad t, \quad p_x, \quad \dot{e}/e, \lambda(.))$$
$$(+) \quad (-) \quad (-) \quad (\pm) \tag{12}$$

where ϕ^* denotes the premium in the steady state and the signs of the comparative static results are shown below each determinant. The function $\lambda(.)$ summarizes money and demand preferences. The comparative static results are intuitive. A rise in the fiscal deficit will tend to raise the premium, because dollars become relatively more attractive, while an improvement in the terms of trade (rise in p_x) will have the opposite effect, because the supply of dollars eases. As discussed copiously above, an acceleration in the rate of depreciation ($\dot{e}/e$) has ambiguous effects.

Lastly, the determinants of the premium in equation (12) omit the level of the official exchange rate e. This implies that discrete, one-shot devaluations (say, every few months) will reduce the premium only temporarily but will not affect its steady-state value (see Figure 12.1a and 12.1b above, as well as Dornbusch et al. 1983, Lizondo 1987a, and Pinto 1986). Devaluations will permanently reduce the premium only in the uninteresting case where the government runs a balanced budget (that is, $g = t$). However, devaluations are valuable when they accompany reductions in the real deficit or as a signal of intent to introduce more basic reforms in fiscal, monetary, and exchange rate policy.

Country Experiences with Unification

Ghana

The experience of Ghana typifies an extreme, eventually unsustainable, case of the foregoing model. The official exchange rate was kept fixed for long periods ($\dot{e}/e = 0$). This fact, combined with considerable and consistent reliance on the inflation tax, created a situation where the black market premium grew monotonically, reflecting the depreciation of the black market rate, as the domestic money stock grew and strict foreign exchange rationing was implemented.

Between 1976 and 1983, average inflation exceeded 50 percent a year, attaining triple-digit levels in 1977, 1981, and 1983. These high rates of inflation were traceable to large fiscal deficits that were financed mainly by printing money, with little or no recourse to external financing or aid. Administrative allocation ensured that the value of import licenses issued did not exceed expected export earnings—more precisely, private sector exports that were surrendered to the authorities. This quantity rationing, combined with capital controls, nullified the issue of whether official reserves might have had to be depleted in order to support the fixed exchange rate.

The official exchange rate was kept fixed from June 1978 until April 1983. There were several quasi-devaluations by means of the erratic imposition and subsequent abolition of import surcharges and export premiums. However, these were of small magnitude, compared with the black market premium that was generally more than 500 percent between 1976 and 1983 and exceeded 2,000 percent in 1982—by far the highest levels in recent economic history.

Table 12.1 presents data pertinent to the Ghanaian macroeconomy between 1970 and the first quarter of 1983. The last period shown in the table refers to the four years of political uncertainty and economic collapse immediately before the introduction of the Economic Recovery Program in April 1983. Sustained inflation, political uncertainty, and unclear economic objectives undermined confidence in the cedi and drastically reduced revenue generation from inflation, as can be seen in Table 12.1. Real base money fell sharply and seigniorage declined from a quarterly average of 848 million 1980 cedis over the second period to 269 million 1980 cedis over the last period.

The demand for cedis was extremely sensitive to inflation. In all likelihood, ready access to dollars through widespread smuggling of cocoa increased the inflation elasticity of the demand for cedis and shrank the real monetary base, as holders of wealth diversified into dollars to escape the inflation tax. The changes in the political regime in

TABLE 12.1   Inflation, Seigniorage, and Tax on Exports through the Black Market Premium in Ghana, 1970–1983

Variable	1970–1974	1975–1978	1979–1983[a]
Average inflation[b] (% per quarter)	3.15	15.60	12.94
Real base money[c] (end-of-quarter averages in billions of 1980 cedis)	7.11	7.80	4.05
Seigniorage[d] (quarterly averages in millions of 1980 cedis)	424	848	269
Average black market premium[e]	1.44	4.64	11.02
Marginal tax on exports (%)[f]	31	78	91
Real GDP (annual averages in billions of 1980 cedis)	42.54	41.57	41.24

a. 1979–1983 refers to the period of political uncertainty and economic collapse immediately preceding the Economic Recovery Program of April 1983 and only includes the first quarter of 1983.
b. Inflation is based on percentage change in consumer price index.
c. Real base money is reserve money divided by the consumer price index.
d. Seigniorage is the change in reserve money divided by consumer price index.
e. Black market premium is the black market rate divided by the official rate.
f. Marginal tax on exports is (black market rate − official rate)/black market rate.
SOURCES: International Monetary Fund, *International Financial Statistics*, various years; International Currency Analysis, *World Currency Yearbook* (black market rates).

1979 and 1982 may also have biased portfolio preferences sharply toward dollars. The increasing difficulty of generating revenue from inflation is perhaps what lay behind the monetary reforms of 1979 and 1982. In 1979, there was an exchange of old bank notes for new ones at a rate of less than 1 to 1, substantially reducing the money stock. In 1982 the 50-cedi note, the largest note in circulation, was demonetized. The fact that the black market premium was allowed to rise to the extent that it did (see Table 12.1) is prima facie evidence of the inability to generate revenue from inflation. In April 1983, the official exchange rate was 2.75 cedis to the U.S. dollar, compared with a black market rate of about 60 cedis.

Given the high levels of taxation implicit in the black market premium (Table 12.1), production of the key exports (cocoa and gold) fell sharply. The resulting scarcity of foreign exchange led to a shortfall in imported intermediate goods, so that real GDP (Table 12.1) stagnated and per capita income declined 30 percent between 1970 and 1982.

The increasing inability to generate revenue from inflation, combined with the unsustainable increase in the premium (unsustainable because of the export tax it represented and the incentives it created for smuggling and the nonsurrender of dollar export earnings) led inevitably to the Economic Recovery Program of April 1983.

What were the exchange rate options realistically open to Ghana in 1983? Some guidance is provided by Johnson et al. (1985). In terms of exchange rate policy, the most popular approach at the time was to attempt to attain some targeted level of the real exchange rate, defined as the official exchange rate multiplied by the ratio of foreign to domestic prices. The first step was to compute a time series on the real exchange rate, next to identify a "normal" year, and then to suggest that the nominal exchange rate be moved so as to attain the real exchange rate of that year.[4] Typically, a devaluation was required to compensate for the fact that past domestic inflation had considerably exceeded past foreign inflation. The second option was to accelerate the rate of depreciation of the official exchange rate above the prevailing inflation rate in order to achieve real depreciation. The third was to float the cedi.

If exchange rate reform aims to stimulate exports, the black market premium must be lowered. Given the considerable black market premium in Ghana in 1983, inflation at about 120 percent a year, and extreme sensitivity of cedi money demand to inflation, neither devaluations nor accelerated crawls would have helped.[5] A float would have been disastrously inflationary. This fact is underscored by the observation of the preceding section that, when the black market premium is high, the link between fiscal and exchange rate reform is direct. There is a conflict between the allocative goal of stimulating exports by reducing the premium and the fiscal goal of financing government spending with a limited choice of available tax instruments. Because the premium had reached unsustainable levels and the ability to raise revenue from inflation was plummeting, there was little choice but to reduce the fiscal deficit.

Ghana's strategy since April 1983 has been one of gradually reducing the fiscal deficit, combined with widely spaced but large devaluations of the cedi. In October 1983, the official exchange rate was moved from 2.75 cedis per dollar to 30 cedis per dollar, with the black market rate at about 90 cedis per dollar. In October 1985, the special import license scheme was reintroduced, permitting those who wished to bring in imports through the black market to do so freely, provided the requisite taxes were paid. This action gave formal recognition to the black market. By January 1986, the exchange rate had been devalued to 90 cedis per dollar, and unification had become a serious quest. The fiscal deficit had been reduced from 2.7 percent of gross domestic product (GDP) in 1983 to 0.7 percent in 1986. Further details may be found in Pinto (1989) and World Bank (1988:Box 3.5).

In September 1986, the official foreign exchange market was split into two tiers: a fixed rate tier, with an officially set rate, and an auction for raw materials and inputs only. The implied segmentation of transactions represented the continued taxation of cocoa and the subsidization of petroleum. The fixed rate and auction markets were unified at the auction rate in March 1987. Consumer goods were subsequently integrated into the auction, unifying the auction and the markets for special import licenses.

Nigeria

Let us recall equation (12) of the preceding section—namely the determinants of the level of the steady-state premium: $\phi^* = \phi(g, t, p_x, \dot{e}/e, \lambda(.))$. In Nigeria,[6] by 1981, oil had become the main determinant of real income, the terms of trade, creditworthiness, and government revenues. Oil accounted for 22 percent of GDP, 81 percent of revenues, and 96 percent of exports. Between late 1981 and September 1986, when Nigeria floated its currency (the naira), events in the foreign exchange market, therefore, were dominated by the collapse of international oil prices. In terms of equation (12), the key changing determinant of the black market premium was the fall in p_x. This fall in dollar prices for oil had two implications: (1) It directly reduced government revenues, since dollars for oil accrue to the government in the first instance. (2) Any rise in the black market premium meant a bigger real transfer from the government to the private sector through the import licensing system. The size of these transfers was proportional to the dollar value of the import licenses issued.

The distinctive feature of Nigeria's experience was that the government, being a net seller of foreign exchange to the private sector, *added* to its fiscal burdens as the premium rose. In other words, given a level of real government spending, the reliance on inflation would increase as the premium rose. There was no scope for a trade-off. The fiscal deficit in real terms was, therefore, dependent on the level of the black market premium. At the same time, the taxation and disincentive effects of the premium would continue to apply to nonoil exports and the tradable goods sector, notably, agriculture.

Table 12.2 summarizes data on Nigerian public finances and oil prices. It divides the subsequent oil glut and price fall into two periods. In the first period, government spending remained roughly the same, so that inflation rose and the black market premium went up considerably as the rationing of foreign exchange was intensified to deal with excess demand for dollars at the official exchange rate. In the second period, administrative control over foreign exchange allocation tightened fur-

TABLE 12.2   Deficit Finance, Inflation, and the Black Market Premium in Nigeria, 1980–1985 (quarterly averages)

Variable	Oil boom period	Oil glut periods	
	1980(1)–1981(3)	1981(4)–1984(3)	1984(4)–1985(4)[a]
Index of real price of oil[b]	116.04	94.57	80.07
Change in net claims on govt./beginning monetary base (%)[c]	2.48	11.59	1.18
Growth rate of monetary base (%)[c]	4.55	5.83	3.00
Inflation, based on consumer price index (%)	4.49	5.78	−0.84
Depreciation (%)			
Official rate	2.36	1.16	4.06
Black market rate	−0.36	12.00	2.18
Black market premium[d]	1.61	2.66	4.24

a. The second oil glut period, 1984(4) to 1985(4), refers to the period of fiscal austerity.
b. Nigerian bonny light petroleum prices deflated by U.S. wholesale price index (1980(1) = 100).
c. Monetary base is reserve money + net claims on government by commercial banks.
d. Premium is black market rate/official rate.
SOURCES: International Monetary Fund, *International Financial Statistics*; World Bank data; International Currency Analysis, *World Currency Yearbook* (black market rates).

ther, but there were two major changes: first, the government implemented a plan of fiscal austerity that greatly reduced spending and inflation, and second, it accelerated the depreciation of a naira/dollar rate. Both measures slowed the growth of the premium. While fiscal austerity did so by slowing the growth of base money, the acceleration in the official rate of depreciation increased the naira payment for dollar-denominated import licenses and, in all likelihood, the proceeds from the inflation tax, owing to the low level of inflation.

As oil prices continued to fall, however, the black market premium continued to rise, thereby increasing the fiscal burden of import license rents. Given a conservative estimate of an average import program of US$3 billion and a black market premium anywhere between 2 and 3 naira per dollar, rents were between naira 6 billion and naira 9 billion, a significant fraction of GDP that was at about naira 70 billion per year at that time.

By the time Nigeria floated the naira in September 1986, it had established a solid record of credible fiscal reform. The float became inevitable, as oil prices fell sharply in 1986 and debt rescheduling and external financing became urgent issues. The float was adopted as the centerpiece of a medium-term restructuring program predicated on market incentives, price signals, and the abolition of the import license system (and the inequity and inefficiency associated with it). From the analytical perspective of the preceding section, three issues are of interest.

First, given the level of real government spending, unification would be expected to lower inflation while the fiscal burden of rents implicit in the black market premium was eliminated. In large measure, this was the case. Although the ceteris paribus assumption may not have held exactly, because oil prices continued to move and real government spending may have changed, inflation in the twelve-month period following the float was lower than in the preceding twelve months.

Second, there was some debate about what naira/dollar rate should emerge from the float. Since the official exchange rate was 1.5 naira per dollar at the time of the float and since official dollars from oil accounted for more than 90 percent of exports, it was argued that an "equilibrium" rate close to 1.5 naira per dollar should emerge. This argument ignored the facts that domestic prices had substantially adjusted to the black market rate and that there was virtually a secondary market in import licenses issued at the official exchange rate. Imports were priced at their opportunity cost—the black market rate. The issue is resolved by the portfolio balance equation (1) of the preceding section. Since the stock of naira (M) and the stock of dollars (F) are predetermined, the outcome for the unified floating rate depends on whether people expect postunification inflation to rise or fall. If they expect it to stay the same, naira assets retain their relative attractiveness, so that, with the stock of M and F given, an equilibrium rate close to the prevailing black market rate would be expected to emerge. The arguments of the preceding paragraph on the favorable inflationary effects of unification suggest that a rate more appreciated than the black market rate should have emerged, ceteris paribus. In fact, a rate close to the black market rate of 5 naira per dollar did emerge. The basic point is that the crucial factor is not the ratio of exports or imports at the official exchange rate, but the expected fiscal and inflationary effects of unification.

Lastly, it was feared that if the official rate registered a substantial one-shot depreciation upon floating, inflation would go up. The response to this concern is similar. The inflationary effects of floating depend on the fiscal effects of unification, rather than on the depreciation of the official rate per se.[7]

Sierra Leone

Sierra Leone's experience provides a graphic illustration of the trade-off between the premium and inflation. When the government is a net buyer of foreign exchange from the private sector and the premium is high, inflation will rise substantially if the currency is floated to achieve unification. When Sierra Leone floated its leone in June 1986, the value of ϕ was between 3 and 4, implying a tax on exports of between 67 percent and 75 percent. Inflation rose from an annual average of 70 percent for the three years before the float to an annual rate of more than 200 percent following the float.

The basic insight that emerges from Sierra Leone's experience is the inseparability of fiscal and exchange rate reform for countries with high black market premiums. Fiscal discipline was weak when the leone was floated in June 1986. After falling to a low of 7 percent of GDP in 1983/84, the fiscal deficit peaked at 14 percent in 1985/86. Three main reasons accounted for this deterioration. First, there was a systematic decline in the tax/GDP ratio from 16.5 percent in 1978/79 to 5.6 percent in 1985/86. Second, the rice and petroleum subsidies that persisted after the float constituted a major fiscal burden. The petroleum subsidy alone accounted for roughly half of the difference between the actual deficit of 14.5 percent of GDP in 1985/86 and its budgeted level of 3 percent. These subsidies were partly financed by the premium (implicit tax on exports) in the dual regime. Third, there were at the time no suitable tax and royalty contracts with the mining companies (a strange omission for a country with a mineral base as rich and diversified as Sierra Leone's) nor any revenue contribution from fishing.

Table 12.3 summarizes budgetary and exchange rate movements for six months following the float (comparative prefloat data are not available). The deficit is expressed in U.S. dollars at the black market rate, because, despite the float, the official rate was "fixed," so that it remained at a discount relative to the black market rate. As a result, there was not even one transaction in the interbank market between June 1986 and March 1987, and the black market rate became the unified rate for all foreign exchange transactions. The data in Table 12.3 show an erratic but upward trend in the deficit, relative to July 1986. The average monthly deficit between August 1986 and January 1987 was about US$4.5 million. The real monetary base was about US$50 million, implying an inflation rate of 9 percent a month to generate the necessary seignorage for the deficit.[8] For the six months ending December 1986, this implied 70 percent inflation (close to actual inflation), and depreciation of the leone that was $(41.5-23)/23 = 80$ percent.

The real monetary base fell over the period shown in Table 12.3. This was partly due to the shift from assets in leones to dollars or even to accounts abroad to avoid the inflation tax. The ratio of quasi-money (time and savings deposits) to M1 (currency outside banks plus demand deposits) fell from 35 percent in 1985 to 31 percent in June 1986 and then to 23 percent by December, suggesting a shift to dollars.

TABLE 12.3   Fiscal Deficits, Monetary Base, and Inflation in Sierra Leone, June 1986–January 1987

Year and month	Deficit (millions of dollars)	Monetary base (millions of leones)	Real monetary base (millions of dollars)	Black market exchange rate (leones per dollar)
1986				
June	n.a.	1,423.28	61.88	23.00
July	2.15			
August	5.10			
September	3.52	1,894.99	57.42	33.00
October	5.39			
November	4.49			
December	3.91[a]	2,122.05	51.13	41.50
1987				
January	4.81	2,064.70	43.93	47.00

n.a. = not available.
a. Excludes a cash grant from Saudi Arabian Monetary Agency of US$5 million.
NOTE: Conversion to U.S. dollars is at black market rate. Monetary base is defined as currency outside banks + commercial bank deposits with Bank of Sierra Leone + cash-in-hand of commercial banks + net claims on the government by commercial banks.
SOURCES: Bank of Sierra Leone, except black market rates, which are World Bank staff estimates.

While there is little doubt that Sierra Leone's float was poorly timed owing to the high premium and low credibility of fiscal policy, another lesson emerges—that fiscal reform becomes much more difficult as inflation rises. Sensitive subsidies may then have to be retained. For example, prior to the float, the rice subsidy could have been eliminated by privatizing the procurement and distribution of rice. However, private traders who were willing to take over this function before the float refused to touch it after the float for fear of being blamed for price hikes. For countries such as Sierra Leone, fiscal reform may not merely have to be undertaken, but also credibly established, before a float is contemplated.

Concluding Remarks

Paradoxically, the first step in exchange rate reform for countries with high black market premiums may have to be a fiscal one—that is, recasting the budget to fix the size of the implicit tax revenues from exports through the premium. The reason is the inseparability and conflict between fiscal reform and exchange rate reform for such countries. The tax-subsidy redistribution within the private sector as a result of foreign exchange rationing through import licenses is also important.

This involves identifying the potential gainers (for example, agriculture) and losers (for example, commerce and protected manufacturing using imported inputs) in the event of unification. Such identification will make plain the political pressure points likely to emerge at the time of unification.

It needs to be stressed that the inflationary effects of unification have nothing to do with any slackening of fiscal discipline. According to the first section of this chapter, inflation can rise permanently and substantially even if the level of real government spending remains constant.

Four distinct issues arise: (1) Can government spending be justifiably reduced? (2) Is there an equitable distribution of the tax burden based on Ramsey-type considerations? (3) Are existing tax instruments apart from the premium and rate of inflation being used to the hilt, or are the latter being used as the easy way out?[9] (4) If the export tax is being used in lieu of land or profits taxes that are more difficult to collect, is the optimal export tax zero, as implied by unification?[10]

The main conclusion is that if the credibility of fiscal reform is low and the initial level of the premium is high, with significant revenue and redistributive implications, the pace of reform should be set by the feasible speed of fiscal reform. Accelerating rates of depreciation above prevailing inflation, in the absence of credible fiscal reform, could raise the black market premium as a result of preemptive portfolio shifts into dollars, thereby jeopardizing the survival of both fiscal and exchange rate reform. Moreover, such policy will not achieve real depreciation unless the premium falls. Likewise, overnight adoption of floats is likely to meet with considerable political and social opposition as inflation rises, creating the possibility of policy reversals, as evidenced by recent events in Sierra Leone, Somalia, and Zambia. The best route, consequently, might be to relax rationing gradually, accompanying this with discrete devaluations, with the pace of reform being set by the speed of fiscal reform.

Some additional guidelines might be helpful. First, commercial transactions can be transferred to the black market. Such legitimization of the black market could be an important step in eventual unification and the removal of rationing. If the ultimate goal is to have a floating interbank market, commercial banks could be permitted to buy foreign exchange from the black market and resell it to importers at a market rate.

Second, in many instances, accounts denominated in foreign currency are created in the domestic banking system to encourage capital reflows (that is, the return of money invested by private citizens abroad). The nature of these accounts is important. For example, are these going to be checking or savings accounts? Are withdrawals going to be made in local or foreign currency? Could such accounts compete with checking accounts in local currency for holding transaction balances?

Permitting imports through the black market provides a channel for repatriating dollars held abroad. Accounts denominated in foreign currency do not augment official reserves. They merely make it easier and cheaper to hold foreign financial assets, rather than domestic financial assets. By increasing substitutability between domestic and foreign assets, such accounts lower the base for the inflation tax, calling for a higher rate of inflation for a given real fiscal deficit. Introducing such accounts, therefore, needs to be carefully considered.

Third, should dual official rates (as distinct from the black market rate) be adopted in the transition—in particular, a two-tier system with a fixed (and more appreciated) first-tier rate and a floating market-determined second-tier rate? If adopted, the dual system should be designed in such a way that incentives for new economic ventures and investment are governed solely by the floating, market-determined rate. This can be done by letting the floating rate apply to all commercial transactions, including those of state-owned enterprises, and restricting the fixed rate to purely government transactions and foreign interest payments on existing (but not new) debt.

Fourth, the transition provides an opportunity to design and implement mechanisms that will speed up information flows in the domestic banking system and the various ministries. This will ensure that information on key macroeconomic variables, such as government spending, domestic credit to the government and private sector, money growth rates, and price data, are available punctually. Such data are basic inputs that must be available in timely fashion to market participants, in addition to other data, such as movements in the terms of trade.

Most important, fiscal reform needs to be designed and implemented in a credible and sustainable manner, with a clear assessment of the taxes and subsidies implicit in the dual exchange rate regime.

Lastly, it would be incorrect to conclude from this study that a developing country should never float its currency. This decision should depend on the credibility of the accompanying fiscal reform and the initial size of the black market premium. Even a country that follows the Ghanaian route described above will, at some stage, need to float its currency to achieve unification. At a minimum, the rationing of commercial transactions has to be eliminated eventually. It is difficult to think of doing this on a sustained basis with fixed exchange rates. Similarly, it would be ineffective to opt for gradual exchange rate unification without matching fiscal reform. This could set off a destabilizing spiral of official depreciations, rising black market premiums, and hence further depreciations and higher inflation unless fiscal policy is simultaneously adjusted. Once unification with or without capital controls is attained, however, there remains the decision of whether to continue with a float as a permanent mechanism. The experience of developing countries over the next few years should give some insights into this issue, but this issue should not be separated from the inflation tax and the credible sustainability of fiscal reform.

Appendix

Mathematical Derivation

Linearizing equations (6) and (7) around the steady-state solution (8) and (9) yields:

$$
\begin{vmatrix} \dot{\phi} \\ \dot{m} \end{vmatrix} = \begin{vmatrix} \dfrac{-\lambda(1-\lambda)}{\lambda'} & \dfrac{(1-\lambda)^2}{\lambda'F} \\ 0 & -\pi \end{vmatrix} \begin{vmatrix} \phi - \phi^* \\ m - m^* \end{vmatrix} \tag{A1}
$$

or $x = A.y$, where $x' = (\dot{\phi}, \dot{m})$, etc., and the partial derivatives in A are evaluated at (ϕ^*, m^*). The argument of $\lambda(.)$ in equation (A1) has been suppressed.

Since there is one predetermined variable m and one jump variable ϕ, saddle-point stability requires that $det(A)$ in equation (A1) be negative. This is satisfied since $det(A) = \lambda(1-\lambda)\pi/\lambda' < 0$. Let μ be the negative eigen value and let $(r, 1)'$ be the normalized eigen-vector corresponding to μ. Along the saddle path SS, $\phi = rm$ (see Figure 12.1a). First, it is seen immediately that $\mu = -\pi$. Second, using standard techniques, it can be shown that

$$
r = (1-\lambda)^2/F[-\lambda'\pi + \lambda(1-\lambda)]. \tag{A2}
$$

Lastly, the slope of the line PP, denoted by s, is given by the expression:

$$
s = \frac{d\phi}{dm}/\dot{\phi} = 0 = -\dot{\phi}_m/\dot{\phi}_\phi = (1-\lambda)^2/F\lambda(1-\lambda). \tag{A3}
$$

Comparing equations (A2) and (A3), it is seen that $0 < r < s$ because λ' < 0. In other words, the saddle path SS is flatter than the portfolio balance line PP.

Notes

This chapter is a synthesis of Pinto (1986, 1989). The views herein are the author's and are not necessarily those of the World Bank or affiliated institutions.

1. A rigorous analytical treatment may be found in Pinto (1991).

2. The approach here follows Kharas and Pinto (1989).

3. We have not mentioned the terms of trade directly above. It enters into the steady-state determination of F through the current account. A more complete model would consist of three state variables—ϕ, M/b, and F. The dynamic equations are (1), (2), and the current account. The equations and their solution are fully developed in Pinto (1991). Some features of the basic model come from Lizondo (1987a, 1987b) and Pinto (1986).

4. Formulating exchange rate adjustments based on the difference between the actual and a postulated equilibrium level of the official real exchange rate, defined as the exchange rate adjusted for foreign relative to domestic prices, was common in 1983. This approach included the idea that for high-inflation countries, the rate of crawl be allowed to exceed prevailing inflation (see Johnson et al. 1985). Edwards (1985) emphasized that the equilibrium exchange rate changes over time and is endogenous, depending on fiscal, monetary, external debt, and trade policy. Deciding what this level is, based on a historical time series, is more art than science.

5. Strictly speaking, the inflation elasticity of the portfolio share of cedi demand (the parameter $\lambda(.)$ in equation (1)) has to be estimated. As discussed in the first section, if this exceeds unity, an accelerated crawl at a rate exceeding prevailing inflation would actually raise the premium, worsening the situation. Unfortunately, data on dollar holdings in private portfolios are not available, preventing this estimation.

6. A discussion of Nigerian economic policy during and soon after the oil boom may be found in Pinto (1987b). An excellent account of the oil boom and its aftermath is contained in "Structural Adjustment Programme, July 1986–June 1988," a Nigerian government document presented to the London Club in June 1986. This insightful paper discusses key corrective measures in the areas of trade and exchange rate policy, public investment, agriculture, and external debt. This chapter concentrates exclusively on Nigeria's unification experience.

7. Ironically, in interviews it became apparent that members of the private sector had a keen appreciation of this. They did not anticipate any inflationary effects of floating the naira, but they bemoaned the imminent reduction in their profit margins from 400 percent (representing the premium) to more "modest" levels of 20 percent.

8. By issuing noninterest or, relative to inflation, low nominal interest-bearing debt, such as currency and treasury bills, the government inflicts a

capital loss on the holders of its outstanding stock of liabilities, thereby making a revenue gain. It is necessary to make a case-by-case determination of the components of base money, which traditionally includes only the liabilities of the central bank—namely, currency outside banks and commercial bank reserves.

9. See Aizenman (1986) for a welfare analysis of a related problem.

10. Suppose $\phi = 3$ to start with, implying a tax rate of 67 percent, and suppose that the export is bought by a commodity board that sets domestic prices with reference to the official exchange rate. Upon unification, the government might find it difficult to justify an explicit tax of 67 percent. It may however, decide on a lower tax of, say, 15 percent. This has the advantage of eliminating the misallocation costs associated with cheap imports in the erstwhile dual regime, since importers must now pay the unified rate.

Comments

FRIEDRICH L. SELL

Brian Pinto's paper provides additional and very interesting insights into what many economists have kept telling governments in developing countries for years—that exchange rate policy alone will seldom cure the diseases of highly inflationary economies with high black market premiums and with dual markets for foreign exchange. If the unification of official and black market exchange rates, or at least a reduction in the black market premium is a goal for improvement of resource allocation, manipulations of the official exchange rate may well fail in this respect and also cause higher inflation. One-shot devaluations in the absence of more fundamental reforms can alter the premium only temporarily. A rise in the rate of crawl (if domestic money demand is less inflation-sensitive) may lead to a lower premium, but at the cost of higher inflation. The latter also applies to an overnight float of the currency. Where the premium disappears by definition, the burden of the inflation tax will go up, ceteris paribus, and so will the inflation rate, as long as the money inflation elasticity is small enough (less than one).

In contrast to exchange rate policy, a credible reduction of government spending is effective by itself (lowering the premium without increasing inflation) and, furthermore, it can make devaluations valuable and exchange rate unifications successful, bringing the inflation rate down. However, unless government spending is cut, there will be a trade-off between the resource allocation benefits and the inflation costs of unification.

It may be pedantic to start the discussion of Pinto's paper by making use of his note 10. Therein he argues that, upon exchange rate unification, a government may substitute the earlier prevailing implicit tax rate on exports by an explicit, though lower, export tax. This consideration gives rise to the fundamental question as to what concept is underlying the implicit export tax that is at the center of Brian Pinto's model. Three issues, in my view, should be discussed:

First, does an implicit export tax exhibit the same properties as ordinary taxes? As explained in the chapter, the case of implicit export taxes favors governments that are net buyers of foreign exchange from the private sector and maintain an overvalued official exchange rate. As equation (5) shows, the implicit export tax revenue is given by the product of government spending g (equal to the *tax base*) and the tax rate $(1-1/\phi)$, which is positively related to the black market premium.[1]

Surprisingly enough, it is not the tax base (as in most cases) that is endogenous, but the tax rate that is dependent only on the black market premium ϕ. As Pinto shows, the premium "is determined endogenously by the general equilibrium of prices of assets and goods in the economy." The tax base, on the other hand, equals the size of government spending g. Thus, we get the striking result that the authorities may increase their implicit tax revenues ceteris paribus by spending more. This makes us think of Keynes's theory of income distribution, explaining that the profits of entrepreneurs are positively affected by their consumption expenditures. This outcome will even be strengthened by the induced rise in the tax rate. As "a permanent reduction in real government spending g permanently lowers the premium," mutatis mutandis, a permanent increase in government spending has to elevate the premium and, thus, the tax rate.[2]

Second, do we find similarities to the inflation tax and what would an optimal implicit export tax mean? (The latter point is briefly addressed in Pinto's concluding remarks.) This is quite different from the inflation tax where usually real money holdings (the tax base) will be negatively affected by a higher rate of nominal money growth or a higher inflation rate (the tax rate). Similarities to the inflation rate do stem from the "hidden nature" of both taxes, as neither of them is obvious in the fiscal accounts and both of them are calculated ex post as a residual when the data for real government spending and real fiscal revenues are known.

Formally, the revenue-maximizing black market premium, analogously to the concept of the optimal inflation rate, is one that goes to infinity. This result, however, is not convincing in a general equilibrium view. As equation (5) shows, both the inflation tax base[3] and the ordinary tax revenues will be negatively affected, in real terms.[4]

Third, if both explicit and implicit export taxes exist *before* an exchange rate unification, would it be possible to compensate losses in one category of tax receipts by tax gains in the other, thereby not increasing the need for inflationary finance and, at the same time, reducing the black market premium? Let us consider now the case of an explicit export tax that accompanies the implicit tax defined by Pinto. As we know from Bhagwati (1974b:66–83) and others, such an explicit export tax, when it accompanies an overvalued official exchange rate and a government that is a net buyer of foreign exchange, gives incentives to underinvoice exports.[5] The tax-based incentives add to the black market premium. These transactions, however, will create a net supply of illegal foreign exchange and their effect will be to reduce the black market premium, ceteris paribus.

Hence, there would be the following export tax revenue (both from implicit and explicit taxes) puzzle for the government: there may exist an optimal explicit export tax rate (t^{ex}) that maximizes the total revenue from both explicit and implicit export taxes. If it is above (below) the existing rate, any increase (decrease) toward the optimal rate will tend to reduce (elevate) the black market premium. This, in turn, will make the deficit smaller, and at the same time, ceteris paribus, make the burden of the inflation tax go down.[6] In this case we find a situation where reductions of the premium are compatible with a drop in the inflation rate, if money inflation elasticity is *less than one*. Thus, there is a case of tax policy in which Pinto's trade-off between resource allocation benefits and inflation costs of unification (reduction of the premium) vanishes.

These effects do not appear in Brian Pinto's model, as he has assumed the government's taxes as fixed in dollars, raised in lump-sum form (Kharas and Pinto 1989:439). If these revenues were endogenized (if they were dependent, for example, on an explicit tax rate t^{ex} and the black market premium ϕ), the fiscal accounts of this model, given by equation (5), would be modified and the vertical line MM, which denotes the financing of the deficit, would become elastic.[7]

Another observation refers to Pinto's expectations-forming assumption. First, I have some doubt whether the rational expectations hypothesis used in the chapter in its strongest version (perfect foresight) is applicable to most developing countries, let alone the case of Sub-Saharan countries. Second, Nowak (1984) and others have shown that, in comparison with rational expectations, the very plausible assumption of static expectations leads to quite different price-level effects of devaluation in a general equilibrium framework.[8] Of course, Nowak's and Pinto's models differ in many aspects, but they have in common the general equilibrium approach, and Nowak's contribution "illustrates the importance of assumptions about expectations in any empirical analysis of price and exchange rate movements" (Nowak 1984:419–20).

Before turning to the country experiences, I would like to focus on a minor point in Pinto's chapter—that is, the assumptions he makes on smuggling and the implied return to exporters. As Pinto puts it: "the marginal cost of smuggling increases with the volume of exports smuggled." Here I have some doubts, unless empirical proof is given. Why should there not be increasing returns to scale that lead to both falling marginal and average costs of smuggling? As a result, exporters may face two different prices (or marginal returns). As the total marginal return is a weighted average, "with the weights dependent on the share of exports through each market," Pinto is worried that these shares might not be known ex ante. But even without any clear-cut government scheme, exporters may quite well foresee that "it is a sensible precaution to keep the marketing board happy and off one's neck by selling it some (or better: a precise amount of) cocoa" (Deardorff and Stolper 1990:123), in the case of Ghana, for example. Also, it would be interesting to see what events or outcomes the model would predict, if other possibilities to merge parallel markets of foreign exchange are discussed—such as a reduction of domestic credit or the sale of official foreign exchange reserves.[9]

In his chapter, Pinto reports the experiences of three Sub-Saharan African countries with the unification of dual exchange rates. As a direct empirical test of his model seems to be difficult (if not impossible) because data on dollar holdings in private portfolios are not available, for example, thus preventing an estimation of the inflation elasticity, he chooses selected indicators that should follow the main strands of his theoretical conclusions.

In the case of Ghana the data (see Table 12.1) tend to support prima facie, as Pinto puts it, the view of a substitutionality between the revenues from the inflation tax and those from the implicit export tax, as "the black market premium was allowed to rise to the extent that it did . . . is prima facie evidence of the inability to generate revenue from inflation."

The case of Nigeria serves as an example in which the government is a net seller of foreign exchange to the private sector. Here, the model states that a "unification would eliminate the subsidy on foreign exchange to the private sector, improving the deficit." Table 12.2 does not disclose any data on the deficit, but Pinto infers from a rise in the premium (in 1984–1985 compared with 1981–1984) a fiscal burden that was matched by fiscal austerity and "in all likelihood" by increasing proceeds from the inflation tax at a lower rate of money growth. The latter implies that Pinto assumes Nigeria to have exceeded its optimal inflation rate before.

Sierra Leone is another example for governments in the position of net buyers of foreign exchange. Monthly figures taken from periods directly after an exchange rate unification in 1986 (Table 12.3) reveal an upward trend in the deficit that was accompanied by an erosion of the real monetary base and rising inflation. Pinto's point that "fiscal reform becomes much more difficult as inflation rises" is a lesson that can be learned not only from Sierra Leone but in particular from Latin American countries such as Argentina and Brazil.

Concluding remarks

In his concluding remarks, Pinto goes far beyond a mere synthesis of his theoretical and empirical findings. Moreover, he designs a sort of agenda or "sequencing" for how to implement exchange rate unification gradually. Provided that the credibility problem can be solved in a gradual reform (which, by the way, gives the affected political and economical pressure groups time to oppose it), his "guidelines" seem to be appropriate with the exception of his third. Why should the fixed rate be restricted to foreign interest payments on existing debt? This represents an implicit subsidy to debtors that lowers the need to earn a sufficient return on capital, whenever the credits have led to real investment.

Finally, Pinto defends the idea of a hypothetical withdrawal of a unified exchange rate, that is not to continue "with a float as a permanent mechanism." Unfortunately, he does not explain why such a turnaround could be welfare-increasing. Among other things, I guess that severe credibility problems would then arise.

These minor points of criticism should not blur the view that Pinto's chapter contains excellent and refreshing arguments in how closely fiscal and exchange rate policy interact and how they should be harmonized, with a clear priority in favor of fiscal restraint, in order to overcome crises in countries with high inflation and high black market premiums.

Notes

1. Therefore, in the case of $\phi = 1$, the tax rate is zero and the government's gross revenue loss equals $g(1 - 1/\phi)$.
2. To some limit, as $\phi = \phi(g, t, p_x, \dot{e}/e, \lambda(.))$ and $X(\phi) \gtreqless g$.
3. So far as an increase in ϕ implies a rising b.
4. Since $\phi = \phi(g, \ldots)$ and as $X = X(\phi)$ and $X' < 0$, there are sustainability

issues. Exceeding of ϕ will force the government to a discontinuous policy change.

5. Bhagwati considers smuggling, which is incorporated in Brian Pinto's model, to belong to a class of illegal trade that occurs through illegal entry points, whereas the faked invoicing of exports or imports (either by misinvoicing prices or by misinvoicing quantities) is associated with illegal trade through legal entry points. He finds arguments, in the latter case, for the need of using bribes but also for no need of using them (Bhagwati 1981:409–27).

6. There are two effects: (1) total export production effects: $X = X(\phi)$, $X' < 0$; and (2) allocation effects between official and unofficial markets.

7. It seems to me that Brian Pinto has considered these effects later in this chapter in the section "Country Experiences with Unification." In the case of Ghana, he finds an "unsustainable increase in the premium (unsustainable because of . . . the incentives it created for smuggling and the nonsurrender of dollar export earnings)."

8. With static exchange rate expectations, the LM-curve remains stationary after any devaluation, and the price level is therefore unchanged. Under rational expectations, an anticipated devaluation raises the demand for domestic currency and brings about a temporary decline in the price level (Nowak 1984: 417–19).

9. In Brian Pinto's model, domestic credit is directly linked to g. Also, he takes R (foreign exchange reserves) as nonexistent.

YUNG CHUL PARK AND
WON-AM PARK

CHAPTER THIRTEEN

Exchange Rate Policies
for the East Asian
Newly Industrialized Countries

The apparent misalignment of currencies and inappropriate monetary and fiscal policies of the major industrial countries that have precipitated the current global imbalance continue to remain as obstacles to sustained world economic growth. These global imbalances, coupled with steady progress toward a united Europe, reforms in the Soviet Union and Eastern Europe, and the economic rise of Japan have created a need for reform of the international monetary system, with focus on the realignment of currencies and coordination of macroeconomic policies of the major industrial countries.

Along with these global transformations, there have been a number of significant changes in the trade and industrial structures of economies in the Asian Pacific region. The rapid rise of the Japanese yen since the Group of Five's Plaza Agreements in September 1985 and Japan's expansion of its internal demand have brought about closer ties among countries in the Asian Pacific region and have contributed to an expansion of intraregional trade and capital flow. These developments have also stimulated discussion of an economic integration in the Asian Pacific region and of the role of the yen as a major reserve currency in the 1990s.

The growth and industrial transformation of the four East Asian newly industrialized countries (NICs)—Hong Kong, Singapore, South

Korea, and Taiwan—over the last two decades have been impressive by any standards. They have sustained a rapid growth of almost 10 percent a year, along with price stability. As a group, they account for more than 7 percent of the world's total exports. They no longer specialize in exports of labor-intensive products but have developed into major producers of skill-intensive and technology-intensive manufactures. Over the past decade, they have amassed a large trade surplus, particularly in their trade with the United States. Together with Japan, they account for the bulk of the U.S. trade deficit. Mainly because of this surplus, their trade relations with the United States have deteriorated to a dangerous level.

These East Asian NICs have been accused of conducting unfair trade practices by keeping tariff and nontariff trade barriers high and, recently, of manipulating their exchange rates to gain export competitiveness. Under pressure from the United States and European countries, these four countries—Taiwan and Korea, in particular—have continued to appreciate their currencies in relation to the U.S. dollar in recent years, and they have reformed their exchange rate system so that changes in the exchange rate reflect changes in the conditions of the foreign exchange market. Despite the large amount of literature on exchange rate policy in developing countries, there is little agreement on an optimal exchange rate regime for newly industrialized countries.

This chapter examines the future direction of exchange rate policy in these four countries from several different perspectives. For this purpose, the first section surveys briefly the existing literature on exchange rate policy. The second section assesses the relative performance of different exchange rate regimes adopted by these countries by focusing on the movement of the real effective exchange rates of their economies. The third section discusses the effects of exchange rate changes on the currenct account and other macroeconomic variables to gain more insight into the channel through which exchange rate policy operates in Taiwan and Korea. This discussion will facilitate an understanding of the role of exchange rate policy in developing economies. The fourth section discusses the possibility of forming a yen currency bloc in Asia with these four countries as important members. The analysis makes it clear that a common currency scheme, with Japan as the key country, is not likely to solve the internal and external economic problems of the member countries and would be politically unacceptable to many other Asian countries. In view of this conclusion, this chapter turns in the fifth section to other exchange rate arrangements that these four countries may choose for the future. Brief concluding remarks make up the final section.

Exchange Regimes and Optimum Currency Areas

Voluminous literature exists on the proper choice of exchange rate regimes in developing countries. According to Wickham (1985), there are two major issues concerning exchange rate policies for developing countries. One is whether they can (and should) let their currencies float independently. Another is whether they should choose a single currency peg or a basket peg, if independent floating is excluded.

The arguments in favor of exchange rate flexibility in developing countries rest on the downward rigidity of domestic wages and the susceptibility of the domestic economy to internal and external shocks (Flanders and Helpman 1978). The arguments against flexible exchange rates focus on the structural characteristics of developing countries, such as underdeveloped domestic financial markets, restrictions on trade and capital flows, and a thin foreign exchange market. Given these characteristics, free floating is likely to increase exchange rate volatility (Black 1976; Branson and Katseli-Papaefstratiou 1981). If pegging is chosen, the next question is to decide on what peg to use. In a world of generalized floating, pegging to a single currency or basket of currencies implies fluctuation of the pegged currency against all other floating currencies. Many developing countries often adjust their pegs to achieve a number of economic objectives. This leads to the question of an optimal peg (Williamson 1982).

In theory, single currency pegging is similar to creating a common currency area, and therefore discussion of the choice of an exchange rate regime is closely related to the debate on the characteristics of an area for which it is optimal to have a currency in common. Mundell (1961) suggests a high degree of factor mobility as a primary condition for establishing an optimum currency area. McKinnon (1963) stresses the importance of the openness of an economy measured by the proportion of tradables in total output, whereas Kenen (1969) emphasizes the degree of product differentiation as a determining factor. In a survey of the literature on this subject, Ishiyama (1975) presents other criteria, such as the degree of financial integration, rates of inflation, and degree of policy integration.

Mundell's criterion of factor mobility may be divided into labor and capital mobility. Given the barriers to interregional labor mobility, the question remains whether interregional capital flow could correct a payments imbalance without an adjustment of the exchange rate and the interest rate. The experience of the Bretton Woods system provides a negative answer, in that high capital mobility has been responsible for the collapse of a fixed exchange rate regime.

McKinnon's criterion of openness for an economy is relevant to the

Asian Pacific region, where most countries have become integrated into the world economy and highly dependent on foreign trade in the process of pursuing an export-led growth strategy. It is true that the more open an economy, the more likely it is to suffer from price instability when there are exchange rate fluctuations. However, when shocks originate from abroad rather than internally, the exchange rate must be readjusted or floated to insulate the domestic economy from external disturbances. Kenen's criterion of product diversification is generally valid, so that a point of concern is its relationship with other criteria (that is, whether factor mobility or the openness of the economy will facilitate the diversification of products). Other conditions, such as a high degree of financial integration, similar rates of inflation, and a high degree of policy integration, may be prerequisites to the successful establishment of a currency union, but it may be argued that these conditions will be met by setting up a currency union.

Evolution of Exchange Rate Arrangements in the Asian Pacific Region

The Asian Pacific region includes a large number of countries with diverse backgrounds in their political systems, cultural traditions, ethnic origins, and stages of economic development. The region contains industrial countries, such as Japan, Australia, and New Zealand (and the United States and Canada, if North America is included), and many developing economies, including the four East Asian NICs, the members of the Association of South East Asian Nations (ASEAN), the People's Republic of China, and Indochinese countries. The exchange rate systems adopted by these countries are as diverse as their political, social, and economic settings. Table 13.1 summarizes the exchange rate systems chosen by different countries in the region since 1982. All industrial countries float their exchange rates, whereas most developing countries, except the Philippines, opt for pegged or managed exchange rate systems.

Among the four East Asian NICs, Korea maintained a managed floating system until March 1990, when the system was changed into a crawling peg known as a "market average exchange rate system," in which the exchange rate is allowed to vary within a certain limit in the interbank market. Singapore has pegged its exchange rate to a currency composite, although its exchange rate regime was classified as a managed floating one by the International Monetary Fund (IMF) in 1987. Taiwan had had a market-average exchange rate system before switching to a more freely floating system. In contrast, Hong Kong has kept its

TABLE 13.1 Exchange Rate Arrangements of Developing Countries in the Asian Pacific Region as of December 31, 1982, 1985, and 1989

Currency pegged to				More flexible		
U.S. dollar	Special drawing right (SDR)	Other composite	Other currency	Flexibility limited in terms of single currency	Managed floating	Independently floating
Afghanistan (1989)	Burma (1982, 1985)	Bangladesh (1982, 1985, 1989)	Bhutan (1982, 1985, 1989)	Afghanistan (1982, 1985)	Australia (1982)	Australia (1985, 1989)
Lao People's Dem. Rep. (1982, 1985)	Iran (1982, 1985, 1989)	People's Rep. of China (1982, 1985)	Kiribati (1989)	Indonesia (1982)	People's Rep. of China (1989)	Japan (1982, 1985, 1989)
Nepal (1982)	Vanuatu (1982, 1985)	Fiji (1982, 1985, 1989)	Tonga (1985, 1989)	Maldives (1982)	India (1982, 1985, 1989)	Maldives (1989)
Viet Nam (1989)	Viet Nam (1982,1985)	Malaysia (1982, 1985, 1989)		Thailand (1982)	Indonesia (1985, 1989)	New Zealand (1985, 1989)
		Maldives (1985)			Korea (1982, 1985, 1989)	Philippines (1985, 1989)
		Nepal (1985, 1989)			Lao People's Dem. Rep. (1989)	
		Papua New Guinea (1982, 1985, 1989)			New Zealand (1982)	
		Singapore (1982, 1985)			Pakistan (1982, 1985, 1989)	
		Solomon Islands (1982, 1985)			Philippines (1982)	
		Thailand (1985, 1989)			Singapore (1989)	
		Vanuatu (1989)			Sri Lanka (1982, 1985, 1989)	
		Western Samoa (1989)			Western Samoa (1982, 1985)	

Source: International Monetary Fund, *Annual Report on Exchange Arrangement and Exchange Restrictions,* 1983 and 1986; *International Financial Statistics,* March 1990.

exchange rate almost fixed since October 1983. Among the ASEAN members, both Thailand and Malaysia have pegged their currencies to a composite of currencies, including the major currencies, since the early 1980s. Indonesia has been on a managed floating system since 1983, whereas the Philippines switched from managed floating to an independently floating system in October 1984.

The diversity of the exchange rate arrangements in the Asian Pacific region largely reflects the differences in trade structure, degree of trade and financial liberalization, and exchange rate policy objectives among the countries in the region. Since the adoption of generalized floating by industrial countries in 1973, developing countries have been pressured to liberalize their trade and financial regimes and to maintain a more flexible exchange rate system. However, most developing countries have been reluctant to liberalize their economies for fear of the potentially adverse effects of an open market on the exchange rate, given their vulnerability to external influence.

One study by the IMF (Quirk, Christensen, Huh, and Sasabi 1987) has shown that developing countries have chosen floating rates for a number of reasons, but mostly for the purpose of correcting imbalances in the balance of payments. The move of the Philippines to an independently floating regime in October 1984 was motivated by an effort to improve the current account status. In the face of balance of payments difficulties, a market-determined floating rate could better integrate the official foreign exchange market with the unofficial parallel market and hence reduce distortions in resource allocation. In contrast to the case of the Philippines, growing trade surpluses have persuaded both Taiwan and Korea to switch to a free floating system.

Exchange rate policy constitutes one instrument of macroeconomic management. If balance of payments considerations crucially affect the choice of an exchange rate regime, as they often do, it would be logical to examine the changes in the real effective exchange rates of countries to assess the relative performance of different exchange rate systems. This is because changes in the real effective exchange rate reflect not only movement in the nominal exchange rate, but also supporting monetary and fiscal policy.

Figure 13.1 shows the fluctuation of the nominal exchange rates and real effective exchange rates of the United States, Japan, and West Germany. The apparent misalignment of major currencies in the early 1980s and their subsequent realignment since 1985 were responsible for the fluctuation of the real effective exchange rates of the industrial countries over a wide margin. The rate of the United States appreciated by 37 percent during the period 1980 to 1985, and then depreciated another 29 percent from 1985 to 1988. This was matched by a 30 percent real ap-

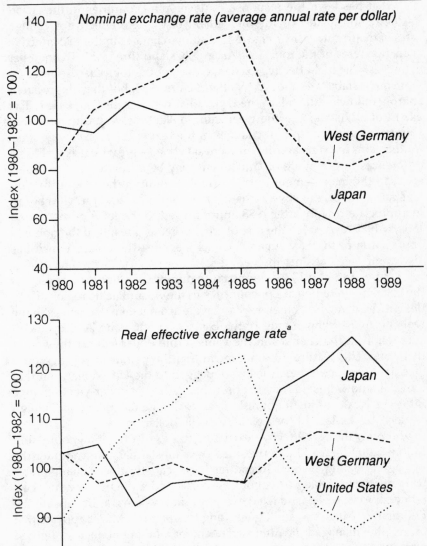

FIGURE 13.1   Nominal and Real Exchange Rates in Japan, the United States, and West Germany, 1980–1989

a. Higher values mean real appreciation. The 1989 value is an average for January–October.
SOURCE: Morgan Guaranty Trust Company, *World Financial Markets*, various issues.

preciation of the yen and 10 percent real appreciation of the German mark during the period 1985 to 1988.

What has been the response of developing countries in the Asian Pacific region to the volatile movement of the real effective exchange rates of major currencies? Figure 13.2 shows changes in the real effective exchange rates of the four East Asian NICs and three ASEAN member countries. The real effective exchange rates of the four East Asian NICs were quite stable and moved together before 1985, but they depreciated sharply following the fall of the U.S. dollar between 1985 and 1987. The extent of adjustment to the weakening dollar was very different from country to country, so that changes in the real effective exchange rates (or the gains in external competitiveness) varied a great deal as well. The differences in the mode of adjustment may be attributed to the differences in the management of the current account in the face of the dollar's fall. The real effective exchange rates of the East Asian NICs began to appreciate rapidly after 1988 and returned to the level of the period 1984 to 1985, except for the rate of Singapore, as a result of the nominal appreciaton of the East Asian currencies against the dollar, which has also appreciated against the yen.

Figures 13.1 and 13.2 demonstrate a number of interesting aspects of the exchange rate policies of countries in the Asian Pacific region. First, despite the diversity of their exchange rate arrangements, changes in the real effective exchange rates of the East Asian NICs and ASEAN members followed the changes in the value of the dollar against the yen in the 1980s. This feature does not mean that the nominal exchange rates of Asian developing countries were pegged to the U.S. dollar, but that they were not adjusted fully to offset changes in the dollar-yen exchange rate. The lack of adjustment reflects an exchange rate policy of "benign neglect" in the face of the volatility of the dollar.

Second, the real effective exchange rates of Korea, Singapore, and Indonesia in Figure 13.2 depreciated by a substantial margin under the managed floating system. In contrast, the real effective exchange rates were relatively stable throughout the 1980s under the free floating, currency composite peg, and fixed exchange rate systems, as in Taiwan, the Philippines, Malaysia, and Hong Kong (see Figure 13.2). It appears that under the managed floating arrangement, judgment factors figured prominently in assessing the appropriate level of the real effective exchange rate indicator and hence in setting the nominal exchange rate. The Asian Pacific region's experience, however, does not reveal which exchange rate system is most effective in stabilizing the real effective exchange rate.

Finally, the high degree of correlation in the pattern of change among the real effective exchange rates suggests that the exchange rate

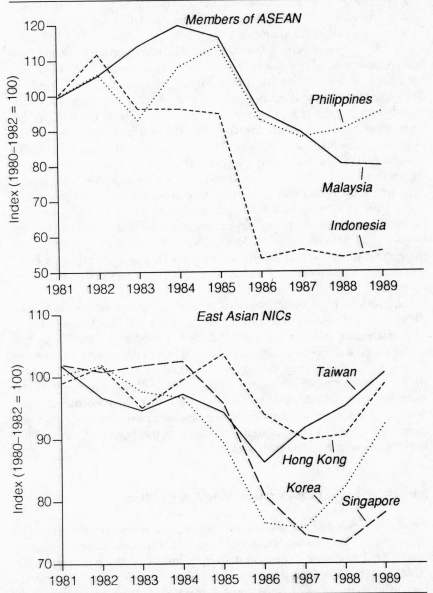

FIGURE 13.2   Real Effective Exchange Rates in the East Asian NICs and Members of ASEAN, 1981–1989 (annual average percentage per U.S. dollar)

NOTE: Higher values mean real appreciation. The 1989 value is an average for January–October.
SOURCE: Morgan Guaranty Trust Company, *World Financial Markets*, various issues.

and monetary and fiscal policies were managed in the same direction to produce a synchronized movement of the real effective exchange rates in the region. Except for Indonesia, fluctuation of the real effective exchange rate in most countries was not as volatile as that of the United States. In particular, the rates of Hong Kong and Taiwan were as stable as the rate of West Germany.

How can we explain the synchronized movement of the real effective exchange rates, especially those of the East Asian NICs? These four countries share many similar structural and institutional characteristics. They are resource-poor economies that have succeeded in industrialization by promoting manufactured exports. The destinations of the exports and supply sources for the imports of these four East Asian economies are also quite similar. They export, mostly to U.S. and European markets, a wide range of manufactured products that are produced by using intermediate parts and technology imported from Japan. This similarity in industrial and trade structures has been detrimental to the expansion of trade within the four countries. Because of fierce export competition, these countries have been reluctant to open their markets to one another and have seldom allowed any of their currencies to depreciate more than those of the others. This competition has been responsible for the similar movement of their real effective exchange rates.

All four of these countries have been running a persistent deficit in their trade with Japan, while running a surplus with the United States. This triangular relation has induced these countries to stay with the dollar when it depreciates against the yen, but to depreciate against the dollar when it becomes stronger. This mode of adjustment is often pointed out as one of the causes of the trade imbalance between these four countries and the United States. In order to increase interdependence and avoid competitive exchange rate adjustments among the four countries, a joint floating system among them has been suggested. This issue is discussed in the fifth section.

Impacts of Rapid Real Exchange Rate Appreciation

As was reviewed in the preceding section, the real effective exchange rates of the East Asian NICs were quite stable and moved together before 1985, but they depreciated sharply following the fall of the U.S. dollar in 1986. Then they began to appreciate rapidly after 1987. From 1986 to 1989, the rates of Taiwan and Korea showed a sharp appreciation of 7 percent and 6 percent a year on average, although the yen appreciated by 6 percent a year on average against the U.S. dollar (see Table

TABLE 13.2   Changes in Nominal and Real Exchange Rates, 1981–1989 (average annual percentage change)

Exchange rate	1981–85	1986	1987	1988	1989	1986–89
Nominal exchange rate (per U.S. dollar)						
Japanese yen	2.0	−29.4	−14.2	−11.4	7.7	−6.4
New Taiwan dollar	2.0	−5.0	−15.9	−10.2	−7.6	−11.3
Korean won	6.3	1.3	−6.7	−11.1	−8.2	−8.7
Real effective exchange rate[a]						
U.S. dollar	5.0	−16.3	−10.4	−4.8	5.0	−3.6
Japanese yen	−1.9	19.0	3.6	5.3	−5.0	1.2
New Taiwan dollar	−1.8	−5.8	6.2	5.8	7.9	6.6
Korean won	−2.9	−14.6	−0.9	8.9	11.9	6.5

a. The negative values mean real depreciation. The 1989 value is an average for January–October.
SOURCES: International Monetary Fund, *International Financial Statistics*, various issues; Morgan Guaranty Trust, *World Financial Markets*, various issues (real effective exchange rates).

13.2). This reversal of exchange rate movements was caused mainly by the nominal appreciation of the New Taiwan dollar and the Korean won against the U.S. dollar by 11 percent and 9 percent a year on average during this period. Currency appreciation was induced by pressure from the United States and Korea, as well as Taiwan's efforts to cut down its current account surpluses.

Overall, the yen's enormous appreciation of 42 percent against the U.S. dollar from 1985 to 1989 produced the New Taiwan dollar's appreciation of 33 percent and the Korean won's appreciation of 23 percent against the U.S. dollar during the same period. Although the magnitude of nominal appreciation was smaller in Taiwan and Korea than in Japan, it must be noted that the real effective exchange rates of both Taiwan and Korea appreciated to surpass their 1985 levels, from which they had depreciated during 1986. If the yen's weakening against the U.S. dollar since 1989 continues in 1990, Taiwan and Korea may be forced to depreciate their currencies to prevent further real appreciation.

It can be called into question whether the rapid nominal appreciation of the New Taiwan dollar and Korean won can be justified, since the real effective exchange rates should be made stable in the face of the enormous nominal appreciation of the yen against the U.S. dollar. It can be asked whether the nominal exchange rates of the New Taiwan dollar and the Korean won, which were both pegged to the U.S. dollar or showed limited flexibility against the U.S. dollar, must be adjusted in line with the volatile movements of the yen-dollar exchange rate. For the purpose of designing appropriate exchange rate policies for these countries, it will be instructive to discover the extent of, and the channel for,

TABLE 13.3   Economic Developments in Taiwan and Korea, 1981–1989 (annual percentage averages)

Economic indicator	1981–85	1986	1987	1988	1989	1986–89
Real GNP growth						
Taiwan	6.7	12.6	11.9	7.8	7.2	8.9
Korea	9.0	12.9	13.0	12.4	6.7	10.7
CPI inflation rate						
Taiwan	1.0	0.7	0.5	1.3	4.4	2.1
Korea	3.8	2.8	3.0	7.1	5.7	5.2
Current account/GNP[a]						
Taiwan	8.9	21.4	18.4	11.7	9.1	13.1
Korea	−2.8	4.5	7.6	8.4	2.4	6.1
M2 growth rate[b]						
Taiwan	23.6	20.7	26.5	18.5	16.1	20.3
Korea	16.2	18.4	19.1	21.5	19.8	20.1
Changes in real wage[c]						
Taiwan	6.3	9.3	9.3	9.5	9.0	9.3
Korea	7.2	6.2	8.3	11.7	18.3	12.7
Changes in real exchange rate[d]						
Taiwan	0.8	2.6	−1.5	−1.3	−4.0	−2.3
Korea	−2.9	−1.3	−6.1	−1.1	−2.3	−3.2
Growth of investment						
Machinery and equipment						
Taiwan	−4.1	12.9	24.6	15.8	12.9	17.7
Korea	7.4	24.4	19.8	13.2	12.1	15.0
Construction						
Taiwan	4.2	7.5	12.3	13.2	12.5	12.7
Korea	13.7	2.9	13.7	13.7	19.9	15.7
Changes in stock price index						
Taiwan	8.0	26.7	126.0	143.7	65.6	108.9
Korea	2.4	64.0	83.3	66.0	32.5	59.2
Changes in land prices						
Korea	10.9	7.3	14.7	27.5	32.0	24.5

a. The 1981–85 value is an average of the ratios from 1981 to 1985. The 1986–89 value is an average of the ratios from 1987 to 1989.
b. End of year.
c. Nominal wage in manufacturing/consumer price index (CPI).
d. Manufacturing GDP deflator/nonmanufacturing GDP deflator.
Sources: Directorate-General of Budget, Accounting, and Statistics, *Quarterly National Economic Trends*, various issues; Bank of Korea, *Economic Statistics Yearbook*, various issues; Ministry of Construction, Republic of Korea, *Trends of Land Prices*, various issues.

the currency appreciation's contribution to reducing currency account imbalances in both Taiwan and Korea.

Table 13.3 shows economic developments in Taiwan and Korea. Several features are evident. First, changes in real effective exchange rates are closely related to changes in the real exchange rate, defined as the tradable goods gross domestic product (GDP) deflator divided by the nontradable goods GDP deflator in Taiwan. With real appreciation in

Taiwan since 1987, the inflation rate of nontradable goods has surpassed the inflation rate of tradable goods since that year. The changes in the real exchange rate in favor of nontradable goods would shift domestic resources from the tradable goods sector into the nontradable goods sector. This is evidenced by the sharp decline in real growth of the manufacturing sector from 16 percent in 1986 to 3.8 percent in 1989 and the sustained real growth of the construction sector from 5.6 percent in 1986 to 11.8 percent in 1989.

In Korea, the real exchange rate in terms of the price of tradable goods relative to the price of nontradable goods continued to decline, as the real effective exchange rate of the Korean won appreciated by a substantial margin from 1986 to 1989. The declining trend of Korea's real exchange rate, in spite of fluctuations in the real effective exchange rate, may be explained by the high productivity of the manufacturing sector as compared with that of the nonmanufacturing sector. Therefore, when the rates of real exchange rate appreciation are examined in consideration of the productivity differential between the two sectors, a relationship is also found between changes in the real effective exchange rate and the rate of real exchange rate appreciation in terms of prices of tradable goods relative to prices of nontradable goods. Korea's domestic resource allocation between the tradable and nontradable sectors has also been affected by the real appreciation since 1987. For instance, the real growth of the manufacturing sector declined sharply from 18.3 percent in 1986 to 3.7 percent in 1989, whereas the real growth of the construction sector increased sharply from 5.0 percent to 15.4 percent during the same period.

A second prominent feature of Table 13.3 concerns the dynamics of real wages and the profitability of capital. In both Korea and Taiwan, real appreciation produced higher growth of real wages and lower growth of investment in machinery and equipment, as shown in Table 13.3. Korea's sharp acceleration in real wage growth, however, could also be attributed to the increased labor disputes since 1987 that accompanied political and economic democratization. We have described a very simple model in the Appendix at the end of this chapter, following Dornbusch (1988), to explain the impact of nominal appreciation on the real wage (and thereby on the real exchange rate) and the profitability of capital.

The model can explain the decline in growth of investment in machinery and equipment and the increase in real wage growth in Taiwan and Korea during the years 1986 to 1989. In particular, Korea's deceleration in growth of investment in machinery and equipment from 24.4 percent in 1986 to 12.1 percent in 1989 and the sharp acceleration in real wage growth from 6.2 percent to 18.3 percent can be attributed to real appreciation and increased home demand during the period 1986 to 1989.

The third development shown in Table 13.3 is related to the dynamics of real exchange rates and the price of real estate. To focus on the relationship between real exchange rates and speculation on real estate, we have set up a simple two-sector general equilibrium portfolio balance model in the appendix, as contained in Park (1987).

When the rate of domestic depreciation is reduced, people want to hold more real domestic money by substituting out of foreign money and real estate in real terms. This is possible with real appreciation and a decline in the real value of real estate. Since the nominal exchange rate will not change instantly, however, real appreciation will be achieved by increases in both the domestic price of commodites and the price of real estate. This result is shown in Table 13.3, where the consumer price index inflation rate continued to increase and land prices (or stock prices, as far as speculation is concerned) shot up, along with real appreciation, since 1987.

An Optimum Currency Area for the Yen?

The recent dramatic growth of Japanese economic and financial power has raised the possibility of elevating the status of the yen to a major reserve currency and possibly making it an anchor for the Western Pacific currency bloc of the 1990s. The debates on a yen currency zone in the Asian Pacific region have been stimulated by several developments, including the expansion of intraregional trade and Japanese foreign direct investment and assistance in the area. Two-way trade between Japan, on the one hand, and other countries in the Asian Pacific region, on the other, has grown more than 40 percent a year over the past three-year period. The East Asian NICs doubled their export market share in the Japanese market to 13 percent in the 1980s. They have done well in exporting all categories of manufactures, but especially in exports of labor-intensive products. On the import side, they have relied on Japan mainly for their supply of capital and intermediate goods. Foreign direct investment by Japanese firms (small and medium-sized firms, as well as multinationals) has also increased rapidly since 1985. For example, Japan's foreign direct investment in these four countries has more than doubled over the past five-year period, although a relatively large share of it has been directed to North America and Europe. Japan's foreign direct investment provides a means of transferring Japanese technology to developing Asian economies and has stimulated intraregional trade in the Asian Pacific region. The expansion of Japan's foreign direct investment has been accompanied by financial assistance in the region. In particular, ASEAN members have begun to borrow heavily in yen. These developments, together with the intraregional trade expansion, have increased the yen's share of Asian countries' foreign exchange reserves.

Despite Japan's growing economic and political influence as an economic superpower, the prospect of the yen's elevation to reserve currency status has been viewed with skepticism. Many skeptics point out that Japan's financial market, in particular its short-term money market and off-shore bond market, is not yet mature enough to support the yen as an international reserve currency. It is also true that there is a relatively small amount of trade and foreign loans denominated in yen and that the yen still accounts for a very small portion of official foreign exchange reserves. Despite these limitations, the growth of the Japanese economy could easily transform the yen into a major reserve currency. Therefore, the yen's future depends on whether or not Japan is ready to allow the yen to play such a role.

If the yen becomes a full-fledged reserve currency, will a yen bloc emerge for the Asian Pacific region? Will Asian developing countries be encouraged to join a yen currency area, where they will peg their currencies to the yen? Although Japanese economic and political influence over the region will constantly increase in the coming decade, it is difficult to believe that Asian developing countries will voluntarily peg their currencies to the yen for a number of reasons. Perhaps the most important reason is that, given their trade dependency on the United States, most Asian countries would have little to gain from joining a currency area that excludes the United States. Indeed, it would be in the interest of Asian developing countries to support a multilateral approach to trade expansion in the Pacific area that would include the United States.

Another reason is related to Japan's limited capacity as a reserve currency country. Japan should be able to replace the United States as the dominant absorber of exports from the Asian Pacific region if it is to serve as the center of any yen block. To absorb a large share of regional exports, Japan would have to increase its capacity to import and lower its high savings rate. In addition, it would have to be prepared to sacrifice domestic growth to maintain price stability and to accept the loss of exchange rate adjustment to maintain internal and external stability. Indeed, there has been no positive sign that Japan is willing to assume the role of center country. Furthermore, the structural characteristics of trade between Japan and other Asian countries could complicate Japan's potential role as a center country.

Since much of the discussion on creating a Western Pacific yen bloc focuses on the rapidly expanding intra-Asian trade and Japan's overseas direct investment, it is important to assess whether these developments could contribute to regional integration in the future. A recent study by Park and Park (1990) shows that there are other factors that cast serious doubt as to the future of regional integration in the Asian Pacific region. As noted before, the recent expansion of intraregional trade and capital flow in Asia has been supported by the appreciation of the yen since 1985. The yen has weakened since 1989. This turnaround in the yen-dollar exchange rate has made it difficult for the East Asian NICs to penetrate further into the Japanese market. Although Japan is the second largest economy in the world, it is highly questionable whether Japan could supplant the United States as a major importer of the products of developing Asian economies.

The expansion in regional trade within the Asian Pacific region is related to an expansion in intraindustry trade between Japan and other developing countries that has been dominated by the exchange of manufactured goods differentiated by different processing stages in the same industry. This type of trade is likely to be determined by comparative advantage based on differences in human capital and technology—that is, factors on the supply side rather than the demand side. Since intraregional trade in the Asian Pacific region includes a relatively small share of the trade in differentiated products, the recent increase in intraregional trade may have been stimulated by the yen's appreciation since 1985. Thus, any reduction in Japan's capacity to absorb Asian imports would be severely detrimental to the growth of intraregional trade in Asia. For example, the weakening of the yen in late 1989 and early 1990 has already considerably slowed the growth of intraregional trade.

A third reason is that the 1990s will witness an increasing currency competition among the U.S. dollar, the Japanese yen, and the deutsche mark, as the new U.S. debtor status, the integration of the European Community, and Japan's rise to a superpower disrupt and challenge the existing international monetary system. In addition, the history of international finance has shown no experience of a harmonious period based on a multiple key currency system. In view of the recent exchange rate developments, it is also likely that the dollar-yen exchange rate will remain unstable in the 1990s. The disappearance of a dominant currency and lender of last resort will bring a period of unstable international finance until a new dominant currency emerges. If Japan maintains its current lead in technological innovation and its high savings rate, the yen will continue to appreciate against other major currencies, and Asian developing countries will have to readjust their exchange rates against the yen to prevent a deterioration of their current account. This, together with the possibility of a protracted period of international financial instability, suggests that developing countries in the Asian Pacific region would be better off remaining outside of a yen block.

A fourth reason is that the developing countries could not easily afford to lose monetary autonomy. The loss of monetary autonomy from joining a monetary union would severely disrupt any economy, but the disruptive effects would be more pronounced in a developing country, where the trade regime is protected and domestic financial and factor markets are regulated. The East Asian NICs and other developing countries in the region could benefit from having a common currency, as they would save the costs of holding large reserves and would be spared exchange rate instability and speculative capital flow. However, they might rely more on fiscal adjustment to offset the loss of monetary autonomy or might have to tolerate a worsening of the inflation-unemployment trade-off.

A fifth reason is related to the question of whether regional monetary integration could narrow inflation differentials in the region. We have calculated the consumer price index inflation rates and M2 growth rates of the East Asian NICs and ASEAN members in the 1980s in Figures 13.3 and 13.4. These show persistent differences in the rates of inflation among these countries. However, a similar trend can be observed in price movements for all countries, excluding the Philippines. Compared with the trend for inflation, the M2 growth rates of countries in the Asian Pacific region diverged—especially among the members of ASEAN (see Figure 13.4). In addition, a higher monetary growth rate was not related to a higher inflation rate. This evidence suggests that monetary union alone could not bring about a uniform rate of inflation in the region.

Finally, the lessons drawn from the evolution of the European Monetary System (EMS) show that the institution of a fixed exchange rate alone cannot assure successful regional monetary cooperation, as long as there remains the so-called nth country probem. Ten years of operation of the EMS reveals that the member countries have tried to retain monetary independence by readjusting their pegging rates and controlling capital flow, while the center country has pursued its own nominal targets. Reflecting on actual economic cooperation in the EMS, some authors argue that monetary union is only one aspect of political union (de Grauwe 1984; Giavazzi and Giovannini 1988). If an optimal currency area for the yen has any political implications, establishment of such a union would be strongly resisted by other countries in Asia.

If the political implications of creating a yen currency zone are indeed as repulsive as it has been suggested that they would be, the East Asian NICs may consider adopting a joint floating system before

FIGURE 13.3 Consumer Price Inflation Rates in the East Asian NICs and Members of ASEAN, 1980–1988

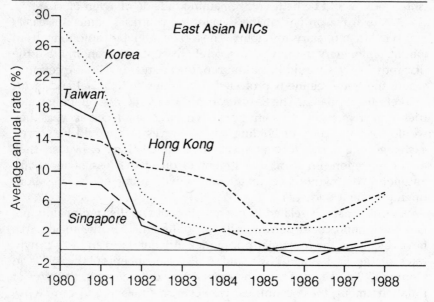

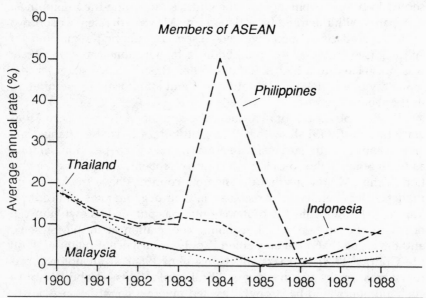

SOURCE: International Monetary Fund, *International Financial Statistics,* various issues.

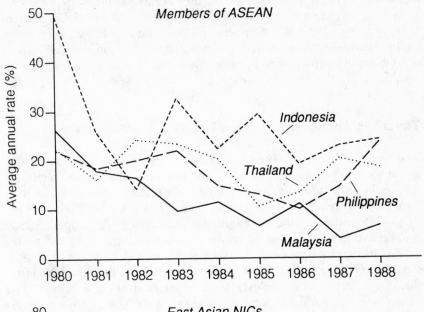

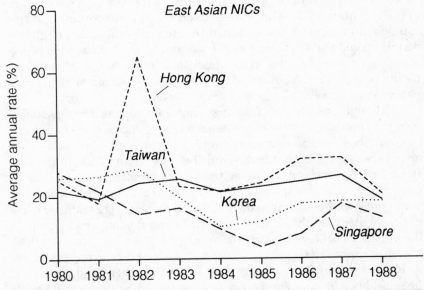

SOURCE: International Monetary Fund, *International Financial Statistics*, various issues.

pegging to the yen. To promote higher trade and financial interdependence among Asian developing economies, de Macedo (1986) suggested a joint float similar to the one followed by Malaysia and Singapore. The possibility of setting up a joint float among the East Asian NICs could in theory be extended to the members of ASEAN and could lead eventually to the creation of a loosely defined currency union. However, without a strong center country, it is questionable whether such a union could be established in the first place.

Toward an Appropriate Exchange Rate Policy

The past fifteen years have seen extremely volatile movements in the exchange rates of major currencies, and it is now agreed that free floating could lead to a serious exchange rate misalignment, unless it is supported by macroeconomic policy coordination among the major industrial countries. If the misalignment is caused by improper macroeconomic policies pursued by major currency countries rather than by an insufficient exchange rate floating, it is not at all clear whether less-developed countries, including the East Asian NICs, should adopt a free floating system. Nevertheless, some economists of the laissez-faire school still argue for the floating exchange rate system even for developing countries.[1] The laissez-faire advocates place importance on free competition and market-determined resource allocation. Although it is widely agreed that liberalization of trade and capital transactions is necessary to increase market competition and efficiency, the same can hardly be said for a free floating system, as excessive capital flow could easily destabilize the foreign exchange market.

Although the choice of an exchange rate regime for developing countries remains an unresolved issue, a higher degree of exchange rate flexibility has been advocated as a means of correcting the trade imbalance between the United States and the East Asian NICs. In general, these East Asian countries are accused of manipulating their exchange rates to gain unfair competitive advantage, and at the same time they are being pressured to liberalize their financial markets. Therefore, it is not clear whether they should move toward a clean floating arrangement or toward financial liberalization. If more emphasis is placed on clean floating, then exchange rate changes will not produce correct market signals as long as capital flow is controlled. If, on the other hand, trade and financial liberalization are the priority reforms, then they should try to maintain a correctly aligned exchange rate, taking into consideration the possible effects of financial liberalization.

Few would advocate simultaneously undertaking a free floating system and economic liberalization in a developing economy. The current debate on the new international monetary system does not advocate the adoption of free floating as much as it did in the past, even for industrial countries. There would be little economic justification for developing countries to float their currencies. As Frankel (1989) points out, it may indeed be misguided to appeal to free-market principles to justify pressure on East Asian countries to allow their currencies to appreciate against the dollar. Indeed, it is perfectly appropriate for a small country to seek exchange rate stability if it wishes to seek it. Instead, East Asian countries would perhaps be better advised to concentrate on the liberalization of trade in goods and services, where the appeal to principle is on a secure ground.

This discussion has indicated that the single currency peg and free floating are the least desirable choices for the East Asian NICs.[2] If the single currency peg is not acceptable, the next best alternative may be a flexible basket peg. The determination of the optimal level of such a basket peg remains a controversial issue, with differing objectives and rules. Such an arrangement could also restrict capital flow, because exchange rate authorities could try to adhere to the peg by strengthening capital controls.

The discussion in the preceding section finds some justification for adopting a joint floating system among the East Asian NICs. The joint floating could serve as a first step toward the establishment of an optimum currency area in the Asian Pacific region, since it would promote trade and financial interdependence among these four countries. It would also eliminate the problem of competitive depreciation among them. They would find it easier to accept a joint float than an independent float. However, there is no political leadership strong enough to bring them to an agreement on such a scheme.

Regional interdependence, although important, may be of secondary importance, compared with the issue of the imbalance in their trilateral trade with the United States and Japan. If the trilateral trade imbalance is the most pressing issue, then attention should be directed toward insuring a correct alignment of the exchange rate in each country. Following the "indicators" approach agreed upon by major industrial countries at the Tokyo and Venice summit meetings in 1986 and 1987, the East Asian NICs could estimate a real effective exchange rate consistent with the simultaneous internal and external balance in the medium term. To maintain an equilibrium real exchange rate, the nominal exchange rate that is pegged to a basket of currencies should be adjusted gradually to offset differential inflation. However, the exchange rate can be allowed to float in the foreign exchange market within some margins around the peg. The determination of the equilibrium real exchange rate is the most difficult aspect of instituting the indicator approach.

The indicator approach should be distinguished from the target zone proposal. The center of a target zone could be established by estimating a real exchange rate that will maintain external and internal balance. However, as Williamson (1989) emphasizes, the choice of the basket to which a currency is pegged and any gradual change in the peg should be made on a preannounced basis. His proposal for a target zone differs from the indicator approach with respect to the width of the allowable margins and the techniques for enforcing the margins. In a target-zone approach, margins would be wide and enforced by sterilized (or unsterilized) intervention in the foreign exchange market, as well as by a deliberate supporting change in interest rates and fiscal policy.

Concluding Remarks

This chapter has examined the future direction of exchange rate policy in the East Asian newly industrialized countries from several different perspectives. After reviewing alternative exchange rate regimes, it has been suggested that they follow the indicator approach agreed upon by major industrial countries at the Tokyo and Venice summit meetings in 1986 and 1987.

In recognition of the recent substantial appreciation of the nominal and real exchange rates of the New Taiwan dollar and the Korean won against the U.S. dollar, this chapter has also discussed the impacts of this real appreciation. It has shown that the rapid appreciation in these four countries could lead to the sharp acceleration of real wage growth, deceleration of investment in machinery and equipment, and land speculation, thereby threatening the potential for their stable growth.

Appendix

Model of the Impact of Appreciation on the Real Wage Rate and on the Profitability of Capital

Investment is a function of Tobin's real price of installed capacity (q):

$$I = I(q) \; ; Iq > 1. \tag{A1}$$

Capital accumulation is defined by the difference between investment and depreciation:

$$\dot{K} = I(q) - \delta K = \dot{K}(q.K) \qquad (A2)$$

where δ is the rate of depreciation.

The return on domestically installed capital—that is, the sum of domestic dividend yield of capital and capital gains—must be equal to the rate of return in the world market (i^*), assuming that capital is internationally mobile:

$$\dot{q}/q = i^* - \phi(w)/q = h(q, K : i^*, G) \qquad (A3)$$

where $\phi(w)$ as a function of real wage w is the marginal product of capital in the traded goods sector and G is the home demand by the government.

The equilibrium real wage is a function of the capital stock (K), employment (L), government spending on home goods (G), and currency depreciation ($\dot{E}$):

$$w = w(K, L, G, \dot{E})\colon w_K > 0,\ w_L < 0,\ w_G > 0,\ w_{\dot{E}} < 0 \qquad (A4)$$

Substituting equation (A4) into (A3) produces the phase diagram in Figure 13.5, which shows the dynamics of the capital stock and the real price of capital. The locus of $\dot{K} = 0$ is upward sloping, since an increase in investment owing to an increase in q must be offset by an increase in capital depreciation. The locus of $\dot{q} = 0$ is downward sloping, since an increase in q must be accompanied by an increase in the marginal product of capital. There exists a downward-sloping unique saddle path to the equilibrium.

An increase in home demand or currency appreciation raises the equilibrium real wage and hence reduces the yield of capital. Therefore, the $\dot{q} = 0$ locus shifts downward. The forward-looking real price of capital declines immediately. The profitability of capital declines because of both the reduction in the marginal product of capital and the decline in the asset price in the short term. Over time, the capital stock declines and real wage falls until a new equilibrium is reached. In sum, an adverse shock on real wages, created by currency appreciation and increased home demand, reduces the yield of capital and hence immediately reduces the real price of capital. This will be followed by a decline in the capital stock and in the real wage over time.

FIGURE 13.5   Impact of Currency Appreciation on Capital
Accumulation

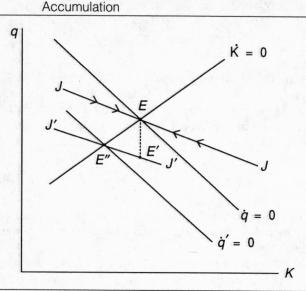

SOURCE: Author, following R. Dornbusch, "Real Exchange Rates and Macroeconomics: A Selective
Survey," National Bureau of Economic Research Working Paper no. 2775 (November 1988).

Model of the Dynamics of the Real Exchange Rate and the Price of Real Estate

The real exchange rate (q) is defined by the relative price of tradable
goods (E) and home (nontradable) goods (P^H):

$$q = \frac{E}{P^H} \tag{A5}$$

The production (Y) and demand (C) functions for both goods are
specified as functions of the real exchange rate (q) and real wealth (a):

$$Y^T = Y^T (q) \; ; Y^T_q > 0 \; , \; Y^H = Y^H(q) \; ; Y^H_q < 0$$

$$C^T = C^T (q, a) \; ; C^T_q < 0, \; C^T_a > 0, \; C^H = C^H(q, a); \; C^H_q > 0, C^H_a > 0. \tag{A6}$$

The real wealth of the public, measured in units of tradable goods,
is composed of domestic money (M), foreign money (F), and real estate
(Z), whose physical stock is fixed and whose price is denoted as P^Z:

$$a = \frac{M}{E} + F + \frac{P^z Z}{E}. \tag{A7}$$

Equilibrium in the market for home goods ($Y^H = C^H$) requires a negative relationship between the real wealth of the public and the real exchange rate:

$$a = V(q) \; ; \; Vq < 0. \tag{A8}$$

The stock of foreign money changes according to an excess demand or supply of tradable goods:

$$\dot{F} = Y^T - C^T = f(q) \; ; \; fq > 0. \tag{A9}$$

The demand for each asset depends on the expected relative rates of return on the two assets:

$$\frac{EF}{M} = L(\hat{E}) \; ; \; L_{\hat{E}} > 0, \quad \frac{P^z Z}{M} = H(\hat{P}^z) \; ; \; H_{\hat{P}^z} > 0,$$

$$\tag{A10}$$

$$\frac{P^z Z}{EF} = J(\hat{P}^z - \hat{E}) \; ; \; J_{\hat{P}^z - \hat{E}} > 0$$

where a circumflex denotes the percentage change in a variable.

Since $\hat{E}$ is assumed to be exogenously controlled, the demand for domestic money relative to foreign money is also exogenously fixed as α from equation (A10). Therefore, equation (A7) can be transformed into:

$$a = (1 + \alpha)F + h \tag{A11}$$

where $h = P^z/E$.

The system can be represented by either a set of state variables of F and q or a set of F and h. Figure 13.6 illustrates the phase diagram for two sets of state variables. In the (F,q) space, the $\dot{F} = 0$ locus should be horizontal at $\bar{q}$. The slope of the $\dot{q} = 0$ locus is not determined, but it does not affect the negativity of slope of the saddle path to the equilibrium. In the (F, h) space, the $\dot{F} = 0$ locus should be downward-sloping, since q and a are fixed in the steady state in equations (A9) and (A11). The $\dot{h} = 0$ locus is upward-sloping from (A10). Thus, the saddle path of (F, h) must be upward-sloping.

A decline in the rate of home currency depreciation through disinflation (or nominal appreciation) will shift the $\dot{q} = 0$ locus

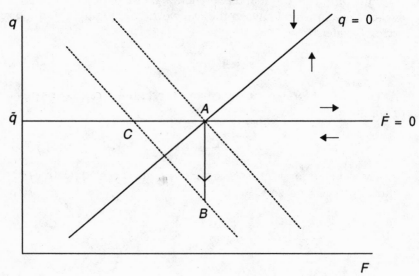

Real exchange rate

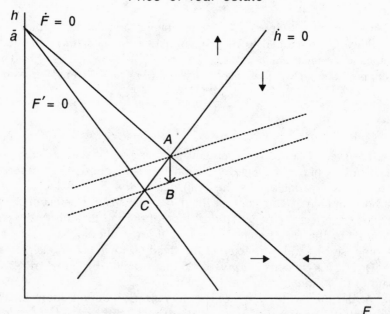

Price of real estate

downward in Figure 13.6 (top) and will rotate the $\dot{F} = 0$ locus downward in Figure 13.6 (bottom), resulting in real appreciation and a decline in the real value of real estate.

Notes

1. Countries with protracted balance of payments difficulties may consider floating their exchange rates in order to unify the legal and illegal markets and to shed political responsibility for the mismanagement of the exchange rate (Quirk, Christensen, Huh, and Sasabi 1987). However, there is little point in recommending free floating to those countries that have managed their monetary, fiscal, and exchange rate policies successfully enough to bring about a current account balance and price stability.

2. Taiwan moved to a free floating regime in 1989, but it is not regarded as "free floating" by outsiders, since the New Taiwan dollar market is confined to Taipei and foreign banks are allowed to hold only a limited amount of the New Taiwan dollar.

Comments

Helmut Reisen

Once upon a time (up to 1985), the East Asian newly industrialized countries (NICs)—Hong Kong, South Korea, Singapore, and Taiwan—were generally applauded for their exchange rate management. It was then characterized by a strong orientation toward the U.S. dollar and by keeping to a minimum the variation in the real effective exchange rates.

In stark contrast to most of Latin America, exchange rate policies of East Asian NICs avoided discrimination against export industries, they never allowed substantial black market premiums to develop, and they generally supported the successful attainment of external and internal balance.

Beginning in the first half of 1985 and especially after the September 1985 Plaza Agreement among the industrialized countries, there has been a growing discrepancy between the real exchange rate movements of the East Asian NICs and Japan (see Figure 13.7). This was caused by the sharp depreciation of the U.S. dollar against key currencies (such as

FIGURE 13.7   Index of Real Effective Exchange Rates for Japan and the East Asian NICs, 1985–1990

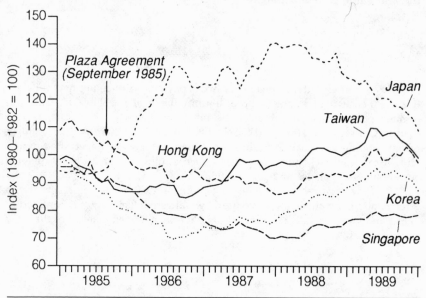

NOTE: A rise of the index denotes appreciation. Calculated on six-month averages.
SOURCE: Morgan Guaranty Bank, *World Financial Markets.*

the yen and deutsche mark) since 1985. On the other hand, the East Asian NICs maintained either a de facto peg to the U.S. dollar or appreciated significantly less against the U.S. dollar than the yen did, leading to a depreciation of the currencies of the NICs in real effective terms. This was the end of the applause for them. Since then, Korea and Taiwan, in particular, have been blamed with (1) preventing the global adjustment process toward financeable trade balances, (2) reaping windfall profits behind the shield of the yen appreciation, (3) exercising exchange rate protection, and (4) keeping the capital account too closed.

These criticisms, however, can hardly be substantiated, except for Taiwan. Exchange rate protection is characterized by the preferential treatment the tradable sector receives in relation to the nontradable sector through maintaining an undervalued exchange rate or effectively preventing its appreciation. If the subsequent shift toward the tradable sector is accompanied by a decrease in absorption in order to balance supply and demand in the nontradable sector, a current account surplus and higher stocks of foreign reserves will be the logical consequences. Table 13.4 reveals, however, that Korea's foreign reserves remained re-

TABLE 13.4   Economic Characteristics of the East Asian NICs, 1980–1988

Economic indicator	Period	Japan	Hong Kong	Korea	Singapore	Taiwan
GDP per capita						
(current U.S. dollars)	1988	23,190	9,550	3,725	8,860	5,600
Relative, PPP-adjusted	1985	69.6	70.4	23.3	69.7	27.5
(United States = 100)						
Consumer prices (annual	1985–88	0.5	5.0	4.3	0.2	0.8
inflation rate)						
Unemployment (% of	1985–88	2.7	2.3	3.4	4.2	2.3
labor force)						
Share in NIC exports (%)	1985–88					
United States			38.2	37.6	20.4	43.8
European Community			20.9	12.6	11.9	11.8
Japan			4.2	15.5	6.6	12.8
Share in NIC imports (%)	1985–88					
United States			7.7	18.3	14.7	24.0
European Community			11.0	9.0	11.8	11.4
Japan			19.4	29.7	20.0	31.5
Foreign reserves (months	1980–84	2.2	n.a	2.8	4.6	4.3
of imports)	1985–88	4.1	n.a	1.5	5.4	20.2

n.a. = not available.
SOURCES: Hong Kong: *Monthly Digest of Statistics;* Korea: Economic Planning Board, *Major Statistics of Korean Economy;* Singapore: *Yearbook of Statistics,* and Ministry of Trade and Industry, *Economic Survey of Singapore;* Taiwan: Council of Economic Planning and Development, *Taiwan Statistical Data Book;* Japan: International Monetary Fund, *Direction of Trade Statistics Yearbook;* Organization for Economic Cooperation and Development; *Economic Survey of Japan,* various issues.

markably stable in terms of imports throughout the 1980s. Since 1986, Korea has been using its current account surplus to pay off part of its massive foreign debt, benefiting from favorable external conditions, such as lower interest rates and raw material prices. Neither Korea nor Hong Kong and Singapore are traditional surplus countries. The current accounts of Hong Kong and Singapore fluctuated between –US$1.5 billion and +US$2 billion during the 1980s, while Korea's current account has switched back to deficit in early 1990.

The monetary focus on exchange rates provides little explanation for the recent surpluses of the East Asian NICs and no explanation for the global imbalances. Current account imbalances have been associated with disparities between national savings and investment rates, largely determined by intertemporal optimization within the private sectors and by changed government savings (with little evidence for "Ricardian equivalence"). While investment ratios have been quite stable since 1985 in the East Asian NICs, variations in savings ratios were closely related to deviations from potential gross national product (GDP) growth. But the current accounts of these countries reflect not only the internal but also the external savings-investment balances, in particular that of the United States. Global current account imbalances are likely to persist as long as the United States fails to raise its savings and to resolve its deficits.

Even if the link between global imbalances and exchange rate policies of the East Asian NICs is not a matter for serious concern, there are other important new developments that warrant a new look at optimal exchange regimes in East Asia. While the growing trade and production integration among the East Asian NICs and Japan has turned the earlier de facto peg to the U.S. dollar into a destabilizing policy, the same pitfalls would hold for a peg to the yen. I will argue that fixed nominal rates have also become obsolete for other reasons—namely, the growing capital mobility caused by financial liberalization and the need for long-term appreciation of real exchange rates in the process of catching up. Assuming that the East Asian NICs will be subject to both foreign monetary and real domestic shocks, I will make the case for a managed float as the best policy response. In a departure from the entrenched short-termism in the exchange rate literature, the chapter will emphasize the longer view for countries in a rapid industrializing process.

Exchange rate policies for catching up

Governments of countries that have experienced a sustained period of export-led growth (such as Korea and Taiwan now, and Germany in the 1960s) are likely to eagerly avoid *any* real appreciation of their exchange rate. They may ignore that real appreciation will come at any rate, with rising wages and prices in the nontradable sector if nominal appreciation is delayed.

When a country "catches up" with initially richer countries, its goods become more expensive because productivity in the tradable sector rises more than in the nontradable sector (where the lack of external competition introduces slack). The prices of nontradables (such as housing) therefore rise faster than those of tradable goods, reflecting the increasing scarcity of the former. Comparing productivity growth between the tradable sectors of the country that is catching up and a rich country, the former will exceed the latter. Also, assuming equal inflation of tradables worldwide, real wages will hence rise faster in the country that is catching up than they will in the rich country. With lower productivity growth in the nontradable sector in both countries and dependent on their weight in the purchasing power parity (PPP) basket, general prices will rise faster in a country such as Korea than in Japan or

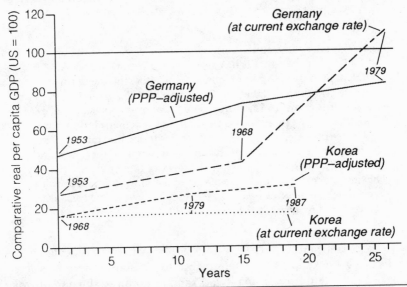

FIGURE 13.8   Deviations from Purchasing Power Parity (PPP) in Germany, 1953–1979, and in Korea, 1968–1987

SOURCES: Robert Summers and Alan Heston, "Improved International Comparisons of Real Product and Its Composition: 1950–1980," *Review of Income and Wealth* 30 (June 1984): 207–62; and Angus Maddison, *The World Economy in the 20th Century,* OECD Development Centre Studies (Paris: Organization for Economic Cooperation and Development, 1989).

the United States, in order to balance the impact of higher money wages on the nontradable sector.

Figure 13.8 presents real per capita income levels (relative to the United States) for Germany (1953–1979) and for Korea (1968–1987). Since nontradables tend to be cheaper in poorer countries, a purchasing-power parity adjustment is essential to make meaningful international comparisons of income levels. By comparing PPP-adjusted real income with real income in current dollars, I implicitly derive the deviations from PPP at different years. In a smooth path (not drawn here), comparative real per capita GDP in dollars should deviate negatively from PPP-adjusted income at the beginning of the catching-up process. With PPP-adjusted income approaching the benchmark country level (100), the negative deviation should gradually become smaller and disappear when the developing country has reached the benchmark country.

Figure 13.8 clearly suggests that Korea has stayed a "cheap" country in PPP terms, although it experienced *relative* growth with a move of real per capita income from a sixth to a third of that of the United States.

Should a country such as Korea cease to stay cheap in PPP terms, and should a gradual appreciation be brought about by an upward float? The German experience may provide some answers, as recalled by Herbert Giersch (1984:6):

> Sooner or later the country will—like West Germany at the end of the 1960s—discover that it has an oversized export sector. An adjustment process will gather momentum either in the form of a domestic cost push—higher wages and costs at the given exchange rate—or in the form of a currency revaluation at constant prices. This adjustment process amounts to an improvement in the country's terms of trade. All rents from superior design and quality, from reliability and punctuality which were formerly used for promoting volumes will then be collected in the form of higher export prices. This improvement in the terms of trade goes along with an upward deviation from the previous real exchange rate, most likely also with an overshooting compared to long-run PPP.

In fact, Germany's exchange rate adjustment was repeatedly delayed during 1968 and 1973 (when the Bretton Woods system was abandoned). Wages and profits "exploded" and announced the end of wage restraint in Germany, leading to an upsurge of strikes and fierce distribution fights and, finally, to persistent unemployment caused by low capital profitability and capital shortage. Hence, Korea today resembles the German situation in the 1970s. In the judgment of the former president of the Deutsche Bundesbank, Ottmar Emminger (1976), the delayed revaluation of the deutsche mark bears an important responsibility for the subsequent German "stagflation." Thus, instead of pegging nominal exchange rates and accommodating the inevitable real appreciation through rising wages and rising prices of nontradables, a nominal upward float is suggested by historical evidence as the only operational policy to attain external and internal balance during a rapid industrialization. Also Singapore's failed wage experiment in the early 1980s suggests that industrial upgrading is achieved with smaller risks when nominal rate flexibility quickly accommodates *relative* productivity growth while wages lag behind.

The case against premature Asian monetary integration

In search of alternatives to the past dollar peg of the East Asian NICs, those calling for closer monetary cooperation among Asian countries have been becoming louder (for a more extensive discussion, see Reisen and van Trotsenburg 1988). There are essentially two proposals: a kind of Asian monetary system around Japan on the pattern of the European Monetary System (EMS), or joint independent floating by the East Asian NICs (excluding Japan). A point in favor of closer monetary ties to the yen is that it would strengthen the yen as an international currency and thus would help to counter inflationary pressures on Japan and the NICs, if they were to emerge again from dependence on the U.S. dollar. In this way, the Asian region could restore the independence of collective monetary control. The problem, of course, is that monetary policy would no longer be decided by the NICs but in Japan. But that eventuality is less dramatic than it sounds because the Parks reject a pure float—the only means to determine independently the domestic money supply.

In a static view and thus ignoring different income levels, the East Asian NICs and Japan share some common characteristics that qualify them to be appropriate candidates for a joint currency area (see Table 13.4). Inflation differentials have narrowed during the 1980s below the margins among EMS countries, and low inflation accompanied low unemployment and high income growth. Also, important for expected long-term price trends and tax liabilities, all East Asian countries (with the notable exception of the Philippines) are characterized now by a low debt burden and the absence of noninterest budget deficits that would risk being monetized eventually. Hence, low inflation differentials would be likely to obviate the need for frequent *nominal* exchange rate adjustment within the proposed Asian monetary system.

In a dynamic setting, the outlook is different. As has been argued in the preceding section, the further economic development of the East Asian NICs (relative to Japan) not only requires trend flexibility in *real* exchange rates but also in *nominal* rates, if inflationary pressures are to be avoided. Countries with divergent rates of productivity growth cannot have the same inflation rate under fixed exchange rates, hence the proposed Asian monetary system would experience considerable inflation differentials—a clear invitation for speculative attacks against the system. Figure 13.9 demonstrates that, although productivity growth is still high in Japan, it has been largely exceeded by Korea's long-term productivity trend.

The intention of the Korean and Taiwanese governments to proceed with external financial liberalization adds a second important case for nominal exchange rate flexibility. Maintaining effective domestic monetary control is difficult when the authorities simultaneously peg the domestic currency and permit free international capital flows. A case in point is again the German experience in the 1960s and early 1970s, where changes in the domestic credit component of the money supply generated offsetting movements in foreign exchange assets through balance of payments imbalances, rendering stabilization policy

FIGURE 13.9   Index of Productivity Growth in Manufacturing in Japan and Korea, 1970–1988

SOURCES: B. Balassa and J. Williamson, *Adjusting to Success: Balance of Payments Policy in the East Asian NICs* (Washington, D.C.: Institute for International Economics, 1989); Economic Planning Board, *Monthly Statistics of Korea* (1989); U.S. Department of Labor, *Monthly Labor Review* (February 1990).

"self-defeating" (Emminger 1976). While sterilization of international capital flows is always possible in a technical sense, the sustainability of such a policy depends on the cost of reducing central bank domestic credit and on the scope and persistence of the inflows (Mathieson 1988).

A clear case against premature Asian monetary integration is based on the small integration of trade among the Asian economies, as Park and Park rightly emphasize. Let us assume that any exchange rate arrangement between small middle-income countries and a large industrial (reserve-currency) country is bound to become asymmetrical. Japan would keep monetary independence and the four East Asian NICs would peg their currencies to the yen. By pegging to a single currency, floating rates among key currencies destabilize the effective exchange rates and increase the macroeconomic effects of external shocks for the East Asian NICs, as theoretical and empirical evidence on the optimal peg has abundantly shown (Black 1976). With a peg to the yen, the NICs would find themselves forced to revalue their currencies against nonyen currencies if the yen appreciated sharply in the foreign exchange market. By pegging to a trade-weighted basket instead, the NICs can reduce the effect on their international trade of large swings in the values of the individual currencies in the basket.

Fluctuations in the value of the currency to which a particular currency is pegged would matter little as long as most foreign exchange transactions in trade and services (including foreign debt service) were denominated in the pegged currency. That is clearly not the case for the East Asian NICs with respect to the yen, nor will it be true in the foreseeable future. To be sure, there has recently been rapid integration of trade and foreign direct investment among the five countries. Japan is shifting assembly and low technology production to the East Asian region at a rapid pace. The NICs are narrowing or even reversing their chronic trade deficits with Japan in standardized products, such as textiles, steel, and television sets. But even if Korea, Taiwan, and Japan would quickly abolish existing trade restrictions, there would still be a long way to go before intraregional trade replaced the existing dominance of the U.S., European, and raw-commodity-producing trade partners. Trade integration among the Asian economies is weak, even when compared with that existing among European economies before the European Economic Community (EEC) was founded.

Moreover, similar production structures, considerable supply diversification, and proven adjustment flexibility reduce the need for swings in the real exchange rates only among Korea, Taiwan, and Japan. The other countries are still commodity-dependent (Malaysia and Indonesia), or are dependent on these countries (Singapore), or form a special political case (Hong Kong). The different structure of these countries fails to protect them from divergent swings in real exchange rates in response to external shocks. Hence, there is little scope for monetary integration in East Asia, with or without Japan.

The case for a managed float under stochastic shocks

Park and Park focus on fluctuations among key currencies, such as the U.S. dollar and the yen, as the likely major disturbance to the economies of the East Asian NICs. If their concern is correct, it adds another case for nominal exchange rate flexibility, since fluctuations among third currencies act like a monetary shock on the affected economies. Fischer (1976) has demonstrated that when exogenous shocks are monetary, the variance of steady-state consumption is lower under a flexible exchange rate system than under a fixed rate system. On the other hand, when the exogenous shocks are real, the fixed rate system is preferred, relying on borrowing and lending as the most efficient buffer for the domestic economy. The use of an appropriate basket peg would then also stabilize the real effective exchange rate.

However, the recent upsurge of labor unrest may suggest that wage disturbances will become important, too. Pursuit of PPP-oriented exchange rate policies, implicitly placing a high cost on the variability of real exchange rates, will generate macroeconomic costs when wage disturbances are predominant—that is, increased instability of domestic prices and potentially increased instability of output (Dornbusch 1982). With monetary accommodation of higher wage costs, by contrast, output is stabilized directly and indirectly by dampening the costs of imported intermediate goods.

A third source of disturbance is varying levels of protectionism by the Organization for Economic Cooperation and Development (OECD). It will consequently be difficult (if not impossible) for the authorities in the East Asian NICs to observe and identify separately monetary and real disturbances. The optimal exchange rate regime will thus involve a system of managed floating with a degree of intervention that allows the external economy of the East Asian NICs to serve as the most efficient buffer for the domestic economy (Frenkel and Aizenman 1982).

PART FOUR

CONCLUSION

CHAPTER FOURTEEN

Advice on the Choice
of an Exchange Rate Policy

This chapter describes the advice on exchange rate policy that I have come to offer over the years. While this advice depends on a country's situation, it does not depend per se on whether the country is classified as industrial or developing, so the discussion is not restricted to developing countries. It concludes with a brief assessment of whether the advice seems appropriate for the countries of Eastern Europe.

Fixed, Floating, or Managed Exchange Rates

The first issue is the traditional one of the choice between fixed and floating exchange rates, enriched by adding the choice of a managed exchange rate. There are circumstances in which a fixed exchange rate provides a sensible policy regime. Specifically, I would recommend a fixed rate to a country that satisfies all of the following four conditions.

1. The economy is small and open, so that it satisfies the conditions for being absorbed in a larger currency area according to the traditional literature on optimum currency areas.

2. The bulk of its trade is undertaken with the trading partner(s) to whose currency (or whose mutually-pegged currencies) it plans

to peg. This is necessary if stability of the bilateral exchange rate is to secure a reasonable measure of stability of the effective exchange rate that is essential for macroeconomic stability. What is meant by "the bulk of its trade"? I would settle for a 50 percent threshold as a working figure, because 60 percent seems more than enough and 40 percent seems too little.

3. The country wishes to pursue a macroeconomic policy that will result in an inflation rate consistent with that in the country (or countries) to whose currency (or currencies) it plans to peg. This policy will be sensible if the center currency provides a stable anchor and the domestic economy is capable of living comfortably with price stability. Conversely, it will be foolish if the center currency suffers rapid inflation or the domestic price level has a life of its own, either because fiscal indiscipline entails reliance on the inflation tax or because cost-inflationary pressures are entrenched.

4. The country is prepared to adopt institutional arrangements that will assure continued credibility of the fixed rate commitment. This may best be established by replacement of a central bank, having the ability to finance fiscal deficits, with a currency board. Alternatively, an independent central bank committed to the fixed rate (for example, that of Austria), or participation in an international agreement that has established credibility such as the European Monetary System (EMS), may suffice, especially if such agreement is extended as suggested by the Delors Commission report to embody a ceiling on the fiscal deficit that is approved by the European Community (EC). A common currency, of course, will guarantee total credibility.

The only pro-floating argument that remains when all of the above four conditions are satisfied is that an exchange rate change can soften the adjustment to a real shock, but this is of modest importance when the economy is small and open and the domestic price level is flexible (conditions one and three). Difficulties start to arise when not all the conditions are satisfied. For example, should the United Kingdom join a European monetary union (EMU)?[1] The U.K. economy is not particularly small, and it certainly suffers from entrenched cost-inflationary pressures. The key question is whether a commitment to an EMU could be a useful component of a strategy for eradicating inflation (as the commitment to a strong exchange rate, meaning a stable nominal rate against the deutsche mark, appears to have been in Austria, and as the EMS commitment seems to have been in France and Italy). In my opinion, an EMU commitment could also be a useful *component* of such a strategy in the United Kingdom, but the assumption among U.K. pro-EMS circles that membership would *constitute* an adequate strategy strikes me as naive and dangerous.

Are there also circumstances in which I would recommend that a country adopt a floating exchange rate? Fifteen years ago, the answer would have been (unenthusiastically) *yes;* today, in the light of experience with floating rates, the answer is unambiguously *no.* Floating rates have not operated as the models of the 1970s (let alone the 1960s) would lead us to expect, with modest deviations from fundamental equilibrium exchange rates explicable by interest differentials or net external wealth positions and changes largely explained by "news."[2] Instead, misalignments have been huge and certainly damaging. Speculative "bubbles" and fads have been perceived more and more as realistic descriptions rather than as fantasies whose mention merits excommunication from the profession. Now de Grauwe and Vansanten (1990) have shown how a seemingly inoffensive four-equation model of the foreign exchange market can generate "chaotic" behavior of exchange rates, in the chaos theory sense that small changes in initial conditions can make large differences to subsequent trajectories, and these exhibit no tendency to converge to a steady state. Their analysis suggests that the only circumstances under which exchange rates are likely to behave as the models imply is when governments manage them with that end in view[3]—and, indeed, that is what I tend to recommend that they should do.

Hence, for countries that do not satisfy the conditions for having a fixed exchange rate, I recommend a managed rate. That recommendation obviously raises the question as to how a rate should be managed. The discussion of this topic first considers how the target exchange rate should be chosen and then how the rate should be managed to keep it appropriately close to the target.

The Fundamental Equilibrium Exchange Rate

I argued in Williamson (1985) that the appropriate target for the exchange rate was what I termed the "fundamental equilibrium exchange rate." By this I meant the exchange rate consistent with macroeconomic equilibrium—that is, the rate expected to reconcile internal and external balance in the medium term.[4] Internal balance is relatively easily defined as the highest level of activity consistent with the continued control of inflation. External balance is much more difficult to define. At a minimum, it requires that the current account deficit be safely sustainable, rather than at a level likely to lead to a crisis (Krugman 1985). This criterion is, however, unlikely to lead to a unique target. The range may be further narrowed by appeal to an optimality criterion (that current account imbalance that maximizes intertemporal welfare), but it is likely to remain ambiguous nonetheless. The result will be a corresponding range of indeterminacy in the estimate of the fundamental equilibrium exchange rate. (See Williamson 1991 for an extended discussion.)

The method for estimating a fundamental equilibrium exchange rate depends on the country and models available. In the case of the Group of Seven countries, it is necessary to estimate all the exchange rates simultaneously, because feedbacks are sufficiently important to preclude meaningful estimates for one country at a time. The project mentioned above involves solving a series of global macroeconometric models to estimate the (real) exchange rate trajectories implied by the objective of achieving simultaneously a set of current account targets by 1995 (while maintaining internal balance).

For other countries, it is sensible to make such estimates for one country at a time (or, at most, for several closely competing countries at one time). Ideally, we would solve a macroeconometric model of the country in the same way as described in the preceding paragraph for the Group of Seven. Failing such a model, a "back-of-the-envelope" elasticities calculation may be employed. At the most casual level, the question I ask in a developing country is always: what is happening to nontraditional exports? If these are nonexistent, stagnant, or declining, it is prima facie evidence of overvaluation and a medium-term inability to sustain growth without running into balance of payments problems. (I am highly resistant to assertions that the stagnation or decline is unimportant because the price of oil—or copper, or aluminum, or coffee, or whatever the principal staple happens to be—is high, or because the deficit is easily financed by a capital inflow on private account, or that it is irrelevant because there is absolutely nothing nontraditional the country could conceivably export. So far my skepticism has stood me in good stead.) If nontraditional exports are booming without the economy overheating, that is a good omen. If these exports are booming, but at the cost of a hypercompetitive exchange rate that is fueling an accelerating inflation, something is wrong. We need to ask such questions as these: Will a real appreciation still allow sufficient export growth to enable the economy to grow at its supply-side potential without the payments deficit becoming unmanageable? If not, is the real wage being held above a market-clearing level by union power or indexation? Or must the economy be operated at a lower pressure of demand?

Exchange Rate Management

The objective of exchange rate management is to keep the actual exchange rate reasonably close to the target, in order to give the correct price signals to a market economy. How this is best accomplished depends greatly on a country's situation. The simplest case is that of a country with limited financial markets that are effectively insulated against the rest of the world by exchange controls. In this case, the authorities can choose a pair of buying and selling rates against the intervention currency, which is universally the dollar, and the only question is how to change those rates over time. This question is treated in detail below.

As financial markets become more sophisticated, it becomes less likely that exchange controls will permit complete insulation against the rest of the world. Instead, they will guarantee a parallel market with a black market rate that differs from the official rate, typically with the dollar at a premium. Should this be tolerated? Yes,[5] provided the premium is generally small. At the very least, capital controls can provide a useful constraint on the speed of capital flight. Satisfactory operation of a system of capital controls does, however, require that the authorities treat a substantial premium on the black market as an indicator that their policies lack credibility with the private sector. At times they may decide that the cause is some temporary factor that will reverse itself in due course, but unless they can convince themselves—and the International Monetary Fund (IMF)—that this is the case, prudence suggests a policy adjustment. This will typically involve higher domestic interest rates, although it might also suggest some depreciation of the target exchange rate.

In the case of a country with a developed financial system and no capital controls, the exchange rate will be market-determined. The authorities may still operate a fixed-rate system in such a context by posting buying and selling rates suitably close to one another (as in the EMS), or they may allow wide bands with hard or soft margins (as envisaged by the target zone proposal). In both cases, they can manage their exchange rate to any desired degree of accuracy, provided they are prepared to do what is necessary in terms of directing monetary policy to exchange rate management (for example, by means of unsterilized intervention). Conversely, where monetary policy needs to be directed primarily to domestic macroeconomic management (as in the United States, Japan, and collectively in the EMS), it is necessary to accept wide bands.

Whatever the form of management chosen as suitable to a country's situation, the question arises as to how the target rate should be adjusted over time. The objectives that should guide this exercise are (1) to prevent capricious changes in the incentive structure, and (2) to change the incentive structure in response to persistent real shocks that require payments adjustment or evidence that the existing target is incompatible with macroeconomic equilibrium.

The objective of avoiding capricious changes in the incentive structure raises two issues. The first is whether to peg to (or target) a single currency or a basket of currencies. This issue essentially involves a trade-off between micro and macro stability. A basket peg gives macro stability but involves capricious changes in each individual bilateral exchange rate, while a peg to a single currency can stabilize the bilateral rate against that currency but results in capricious changes in the effective exchange rate (the rate that is important for macro stability). In a world where the major currencies float against one another, a choice must be made as to the form of stability to pursue. This issue has already arisen in the discussion of the conditions under which a fixed exchange rate makes sense, where condition two above required that at least half a country's trade be with the prospective peg-currency country (or bloc). I would use a similar threshold in this context—that is, a country should peg to a single currency if at least half of the country's trade is with that peg-currency country (or currency bloc); otherwise, the country should peg to a basket.

A substantial literature developed in the 1970s and early 1980s about the choice of a currency basket to which to peg (for a survey, see Williamson 1982). My impression now is that the choice of a formula for the basket is not really a major issue, and I am comfortable in recommending the use of crude trade weights that are easy to calculate. A more important issue may be whether countries that are close competitors (for example, the East Asian newly industrializing countries) should not peg to a *common* basket, in order to eliminate capricious changes in their mutual competitiveness and to overcome the fear of their competitiveness being eroded if they respond rationally to changes among third currencies.

The second issue raised by the objective of avoiding capricious changes in competitiveness is whether this requires adjustment of the peg or target to offset differential inflation. The argument in favor of doing this—that is, adopting a real exchange rate target—is that it is the real rather than the nominal exchange rate that determines the incentive to export (or import), and it is not desirable to erode that incentive just because domestic inflation is high. Not only is actual erosion bad for nontraditional exports, but *uncertainty* about the future real exchange rate is damaging. The argument against adjustment of the peg or target was first developed at the 1979 conference on the crawling peg (Williamson 1981, especially the Dornbusch paper). It states that such a policy can be macroeconomically destabilizing. An overcompetitive target for the real exchange rate can generate an ever-accelerating inflation, just as can an unemployment target below the natural rate. Jeffrey Sachs claims that it was exactly such a policy, urged by the IMF, that led Yugoslavia into hyperinflation in 1989 (Lipton and Sachs 1990).

As already indicated in the discussion of the case for fixed exchange rates, a crucial question is whether prices are sufficiently flexible to permit a fixed peg without excessive unemployment. Even if they are, I would recommend a fixed nominal rather than a real exchange rate target only if the single currency or the basket can be relied on to remain noninflationary. Otherwise, I recommend a crawling rate appreciation to maintain a target for the real rate and to permit the country in question to achieve price stability. Where the inflation rate has too much momentum to be stopped by an exchange rate commitment (a situation that is fairly common), I recommend a real target even at the cost of a crawling depreciation that ratifies the existing inflation.

I offer two responses to the objection to a fixed real exchange rate target. One response is to urge the necessity of a responsible demand management policy (meaning, above all, fiscal discipline) as a sine qua non for *any* exchange rate regime to operate satisfactorily. The objective of demand management policy can usefully be encapsulated into a target for the growth of nominal income (or, better, of nominal domestic demand) to provide an alternative nominal anchor to the nominal exchange rate (Williamson and Miller 1987), and one that is compatible with a real exchange rate target.

My other response to the objection that a fixed real exchange rate target can destabilize the price level is to accept that the target may need to change at times. This brings us to the second of the conditions that were suggested above to guide the change in the target exchange rate over time. Even if the target is initially set correctly, it will need to change if a permanent real shock creates a need for payments adjustment. (This will also, in general, require a supporting adjustment in fiscal policy.) However, no one can guarantee that the target will always be set correctly. That the target is insufficiently competitive becomes apparent when persistent difficulties arise in maintaining a viable payments position without suppressing growth below its supply-side potential. Similarly, accelerating inflation should raise the question as to whether the target may not be excessively competitive. It is not axiomatic even then that the real exchange rate target should be adjusted. It may be better to tighten fiscal and monetary policy, to modify wage indexation formulas, or to make the labor market more flexible.

Let me add two final observations about my advice in this chapter. The first concerns stepwise versus crawling adjustments in exchange rates. It is not possible to totally rule out stepwise adjustments, any more than we can totally forswear currency reforms; if the inherited situation is sufficiently disastrous, there may be no alternative. I would, however, always urge that policy be based on the premise that *future* stepwise changes are unacceptable, since the expectation that such changes may occur creates private incentives for antisocial behavior and generates crises. In my opinion, the IMF pays far too little attention to investment in governmental credibility, which is an inevitable casualty of stepwise devaluations. I am happy to say that, despite resistance from the IMF, the case for preferring crawling to stepwise adjustments seems to have become quite widely accepted in the quarter of a century since I first argued the point (Williamson 1965).[6]

At the other extreme, my most consistently ignored advice has been that it is desirable to publish details of target zones and the calculation of target exchange rates. Most officials seem to believe that public knowledge of the limits of a target zone would encourage speculation against the zone, rather than provide a focus for stabilizing speculation (as demonstrated by Krugman 1987). This belief may be a cultural lag from the days of the adjustable peg when officials were duty-bound to defend disequilibrium exchange rates rather than medium-term equilibriums, but the lag is proving to be very long.

Implications for Eastern Europe

In Latin America, the conventional wisdom now seems to hold that a temporary fix of the exchange rate can help to establish the price structure when a stabilization plan is introduced, but that the exchange rate should, if necessary, start to be adjusted within six months or so in order to avoid any buildup of expectations of a subsequent jump (van Wijnbergen 1990). This factor may be of great relevance to Eastern Europe, an area that inherited extremely distorted price structures after forty-five years of central planning. In Poland, coal cost some 6 percent of the world price, resulting in the country's becoming an exporter of semitropical flowers (Lipton and Sachs 1990). The most promising way of quickly achieving a price structure capable of providing a rational basis for decentralized decision making was to "import" it, by making the zloty convertible. Given that the world does not exhibit the instantaneous perfect arbitrage that was formerly built into many monetarist models, this process was probably aided by Poland's declaration of a fixed exchange rate (although the dollar was an odd unit in terms of which to fix it).

Perhaps price inertia will prove so much less in Eastern Europe that it will be possible and sensible to maintain a fixed peg indefinitely. Only time will tell. What would be unforgivable would be the unthinking slide into overvaluation that has so often occurred elsewhere. A real exchange rate target has its dangers, but at least it gives time to diagnose that something is amiss and permits the government to take corrective action that does not involve the debilitating act of abandoning what was supposed to be the foundation of macroeconomic stability. My advice to Eastern Europe is to think hard and long before making a commitment to a fixed nominal exchange rate for the indefinite future, even if the commitment is to fix in terms of an appropriate unit, such as the European currency unit (ECU) or a basket of the ECU, dollar, yen, and pound sterling. Credibility is too precious to be squandered.

Notes

1. I pose the question in terms of membership in an EMU, rather than the EMS, because the latter has until now acted as a hybrid between a system of fixed nominal and fixed real exchange rates and, as long as it remains possible to devalue to offset differential inflation, the conditions for U.K. membership to be beneficial are much less demanding.

2. See below or Williamson (1985) for the concept of the fundamental equilibrium exchange rate. See Dornbusch (1976), Kouri (1976), and Frenkel and Mussa (1985) for the main theories of the 1970s, and Meese and Rogoff (1983) for the classic evidence that the models do not explain actual exchange rate behavior.

3. In view of this, it is time for the U.S. Treasury to abandon its pressure on Korea and Taiwan to float—a step that the Treasury seems to treat as a necessary part of growth and development and a sufficient excuse for having a misaligned exchange rate.

4. Edwards (1989a) utilized the same concept, though he labeled it the "equilibrium real exchange rate" (and he prefers to measure it as the relative price of tradable goods rather than the relative price of national outputs). Also see Chapter 9.

5. I would never recommend a system of multiple official rates. To the extent that a government wishes to discriminate among transactions (usually, more than it ought to), this should be done by means of trade taxes.

6. I define a crawl as occurring when the parity change is less than the width of the band, so that there is no forced discontinuity in market rates (as first suggested by Johnson 1970). On that basis, most EMS realignments have involved a crawl.

Comments

Herbert G. Grubel

John Williamson's writings about exchange rate policies have undergone many changes over the years, most of which represent refinements and extensions of technical matters. At the same time there has also been an important and fundamental change in emphasis. In his widely discussed 1985 and 1981 publications, he proposes the adoption of an international system of target zones for the world as a whole. In the present chapter, he merely gives advice to individual governments about the choice of optimal exchange rate systems and policies.

As Williamson knows better than anyone else, his recommendations for the adoption of a new collective, global agreement on international exchange rate management have been rejected by the mainstream economists of his era.[1] The main reason for this position of mainstream economists is practical, but it has strong ideological overtones.

Most economists have emerged from the age of Keynes with a profound distrust of the technical ability of governments to manage exchange rates, and from the age of Musgrave skeptical of their ability to resist the blandishments of political and bureaucratic interest groups. As Corden (1983) noted, the international monetary "non-system"[2] without global collective agreements on exchange rate determination can usefully be seen as an application of free-market principles to the determination of exchange rates by individual nations. Friedman's essay (1953) in favor of flexible exchange rates rests on the basic premise that market-determined rates are inherently more efficient than those determined by bureaucrats. Former U.K. Prime Minister Thatcher's opposition to a European monetary union was founded on her concerns about the politicization of the management of the proposed common currency for the continent—concerns that can readily be found in the writings of Alan Walters.

I welcome Williamson's advice to governments on the management of their exchange rates, even if his recommended reliance on sophisticated econometric models is perhaps somewhat naive, given the performance record of such models. The view that there is a strong presumption in favor of market solutions does not indicate an absence of opportunities for improvements of markets, in particular the totally free float of national currencies. The question of optimum currency areas, first raised by Mundell (1961) and McKinnon (1963), continues to represent a major qualification to the arguments in favor of freely floating rates, and it is raised appropriately by Williamson.[3] I have (Grubel 1973, 1977) used the same arguments on an optimum currency area to make the price-theoretic case for optimum stability of exchange rates through time by smoothing and "leaning against the wind."

Today, however, I view the problem of exchange rate policy differently as part of a more fundamental problem besetting Western democracies. The problem is the lack of institutional restraints on economic legislation by politicians and bureaucrats who are motivated not by public interest but by self-interest. One interesting and important implication of Williamson's recommendations is that they will restrain the freedoms of these agents.

One of the most powerful arguments against the use of target zones made by almost every critic is that such policies cannot succeed unless monetary and fiscal policies within each country are stable and unless the trend of these policies is coordinated internationally. Some critics go so far as to say that if such internal stability and international coordination did exist, exchange rates would be stable and there would be no need for target zones. This argument has the interesting implication that international agreement on, or even the national adoption of, target zones implies that national governments accept severe limitations on the use of monetary and fiscal policies for their narrow self-interests. In other words, an international agreement on exchange rate targets, in principle, constrains politicians in the same manner as a set of rules on monetary growth and constitutional limitations on spending deficits or levels.[4]

Williamson in his own writings does not discuss this implication of his proposals, but I think it deserves further attention. One fundamental problem surrounding it concerns the potential for abuse by exactly the kinds of special interest groups that, in principle, it could restrain. As an example of the issue, consider the future of the European Monetary System (EMS).

On the one hand, the Delors Commission report and the movement toward a European monetary union can be interpreted as evidence that politicians are prepared to accept national monetary discipline through external treaty obligations. If the new central bank of Europe operates according to principles and constitutionally guaranteed freedoms like those of the Deutsche Bundesbank, national politicians will have effectively lost their ability to manipulate monetary policy for their own, narrow ends.

On the other hand, it is also possible that the new central bank of Europe will operate under the same principles as the Bank of England, or even the Bank of France. Under these conditions, a European monetary union will have removed the equivalent of the constitutional anchor that now restrains member countries indirectly through the actions of the Bundesbank. Under these conditions, the winners will be politicians and bureaucrats, particularly those in Brussels. The loser will be the public interest.[5]

Whatever may be the fate of the European monetary union, the same types of alternatives will exist with respect to the use or abuse of exchange rate targets. In my view, Western democracies would be served better if national governments attacked the problems of imperfect knowledge and political competition directly, through appropriate constitutional restraints on economic policy making.

Proper public debate over the formulation and operation of constitutional clauses would be more democratic, and therefore acceptable to the public, than international treaties concluded by technical elites. Such national solutions would maximize the freedom of individual countries to choose according to their national differences and intertemporal changes in the rules; they would be more permanent than the international organizations that are subject to capture; and, technically, they would be efficient through the direct attack on the fundamental problem of democracy. There is no doubt that they would reduce considerably the need for the bureaucratization and politicization of the globe through international organizations and agreements.

Perhaps I am too idealistic in believing that modern Western legislatures are prepared to adopt policies that take away the most useful and powerful tools of their trade. A cynic might argue that the world can move toward more constitutional constraints only through the work of (and agreement among) intellectual and technical elites in international organizations and research institutes. Through international agreements, it might be possible to get national legislatures to pass, in the name of global externalities and technical improvements, restrictions for which a qualified majority could never be attained in national legislatures.

What has just been said about international organizations, of course, also applies to the countries of Eastern Europe. Williamson suggested that these countries should consider the adoption of targets for exchange rate management. I strongly urge them to put into their constitutions clauses assuring the personal and economic liberties of their people. In particular, they should constitutionally protect the property rights of their citizens through limits on the manipulation of the money supply, spending, deficits, taxation, and regulation. Such action would create necessary conditions for economic growth and social development. Stable exchange rates would be a happy and simple by-product of such a system of limits on government activities in the economy.

Notes

1. Suffice it to mention as examples the comments made by Frenkel (1987) and Kenen (1987) at the meeting of the American Economics Association in New Orleans in 1986 and the review article by Marston (1988)

2. According to Corden, the concept of a "non-system" originated with Williamson (1976), who in that publication deplored this state of affairs.

3. During the 1970s, I elicited from Milton Friedman his view on the theory of optimum currency areas by asking him whether he thought that a small country like Guatemala should have freely floating exchange rates. He responded by saying that Guatemala should not have freely floating exchange rates, but that the country should also not have its own currency. Thus, even Friedman acknowledged that the case for freely floating rates is modified by the need to endogenize the geographic domain of national currency regimes.

4. This is not strictly correct, since targets could be chosen to be consistent with large deficits and inflationary monetary policies. However, the design of the targets will (at the very least) make transparent the planned monetary and fiscal policies. In addition, it is likely to be difficult to change the magnitudes of targets and related policies, once they have been agreed upon, so that the system increases the stability of the national macroeconomic environment, at the very least.

5. The establishment of a European monetary union represents a puzzle in terms of the public choice theory, because even if the new central bank has very little independence from the European Commission, or ultimately a European parliament and government, national politicians will still lose one of their traditional instruments of manipulation. Or, perhaps there is no puzzle because experience with the use of the instrument has shown national politicians that their own gains are small and transitory, while the genuine public costs are large? These issues are discussed further in Grubel (1990).

References

Adams, Charles, and Daniel Gros. 1986. "The Consequences of Real Exchange Rate Rules for Inflation: Some Illustrative Examples." *IMF Staff Papers* (September):439–76. Washington, D.C.: International Monetary Fund.

Aganbegyan, Abel. 1988. *The New Stage of Perestroika*, 25–44. New York: Institute for East-West Security Studies.

Aghevli, Bijan B. 1981. "Experience of Asian Countries with Various Exchange Rate Policies." In *Exchange Rate Rules: The Theory, Performance, and Prospects of the Crawling Peg*, edited by John Williamson, 298–318. London: Macmillan.

Aghevli, Bijan B., and Mohsin S. Khan. 1977. "Inflationary Finance and Dynamics of Inflation: Indonesia, 1951–72." *American Economic Review* (June): 390–403.

Aizenman, Joshua. 1986. "On the Complementarity of Commercial Policy, Capital Controls and Inflation Tax." *Canadian Journal of Economics* 19, no. 1:114–33.

Angell, Wayne. 1989. *Monetary Policy in a Centrally Planned Economy: Restructuring toward a Market-Oriented Socialist System*. Moscow: Institute of USA and Canada Studies, September 4.

Anjaria, Shailendra J., Sena Eken, and John F. Laker. 1982. *Payments Arrangements and the Expansion of Trade in Eastern and Southern Africa*. Washington, D.C.: International Monetary Fund (July).

Aslund, Anders. 1989. *Gorbachev's Struggle for Economic Reform*. Ithaca, N.Y.: Cornell University Press.

Auerbach, S. 1990. "Soviets Say CIA Picture of Economy Was Too Rosy." *Washington Post*. Reprinted in *The Gazette*, April 24.

409

Auernheimer, Leonardo. 1974. "The Honest Government's Guide to the Revenue from Creation of Money." *Journal of Political Economy* 82:598–606.

Ausch, Sandor. 1972. *Theory and Practice of CMEA Cooperation*. Budapest: Akademiai Kiado.

Balassa, B. 1984. "Adjustment Policies in Developing Countries: A Reassessment." *World Development* 12, no. 9 (September):955–72.

Balassa, B., and John Williamson. 1989. *Adjusting to Success: Balance of Payments Policy in the East Asian NICs*. Washington, D.C.: Institute for International Economics.

Barro, Robert J., and David B. Gordon. 1983. "Rules, Discretion, and Reputation in a Model of Monetary Policy." *Journal of Monetary Economics* (July): 101–21.

Bernstein, Edward M., et al. 1976. *Reflections on Jamaica*. Essays in International Finance (April). Princeton, N.J.: Princeton University Press.

Bevan, D., P. Collier, and J. Gunning. 1990. "Indonesia and Nigeria." In *The Political Economy of Poverty, Equity, and Growth*, edited by D. Lal and H. Myint. Oxford: Oxford University Press. Forthcoming.

Beveridge, S., and C. R. Nelson. 1981. "A New Approach to Decomposition of Economic Time Series into Permanent and Transitory Components." *Journal of Monetary Economics*, no. 7:151–74.

Bhagwati, J. N. 1974a. ed. *Illegal Transactions in International Trade: Theory and Measurement*. Amsterdam: North-Holland.

———. 1974b. "Fiscal Policies, the Faking of Foreign Trade Declarations, and the Balance of Payments." In *Illegal Transactions in International Trade*, edited by J. N. Bhagwati, vol.1:66–83. Amsterdam: North-Holland.

———. 1981. "Alternative Theories of Illegal Trade: Economic Consequences and Statistical Detection." *Weltwirtschaftliches Archiv* 117:409–27.

Birman, I. 1981. *Secret Incomes of the Soviet State Budget*. The Hague: Martinus Nijhoff Publishers.

Black, Stanley W. 1976. "Exchange Rate Policies for Less Developed Countries in a World of Floating Rates." Essays in International Finance no. 119. Princeton, N.J.: Princeton University Press.

Blanchard, Olivier, and Stanley Fischer. 1989. *Lectures on Macroeconomics*. Cambridge, Mass.: MIT Press.

Blejer, Mario I., and Adrienne Cheasty. 1988. "High Inflation, Heterodox Stabilization, and Fiscal Policy." *World Development* 16, no. 8:867–81.

Blejer, Mario I., and Gyorgy Szapary. 1989. "The Evolving Role of Fiscal Policy in Centrally Planned Economies under Reform: The Case of China." IMF Working Paper 0407 (March 31). Washington, D.C.: International Monetary Fund.

Bofinger, Peter. 1990. "A Multilateral Payments Union for Eastern Europe?" Discussion paper no. 458, Centre for Economic Research, London.

Branson, William H., and Louka T. Katseli-Papaefstratiou. 1981. "Exchange Rate Policy in Developing Countries." In *The World Economic Order: Past and Prospects*, edited by S. Grassman and E. Lundberg, 391–419. London: Macmillan.

Brenner, R. 1985. *Betting on Ideas: Wars, Invention, Inflation*. Chicago: University of Chicago Press.

_____. 1987. *Rivalry: In Business, Science, among Nations*. Cambridge: Cambridge University Press.

_____. 1989. "Don't Frighten the East Bloc Bureaucrats." *Wall Street Journal*, December 26.

_____. 1990a. "The Long Road from Serfdom and How to Shorten It." *Canadian Business Law Review* 14, no. 2 (December):195–226.

_____. 1990b. "Debts, Deficits and the Government's Expenditures." *Revista Economica*. Also in *Fiscal Policy*, edited by J. McCallum and R. Mundell. Montreal: McGill University Press.

_____. 1990c. "Numbers out of a Hat." Mimeo.

Brenner, R., and G. A. Brenner. 1990. *Gambling and Speculation*. Cambridge: Cambridge University Press.

Brock, Philip. 1989. "Reserve Requirement and the Inflation Tax." *Journal of Money, Credit and Banking* 21 (February).

Bruno, Michael, and Stanley Fischer. 1987. "Seigniorage, Operating Rules and the High Inflation Trap." NBER Working Paper, no. 2413 (October). Cambridge, Mass.: National Bureau of Economic Research.

Buiter, Willem. 1986. "Fiscal Prerequisites for a Viable Managed Exchange Rate Regime: A Non-Technical Eclectic Introduction." NBER Working Paper no. 2041 (October). Cambridge, Mass.: National Bureau of Economic Research.

Bush, K. 1990. "Soviet's Credit Rating Slips." *Wall Street Journal*, March 12.

Cagan, Phillip. 1956. "The Monetary Dynamics of Hyperinflation." In *Studies in the Quantity Theory of Money*, edited by Milton Friedman. Chicago: University of Chicago Press.

Calvo, G. 1986. "Factured Liberalism: Argentina under Martinez de Hoz." *Economic Development and Cultural Change* 34:522–34.

Calvo, G., and Roque B. Fernández. 1983. "Competitive Banks and the Inflation Tax." *Economics Letters* 12.

Calvo, G., and Carlos Alfredo Rodriguez. 1977. "A Model of Exchange Rate Determination under Currency Substitution and Rational Expectations." *Journal of Political Economy* 85:617–25.

Calvo, G., and Carlos Vegh. 1990. "Interest Rate Policy in a Staggered-Prices Model." Washington, D.C.: International Monetary Fund. Mimeo.

Canavese, A. J., and G. Di Tella. 1988. "Inflation Stabilization or Hyperinflation Avoidance? The Case of the Austral Plan in Argentina: 1985–87." In *Inflation Stabilization*, edited by M. Bruno, G. Di Tella, R. Dornbusch, and S. Fisher. Cambridge, Mass.: MIT Press.

Collier, I. L., Jr., and D. H. Papell. 1988. "About Two Marks: Refugees and the Exchange Rate before the Berlin Wall." *American Economic Review* (June):531–42.

Corbo, V., and J. de Melo. 1987. "Lessons from the Southern Cone Policy Reforms." *World Bank Research Observer* 2:111–42.

Corden, W. M. 1983. "The Logic of the International Monetary Non-System." In

Reflections on a Troubled World Economy, Essays in Honor of Herbert Giersch, edited by F. Machlup, G. Fels, and H. Mueller-Groeling. London: Macmillan.

Corden, Max, and J. Peter Neary. 1982. "Booming Sector and De-Industrialization in a Small Open Economy." *Economic Journal* (December):825–48.

Cottani, J., and R. García. 1989. "The Determinants of the Real Exchange Rate in Argentina, 1976–1985." Buenos Aires: Fundación Mediterránea.

Cuddington, J. T., and C. M. Urzua. 1989. "Trends and Cycles in Colombia's Real GDP and Fiscal Deficit." *Journal of Development Economics* 30, no. 2 (April):325–43.

de Grauwe, Paul. 1984. "Political Union and Monetary Union." In *Currency Competition and Monetary Union*, edited by Pascal Salin, 260–62. The Hague: Martinus Nijhoff Publishers.

de Grauwe, Paul, and Kris Vansanten. 1990. "Deterministic Chaos in the Foreign Exchange Market." CEPR Discussion Paper no. 370. London: Centre for Economic Policy Research.

de la Cuadra, S. 1981. "Política Cambiaria y Deuda Externa." *Boletín Económico del Banco Central de Chile*. Santiago: Banco Central de Chile.

de Macedo, Jorge B. 1986. "Trade and Financial Interdependence under Flexible Exchange Rates: The Pacific Area." In *Pacific Growth and Financial Interdependence*, edited by Augustine H. H. Tan and Basant Kapur, 227–91. Sydney: Allen and Unwin.

de Soto, H. 1989. *The Other Path*. New York: Harper and Row.

Deardorff, A. V., and W. F. Stolper. 1990. "Effects on Smuggling under African Conditions: A Factual, Institutional and Analytical Discussion." *Weltwirtschaftliches Archiv* 126:117–41.

Desai, P. 1989. "Perestroika, Prices, and the Ruble Problem." *The Harriman Institute Forum* 2, no. 11 (November).

———. 1990. "Perestroika: Is It on Track?" Department of Economics, Columbia University, New York, N.Y. Mimeo.

Deutsches Institut für Wirtschaftsforschung. 1990. *Wochenbericht* (April 12).

Diaz-Alejandro, Carlos. 1970. *Essays on the Economic History of the Argentine Republic*. New Haven, Conn.: Yale University Press.

———. 1976. *Foreign Trade Regimes and Economic Development*. New York: Columbia University Press.

———. 1982. "Exchange Rates and the Terms of Trade in the Argentine Republic, 1913–1976." In *Trade, Stability, Technology and Equity in Latin America*, edited by M. Syrquin and S. Teitel. New York: Academic Press.

Dobbs, M. 1990. "Gorbachev to Speed up Economic Reform." *Washington Post*. Reprinted in *The Gazette* (Montreal), A9, April 11.

Dornbusch, R. 1974. "Tariffs and Nontraded Goods." *Journal of International Economics* 4:177–85.

———. 1976. "Expectations and Exchange Rate Dynamics." *Journal of Political Economy* (December).

———. 1982. "PPP Exchange Rate Rules and Macroeconomic Stability." *Journal of Political Economy* 90, no. 1 (February):158–65.

_____. 1983. "Remarks on the Southern Cone." *IMF Staff Papers* (March). Washington, D.C.: International Monetary Fund.

_____. 1985. "Multiple Exchange Rates for Commercial Transaction." CPD Discussion Paper 1985-23. Washington, D.C.: World Bank.

_____. 1986. "Special Exchange Rates for Capital Account Transaction." *World Bank Economic Review* 1, no. 1:3-33.

_____. 1987. "Lessons from the German Inflation Experience of the 1920s." In *Macroeconomics and Finance: Essays in Honor of Franco Modigliani,* edited by R. Dornbusch and S. Fischer. Cambridge, Mass.: MIT Press.

_____. 1988. "Real Exchange Rates and Macroeconomics: A Selective Survey." NBER Working Paper no. 2775 (November). Cambridge, Mass: National Bureau of Economic Research.

Dornbusch, R., D. V. Dantas, C. Pechman, R. Rocha, and D. Simoes. 1983. "The Black Market for Dollars in Brazil." *Quarterly Journal of Economics* 98, no. 1:25-40.

Dornbusch, R., and J. de Pablo. 1989. "Debt and Macroeconomic Instability in Argentina." In *The Developing Countries' Debt Crisis,* edited by J. Sachs. Chicago: University of Chicago Press.

Dornbusch, R., and Stanley Fischer. 1986. "Stopping Hyperinflations Past and Present." *Weltwirtschaftliches Archiv* (February).

Drazen, Allan, and Elhanan Helpman. 1989. "Inflationary Consequences of Anticipated Macroeconomic Policies." *Quarterly Journal of Economics* 102, no. 4 (November).

Economic Commission for Europe. 1990. *Economic Survey of Europe 1989-1990.* New York: United Nations.

Edwards, S. 1985. "Real Exchange Rate Misalignment in Developing Countries: Analytical Issues and Empirical Evidence." CPD Discussion Paper 1985-43. Washington, D.C.: World Bank.

_____. 1986a. "Are Devaluations Contractionary?" *Review of Economics and Statistics* (August):501-508.

_____. 1986b. "Commodity Export Prices and the Real Exchange Rate: Coffee in Colombia." In *Economic Adjustment and Exchange Rates in Developing Countries,* edited by S. Edwards and L. Ahamed. Chicago: University of Chicago Press.

_____. 1986c. "Monetarism in Chile: 1973-1983: Some Economic Puzzles." *Economic Development and Cultural Change* 34:535-60.

_____. 1988a. "Exchange Rate Misalignments in Developing Countries." World Bank Occasional Papers, New Series, no. 2. Baltimore, Md.: Johns Hopkins.

_____. 1988b. "Real and Monetary Determinants of Real Exchange Rate Behavior: Theory and Evidence from Developing Countries." *Journal of Development Economics* 29:311-41.

_____. 1989a. *Real Exchange Rates, Devaluation and Adjustment: Exchange Rate Policy in Developing Countries.* Cambridge, Mass.: MIT Press.

_____. 1989b. "Macroeconomic Environment and Trade Policy." UCLA Working Paper. Los Angeles, Calif.: University of California.

_____. 1989c. "Real Exchange Rates in Developing Countries: Concepts and

Measurements." NBER Working Paper no. 2950. Cambridge, Mass.: National Bureau of Economic Research.

Edwards, S., and A. Cox-Edwards. 1987. *Monetarism and Liberalization: The Chilean Experience*. Cambridge, Mass.: Ballinger.

Edwards, S., and S. van Wijnbergen. 1987. "Tariffs, the Real Exchange Rate and the Terms of Trade: Two Popular Propositions in International Economics." *Oxford Economic Papers* 39, no. 3 (September):458–64.

Emminger, Ottmar. 1976. "Deutsche Geld- und Währungspolitik im Spannungsfeld zwischen innerem und äusserem Gleichgewicht (1948–1975)." In *Währung und Wirtschaft in Deutschland 1876–1975* by Deutsche Bundesbank, 485–554.

Englebrekt, Kjell. 1990. "Agreement with the USSR on Step-by-Step Transition to Hard Currency Trade." Radio Free Europe, Report on Eastern Europe, May 13.

Favaro, E., and P. Spiller. 1989. "The Determinants of the Real Exchange Rate in Post-War Uruguay." Washington, D.C.: World Bank.

Feldstein, Martin. 1988. *International Cooperation*. Chicago: University of Chicago Press.

Fernández, Roque B. 1985. "The Expectation Management Approach to Stabilization in Argentina during 1976–1982." *World Development* 13, no. 8:871–92.

———. 1990a. "What Have Populists Learned from Hyperinflation?" IMF, Fiscal Affairs Department. Washington, D.C.: International Monetary Fund. Mimeo.

———. 1990b. "Real Interest Rate and the Dynamics of Hyperinflation." IMF Research Department. Washington, D.C.: International Monetary Fund. Mimeo.

Fernández, Roque B., and Rolf Mantel. 1988. "Fiscal Lags and the Problem of Stabilization: Argentina's Austral Plan." In *Latin American Debt and Adjustment*, edited by P. Brock, M. Conolly, and C. González. Praeger Publishers.

Fischer, Stanley. 1976. "Stability and Exchange Rate System in a Monetarist Model of the Balance of Payments." In *The Political Economy of Monetary Reform*, edited by R.Z. Aliber, 59–73. Montclair, N.J.: Allanhel, Osmum and Co.

———. 1986. "Economic Growth and Economic Policy." In *Growth-Oriented Adjustment Programs*, edited by V. Corbo, M. Goldstein, and M. Khan, 151–78. Washington, D.C.: International Monetary Fund and World Bank.

Flanders, M. June, and Elhanan Helpman. 1978. "On Exchange Rate Policies for a Small Country." *Economic Journal* 46 (March):44–58.

Frankel, Jeffrey A. 1989. "And Now Won/Dollar Negotiations? Lessons from Yen/Dollar Agreement of 1984." In *Korea's Macroeconomic and Financial Policies*, Korea Development Institute (December):109–29.

Frenkel, J. 1987. "The International Monetary System: Should It Be Reformed?" *American Economic Review Papers and Proceedings* (May).

Frenkel, Jacob A., and Joshua Aizenmann. 1982. "Aspects of the Optimal Management of Exchange Rates." *Journal of International Economics* 13, no. 3/4 (November):231–56.

Frenkel, J., and Morris Goldstein. 1988. "The International Monetary System:

Developments and Prospects." NBER Working Paper no. 2648 (July). Cambridge, Mass.: National Bureau of Economic Research.

Frenkel, J., and M. Mussa. 1985. "Asset Markets, Exchange Rates and the Balance of Payments." In *Handbook of International Economics*, Vol. 2, edited by R. W. Jones and P. B. Kenen. Amsterdam: North Holland.

Friedman, Milton. 1953. "The Case for Flexible Exchange Rates." In *Essays in Positive Economics*, edited by M. Friedman. Chicago: University of Chicago Press.

García-García, J. 1989. "Exchange Rate Determinants and Exchange Rate Policy in Colombia." Unpublished paper. Bogotá, Colombia.

Giavazzi, F., and Alberto Giovannini. 1988. "Can the European Monetary System Be Copied outside Europe? Lessons from Ten Years of Monetary Policy Coordination in Europe." NBER Working Paper no. 2786 (December). Cambridge, Mass.: National Bureau of Economic Research.

Giavazzi, F., and Marco Pagano. 1986. "The Advantage of Tying One's Hands: EMS Discipline and Central Bank Credibility." Discussion Paper no. 135 (October). London: Centre for Economic Policy.

Giersch, Herbert. 1984. "Real Exchange Rates and Economic Development." Kiel Working Paper no. 218 (November).

_____. 1990. *The Consequences of European Unification 1992*. Proceedings of the 1989 Kiel Conference. Tübingen: Mohr.

Gigot, Paul A. 1990. "Gorbo Goes out of Fashion in Washington." *Wall Street Journal*, April 12.

Goldman, M. I. 1990. "Gorbachev's Other Crisis." *New York Times*, April 22.

Gomulka, Stanislaw. 1990. "Reform and Budgetary Policy in Poland, 1989–1990." Paper presented at the meeting of the European Economic Community Panel on Poland and Hungary, Brussels, February 6. Mimeo.

Grossman, Gregory. 1989. "Monetary and Financial Aspects of Gorbachev's Reform." In *Financial Reform in Socialist Economies*, edited by C. Kessides, T. King, M. Nuti, and C. Sokil. Washington, D.C.: World Bank.

_____. 1990. "Problems of Monetary Reform." Hoover-Rand Symposium, Rand Corporation, Santa Monica, Calif., March 29–30.

Grubel, Herbert. 1973. "The Case of Optimum Exchange Rate Stability." *Weltwirtschaftliches Archiv* 109, no. 3.

_____. 1977. "How Important Is Control over International Reserves?" In *The New International Monetary System*, edited by R. Mundell and J. Polak. New York: Columbia University Press.

_____. 1990. "Some Thoughts on the Future of the European Monetary Union: Comment on a Paper by Niels Thygesen." In *The Consequences of European Unification 1992*, edited by H. Giersch. Proceedings of the 1989 Kiel Conference. Tübingen: Mohr.

Gruen, F. H., and W. M. Corden. 1970. "A Tariff That Worsens the Terms of Trade." In *Studies in International Economics: Monash Conference Papers*, edited by I. A. McDougall and R. H. Snape, 55–58. Amsterdam: North-Holland.

Guglielmi, J. L., and Marie Lavigne. 1978. *Unités et Monnaies de Compte*. Paris: Economica.

Guillaumont, Patrick and Sylvianne. 1984. *Zone Franc et Développement Africain.* Paris: Economica.

Gumbel, P. 1990. "Soviets May Gain in Comecon Overhaul." *Wall Street Journal,* January 27.

Hachette, D. 1989. "The Opening of the Capital Account, the Case of Chile: 1974–1982." Catholic University of Chile, Santiago.

Halevi, N. 1989. "Trade Liberalization in Adjustment Lending." Hebrew University, Jerusalem.

Haque, Nadeem, Peter Montiel, and Steven Symanski. 1990. "A Forward-Looking Macoeconomic Stimulation for a Developing Country." *Journal of Policy Modeling* 13, no. 1:41–65.

Harberger, A. 1985. "Observations on the Chilean Economy." *Economic Development and Cultural Change* 33, no. 3 (April): 451–62.

_____. 1987. "A Primer on Inflation." *Journal of Money Credit and Banking* 10, no. 4 (November):505–21.

Harris, J. R., and M. P. Todaro. 1970. "Migration, Unemployment and Development: A Two-Sector Analysis." *American Economic Review* (March):126–42.

Heymann, D. 1990. "From Sharp Disinflation to Hyper and Back: The Argentine Experience, 1985–1989." Paper presented at the conference on Lessons of Economic Stabilization and Its Aftermath, organized by the Bank of Israel and the Inter-American Development Bank. Mimeo.

Hewett, Ed. 1988. *Reforming the Soviet Economy.* Washington, D.C.: Brookings Institution.

Hinds, Manuel. 1990. "Issues in the Introduction of Market Forces in East European Socialist Economies." Internal Discussion Paper 0057 (April). Washington, D.C.: World Bank.

Hopkins, J. 1988. "Real and Monetary Determinants of Real Exchange Rate Behaviour: Theory and Evidence from Developing Countries." *Journal of Development Economics* 29, no. 3 (November): 311–41.

Il'in, O. 1990. "The Means of Restructuring the Mechanism of Economic Integration of the CMEA Member Countries." *Planovoe Khoziaistvo,* no. 2:105–10.

Ishiyama, Yoshihide. 1975. "The Theory of Optimum Currency Areas: A Survey." *IMF Staff Papers* 22 (July):344–83. Washington, D.C.: International Monetary Fund.

Jackson, Marvin, and Barbara Donovan. 1990. "Economic Issues Raised by German Unification." Radio Free Europe, Report on Eastern Europe, May 11.

Johnson, G. G., et al. 1985. "Formulation of Exchange Rate Policies in Adjustment Programs." IMF Occasional Paper, no. 36. Washington, D.C.: International Monetary Fund.

Johnson, Harry G. 1970. "A Technical Note on the Width of Band Required to Accommodate Parity Changes of Particular Size." In *Approaches to Greater Flexibility of Exchange Rates: The Buergenstock Papers,* edited by C. Fred Bergsten, George N. Halm, Fritz Machlup, and Robert V. Roosa. Princeton: N.J.: Princeton University Press.

Kafka, Alexandre. 1969. "Regional Monetary Integration of the Developing Countries." In *Monetary Problems of the International Economy,* edited by Robert

Mundell and Alexander K. Swoboda, 135–43. Chicago: University of Chicago Press.

Kenen, Peter. 1969. "The Theory of Optimum Currency Areas: An Eclectic View." In *Monetary Problems of the International Economy*, edited by Robert Mundell and Alexander K. Swoboda, 41–60. Chicago: University of Chicago Press.

_____. 1987. "Exchange Rate Management: What Role for Intervention?" American Economic Review, Papers and Proceedings (May).

_____. 1990. "Transitional Arrangements for Trade and Payments among the CMEA Countries." IMF Working Paper (September). Washington, D.C.: International Monetary Fund.

Khan, Moshin S., and Peter Montiel. 1987. "Real Exchange Rate Dynamics in a Small Primary-Exporting Country." *IMF Staff Papers* (December). Washington, D.C.: International Monetary Fund.

Kharas, H., and B. Pinto. 1989. "Exchange Rate Rules, Black Market Premia and Fiscal Deficits: The Bolivian Hyperinflation." *Review of Economic Studies* 56: 435–48.

Kiguel, M. A., and N. Leviatan. 1990. "The Inflation Stabilization Cycles in Argentina and Brazil." Paper presented at the conference on Lessons of Economic Stabilization and Its Aftermath, organized by the Bank of Israel and the Inter-American Development Bank. Mimeo.

Kornai, Janos. 1980. *Economics of Shortage*. Vols. 1 and 2. The Hague: North-Holland.

_____. 1982. *Growth: Shortage and Efficiency*. Oxford: Basil-Blackwell.

_____. 1986a. *Contradictions and Dilemmas: Studies on the Socialist Economy and Society*. Cambridge, Mass.: MIT Press.

_____. 1986b. "The Hungarian Reform Process: Visions, Hopes, and Reality." *Journal of Economic Literature* (December).

_____. 1990. *The Road to a Free Economy*. New York: W. W. Norton.

Kouri, Pentti J. K. 1976. "The Exchange Rate and the Balance of Payments in the Short Run and in the Long Run: A Monetary Approach." *Scandinavian Journal of Economics*, no. 2.

Krueger, A. O. 1977. *Growth, Distortions and Patterns of Trade among Many Countries*. Princeton Studies on International Finance no. 40. Princeton, N.J.: Princeton University Press.

Krugman, P. 1979. "A Model of Balance of Payments Crisis." *Journal of Money, Credit and Banking* (August):311–25.

_____. 1985. "Is the Strong Dollar Sustainable?" In *The US Dollar: Prospects and Policy Options*. Kansas City: Federal Reserve Bank of Kansas City.

_____. 1987. "The Bias in the Band: Exchange Rate Expectations under a Broad-Band Exchange Rate Regime." Paper presented at a conference on the European monetary system, NBER Working Paper. Cambridge, Mass.: National Bureau of Economic Research.

Lal, D. 1980. "A Liberal International Economic Order: The International Monetary System and Economic Development." Princeton Essays on International Finance no. 139 (October). Princeton, N.J.: Princeton University Press.

_____. 1984. "The Real Aspects of Stabilization and Structural Adjustment Policies: An Extension of the Australian Adjustment Model." World Bank Staff Working Paper no. 636. Washington, D.C.: World Bank.

_____. 1985. "The Real Exchange Rate, Capital Inflows and Inflation: Sri Lanka, 1970–1982." Weltwirtschaftliches Archiv 121, no. 4:682–702.

_____. 1986. "Stolper-Samuelson-Rybczynski in the Pacific—Real Wage and Real Exchange Rates in the Philippines, 1956–1978." Journal of Development Economics 21, no. 1 (April).

_____. 1987. "The Political Economy of Economic Liberalization." World Bank Economic Review 1, no. 2. (January). Washington, D.C.: World Bank.

_____. 1989a. "After the Debt Crisis: Modes of Development for the Longer Run in Latin America." In Debt, Adjustment and Recovery, edited by S. Edwards and F. Larraine. Oxford: Basil Blackwell.

_____. 1989b. "A Simple Framework for Analyzing Real Aspects of Stabilization and Structural Adjustment Policies." Journal of Development Studies (April).

Lal, D., and Martin Wolf, eds. 1986. Stagflation, Savings and the State. New York: Oxford University Press.

Lavigne, Marie. 1989. "Prospects for Soviet Foreign Trade Reform." In Gorbachev's Agenda: Changes in Soviet Domestic and Foreign Policy, edited by Susan L. Clark, 129–60. Boulder, Colo.: Westview Press.

Leamer, E. 1987. "Patterns of Development in the Three-Factor n-Goods General Equilibrium Model." Journal of Political Economy 95, no. 5 (October).

Lehment, Harmen. 1984. "Freely Flexible Exchange Rates or a Common Currency." In Currency Competition and Monetary Union, edited by Pascal Salin, 247–60. The Hague: Martinus Nijhoff Publishers.

Lipton, David, and Jeffrey Sachs. 1990. "Creating a Market Economy in Eastern Europe: The Case of Poland." Brookings Papers on Economic Activity 2 (Fall). Washington, D.C.: Brookings Institution.

Litwack, John. 1991. "Discretionary Behavior and Soviet Economic Reform." Soviet Studies, Stanford University, Stanford, Calif. (March).

Lizondo, J. Saul. 1987a. "Exchange Rate Differential and Balance of Payments under Dual Exchange Markets." Journal of Development Economics 26:37–53.

_____. 1987b. "Unification of Dual Exchange Markets." Journal of International Economics 22:57–77.

_____. 1989. "Real Exchange Rate Targets, Nominal Exchange Rate Policies and Inflation." Unpublished paper, University of Tucumán, Tucumán, Argentina.

Lizondo, J. Saul, and Peter Montiel. 1989a. "Contractionary Devaluation in Developing Countries: An Analytical Overview." IMF Staff Papers (March):182–227. Washington, D.C.: International Monetary Fund.

_____. 1989b. "Dynamics of Devaluation and 'Equivalent' Fiscal Policies for a Small Country with Optimizing Agents." Washington, D.C.: International Monetary Fund. Unpublished paper (August).

Machinea, J. L., and J. M. Fanelli. 1988. "Stopping Hyperinflation: The Case of the Austral Plan in Argentina, 1985–87." In Inflation Stabilization, edited by

M. Bruno, G. Di Tella, R. Dornbusch, and S. Fisher. Cambridge, Mass.: MIT Press.

Machlup, Fritz, Gerhard Fels, and Hubertus Mueller-Groeling. 1983. *Reflections on a Troubled World Economy*. London: Macmillan.

Maddison, Angus. 1989. *The World Economy in the 20th Century*. OECD Development Centre Studies. Paris: Organization for Economic Cooperation and Development.

Manuelli, Rodolfo, and Thomas Sargent. 1987. *Exercises in Dynamic Macroeconomic Theory*. Cambridge, Mass.: Harvard University Press.

Marston, Richard. 1988. "Exchange Rate Coordination." In *International Cooperation*, edited by M. Feldstein. Chicago: University of Chicago Press.

Mathieson, Donald J. 1988. "Exchange Rate Arrangements and Monetary Policy." In *Monetary Policy in Pacific Basin Countries*, edited by Hang Sheng Cheng, 43–80. Boston: Kluwer Academic Publishers.

Mayer, T., and G. Thumann. 1990. "Radical Currency Reform: Germany, 1948." *Finance and Development* (March).

McKinnon, R. 1963. "Optimal Currency Areas." *American Economic Review* 53 (September):717–25.

_____. 1973. *Money and Capital in Economic Development*. Washington, D.C.: Brookings Institution.

_____. 1982. "The Order of Economic Liberalization: Lessons from Chile and Argentina." In *Economic Policy in a World of Change*, edited by K. Brunner and A. Meltzer. Amsterdam: North-Holland.

_____. 1989. "The Order of Liberalization for Opening the Soviet Economy." Prepared for the International Task Force on Foreign Economic Relations (April). Unpublished paper.

_____. 1990. "Stabilizing the Ruble." *Communist Economies* (June).

_____. 1991. *The Order of Economic Liberalization: Financial Control in the Transition to a Market Economy*. Baltimore: Johns Hopkins University Press.

Meese, Richard, and Kenneth Rogoff. 1983. "Empirical Exchange Rate Models of the 1970s: Do They Fit out of Sample?" *Journal of International Economics* (February).

Metzler, L. A. 1979. "The Colm-Dodge-Goldsmith Plan (1946), Appendix N: Considerations regarding the Foreign Exchange Rate for the Deutsche Mark." *Zeitschrift für die Gesamte Staatswissenschaft* (September).

Michaely, M. 1991. "The Lessons of Experience: An Overview." In *Trade Reform*, edited by G. Shepherd and C. Langoni. San Francisco: ICS Press.

Milanovic, B. 1990. *Liberalization: The Political Economy of Reform*. New York: M.E. Sharpe.

Moeller, H. 1976. "Die Westdeutsche Währungsreform von 1948." In Deutsche Bundesbank, *Währung und Wirtschaft in Deutschland 1876–1975*. Frankfurt am Main: Knapp.

Morande, F. 1988. "Domestic Currency Appreciation and Foreign Capital Inflows: What Comes First?: Chile 1977–1982." *Journal of International Money and Finance* (December).

Morgenstern, O. 1965. *On the Accuracy of Economic Observations.* Princeton, N.J.: Princeton University Press.

Mundell, R. 1961. "A Theory of Optimal Currency Areas." *American Economic Review* 51 (September):657–65

———. 1962. "The Appropriate Use of Monetary and Fiscal Policy for Internal and External Stability." *International Monetary Fund Staff Papers* 9:70–77.

———. 1990. "The Global Adjustment Problem." *Rivista di Politica Economica* (March).

Mundell, R., and Jacques Polak. 1977. *The New International Monetary System.* New York: Columbia University Press.

Mussa, Michael. 1986. "Nominal Exchange Rate Regimes and the Behavior of Real Exchange Rate: Evidence and Implications." Carnegie-Rochester Conference Series on Public Policy, Real Business Cycles, Real Exchange Rates and Actual Policies, vol. 25:117–213.

Neary, J. P. 1988. "Determinants of the Equilibrium Real Exchange Rate." *American Economic Review* (March):210–15.

Neary, J. P., and S. van Wijnbergen. 1986. *Natural Resources and the Macroeconomy.* Oxford: Basil Blackwell for Centre for Economic Policy Research.

Nelson, C.R., and C. I. Plosser. 1982. "Trends and Random Walks in Macroeconomic Time Series." *Journal of Monetary Economics* 8:129–62.

Nowak, M. 1984. "Quantitative Controls and Unofficial Markets in Foreign Exchange." *IMF Staff Papers* 31 (June):404–31. Washington, D.C.: International Monetary Fund.

Nuti, D. M. 1990. *Internal and International Aspects of Monetary Disequilibrium in Poland.* Paper presented at the meeting of the Working Group on Aid Programs for Hungary and Poland, Brussels, February 6. Mimeo.

Obstfeld, M. 1984. "Balance of Payments Crises and Devaluation." *Journal of Money, Credit and Banking* (May):208–17.

———. 1986. "Capital Controls, the Dual Exchange Rate and Devaluation." *Journal of International Economics* (February).

Obstfeld, Maurice, and Kenneth Rogoff. 1983. "Speculative Hyperinflations in Maximizing Models: Can We Rule Them Out?" *Journal of Political Economy* 91:675–87.

———. 1986. "Ruling Out Divergent Speculative Bubbles." *Journal of Monetary Economics* 17:349–62.

O'Hearn, D. 1980. "The Consumer Second Economy: Size and Effects." *Soviet Studies,* no. 2 (Summer):218–314.

Okolicsanyi, Karoly. 1990. "Exports to the Soviet Union Cut Back." Radio Free Europe, Report on Eastern Europe, May 18.

Olivera, Julio. 1967. "Money, Prices and Fiscal Lags: A Note on the Dynamics of Inflation." *Banca Nazionale del Lavoro Quarterly Review* (September):258–67.

Palankai, Tibor. 1990. *Integration of Central and Eastern Europe into European Economy with Special Emphasis on EC-Hungarian Relations.* New York: Institute for East-West Security Studies.

Park, Won-Am. 1987. "Crawling Peg, Inflation Hedges, and Exchange Rate Dynamics." *Journal of International Economics* 23:131–50.

Park, Yung Chul, and Won-Am Park. 1990. "Changing Japanese Trade Patterns and the East Asian NICs." Korea Development Institute Working Paper no. 9003. Also in *The U.S. and Japan: Has the Door Opened Wider?* edited by Paul Krugman. Chicago: University of Chicago Press (forthcoming).

Parks, Michael. 1990. "Gorbachev Slows Down Pace of Change: Conservatives See Risk of Upheaval If Reforms Go Ahead." *Los Angeles Times*. Reprinted in *The Gazette*, April 24.

Pecsi, Kalman. 1989. "Rendre la Coopération Economique plus Performante." *Socialisme: Théorie et Pratique*, no. 9.

Pfleiderer, O. 1976. "Die Reichsmark in der Zeit der grossen Inflation, die Stabilisierung der Mark und die Aufwertung von Kapitalforderungen." In Deutsche Bundesbank, *Währung und Wirtschaft in Deutschland 1876–1975*. Frankfurt am Main: Knapp.

Pinto, B. 1986. "Fiscal Deficits, Inflation and Parallel Exchange Markets in Ghana: Monetarism in the Tropics?" CPD Discussion Paper 1986–57. Washington, D.C.: World Bank.

_____. 1987a. "Exchange Rate Unification and Budgetary Policy in Sub-Saharan Africa." Washington, D.C.: World Bank. Mimeo.

_____. 1987b. "Nigeria during and after the Oil Boom: A Policy Comparison with Indonesia." *World Bank Economic Review* 1, no. 3:419–45.

_____. 1989. "Black Market Premia, Exchange Rate Unification and Inflation in Sub-Saharan Africa." *World Bank Economic Review* 3 (September):32–38.

_____. 1991. "Black Markets for Foreign Exchange, Real Exchange Rates and Inflation." *Journal of International Economics* 30:121–35.

Poland, Council of Ministers. 1989. *Outline Economic Program*. Warsaw (October). Mimeo.

Quirk, Peter J., B. V. Christensen, K. Huh, and T. Sasabi. 1987. "Floating Exchange Rates in Developing Countries." Occasional Paper no. 53. Washington, D.C.: International Monetary Fund.

Reisen, Helmut, and Axel van Trotsenburg. 1988. "Should the Asian NICs Peg to the Yen?" *Intereconomics* (July/August):172–77.

Ricoeur, N. 1990. "La Convertibilité du Rouble." *Le Courrier des Pays de l'Est*, no. 346 (January):49–57.

Rimmer, D. 1990. "Ghana." In *The Political Economy of Poverty, Equity, and Growth*, edited by D. Lal and H. Myint. Oxford: Pergamon Press. Forthcoming.

Robinson, R. W. 1990. "Gorbachev's Empire on the Cheap." *Wall Street Journal*, March 16.

Rogoff, Kenneth. 1985. "The Optimal Degree of Commitment to an Intermediate Monetary Target." *Quarterly Journal of Economics* (November):1169–89.

Roth, T. 1990. "The Next Step: East German Winners in Election Now Seek Fast Monetary Union." *Wall Street Journal*, March 20.

Rowen, Henry S., and Charles Wolf, Jr., ed. 1990. *The Impoverished Superpower: Perestroika and the Soviet Military Burden*. San Francisco: ICS Press.

Sachs, Jeffrey. 1987. "Trade and Exchange-Rate Policies in Growth-Oriented Adjustment Programs." In *Growth-Oriented Adjustment Programs*, edited by V. Corbo, M. Goldstein, and M. Khan. Washington, D.C.: International Monetary Fund and World Bank.

_____. 1988. "The Debt Overhang of Developing Countries." In *Debt, Stabiliza-*

tion and Development, edited by G. Calvo, R. Findlay, P. Kouri, and J. Braga de Macedo. Oxford: Basil Blackwell for WIDER.

Sarafonov, Mikhail. 1990. "Wholesale Trade: Problems and Prospects." *Foreign Trade* (USSR) no. 3:8–10.

Sargent, T., and N. Wallace. 1981. "Some Unpleasant Monetarist Arithmetics." *Federal Reserve Bank of Minneapolis Quarterly Review* 5, no. 3:1–17.

Sayers, R. 1976. *The Bank of England, 1881–1944.* Vol.3. Cambridge: Cambridge University Press.

Schroder, K. 1988. "La Politique d'Exportation d'Or de l'Union Sovietique." *Problèmes Economiques* 2 (May):16–20.

Sergeev, B. 1989. "Through Currency Gluts." *Ekonomicheskaia Gazeta*, no. 29 (July).

Shelton, J. 1990. "Only Gold Can Save the Soviets." *Wall Street Journal*, February 27.

Shmelev, Nikolai. 1987. "Assets and Liabilities." *Novyi Mir*, no. 6.

Shmelev, Nikolai, and Vladimir Popov. 1989. *The Turning Point: Revitalizing the Soviet Economy.* New York: Doubleday.

Stefanowski, Roman. 1990. "Polish-Soviet Trade Relations." Radio Free Europe, Report on Eastern Europe, May 11.

Stock, J. H., and M. W. Watson. 1988. "Variable Trends in Economic Time Series." *Journal of Economic Perspectives* 2, no. 3:147–74.

Stucken, R. 1964. *Deutsche Geld-und Kreditpolitik.* 3d ed. Tübingen: Mohr.

Summers, Robert, and Alan Heston. 1984. "Improved International Comparisons of Real Product and Its Composition: 1950–1980." *Review of Income and Wealth* 30 (June):207–62.

Tanzi, Vito. 1977. "Inflation, Lags in Collection, and the Real Value of Tax Revenue." *IMF Staff Papers* (March):154–67. Washington, D.C.: International Monetary Fund.

Tinbergen, J. 1952. *On the Theory of Economic Policy.* Amsterdam: North Holland.

Thomas, V. 1985. *Linking Macroeconomic and Agricultural Policies for Adjustment with Growth.* Baltimore, Md.: Johns Hopkins University Press.

Urrutia, M. 1981. "Experience with the Crawling Peg in Colombia." In *Exchange Rate Rules*, edited by J. Williamson. London: Macmillan.

U.S. Central Intelligence Agency. 1989. *USSR: Estimates of Personal Income and Savings.* Directorate of Intelligence, SOV 89-10035. Washington, D.C.: Government Printing Office (April).

van Brabant, Jozef. 1987. *Adjustment, Structural Change and Economic Efficiency— Aspects of Monetary Cooperation in Eastern Europe.* New York: Cambridge University Press.

———. 1989. *Economic Integration in Eastern Europe: A Handbook.* New York: Harvester Wheatsleaf.

———. 1990. "On Reforming the Trade and Payments Regime in the CMEA." *Jahrbuch der Wirtschaft Osteuropas.* Munich: Osteuropa Institut.

van Wijnbergen, S. 1984. "The Dutch Disease: A Disease after All?" *Economic Journal* 94:41–55.

van Wijnbergen, Sweder. 1990. "Comment." In *Latin American Adjustment: How*

Much Has Happened?, edited by John Williamson. Washington, D.C.: Institute for International Economics.

Vanous, Jan, ed. 1990. *PlanEcon Report*, February 21. Washington, D.C.: Plan Econ Inc.

Vittori, J. M. 1990. "Disparition Progressive du Franc CFA." *L'Expansion*, April 19/May 2.

Walsh, Carl E. 1984. "Optimal Taxation by the Monetary Authority." NBER Working Paper No. 1375. Cambridge, Mass.: National Bureau of Economic Research.

Wanniski, Jude. 1989. "Gold-Based Ruble." *Barron's*, September 25.

Whitney, C. R. 1990. "The Revolution Is Today; Bureaucracy Is Forever." *New York Times*, April 15.

Wickham, Peter. 1985. "The Choice of Exchange Rate Regime in Developing Countries." *IMF Staff Papers* (June):248–88.

Wiesner, E. 1978. *Política Monetaria y Cambiaría en Colombia*. Bogotá: Asociación Bancaria de Colombia.

Williamson, John. 1965. *The Crawling Peg*. Essays in International Finance no. 50. Princeton, N.J.: Princeton University Press.

_____. 1976. "The Benefits and Costs of an International Monetary Non-System." In *Reflections on Jamaica*, edited by E. M. Bernstein, Princeton, N.J.: Princeton University Press.

_____. 1981. *Exchange Rate Rules*. London: Macmillan.

_____. 1982. "A Survey of the Literature on the Optimal Peg." *Journal of Development Economics* 11:39–61.

_____. 1985. *The Exchange Rate System*. Washington, D.C.: Institute for International Economics.

_____. 1989. "The Korean Exchange Rate System." Paper presented at the joint KDI/IIE Conference on Korean Financial Policy. In *Korea's Macroeconomic and Financial Policies*, Korea Development Institute (December):97–103.

_____. 1991. *Equilibrium Exchange Rates: An Update*. Washington, D.C.: Institute for International Economics.

Williamson, John, and Marcus Miller. 1987. *Targets and Indicators: A Blueprint for the Coordination of Economic Policy*. Washington, D.C.: Institute for International Economics.

Winston, G. C. 1974. "Overinvoicing, Underutilization, and Distorted Industrial Growth." In *Illegal Transactions in International Trade*, edited by J. N. Bhagwati, 49–66. Amsterdam: North-Holland.

Wood, A. 1988. "Global Trends in Real Exchange Rates, 1960–1984." World Bank Discussion Paper no. 35. Washington, D.C.: World Bank.

World Bank. 1987. *Poland: Reform, Adjustment and Growth*. Vols. 1 and 2. Washington, D.C.: World Bank,

_____. 1988. *World Development Report 1988*. New York: Oxford University Press.

_____. 1989. *Poland: Policies for Trade Promotion*. Washington, D.C.: World Bank.

Yeager, Leland B. 1966. "From Bilateralism through the European Payments Union to Convertibility." In University of Virginia, *International Monetary Relations*, 359–77. New York: Harper and Row.

About the Contributors

Emil-Maria Claassen is professor of monetary and international economics at the University of Paris-Dauphine. During the 1980s he held academic positions at INSEAD (Fontainebleau), the European University Institute (Florence), and New York University. He was the Bundesbank Professor at the Freie Universität Berlin. Among his previous works are four edited volumes on international economics: *Stabilization Policies in Interdependent Economics; Recent Issues in International Monetary Economics; Recent Issues in the Theory of Flexible Exchange Rates;* and *International and European Monetary Systems.*

Bijan B. Aghevli is a senior adviser in the Research Department of the International Monetary Fund. He has a Ph.D. from Brown University.

Dieter Bender is professor of economics and director of the Institute of Development Research and Development Policy at the Ruhr-Universität Bochum, Germany. His main fields of research are international finance and macroeconomics, exchange rate theory, and international trade and developing countries.

Reuven Brenner holds the Repap Chair in Economics at McGill's School of Management and is associate fellow at the Centre de Recherche et Développement en Economique (CRDE), Université de Montréal.

Brenner is the author of four books: *History: The Human Gamble* (1983); *Betting on Ideas: Wars, Invention, Inflation* (1985, paperback 1989); *Rivalry: In Business, Science, among Nations* (1987, paperback 1990); and *Gambling and Speculation* (with Gabrielle Brenner, 1990). He has also written articles on macroeconomics and legal-constitutional issues in the Eastern Bloc, where he grew up.

Juan L. Cariaga is the executive director of the Inter-American Development Bank for Bolivia, Paraguay, and Uruguay. He was the finance minister of Bolivia during the implementation of the stabilization program of 1985. He has written five books and numerous articles on economics in Latin America and the United States.

Apostolos Condos received his Ph.D. in economics from Iowa State University. He taught at Duke University and has been a member of the staff of the World Bank. He is presently senior economist in the Policy Analysis Division of the Food and Agriculture Organization of the United Nations.

Juergen B. Donges is professor of economics at the University of Cologne, Germany, and codirector of the Institut für Wirtschaftspolitik in Cologne. He has been an adviser to economic research institutes and government agencies in Germany and elsewhere as well as to the World Bank, the United Nations Industrial Development Organization, the United Nations Conference on Trade and Development, and other international organizations. His many publications focus on trade policy, development economics, economic growth and structural change, and the economics of European integration.

Sebastian Edwards is the Henry Ford II Professor of International Business Economics at the Anderson Graduate School of Management of the University of California, Los Angeles (UCLA). He is also a professor of economics at UCLA, a research associate of the National Bureau for Economic Research, and a senior fellow of the Institute for Policy Reform. He is a coeditor of the *Journal of Development Economics*. Edwards's main fields of research are international economics and the economics of developing and Eastern European countries. His most recent books are *Debt, Adjustment and Recovery: Latin America's Prospect for Growth and Development* (1988) and *Real Exchange Rates, Devaluation and Adjustment* (1989).

Roque B. Fernández is president of the Central Bank of Argentina and a member of the Board of Directors of the Centro de Estudios

Macroeconómicos de Argentina (CEMA). Fernández received a Ph.D. in economics from the University of Chicago in 1975. He is the author of two books and more than fifty articles in books and professional journals.

Roman Frydman holds a Ph.D. in economics from Columbia University and is associate professor of economics at New York University. He has written extensively on the theory of market behavior under uncertainty and expectations formation. He is a coeditor, with Edmund S. Phelps, of *Individual Forecasting and Aggregate Outcomes* (Cambridge University Press, 1983). Since the changes in Eastern Europe he has been investigating the problems of making a transition to a market economy. Frydman proposed, with Andrzej Rapaczynski, an approach to the privatization of Polish industry, which has been incorporated into the privatization program announced by the Polish government.

Daniel Gros is a senior research fellow at the Centre for European Policy Studies, Brussels. He teaches at the University of Leuven and serves as an academic adviser to the European Commission.

Herbert G. Grubel is a professor of economics at Simon Fraser University in Canada. He has taught at Stanford University, the University of Chicago, and the University of Pennsylvania and has held temporary research and teaching positions at the U.S. Treasury, the Australian National University, Oxford University, the University of Cape Town, the Institute of Southeast Asian Studies in Singapore, the University of Nairobi, and the Free University of Berlin. Grubel is the author or editor of fifteen books and has published over two hundred professional articles and chapters in compendia. He received his Ph.D. from Yale University.

Grzegorz W. Kolodko is a professor of economics at the Central School of Planning and Statistics in Warsaw and director of the Research Institute of Finance, the leading think tank in Poland. He is also a member of the government's Economic Council and has helped plan Poland's stabilization programs. From 1982 to 1988, Kolodko was an adviser to the governor of the National Bank of Poland. He has published six books in Polish. His most recent book, *Hyperinflation and Stabilization in Postsocialist Economies*, has been published in English and Russian.

Deepak Lal is professor of political economy at University College London and James S. Coleman Professor of International Development Studies at the University of California, Los Angeles. Educated at St.

Stephen's College, Delhi, and at Oxford, he served in Tokyo as a member of the Indian foreign service. He has taught development economics at universities in the United Kingdom, Australia, and the United States and has advised governments in developing countries worldwide. From 1984 to 1987, he was research administrator, economics and research, for the World Bank. His recent books include *Prices for Planning: Towards the Reform of Indian Planning* (1980); *The Poverty of Development Economics* (1983); and *The Hindu Equilibrium*, in two volumes (1989).

Marie Lavigne is a professor of economics at the University of Paris 1 (Panthéon-Sorbonne). She is also director of the European Studies Center at Stirin, Czechoslovakia, a branch of the Institute for East-West Security Studies in New York. Her most recent book is *International Political Economy and Socialism*, Cambridge University Press (1991).

Ronald I. McKinnon is William Eberle Professor of Economics at Stanford University, where he has taught since 1961. He is an internationally known expert on international and development finance, and his current research focuses on financial processes in liberalizing socialist economies. In addition to many articles and essays, he has published three books: *Money and Capital in Economic Development* (1973); *Money in International Exchange: The Convertible Currency Sytem* (1979); and *The Order of Economic Liberalization: Financial Control in the Transition to a Market Economy* (1991).

Peter J. Montiel is deputy division chief of the Developing Country Studies Division in the Research Department of the International Monetary Fund. He has a Ph.D. from the Massachusetts Institute of Technology (MIT).

Robert A. Mundell is professor of economics at Columbia University and an authority on international economics and macroeconomics. After receiving his Ph.D. at the Massachusetts Institute of Technology (MIT), Mundell worked at the International Monetary Fund and then became a professor of economics at the University of Chicago and editor of the *Journal of Political Economy*. Mundell is known as the father of the theory of optimum currency areas and an originator of the theory of the international macroeconomic policy mix, the monetary approach to the balance of payments, and supply-side economics. His books include *International Monetary Conflict and Reform* (1965); *Man and Economics* (1968); and *International Economics* (1971). He has also written over one hundred articles for professional journals.

J. Peter Neary is professor of political economy at University College Dublin. Educated at University College Dublin and Nuffield College, Oxford, he has been a visiting professor at Berkeley, Princeton, and Queen's (Ontario), and a visiting scholar at the Massachusetts Institute of Technology (MIT) and the International Institute for Applied Systems Analysis (Vienna). He has published extensively, especially on international trade theory, and edited *Natural Resources and the Macroeconomy* (1986) with Sweder van Wijnbergen. He is a former editor of the *European Economic Review*, a fellow of the Econometric Society and the Centre for Economic Policy Research (London), and a member of Academia Europaea.

Won-Am Park is a fellow at the Korea Development Institute. He is a graduate of Seoul University and the Massachusetts Institute of Technology (MIT). He was formerly a member of the Research Department of the Central Bank of Korea. Park has written papers on Korean macroeconomic policies, the East Asian NICs, trade with Japan, and other topics.

Yung Chul Park is professor of economics at Korea University. A graduate of the University of Minnesota, Park has served as president of the Korea Development Institute.

Edmund S. Phelps has been McVickar Professor of Political Economy at Columbia University since 1982. He is an adviser to the European Bank for Reconstruction and Development (EBRD) and was a member of the EBRD mission to Moscow for the Joint Study of the Economy of the Soviet Union in 1990. His most recent books are *The Slump in Europe: Open Economy Theory Reconstructed* (with Jean-Paul Fitoussi); *Seven Schools of Macroeconomic Thought: The Arne Ryne Lectures;* and *Modern Readings in Macroeconomic Theory.*

Brian Pinto received his B.A. from Loyola College, Madras, India; his M.B.A. from the Indian Institute of Management, Ahmedabad; and his Ph.D. in economics from the University of Pennsylvania. He has held assignments on macroeconomic policy research and international finance at the World Bank. He helped launch the World Bank's Financial Technical Assistance program, designed to transfer high-tech finance (swaps, options, futures) to developing countries. He has written for many well-known professional journals. Currently, he is resident economist at the World Bank mission in Poland.

Helmut Reisen is a senior economist at the Development Centre of the Organization for Economic Cooperation and Development (OECD) in Paris. He previously worked at the Kiel Institute of World Economics and the German Ministry of Economics. He has written primarily on international monetary economics, with particular reference to advanced developing countries. His most recent monograph is "Public Debt, External Competitiveness, and Fiscal Discipline in Developing Countries," Princeton Studies in International Finance no. 66. He is also coauthor of a forthcoming OECD Development Centre study entitled *Financial Opening in Dynamic Asian Economies: Pitfalls, Prerequisites, and Perspectives.*

Friedrich L. Sell is a professor of international and development economics at the University of Giessen, Germany. Previously, he was division chief of the research group on international resource transfer at the Kiel Institute of World Economics and leader of the project "Present Problems and Future Prospects of the Brazilian Economy in the International Division of Labor" at the Kiel Institute.

Stanislaw Wellisz is a professor of economics at Columbia University. A native of Poland, Wellisz received his Ph.D. from Harvard University. He has been a consultant to many developing country governments, including Cameroon, Venezuela, Mauritius, and Jamaica, and in 1990–1991 was an adviser to Poland's Ministry of Finance. He is the author of *The Economies of the Soviet Bloc* and coauthor of *The Political Economy of Poverty, Equity and Growth: Five Small Open Economies* (forthcoming).

John Williamson is a senior fellow at the Institute for International Economics in Washington, D.C. He has held various teaching positions and has served as a consultant to the U.K. Treasury and an adviser to the International Monetary Fund. He has written extensively on international monetary issues, and his publications include *The Open Economy and the World Economy; Political Economy and International Money; The Exchange Rate System;* and *Targets and Indicators: A Blueprint for the International Coordination of Economic Policy* (with Marcus H. Miller).

Conference Participants

Bijan B. Aghevli, International Monetary Fund, Washington, D.C.
Gerhard Michael Ambrosi, Freie Universität Berlin
Carlos Gonzales-Arévalo, Asociación de Investigación y Estudios Sociales, Guatemala
Dieter Bender, Ruhr-Universität Bochum
Reuven Brenner, Université de Montréal
Juan L. Cariaga, Inter-American Development Bank, Washington, D.C.
Emil-Maria Claassen, Freie Universität Berlin and Université de Paris-Dauphine
Apostolos Condos, Food and Agriculture Organization, Rome
Juergen B. Donges, Universität Köln
Sebastian Edwards, University of California, Los Angeles
Roque Fernández, Banco Central de la República Argentina, Buenos Aires
Stephen Frowen, London
Roman Frydman, New York University, New York
Daniel Gros, Centre for European Policy Studies and European Economic Community, Brussels
Herbert G. Grubel, Freie Universität Berlin and Simon Fraser University, Vancouver
Dieter Hiss, Landeszentralbank Berlin
Grzegorz Kolodko, Research Institute of Finance, Warsaw

Deepak Lal, University College, London
Marie Lavigne, Université de Paris (Panthéon-Sorbonne)
Ronald I. McKinnon, Stanford University, Stanford, California
Peter J. Montiel, International Monetary Fund, Washington, D.C.
Robert R. Mundell, Columbia University, New York
J. Peter Neary, University College, Dublin
Mario Nuti, European University Institute, San Domenico di Fiesole, Florence
Won-Am Park, Korea Development Institute, Seoul
Yung Chul Park, Korea University, Seoul
George Petty, Repap Enterprises Inc., Montreal
Edmund S. Phelps, Columbia University, New York
Brain Pinto, World Bank, Washington, D.C.
Helmut Reisen, Organization for Economic Cooperation and Development, Paris
Hajo Riese, Freie Universität Berlin
Friedrich Sell, Universität Giessen
John Sullivan, International Center for Economic Growth, Washington, D.C.
Eirik Svindland, Deutsches Institut für Wirtschaftsforschung, Berlin
Aaron Tornell, Columbia University, New York
Jaroslaw Vostatek, Office of the Prime Minister, Prague
Stanislaw Wellisz, Columbia University, New York
John Williamson, Institute for International Economics, Washington, D.C.
Andreas Wörgötter, Institut für Höhere Studien, Vienna

INDEX

ICEG Academic Advisory Board